ANATOMY OF A PERSONAL INJURY LAWSUIT

3rd Edition

Edited by James S. Rogers

ATLA Press

Published by
ATLA Press
1050 31st Street, NW
Washington, DC 20007

First Edition published 1968

Library of Congress Catalog Number 91-312-56
ISBN 0-941916-61-8

Table of Contents

ABOUT THE AUTHORS

Douglas B. Abrams is a partner of Blanchard, Twiggs, Abrams & Strickland, P.A., in Raleigh, N.C. He received his B.A. and J.D. degrees from Wake Forest University and was elected Phi Beta Kappa. Abrams has written and lectured extensively on products liability and law-related subjects, including the use of computers in litigation.

Linda Miller Atkinson is on the editorial board of the *Federal Litigation Reporter*. She has published articles in *TRIAL* magazine and is a distinguished speaker at conventions and seminars across the country. After graduating from Oberlin College, Atkinson received her J.D. from Wayne State University in 1973. She is a partner in the law firm of Philo, Atkinson, Steinberg, Stephens & Whitaker in Detroit and Channing, Mich., and she serves on the ATLA Board of Governors.

David B. Baum heads a three-lawyer firm in San Francisco, Calif. He graduated with a B.S. from the University of Wisconsin and received his L.L.B. from Northwestern University School of Law. He has written "Preparation of the Case" as part of the Art of Advocacy series and served as editorial advisor to *TRIAL* magazine. He is a former president of the California Trial Lawyers Association and has been appointed Judicial Counsel of California.

Arthur H. Bryant has extensively litigated protective order issues and has spoken on secrecy in the courts at numerous educational seminars and meetings. He practices law in Washington, D.C. A graduate of Swarthmore College, Bryant went on to receive his J.D. from Harvard University. He is the executive director of Trial Lawyers for Public Justice and is co-chairperson of ATLA's Protective Order Litigation Group.

Roxanne Barton Conlin has served as president of both the Civil Justice Foundation and the NOW Legal Defense and Education Fund.

She received her B.A., J.D., and M.P.A. from Drake University. Conlin has written numerous articles and has been a frequent lecturer on litigation and the civil justice system. She practices law in Des Moines, Iowa, and she is the 1991-1992 President-Elect of ATLA.

Philip H. Corboy is well known for his published works, including *Final Arguments* and articles on issues of litigation, practice, damages, and evidence. He attended Notre Dame University and went on to receive his law degree from Loyola University and an Honorary Doctor of Law degree from St. Ambrose College. A partner of Corboy & Demetrio in Chicago, Ill., Corboy is also past president of the Illinois Trial Lawyers Association.

Abraham Fuchsberg is editor-in-chief of the *Trial Lawyers Quarterly*. A senior partner of Fuchsberg & Fuchsberg in New York City, he has lectured at national conventions and at various universities. He is a regular contributor to the *New York Law Journal* and is the author of *Modern New York Discovery, New York Courtroom Evidence*, and a collection of poems titled *Poetic Justice*. Fuchsberg is the vice president of ATLA's Civil Justice Foundation and a patron founder of Trial Lawyers for Public Justice.

Michael S. Gillie is the executive director and founder of United States Arbitration and Mediation, Inc. (USA & M), headquartered in Seattle, Wash. USA & M has 48 offices in the United States, plus offices in Canada and Europe. Gillie is a graduate of Western Washington University and the University of Puget Sound School of Law. He is a nationally recognized speaker and author on alternative dispute resolution.

Carole L. Gutterman, Ph.D., C.U.R.N., is a nurse consultant to the law firm of Pegalis & Wachsman, P.C., in Great Neck, N.Y. She received her Ph.D. from the Marion A. Buckley School of Nursing at Adelphi University. She is a Charter Member of the American Association of Legal Nurse Consultants and is the author of several articles in the area of legal medicine.

Dale Haralson is a senior partner in the Tucson law firm of Haralson, Kinerk & Morey, P.C. He has held offices in ATLA and has served as president of the Arizona Trial Lawyers Association and the Western

Trial Lawyers Association. He has been a frequent lecturer at ATLA's national and circuit seminars. His degrees are from Hardin-Simmons University and the University of Arizona College of Law.

Mitchell A. Karton, M.D., is on the clinical faculty of the University of Washington Medical School. He received his B.A. from Harvard and his medical degree from the University of California-Davis Medical School. Karton's practice specializes in internal medicine, and he has written numerous articles for both medical and law journals.

James J. Leonard, Jr., a partner of Leonard & Clancy in Phoenix, Ariz., has been a practicing trial lawyer for 26 years. Leonard is a graduate of Brown University and Notre Dame Law School. He is a past president of the Phoenix Trial Lawyers Association and has written and lectured extensively on civil litigation issues.

Paul N. Luvera of Mount Vernon, Wash., is the author of four law books, a contributing author to five additional books, and the author of more than fifty articles in legal journals. He is a member of the American College of Trial Lawyers, American Board of Trial Lawyers, Inner Circle of Advocates, and the International Society of Barristers. Luvera is a frequent lecturer to legal groups throughout the country.

Howard L. Nations is a plaintiff's personal injury trial lawyer in Houston, Tex. He has authored many works, including law review articles, *Maximizing Damages in Personal Injury Litigation*, and *Structuring Settlements*. Nations received his undergraduate degree from Florida State University and his law degree from Vanderbilt University. He is chairman of the Board of Trustees of the National College of Advocacy.

Peter Perlman practices in Lexington, Ky. He is a past president of both ATLA and the Kentucky Association of Trial Attorneys. After graduating from the University of Kentucky, Perlman studied law at Duke University. A successful litigator, professor, writer, and editor, he is the author of *Opening Statement*, a contributor to *Crashworthiness*, and the author of many articles.

James S. Rogers is a prominent Seattle attorney whose practice is limited to personal injury cases, with an emphasis on automobile, products liability, and medical negligence cases. A noted lecturer and moderator, Rogers teaches at legal seminars and advocacy courses nationwide. He served as editor-in-chief of the Washington State Trial Lawyers Association's *Trial News* and is known for his articles in *TRIAL* magazine and other legal publications. He received his B.A. degree in history from the University of Washington and his J.D. degree from the University of Arizona College of Law. Rogers is currently president of the Washington State Trial Lawyers Association.

Nicole Schultheis has successfully opposed protective orders in a variety of drug products liability cases. She attended M.I.T. before going on to Boston University for law school. With an office in Baltimore, Md., she is the education coordinator of Project ACCESS, a nationwide campaign sponsored by Trial Lawyers for Public Justice against secrecy in the courts. She also co-chairs ATLA's Protective Order Litigation Group.

Susan J. Schwartz is an associate with Corboy & Demetrio in Chicago, Ill. She attended Georgetown University and Loyola University School of Law. She has lectured in the Chicago area on medical negligence and evidentiary issues.

Deanne C. Siemer is a partner of Pillsbury, Madison & Sutro in Washington, D.C. She received her B.A. degree from George Washington University and her L.L.B. degree from Harvard Law School. She has tried commercial cases in many fields, has taught at seminars and continuing legal education workshops, and has recently written extensively on the use of computers in litigation.

Gerry L. Spence has not lost a jury trial in 22 years. This Jackson, Wyo., lawyer remains committed to representing people in civil and criminal cases. He is the author of *Gunning for Justice*, *Murder and Madness*, *Trial by Fire*, and *With Justice for None*. Spence graduated from the University of Wyoming and the University of Wyoming Law School. He has lectured at law schools and conducted seminars around the country.

Victoria C. Swanson is a nationally recognized aviation lawyer practicing in Denver and Colorado Springs, Colo. Swanson is a graduate of the University of Detroit School of Law and received her undergraduate degree from Ohio State University. She has served as a faculty member of the National College of Advocacy, co-authored the book *Product Design Liability*, and written numerous articles for law journals and legal magazines. She is past chair of ATLA's Aviation Section and ATLA's Women's Caucus.

Harvey F. Wachsman, M.D., J.D., F.C.L.M., is a neurosurgeon and partner in the law firm of Pegalis & Wachsman, P.C., in Great Neck, N.Y. He is a member of ATLA's Board of Governors and president of the American Board of Professional Liability Attorneys. Wachsman is the co-author of the three-volume text *American Law of Medical Malpractice* and has written many articles. He has lectured nationally and internationally in the fields of medicine and law.

Contributors to the First Edition

Editor-in-Chief
Robert M. Dudnik

Assistant Editors
James Leonard
C. Glennon Rau

Chairman
John E. Norton

Authors

Thomas T. Anderson
Wade J. Dahood
Robert M. Dudnik
Francis H. Hare, Jr.
Lex Hawkins
James E. Hullverson
J.D. Lee
James J. Leonard, Jr.
Stanley E. Preiser
C. Glennon Rau
Paul D. Rheingold
Lawrence J. Smith
Shannon Stafford
Ward Wagner, Jr.

Contributors to the Second Edition

Editor-in-Chief
John E. Norton

Assistant Editors
Francis H. Hare, Jr.
Edward M. Ricci
Mary Frances Edwards

Chairman
Lawrence J. Smith

Authors

Scott Baldwin
Sidney Bernstein
Michael F. Colley
James A. George
Francis H. Hare, Jr.
James E. Hullverson
J.D. Lee
James J. Leonard, Jr.
John E. Norton
Stanley E. Preiser
Paul D. Rheingold
Edward M. Ricci
Lawrence J. Smith
Ward Wagner, Jr.

INTRODUCTION

James S. Rogers

I remember a line from a review of the musical *A Chorus Line*—"If you see only one show this season, this is it." One of my objectives as Editor-in-Chief of the third edition of *Anatomy of a Personal Injury Lawsuit* is to publish a book about which trial lawyers can say, "If you read only one book about litigating a personal injury case, this is it."

We trial lawyers are inundated with books on trial tactics and techniques, materials from a seemingly endless number of legal seminars, audiotapes on all aspects of litigation (that we can listen to as we jog or drive to work), and videos of trial demonstrations not available at our favorite video store (at least not yet, anyway). Our lives would be simpler if we could refer to one highly readable, comprehensive, and helpful book to guide us through every aspect of litigating a personal injury case—a book to keep close at hand during trial preparation. When I was first asked to be Editor-in-Chief of this book, I saw the potential for taking what has long been ATLA's best-selling publication, thoroughly revising and updating it, and making it into the book I've just described—an indispensable addition to a trial lawyer's "short list" of reference aids.

The first edition of *Anatomy of a Personal Injury Lawsuit* was published in 1968. It was written by a committee of trial lawyers, with Robert M. Dudnik acting as Editor-in-Chief. The second edition, also written by a committee, was published in 1981 with John E. Norton as Editor-in-Chief. The names of the committee members and editors of the first and second editions appear at the beginning of this book.

Although some text from the first two editions has been retained, the third edition has been updated and expanded. There are new chapters on subjects that have developed or become timely or prominent since the second edition was published. Doug Abrams's chapter, "Use of Computers in Personal Injury Litigation," would have stirred little interest years ago; today we can't imagine a litigation practice without computers. Abrams provides a primer on the subject, specifically tailored to personal injury practice. Michael Gillie's "Alternatives to Litigation: Mediation and Arbitration" chapter discusses increasingly available methods for resolving lawsuits before trial. Another chapter that is new in this edition, "Fighting Protective and Secrecy Orders," by Nicole Schultheis and Arthur Bryant, discusses attempts by manufacturers and corporate defendants to stop information from reaching consumers and plaintiffs and their counsel.

Gerry Spence's chapter, "How To Be a Trial Lawyer," sets a reflective, invigorating tone for the book and establishes a philosophical context for the chapters that follow. The pretrial and trial chapters, beginning with Victoria Swanson's comprehensive chapter, "Initial Interviews and Investigation of the Case," and continuing through Phil Corboy's and Susan Schwartz's thought-provoking chapter on final argument, are crammed full of information and ideas. Here you'll find Linda Miller Atkinson's mini-treatise on discovery, Dale Haralson's checklist review in "Analysis of the Case," and Paul Luvera's highly informative chapter, "Case in Chief." Roxanne Barton Conlin's verve can be sensed throughout her chapter, "Voir Dire Examination and Jury Selection," and David Baum gives us a wealth of useful techniques in his chapter on the opening statement.

The topic of direct examination is well taught by Deanne Siemer. Peter Perlman gives us new thoughts on the subject of expert testimony, and Howard Nations discusses cross-examination. James Leonard and Abraham Fuchsberg revised the chapter from the second edition on instructions to the jury, while Harvey Wachsman and Carole Gutterman significantly updated the "Medical Examination and Testing" chapter. A Seattle physician and member of the clinical faculty of the University of Washington School of Medicine, Mitchell Karton, has done a masterful job expanding on and clarifying the basic medical anatomy chapter, a significant accomplishment given that human anatomy has not changed since publication of the second edition. Each chapter reflects the opinions of the authors—all masters in their fields of practice. Having the perspectives and sensibilities of these outstanding trial lawyers and medical professionals is one of the strengths of this book.

This book can be used as a checklist for trial preparation and as a reference for learning and reviewing tactics and techniques of personal injury litigation. For the lawyer who will take the time, I believe that reading this book cover to cover will prove highly informative, regardless of the lawyer's level of experience. I have been practicing law in Seattle since 1974. My inspiration has always been the American judicial system, with its commitment to the right to trial by jury and to due process of law. I am disturbed when this system that I value is attacked in the media by insurance and business interests.

Most of us have seen full-page advertisements in national periodicals blaming trial lawyers for the high cost of insurance. *Forbes* magazine, with its readership primarily consisting of people in the business community, has published derogatory pieces about plaintiff personal injury lawyers espousing a distorted view of what we do and why we do it. *Forbes* reports the earnings of a small group of highly successful trial lawyers, giving a false impression about what most personal injury lawyers earn and intimating that the motives of plaintiffs' lawyers are less than honorable.[1]

In my nearly 18 years as a trial lawyer, I have met many committed and compassionate lawyers who care deeply about helping people lead better lives. I know few, if any, tort lawyers who are primarily motivated by fees; the plaintiffs' lawyers I know and have known over the years are driven by a desire to help their clients and to become excellent trial lawyers in the process. Plaintiffs' trial lawyers recognize the importance of the constitution as a cornerstone for the principles of our judicial system. Corporate conservatives who otherwise flaunt the constitution seem to forget their loyalty when the subject is the tort system.

1 Brimelow and Spencer, *The Plaintiff Attorneys' Great Honey Rush*, FORBES, Oct. 16, 1989, at 197.

It would be unrealistic for me not to mention the tort-reform campaigns that insurance companies, business interests, and other entities have waged and continue to wage in states across the country. The rights of injured people have been limited or abrogated in many states through regressive legislation that, for example, eliminates joint and several liability in varying degrees, caps damages, limits contingency fees, mandates structured payments for judgments, or provides increased immunity for governmental entities. We have seen a presidential proposal to Congress encouraging states to, among other things, limit general damages in medical negligence cases. Under the proposed law, states that failed to limit damages would lose some of the federal payments they received under the government's Medicare and Medicaid programs, which pay for health care for the elderly and the poor.

The motivation that is primarily alleged to be behind these anti-victim laws—cheaper and easier-to-obtain insurance—has generally been proven to be without merit. For example, the Washington State Insurance Commissioner's Office issued a lengthy report discussing the effect of Washington's Tort Reform Act of 1986. The report concluded that the comprehensive tort reforms implemented by the state legislature had no significant effect on the affordability or availability of insurance in the state.

Partly in response to legislation and proposed legislation, ATLA and most state trial lawyer associations have become politically sophisticated. However, ATLA's primary objective has been and continues to be helping lawyers who represent injured people to be as effective as possible. ATLA excels in the education of trial lawyers. For example, ATLA's National College of Advocacy has entered into an agreement with San Francisco's Hastings College of the Law to jointly provide continuing legal education programs leading to certification as a Master in Trial Advocacy. The growth of litigation groups within ATLA shows a recognition of the importance of lawyers' sharing information with each other. The ATLA Alert program, established to prevent harm to consumers by informing appropriate regulatory agencies of hazards to public health and safety, is dependent on evidence developed in cases being handled by ATLA members. And ATLA publications, including this book, are written to help trial lawyers improve their skills and represent victims better.

In editing the chapters and reading the techniques and strategies of these litigators, I have had some additional thoughts I'd like to share. First of all, I think that we trial lawyers must slow down and think. Our practices are so busy that we often do our work without pausing to reflect or, as the late Ted Koskoff used to say, to "cerebrate." Many of us believe that we are dysfunctional if we are not constantly doing something "productive"—writing, talking on the phone, dictating, reading documents, or working on a computer. Yet creativity can be tapped in many different ways and often comes to the person who periodically shuts out everything else, focuses on the issues at hand, and lets his or her thoughts roam. We've all had great ideas about a case (or so they seemed at the time) come to us in the middle of the night—a time when we were lying in bed, letting our minds wander. And those of us who are runners know that many creative thoughts come to us while we are jogging (an argument against the "Walkman").

Another observation of mine concerns the growing recognition by trial lawyers that there is much that can be learned from actors. A trial lawyer may learn every technique in this book but not be able to affect or impact a jury without learning communication skills that are within the realm of the actor. Continuing legal education programs featuring actors and other theater professionals who show how the actor's art can be adapted by the trial lawyer are increasingly popular. At these programs, theater professionals discuss and demonstrate subjects such as voice projection and modulation, effective use of language, and successful communication with jurors.

A tactic that I think has been overlooked is that of working with professional directors in staging a trial. The trial lawyer is a director (and producer, too), responsible for directing the trial so that it culminates in jury impact, interest, and persuasion. The director of a play, like the trial lawyer, is responsible for the success or failure of the production. Consider the impact the directors of *L.A. Law* have had, revising the public's expectations of a trial: people now expect brevity—in witness examination, final argument, and overall length of the trial. There are experienced directors in theaters across the country, or, depending on the magnitude of the case, there are film or television directors in Los Angeles or New York, who could be retained to assist in staging the trial in terms of witnesses and evidence.

An instructor at a trial advocacy course I attended as a young lawyer told our small workshop group that we, as trial lawyers, were merely conduits in presenting a case to the jury. He told us that during trial he was not even aware of himself while he gave his opening statement. According to my experience, this instructor was wrong; we are not merely robot-like, albeit technically proficient, conduits. We are human beings with emotions, feelings, and personalities. We must take our acquired technical skills, including those that we learn and reaffirm in this book, and integrate them with our own unique styles.

One of my hopes for this book is that it will inspire and motivate you to perform at a higher level. That's my expectation when I read for educational purposes. I have been conscious of that in editing each chapter of the book, particularly those chapters devoted to litigation skills.

I also hope you will find this book useful in your practice and enjoyable to read. Above all, may it help you obtain full justice for your clients.

My thanks go to those persons from ATLA Press who worked tirelessly to help make this book a reality: Rich Page, for driving us all to meet our deadlines and overseeing the publication; Cathy Kruvant, for her superb editing; April Gustafson and Lianne Best, for meticulous copy editing; Lou Leto, for his production talents and efforts; and Anne Goodwin, for helping wrap up the final details.

I'd also like to give special thanks to Anne Grant for her time spent working with me on developing the concept for the Third Edition and to Arnett Holloway and Christine Griffith for laying the groundwork for this work.

I dedicate my efforts to Theresa and Zoey.

HOW TO BE A TRIAL LAWYER

Gerry L. Spence

A young lawyer once complained to me that he couldn't win cases anymore. Something strange had happened. He felt as if an insidious malady had overtaken him. Fresh out of law school he had won almost everything—then he began to hone his technique. He read books by the experts and attended seminars conducted by the current stars of the courtroom. He became a fine cross-examiner and considered his final arguments just short of masterpieces. "I've gotten good," he said. "Real good. But I don't win anymore." He wanted me to tell him why, but before I could answer he said, "I already know why," and walked away.

Trial lawyers—some like to call themselves "litigators"—are an arrogant lot who see themselves as the vestiges of ancient gladiators, occupying a special high nob from which they peer down on the ignorant and mundane remainder of the human race. Jurors are objects to be fooled and manipulated; a trial is a game. Their clients are not frightened, suffering people but cases and money. The courtroom is the place where, to the amazement of all, they do their legalistic songs and dances, and where justice has become a sophomoric concept that no one can define anyway.

How well I remember my first days in law school, when I was urged by my professors to rise above the emotional pot that steams and simmers in most cases. The law that we were taught was not related to truth or justice, nor was it even related to human beings. The law was rarified stuff, a mysterious logic possessed only by lawyers and judges and adapted to the esoteric science of jurisprudence. In short, we were told to learn to "think like lawyers," which seemed to mean that we must shed our natural ability to think like human beings. The goal was a risk-free, antiseptic profession, one that took the lawyer out of the law, the human out of the human conflict. We were to become surgeons dissecting bodies with no names, faces, personal histories, suffering, fear, or loneliness. We were to become legal machines—sweet, smooth, and uniform—and, like our professors, so far removed from the heart of human struggle that life would take on a new form; a dead word on a dead white page.

The young lawyer who came complaining to me had won his cases early on because he *failed* to learn the lessons of his professors. Without technical skill he had nothing to resort to in the courtroom except his raw, unsophisticated self. He possessed no fine techniques, no tricks, no cute arguments, no pretentious mannerisms. Often he stumbled. At times he stood with his hands in his pockets, his face red, trying to form an unobjectionable question. Sometimes he looked silly. Sometimes his opponent laughed at him, and often the judge lost patience with him. Yet he won.

Now that his techniques were slick and smooth, the juries were rejecting him. He hated the jury. He railed at the gods. His argument, of course, was that he should be judged as he saw himself, a combatant in the pit who delivered the most telling blows with the greatest style. Unfortunately, his professors, most of whom had never peeped into the pit themselves, had neglected to tell him that jurors, though they might be amused, even enthralled, with a lawyer's fancy footwork, see their job as discovering the truth and delivering a just verdict. They failed to tell him that the very persons who would judge his case would demand of him something he had been taught to exclude from the arena—himself.

In my country of vast space and great mountain ranges, we provide guides for the tourist who would otherwise become lost. Such is the role of the trial lawyer with jurors. One would never select a guide based on his glibness or his cute way of walking down the trail. We demand a guide we can trust, one we can follow into dangerous places, who will bring us out again inspired, blooming with new knowledge and glowing with a sense of satisfaction for having made the journey; and, of course, a guide always takes the trip with us.

Those who have struggled through these treacherous journeys called trials know they are hazardous to the soul. By the time trial lawyers walk into the courtroom they have spent many a day and long night inside the skin of their clients. To lose, to share the agony and despair of your client, to know you have laid it all out and the jury has rejected not only your client's case, but you—well, it's like feeling the sword slip through your heart. I have never walked into a courtroom without feeling my guts drawn tight. I have never stood up to cross-examine the principal witness without wondering anew if I was up to it, without the fearsome fantasy of the witness running wild, turning my case into a shambles and revealing me as the fool I sometimes fear I am. It makes no difference how many cases I have won before. Deep in my heart I suspect that, in the past, some magic fell over the jury like hot river fog and that the magical fog will never return to save me again. It's that excruciating pain of loss we guard against, and that very effort causes many lawyers to view their cases as mere legalistic exercises instead of human struggles for justice. Yet the pain-avoidance mechanism at work here almost always guarantees the lawyer will lose.

I have learned over the years that I won most of my cases because I *cared* a great deal, both about myself and my clients. My caring wasn't some high morality not shared by my brothers and sisters of the bar. I couldn't help myself. I tried not to get involved; I admit it. I tried to keep my personhood in my pocket, to be a clever, competent, impersonal technician who could win either side of a case—in the eyes of many, the hallmark of the skillful trial lawyer. But in the end, it was my miserable failure to do so that proved to be the secret to my successes.

The dynamics at work with the jury, like most truths, are embarrassingly simple. What do jurors want? Do they lust for the blood of the witness and long to hear you fill the halls with your glorious oratory? Do they wish to be deeply impressed by your skills, your grace, and your beauty? I say jurors want the truth. They want to know they haven't been fooled and that they've been fair and have rendered as good a brand of justice as they can. Too often clever trial lawyers stand in the way of these goals. So if I have accurately stated the wishes of most jurors, why not fool the jury into believing whatever they want to believe? Offer up a platter of platitudes, rhetoric, and logic that jurors will buy. Why jump into the stew and get cooked along with the missionaries?

I subscribe to the notion that the jury is the most intelligent, the best informed, the wisest collective mind in the courtroom. The average juror is about 40 years old, so the 12 jurors possess among them nearly 500 years of exquisitely varied life experiences. The worker who scrubs the latrines of the saloon for a living and goes home to a cold bowl of cereal and an empty bed knows more about the human condition than all the Harvard Ph.D.'s I can haul into the courtroom at a thousand dollars an hour. The workers who know the fear of being without jobs, and who have witnessed co-workers losing their hands and breaking their backs in those hellholes called the workplace possess a wisdom not taught in universities. Consider what the senior male litigator in the large firm knows about being a woman. Yet nowadays there are usually more women on my juries than men.

Perhaps you can fool this enlightened conglomerate of humanity, the jury, for a while, but the pressure of the trial will almost always squeeze out who you really are and how you really feel—if you have dared to feel at all. After which the jury will ask themselves a simple question: What kind of human being stands in front of honest men and women asking them to do what he refuses to do—to care about his client? After you have lost you can study the transcripts forever, but you will never discover the reason you were unable to fool the jury. It was the sound of your voice, the tempo of your words, the language of your body. They weren't in sync. It's like an expert who can tell a counterfeit hundred dollar bill a mile away, not by its color, not by its print or its paper. It's just that the counterfeiter can never quite get it all together.

We hear a lot about ethics these days, and law students are taught a course by that name. However, I know of no professors who teach that to strut and preen and lay down long trails of pettifoggery emanating from places void of feeling and empty of caring is unbefitting one who purports to serve the cause of the injured, the forgotten, and the damned. I know of no professors who teach that a lawyer must learn to love his client. Yet whenever I begin these uninvited preachings, I am met with a high, whiny protest: "A lawyer can't love every client," and, indeed, I concede that not all clients are lovable. What I hear most often is "How can *I*" (with a capital "I") "love *them*" (with a lower case "t")? The arrogance of the profession is the enemy, the elitist idea that somehow I can take full credit for the gifts that have been showered on me—my good genes, my caring parents, my benevolent surroundings, my cornucopia of opportunity—but my clients, by reason of choice, are stupid, slothful, often immoral, and usually deserving of their lower station in the hierarchy of human worth. Find yourself born deep in the ghetto, your father unknown, your mother selling her flesh by the trick to feed your face, and explain why you haven't attended Exeter and matriculated at Yale and why you're not blinding us with your blazing social graces and charm.

Caring is contagious. After a recent trial in which the jury returned a verdict for my client that surprised the media, the prognosticators, and the public, the client held a party for the jury. After collective hair was let down and souls bared, one juror came up to my client and said, "Do you know why we knew you were right? We knew because your lawyer fought so hard for you. No lawyer would fight like that unless you were right."

I say caring is contagious, but caring begins with lawyers caring about themselves. The lawyer who has withdrawn from the fray has already lost, for even if the jury found for his client, what he takes home from the experience is as empty as eggshells. To the same extent that lawyers must give their clients the gift of themselves, so, too, lawyers are entitled to gifts—their own raw feelings and the knowledge that they are, indeed, alive after all. Such gifts usually contain little joy or peace. The gifts are savage and brim with fear. They manifest themselves with eyes locked open, staring at the ceiling in the dark of night. They countermand one's right to quiet evenings at home with the kids. They leave one open to a variety of difficult questions, like, "How can you put some stranger ahead of your family?" and "Why is an opening statement on Monday more important than fishing on Sunday?" The compromises that are demanded of the trial lawyer come without excuse, without reason. Finally, they come without any justification. One is a trial lawyer only because one has no choice about it, like one cannot change one's weak chin.

The lawyer who never learns to use the tools of his profession—the art of witness examination and of argument and oratory—is like the painter who has never mastered the brush or the surgeon whose brain is full of exotic medical data but who can't safely pare his own fingernails. The most successful trial lawyers are those who have not only acquired the requisite technical skills but who have mastered the highest art of all—truly being themselves. I think of the old cowboys who laughed at the dude who bought a $100 saddle for his $10 horse. All the known techniques of the great trial lawyers can be deposited in some intellectual machine who scored high on the LSAT, stunned the professors at Stanford, and astounded one and all with its score on the Multistate Bar Examination but who could never convince a jury that water is wet. I know an old-time Wyoming lawyer who, after nearly a half-century in the courtroom, has never learned the simple techniques of cross-examination, and who stumbles around in his final arguments like a kid trying to explain the dent in the fender of his father's new car. Yet he wins nearly all of his cases. Over and over he proves to the jury he is trustworthy. Plainspoken, open, and painfully candid, he tells it like it is, with words breaded in the stuff of his soul and soaked in the blood of his being.

I think of the people I have most feared in the courtroom, and they've always been either some young man struggling to get his honest feelings out to the jury or some neophyte self-conscious woman who wishes, for God's sake, that she could be anywhere else. She's only there because she has to be, because she cares. She has no choice, and so she struggles on. Over the years I have learned that the successful trial lawyer does not fit into any pattern of age or size or sex or looks or voice or education or even intelligence. The diminutive personality seems to be as successful as the dynamic spellbinder because the successful trial lawyers of this country have one thing in common—they strive to become whole persons who put all of themselves into their clients' cases, including a deep sense of caring, for no fortress can stave off the onslaught of men and women who have given themselves to the cause of those who need them, God bless them all, our clients, who, through us and only us, seek that ephemeral jewel called justice.

INITIAL INTERVIEWS AND INVESTIGATION OF THE CASE

Victoria C. Swanson

Plaintiffs' personal injury lawyers choose to represent people instead of corporations. They are committed to helping the poor, the injured, the disabled, and the grieving to obtain compensation from a judicial system that can offer only money to ease the tragedy of wrongful personal injury or death.

Such people do not habitually deal with lawyers. The hiring of a lawyer to pursue justice is, to say the least, intimidating to most people. Added to that is the distraction of pain, disability, financial worries, or grief. The personal injury client deserves empathy, concern, honesty, and candor.

FIRST MEETING

For most lawyers and clients, the first meeting is usually a telephone call. Your staff must be trained to recognize the calls of potential clients and to treat these inquiries with courtesy and dispatch. You and your staff must be committed to responding promptly to all client calls—this is inherent in a service profession. Realize that clients are consumers, shopping for the lawyer who will offer the best service for their problem.

The fundamental questions that both you and the prospective client have in this call are (1) is there a case? (2) does this person want to hire you? and (3) how much will your fee be? An initial screening of the client's problem is the only efficient way to decide whether a subsequent meeting is worthwhile. These are some preliminary questions:

- When and where did the injury or death occur?
- Has the statute of limitations expired?
- How did the injury or death happen?
- Has the client contacted an insurance company?
- Is the client switching lawyers? If so, why?
- How did the client learn about you?
- Are the contingent fee arrangement and costs for this kind of case acceptable to the client?

If the matter seems to be one that both you and the client want to pursue, an in-depth personal interview should be scheduled. The client should bring all pertinent material to the interview, including

- medical records and reports;
- records of wage loss;
- insurance information;
- photographs; and
- investigative reports, such as police reports.

Some lawyers ask clients to fill out information sheets and bring them to the interview (see Forms 1 and 2 in the Appendix to this chapter). Other lawyers go over the forms with the clients during the interview and ask the clients to complete them later, possibly with the help of a paralegal.

CLIENT INTERVIEW

This is an important meeting for the client, and you should treat it as such. Time should be set aside for the interview, and no interruptions should be allowed. The interview should be conducted over an uncluttered desk, so the client realizes your attention is undivided.

The interview should be a sympathetic inquisition. While the client may be reluctant to reveal unfavorable aspects of the case, it is exactly these facts that you must gently uncover. Helpful questions are, "You know, the lawyers for the driver are going to ask you ______________ ; how would you answer that question?" or "What do you suppose the other driver will say about where your car was just before the collision?" The client must understand that you need complete information about the case to provide adequate representation.

Explore the client's damages in detail. The data sheets (such as Forms 1 and 2) should be filled out completely. The damages are what the client knows best and needs to talk about. Let the client talk, noting all intangible items for later reference. If the client is particularly involved in the damages, the client should keep a journal reflecting lifestyle changes.

Affirm that you, like the client's family and physician, desire the client's rapid return to good health. A client who develops an obsessive concern for the injury or case is not likely to be satisfied with any result you obtain. In any event, the sooner a client returns to the lifestyle enjoyed before the incident, the sooner he is likely to be happy, secure, and satisfied. Therefore, the injured client should be encouraged to participate in as many former activities as medically possible, including work. It is always good to advise the client not to live for the lawsuit.

Topics that should be covered with the client in the interview for an automobile accident case are discussed below. They can be adapted to virtually all personal injury cases.

Date and Location of the Incident

Knowing the exact date of the accident is essential. This will reveal any problem with the statute of limitations. If the applicable statute already bars the case, immediately and clearly advise the client that the case is proscribed. Write down this advice and the date it was given. If the date of the running of the statute is dangerously near, note that fact in writing also, as well as the action taken (for example, file suit or decline employment).

You should also identify exactly where the incident occurred. This may have important implications on questions of jurisdiction, venue, or conflict of laws.

Potential Plaintiffs

Obtain a complete biography of each potential plaintiff. If minors are involved, this biography should include the names and addresses of the parents or guardian. If the claim involves a wrongful death, each statutory beneficiary should be identified (see Forms 1 and 2).

Potential Defendants

The client should provide any information that might help in identifying potential defendants, including the existence and nature of any agency relationship or ownership of the striking vehicle. If a defendant is a minor, local rules may require appointing a guardian. If a defendant is deceased, you may have to take steps to have a personal representative appointed and to file a claim against the estate. Probate codes vary as to the time available to file a claim against an estate, but it is generally short.

Investigative Agencies

Determine in the interview whether there were police officers at the scene of the incident and, if so, whether they were from the state or city police department or from the county sheriff's office. Workplace injuries are frequently investigated by a workers' compensation carrier, by an employer's safety committee, by a union safety committee, and sometimes by a state or federal Occupational Safety and Health Administration office. Sometimes other state and federal agencies investigate individual incidents; if so, the client may be aware that such an investigation was done.

Identification of Witnesses

The names, addresses, and telephone numbers of all persons who might have knowledge or information about any issue in the case must be obtained. You should explain to the client that there are two types of potential witnesses: persons who have knowledge of the facts and circumstances relating to the incident and persons with knowledge about the existence or effect of the client's injuries. The second type of witness should be used at trial to give a before-and-after description of the plaintiff, showing how the injury has affected the plaintiff's life.

Statements

It is important to determine whether the client has given a statement to anyone, including the client's or potential-defendant's insurance company or employer, or has testified at an investigative hearing. A client may think that she has not given a statement if there was no signed, written document; you need to inquire into this carefully. Take immediate steps to obtain any statement the client may have given, whether oral or written and whether signed or unsigned. Instruct the client not to discuss the case with anyone other than members of her family without your express permission.

The client should describe as accurately as possible all his conversations about the case, including those that might have been overheard at the scene of the incident. Any comments made by the potential defendants should be given close attention because they may be admissible at trial as admissions.

Tangible Evidence and Photographs

Look carefully for any physical object that played a role in the incident.

The existence of any photographs that might be relevant to any issue, whether relating to liability or damages, must be researched. Often, a newspaper or independent photographer may have taken photographs that could be invaluable. A local television news department may have shown the incident on its evening news broadcast. In this case, a videotape of that segment should be quickly obtained. Photographs should be taken before the vehicles involved are repaired.

In all personal injury cases, until a products case is ruled out, the auto, tool, machine, or other product involved in the injury must be preserved, and a new one purchased, if necessary.

Insurance Carriers

Identify the insurance companies for all potential defendants and notify them as soon as possible. Insurance representatives should be requested to address inquiries about the claim to your office. If a representative of the carrier has already been in touch with the client, record in detail the content of these communications. If the client has received an offer of settlement, this fact and the amount of the offer must be confirmed in writing by the carrier. The carrier should be reminded in writing to direct all further communications to you.

Insurance and Other Benefits

Take great care to identify any insurance policy that might provide the client protection or benefits. Specifically request a copy of every such insurance policy for inspection. Information concerning the client's insurance coverage is valuable for several reasons; the carrier must be notified about the incident in case other persons involved institute proceedings against its insured. The insurance company may have already investigated the accident and taken photographs or witnesses' statements. The client may have uninsured motorist's coverage. This might be necessary if a potential defendant was not covered by insurance or was underinsured at the time of the collision. The client may wish to have her insurance company pay the cost of repairing her vehicle. In most incidents, you should direct the client to permit her insurance company to pay the medical expenses; there may be more than one policy that provides benefits or coverage for the payment of medical expenses, but first exhaust the coverage for which there is no subrogation. Similarly, you should determine whether the client has other forms of insurance that will provide additional benefits like disability income and wage loss protection.

You should explore other benefits to which the client may be entitled, such as social security disability benefits, workers' compensation, and veteran's benefits.

Injuries and Damages

Ask the client to list all injuries suffered as a result of the incident. To ensure a detailed description of all the injuries, pain, and discomfort experienced, suggest that the client start with the head and describe the problems down to the toes. The names of all treating doctors and hospitals should be provided. The client must describe in detail all previous injuries, accidents, and claims. Ask whether the client ever sustained an injury at work, in the armed forces, in sports, in a fall, in an auto accident, or anywhere else.

Since many clients are hesitant to provide this information, warn that unsatisfactory verdicts often result from plaintiff's own counsel not being fully informed of prior injuries and claims at the outset. Tell the client that the insurance industry has an index bureau that contains a record of every claim made against a party and covered by insurance. Assure the client that a prior injury or claim does not necessarily jeopardize the case. Such information may be advantageous. For instance, the client's doctor may believe that the present incident aggravated the previous condition. If there has been a prior injury, obtain names of the doctors and hospitals that provided treatment and the dates of treatment.

YOUR ADVICE

After the client has talked, it is your turn. With only the limited information available, you should advise the client of the options for the case. Clients will want to know the following:

- Will I have to go to trial, or can the case be settled?
- How long will the whole process take?
- If a trial is necessary, what are my chances of winning?

Every client's most pressing concern is the dollar value of the case. A case's value should never be declared at the first interview. If a client insists, giving a range of values is the safest avenue, focusing on the conservative end. A client's expectation can always be exceeded if the case turns out better than anticipated, but few lawyers can successfully reduce overblown client expectations and still keep the client happy.

Take a few minutes to acquaint the client with what work you must do and the procedures to be followed. Tell him that any offer of settlement will be made to you, either by the opposing counsel or the defendant's insurance carrier. He should know that any and all such offers will be communicated to him, along with your advice and recommendation. Advise that an accurate evaluation of the claim may itself take a great deal of investigation and analysis but that as soon as you are able to suggest a range of figures for the anticipated results, you will present them to him for consideration and that, in any event, the final settlement decision will be his.

It is also helpful to introduce the client to your staff. Linking a name with a face puts a client at ease and opens lines of communication. A client will often tell your staff important details that she may not want to bother you with.

The interview should end with an offer to answer any additional questions. Clients are grateful for the opportunity to ask questions. Most concerns are easily dealt with, greatly relieving the client.

The client's ultimate sense of satisfaction is often influenced by the underlying motive that led him to hire a lawyer. If there is a mistrust or dissatisfaction with the American judicial system, or if the motive for embarking on litigation is revenge, you will never be able to satisfy the client. The client drops clues: does he want something that the law cannot obtain for him? Will he follow the advice of counsel? You must understand the client's motives not only to decide whether to accept the case but also to present the client's testimony at trial in such a way that the jury identifies with him and his objectives.

Before concluding the initial interview, you should be able to decide whether or not the case has sufficient merit to justify further investigation. If, at the conclusion of the interview, you decide not to take the case for whatever reason (lack of merit or conflict of interest, for example), write a letter to the client clearly and expressly declining the offer of employment. State the existence and effect of the applicable statute of limitations, and keep a record of this letter.

If you cannot determine whether there is a viable case, inform the potential client of that fact and advise her that further investigation will be needed. The file must be carefully managed at this point. All limitation dates must be recorded; promised investigation must be promptly and efficiently conducted. Confirm in writing the client's agreement to pay for this preliminary investigation. Have the potential client sign a special authorization permitting investigation of the claim but clearly stating that no attorney-client relationship exists (see Form 3). Your decision to accept or reject the case should be made as quickly as possible and communicated to the client promptly and candidly.

If you have accepted the case, give the client an instruction sheet outlining some of the things that are likely to occur while the case is pending. This instruction sheet may be given to the prospective client *before* your interview to help reinforce some of the ideas that will be discussed during the interview. Although the instruction sheet is self-explanatory, it should be emphasized that the client must not to talk to anyone except a representative of your office about the case (see Form 4). The instruction sheet may be followed by a pamphlet on the process, mailed within two weeks of the initial interview.

SPECIAL CONSIDERATIONS: PRODUCTS LIABILITY

If the case becomes a products case, you may not have foreseen in the initial interview the significance of small details that have now become paramount to a critical issue in the case.

For example, whether the left rear window was rolled down before impact or was broken out in the collision may ultimately prove to be of pivotal importance in a rear-end gas tank case, but it might not even suggest itself initially as a topic for inquiry. Therefore, in the initial interview, explain to the client that the conference will probably have to be repeated several times. In fact, in many products cases, it may be preferable to defer any exhaustive client examination until after you have conducted a preliminary investigation.

During the first interview, you should get only a general statement about the incident and how it occurred. The reasons for this are simple and practical. In the typical products liability case, the incident involves technical, causative factors of which the client is not fully aware. His recollection of what happened will make sense only after he understands the engineering principles and events involved in the incident. You cannot even ask the right questions until you have investigated, interrogated the witnesses, and acquired a thorough, technical knowledge of the product involved.

Once you determine that the case involves a products claim, you need to cover additional areas:

Product Documentation

All written documents of purchase, owner's manuals, service manuals, and instruction manuals must be obtained. If the case may proceed under the Uniform Commercial Code, warranty notification may be required.

The Product

Obtain the product, and, if it is damaged, get a similar undamaged one. The make, model, and serial number are needed, as well as the ingredients and formula, if possible. The trademark, trade name, and logo need to be preserved, as do all other markings and labels on the product.

Product History

As much as possible, determine the ownership history of the product and all pertinent modifications or repairs. The product designer, manufacturer, seller, distributor, and dealer need to be identified. If the client ever owned a similar product, it should be described in detail. If someone recommended or demonstrated this product to the client, all details should be explored. All statements made by the seller should be discussed, and all prepurchase product inspections should be obtained. The client should disclose everything she knew about the condition of the product, from its manufacture to date of injury.

Advertisements

If the product was purchased while it was being advertised, copies of all print, audio, and video advertisements must be procured immediately. Promotional materials quickly become obsolete and may be unobtainable within two to three years. The client should summarize all representations and explain why he bought or selected this product, as opposed to other competitive products. Even if the client never saw an advertisement, the advertisement may be admissible evidence at trial if a consumer expectation test—a tool that measures the reasonable expectations of the ordinary consumer—is part of the products liability law in the jurisdiction where the lawsuit was filed.

Government Agencies

If the incident was investigated by any state or federal agencies, obtain all reports of the investigations.

Photographs

Photographs of the product before and after the incident are essential.

Client Knowledge

Issues of intended use or foreseeable misuse are common. Any specialized training, education, or skills the client might have had that relate to the product or similar products and how they are built and maintained, function, or are used should be included. The defense of assumption of risk is common.

Warnings

Was the client ever warned of any dangers associated with using the product, or did the client ever see any writing containing a warning, for example, labels, literature with the product, or manuals? Explore with the client all contents of warnings or the names of any person who gave warnings.

Other Malfunctions

The client may know about prior malfunctions or injuries involving the product. Subsequent malfunctions and injuries should also be investigated, as they are relevant to a design defect.

The Injury Incident

The client should describe in detail all uses to which the product was put at the time of injury. Determine whether these uses were abnormal or otherwise contrary to instructions.

Government Standards

The client may know if the product was subject to certain government design, manufacture, or maintenance requirements.

SPECIAL CONSIDERATIONS: MEDICAL NEGLIGENCE

In medical negligence cases, as in products cases, you may not be able to foresee the later significance of small details until the necessary technical facts are known. In such cases, advise the client that the fact-finding initial interview may have to be repeated several times. Since the client in a professional negligence case frequently has personal knowledge of what the health care provider did to cause the injury, the client should be exhaustively examined. The interview may be tape recorded for detailed factual submission to an expert for review. However, the recording may be discoverable as part of the facts on which the expert is relying to form opinions.

With this understanding, the following areas should be discussed in an initial interview involving a claim of medical negligence:

- a complete medical history;
- all symptoms before, during, and after the alleged negligence;
- a complete list of every symptom described to the health care provider by the client or family; this list should be in chronological order, stating the name and identity of each person present when the information was provided;
- a chronological list of all tests and examinations performed by the health care provider; and
- a complete and chronological summary of every statement

made by the health care provider—this summary should identify each person present on each occasion.

FEE AGREEMENT

Before deciding to accept the case, you must weigh a number of factors: the probability of success, the potential value of the claim, the anticipated costs of litigation (especially expert witness fees), and the nature of the case in light of your experience. If you are inexperienced and the case is complex or unusual, consider affiliating with a more experienced attorney or an attorney who practices in the particular field of litigation.

In general, you should not accept employment in a case that you do not expect to try. The wrongful injury or death case will only be resolved for its maximum value if the defense counsel and insurance company face the real threat of a jury trial. You should not take a case of doubtful liability solely on the hope that the case can be settled.

If you decide to accept the case, the client should execute an employment agreement that provides for fees and costs. Contingency fees are appropriate and customary in personal injury cases. The agreed-upon percentage should conform to local bar standards and state statutes in those jurisdictions that have enacted legislation or court rules.

Discuss with the client the items and activity necessary for an adequate investigation, and explain that the investigation will result in expenses. Typically, such items and activities would include photographs, depositions, medical reports, and fees for investigators and experts. The American Bar Association Code of Professional Responsibility and the American Lawyer's Code of Conduct, written by the Commission on Professional Responsibility of the Roscoe Pound–American Trial Lawyers Foundation, permit you to advance these expenses on behalf of a client with the understanding that ultimately they will be borne by the client. It is essential that the client understand this at the outset to prevent a possible misunderstanding at the time of distribution. Also explain that the client's medical bills are the client's personal obligation.

Some states require that a copy of the contract be given to the client (two fee agreements patterned by state statutes are provided as Forms 5 and 6). In an office equipped with word processors, a custom fee agreement (as opposed to a fill-in-the blank one) should be presented to the client.

INVESTIGATION

A lawsuit is no better or worse than the evidence collected. Though methods of presentation may vary, facts control a lawsuit. The first and most important thing the plaintiff's attorney can do is to learn every fact, favorable or unfavorable. The principles of investigation are the same for the attorney's professional investigator.

At the client interview, have releases available for client signature so that the necessary prefiling investigation can begin without delay. These releases include those for medical records, employment and personnel records, tax records, school records, and other documents that may be privileged (see Forms 7 and 8).

When the new client leaves your office, you can begin processing the new file. Typically, four things should be done immediately:

- ► Request the hospital records and physicians' reports.
- ► Notify the potential defendants or their insurance carriers.
- ► Request the police or incident report from the appropriate investigative agencies.
- ► Notify the client's insurance carrier.

Some counsel send a letter simply advising a health care provider that their office is representing the client but that the provider need not send a written report unless and until requested to do so by the attorney at a future date (see Form 9). In some cases it may be preferable to secure the provider's testimony by deposition rather than through a written report, where, for example, the injuries or causation of injuries needs to be carefully stated or explained.

When the appropriate authorization has been executed, the request for records *may* state that the health care provider's unpaid bills will be protected in the event a recovery is ultimately effected, but this is not required. Before requesting hospital records, decide whether to order the full records or merely some portion. Even though the complete record is expensive, it generally gives a thorough medical history and is helpful in informing experts. Nurses' notes also serve as a good indication of the patient's pain and suffering. If a death is involved, the death certificate or report of the coroner's inquest should be ordered.

A letter of notification should be addressed to all potential defendants, informing them that legal action is being contemplated and instructing that they so advise their insurance carriers. If counsel knows the defendants' insurance companies, copies of this letter of notification should go there, too. Prompt notification may be imperative where the defendants are government employees or deceased. Carefully check the law of your jurisdiction to determine when formal notice and presentation of the claim must be made and whether or not the state law requires written notification to set up an attorney's lien.

Be aware that if the case involves a claim of breach of warranty, some jurisdictions still require that the defendant be notified as a condition precedent to the filing of an action for breach of warranty. In fact, some state remedial statutes, such as the Texas Deceptive Trade Practices Act, require notification to the defendants before suit is filed. Likewise, the laws of some states require that, in the event of the death of a potential defendant, a claim be filed against the estate before institution of a lawsuit. Such a letter of notification should *never* be sent to an individual defendant, the defendant's insurance carrier, or any other prospective defendant until an attempt has been made to obtain the statement of the potential defendant. This is because, if informed of impending litigation involving the insured, insurance companies customarily advise their policyholders not to give statements to anyone.

You should immediately request the full and final report of any investigation conducted by a municipal, state, or federal agency, including, where appropriate, the results of any action taken against the defendants or the employer as a result of that investigation.

Some firms regularly employ nonlawyer investigators. A trained professional investigator may be of enormous value in preparing a personal injury case, if only because the investigator devotes full resources to preparing the factual and technical aspects of the case, thereby freeing the attorney to concentrate on legal matters and the implementation of overall strategy.

Cases are often won or lost in the investigation. It is, therefore, essential that the investigator be well-trained in the art of conducting an investigation and carefully briefed in the specific objectives of the particular investigation. Ordinarily, you should not delegate the entire responsibility for the factual preparation of the case to an investigator. In any event, the activities of the nonlawyer investigator should be reviewed periodically. In some cases, a nonlawyer investigator may be more effective than a lawyer in getting witnesses to open up and discuss the relevant facts. Where you personally conduct the investigation, you have the advantage of an intimate and firsthand knowledge of the witnesses.

Every personal injury investigation should be approached with one key question in mind: "How could this accident have been prevented?" This will be important in an automobile case, a "fall-down" case, or a products liability case. For the investigator to probe effectively, she must have some familiarity with principles of tort law, and you should work closely with the investigator—before and after the initial investigation—to determine whether liability can be proven. Together, you and the investigator should periodically review each case file to determine what investigations have been completed and what needs to be done next.

When asked to recount the details of a fortuitous and traumatic event, the typical layperson will describe as *fact* what is actually a personal and inaccurate estimate. Typically, the client's estimates of time, distance, and speed will not reflect the facts. You, as the lawyer, must accurately identify the pertinent facts at the scene of the injury and apply known physical laws to the facts, explaining your conclusions to the client before he commits to a statement describing the occurrence of the incident.

Soon after the initial interview, the investigator may wish to meet with the client at the scene of the incident to take a comprehensive statement of how the accident occurred. In the presence of the client, the investigator should diagram the area; the diagram need not be made to scale, but it should be measured accurately. In an auto case, the investigator should locate the point of impact, if possible, and measure from that point to a known reference point on the scene diagram. This is an easily located point, such as a telephone pole or the corner of a building. The client should show where he was when the other vehicle was first seen, where on the road brakes were first applied, and other important points of reference. Having located the point of impact, the spot at which the brakes were first applied, and other important locations, the investigator should measure the distances involved. In an auto case, the investigator should also measure the width of the roadway pavement where the incident occurred, noting any unusual topographical features. Ultimately, the value of the diagram will depend on the accuracy of the person making it.

At the time of deposition or trial, the client can refer to the diagram to refresh her memory of the scene and the pertinent facts relating to the incident. Remember, though, that opposing counsel is entitled to see any document used to prepare your client for deposition or trial, *if* it is used to refresh her recollection. The time spent by the investigator and the client at the scene of the incident helps prepare the investigator for subsequent investigation of the case.

The investigation should include as complete a photographic history of the incident as possible; photos should be taken as soon as feasible. When taking photos of the scene, the photographer should show various key features from more than one angle. Photographs should show the views available to each potential party. Aerial photographs can be very valuable in certain cases, but their expense often outweighs their value. The investigator should always look for photographs taken by freelance or newspaper photographers or television news videotape. If the case warrants the effort, the investigator may check newspaper archives to see if any pictures appeared in the papers. In an auto case, photographs should also be taken of all vehicles involved in the collision. If photographs were not taken at the scene of the collision, the investigator should locate the vehicles and photograph them from all possible angles. Often, the condition of the interior of the client's vehicle dramatically portrays the force of impact at the time of collision. In all cases, photos should be taken as soon as possible because conditions will change, and automobiles, premises, or machinery will be repaired or destroyed.

Photographs are equally important in more complex litigation such as products liability cases. Everything about the product should be photographed, including warning labels, serial numbers, names of manufacturers, guards or lack thereof, and other such materials that may be relevant to the case. It is extremely important to obtain and preserve custody of the product. If the product exists under an uncooperative third party's control, you should consider what method is available to legally impound the product. Injunctive relief may be available to secure control of it and place it in the custody of the court to prevent alteration without express court approval.

In a case involving an automobile collision, you should obtain copies of repair estimates on the vehicles involved. Whether or not the frame or suspension of the client's car was damaged is important; such damage indicates a major impact. Finally, investigators should obtain information concerning the exact weight of the vehicles involved in the collision (including all baggage, fuel, and occupants), because at trial an engineering expert can use this information in connection with the law of kinetic energy to reconstruct the accident or to prove the amount of force exerted on the client's body.

Witnesses should be interviewed as soon as possible to record their observations. When you or your investigator confronts a witness, make clear that you are only interested in the truth. Explain that our adversary system cannot function without the cooperation of sound-thinking citizens willing to become involved. If witnesses consent to returning to the scene of the incident, interview them there. With the help of the scene diagram, ask these witnesses to go through the sequence of events as they remember them. The place where each person was when the incident occurred should be marked on the scene diagram. If witnesses refuse to go to the scene of the incident, talk to them at home or anywhere else convenient to them. Photographs can be used to orient witnesses to the scene of the incident. These photos should be marked at the points to which witnesses refer, such as their location and where the cars were first seen. In this way, the photographs become permanent records of the witnesses' observations.

No matter where witnesses are interviewed, their observations should, if possible, be recorded. You may choose to have interviews recorded by a court reporter or to take written or recorded statements yourself. Although using a court reporter raises the cost of investigation, the increase may be justified because of the authoritative nature of such statements. That is, the court reporter is a disinterested third party available as a witness at trial to testify if the accuracy of the statements is questioned. Some witnesses, however, do not feel comfortable when a third party, such as a court reporter, is present.

The investigator should have recording devices to tape a witness's statement (or a potential defendant's statement) either in person or on the telephone. After the statement is recorded (with the witness's permission), it should be transcribed and two copies delivered to the witness. The witness should be requested to read the statement and then to sign it after making corrections. The witness should also be permitted to keep a copy of the statement in case anyone else attempts to take another statement. When the witness (or potential defendant) will permit an interview but will not allow remarks to be recorded and will not sign a handwritten statement, the investigator should summarize notes of the interview. This transcript may be sent to the witness with a cover letter stating that the enclosed is a summary of the conversation with the witness and requesting that the witness check it for accuracy, make any corrections, sign it, and return it in a self-addressed envelope. An extra copy of this summary should be furnished to the potential defendant or witness for his own records.

When neither a court reporter nor audio recording equipment is used, the investigator should write down, in longhand, all the comments made by the witness. When the interview concludes, the investigator should ask the witness to read the longhand narrative and make any necessary corrections. If the witness will sign the statement, she should be encouraged to sign each page and initial any changes.

In addition to getting a full account of what happened, the investigator should be certain that in all of these statements the correct names, addresses, dates of birth, telephone numbers, and maiden names, including the addresses and telephone numbers of neighbors, relatives, and employers, are recorded so that several months or even years later, the witnesses can be found. If the defendant or witness refuses to give a detailed statement, it is helpful, if applicable, to get a negative statement. This is an admission by the person: "I don't remember," "I have no idea how fast the driver was going," "I didn't see anything," or "I didn't hear the horn." Negative admissions may be used to impeach if the witness suddenly remembers these things at trial.

It is not unethical to attempt to obtain a statement from the defendant *before* he is represented by counsel. Therefore, you should try to obtain such a statement before filing. Once suit is filed, the defendant will be represented by counsel, and then it would be unethical to approach him for a statement. You should instruct the investigator that, if the defendant is represented by counsel, no statement should be taken.

The police officers who investigated the occurrence should be contacted (investigators would be wise to develop an amicable relationship with law enforcement officers in their area). Police officers are more likely to cooperate if the investigator arranges to meet with them while they are on duty. Frequently, officers agree to meet the investigator at the scene of the incident; you should encourage this approach. Ask them to bring original notes made at the scene of the incident because they may contain information not recorded in the official report. When a traffic signal is involved in the auto case, the time sequence of the signal at the hour of the incident should be checked with the local authorities.

Photographs of an injured client, if they show her disability and indicate discomfort and pain, can be valuable at trial. Such photographs, showing injuries, should be taken either at the hospital or at the home of the injured party—never at the lawyer's office. If photographs are taken at the hospital or at some other location, the investigator should be sure to include in the photograph any special medical equipment now used by the client. It is also imperative that the investigator or photographer note the dates and times that each photograph was taken, as these facts may become important at the trial. Photographs are particularly valuable for showing scars, extensive bruising and swelling, and lacerations. Photographs are also recommended when the client is forced to wear a device such as a cervical collar or to use some form of traction. Many times orthopedic surgeons, plastic surgeons, and other physicians take pictures in the regular course of their medical treatment; these pictures are often accessible to the lawyer.

INVESTIGATION: PRODUCTS LIABILITY

Below is a brief outline of the major topics that should be covered in the investigation process of a products liability case.

- Get the product or a similar one, if possible.
- Photograph the product and the scene of the incident.
- Hire and consult with an appropriate expert as soon as possible.
- Search the technical and trade literature for information relative to the product and the industry involved.
- Carefully trace the path of the product from the date it left the original manufacturer's control until the incident occurred and then forward to the present time. Was there any prior abuse to or alteration of the product?
- Identify all potential witnesses and interview them as soon as possible.
- Identify all potential defendants.

You should attempt to answer the following major questions in this investigation:

- What actual occurrence in the incident caused the client's injury?
- What could the manufacturer have done to avoid the incident?
- What claims or representations has the manufacturer made about the quality or performance of the product?
- Have other similar incidents occurred?
- What do other manufacturers do in the design, construction, or instructions for use or maintenance of similar products?
- What does the technical and trade literature say *should* be done in the design, construction, or instructions for use or maintenance of similar products?
- Has the defendant altered or modified either the product or the instructions for its use and maintenance?
- Was the condition of the product changed at all between the time it left the defendant and the time of the incident?
- Are there any applicable industry or governmental standards or regulations?

INVESTIGATION: PROFESSIONAL NEGLIGENCE

The very bases of liability in professional negligence cases, such as medical or legal negligence, are factually and technically complex. By necessity, therefore, the scope of a basic investigation is much more extensive than in the typical automobile collision.

Medical Negligence

In a medical negligence case, the investigator should immediately photograph and copy all records from the hospital, physician, or other health care provider. After a complete and comprehensive record has been made of your client's version of the facts, a competent physician in the relevant specialty should review all of this material to advise whether or not there was a departure from the applicable standard of care and whether the defendant's negligence proximately caused your client's injuries.

This screening process is extremely important and should be done early in the case. The most important thing that a lawyer should learn is how to turn down a medical negligence case. As in products cases, you must estimate the potential value of a client's loss and compare that with the generally high costs of the experts and case preparation to analyze whether it is economically feasible to proceed with the expense of such a case.

Legal Negligence

In a legal negligence case, the investigator should copy all records from the courthouse or from any legal proceedings. She should attempt to obtain a complete copy of the attorney's office records, all depositions, and every other document or paper involving the potential case. In addition, the investigator should carefully investigate the important witnesses as well as record a complete and comprehensive statement from the client as to the client's version of the facts. In other words, you and the investigator will have to prepare a complete case so that these facts can be submitted with all of the records for review by a competent, well-regarded attorney-expert in the field involved for advice from a technical standpoint on whether to proceed with the suit.

As in medical negligence cases, the screening process is extremely important and should be completed as early as possible. As in products liability and professional negligence cases, a cost-value economic analysis of the case should be made carefully before proceeding. In each instance, if the case is rejected, the client should be notified by a letter that sets forth the reasons for the decision. It is advisable to send such a letter by certified or registered mail.

EXPERTS

In all but the most routine automobile accident or similar cases, both counsel and the investigator need to consult an expert early in the development of the case to acquire the necessary technical background. You need at least basic knowledge of the technical aspects of the case to determine whether the case is meritorious.

This threshold decision should be made early in the development of the case because of the tremendous cost and expense of case development. It is better to withdraw from a case early than to spend a lot of time and money only to withdraw later. You must make an early estimate of the value of the claim and compare that with the expenses that will necessarily be incurred to determine whether the client would be well advised to proceed. Such an analysis may reveal that the prospects of a positive recovery for the client do not justify a decision to proceed. Carefully explain the need for this analysis to the client.

In a products liability case, retain a competent expert to inspect the product thoroughly and to perform nondestructive testing, if appropriate. Destructive testing should only be done with either agreement of all parties or court approval and with another undamaged product in counsel's care.

In a medical negligence case, an expert evaluation of the case is essential before filing and a matter of good practice if not statutorily mandated in the particular jurisdiction.

In all complex cases, you (and your client) can save money if you learn the technical aspects of the issue in question. The experts can direct you to appropriate treatises, technical literature, and industry or government standards. After all, you, not the expert, are the one who will try the case.

APPENDIX

FORM 1

CLIENT DATA SHEET

Please Type or Print Neatly
Client's Name: ______________________________
Address: ______________________________
Telephone number: (H) ______________ (W) ______________
Social Security Number: ______________________________
Date of birth ______________ Birthplace: ______________
Former address: ______________________________

Spouse's Name: ______________________________
Address: ______________________________
Telephone number: (H) ______________ (W) ______________
Social Security Number: ______________________________
Date of birth: ______________ Birthplace: ______________
Date of marriage: ______________ Place: ______________
Was a divorce ever filed? If so, when? ______________
Spouse's employer's name, address, and telephone number: ________
____

Former Spouse's Name (if applicable): ______________
Address: ______________________________
Telephone number: (H) ______________ (W) ______________
Social Security Number: ______________________________
Date of termination of marriage: ________ Where? ______________
Divorce or death? ______________________________

List All Natural Children of Client:
Attach extra pages if necessary.
(A) Name: ______________________________
Address: ______________________________
Telephone number: (H) ______________ (W) ______________
Social Security Number: ______________________________
Date of birth: ______________ Birthplace: ______________

Other parent's name, address, and telephone number: ________
____

(B) Name: ____
Address: ____
Telephone number: (H) ____________(W) ____________________
Social Security Number: ______________________________
Date of birth: ______________Birthplace: ____________________
Other parent's name, address, and telephone number: ________
____

(C) Name: ____
Address: ____
Telephone number: (H) ____________(W) ____________________
Social Security Number: ______________________________
Date of birth: ______________Birthplace: ____________________
Other parent's name, address, and telephone number: ________
____

List Any Other Dependent Children of Client:
Attach extra pages if necessary.
(A) Name: ____
Address: ____
Telephone number: (H) ____________(W) ____________________
Social Security Number: ______________________________
Date of birth: ______________Birthplace: ____________________
Natural parent's name, address, and telephone number: ______
____

(B) Name: ____
Address: ____
Telephone number: (H) ____________(W) ____________________
Social Security Number: ______________________________
Date of birth: ______________Birthplace: ____________________
Natural parent's name, address, and telephone number: ______
____

Did Client Support Any Others Not Listed Above?

(A) Name: ______________________________
Address: ______________________________
Telephone number: (H) ____________ (W) ____________
Relationship to client: ______________________________
What percentage or amount of client's income was provided to this person? ______________________________

(B) Name: ______________________________
Address: ______________________________
Telephone number: (H) ____________ (W) ____________
Relationship to client: ______________________________
What percentage or amount of client's income was provided to this person? ______________________________

Client's Father's Name: ______________________________
Address: ______________________________
Telephone number: (H) ____________ (W) ____________
Date of birth: ____________ Birthplace: ____________
If deceased, state date of death: ______________________________
Place of death: ______________________________
Cause of death: ______________________________

Client's Mother's Name: ______________________________
Address: ______________________________
Telephone number: (H) ____________ (W) ____________
Date of birth: ____________ Birthplace: ____________
If deceased, state date of death: ______________________________
Place of death: ______________________________
Cause of death: ______________________________

Client's Brothers and Sisters (including half-brothers and half-sisters, if any): Attach extra pages if necessary.

(A) Name: ______________________________
Address: ______________________________
Telephone number: (H) ____________ (W) ____________
Date of birth: ____________ Birthplace: ____________
If deceased, state date of death: ______________________________
Place of death: ______________________________
Cause of death: ______________________________

(B) Name: ____________________
Address: ____________________
Telephone number: (H) __________ (W) __________
Date of birth: __________ Birthplace: __________
If deceased, state date of death: __________
Place of death: ____________________
Cause of death: ____________________

(C) Name: ____________________
Address: ____________________
Telephone number: (H) __________ (W) __________
Date of birth: __________ Birthplace: __________
If deceased, state date of death: __________
Place of death: ____________________
Cause of death: ____________________

Economic Losses (Client's Annual Income for Five Years Before Injury):
19__ $__________
19__ $__________
19__ $__________
19__ $__________
19__ $__________

Client's Current Employer:
Name, address, and telephone number: ____________________
____
Title and duties performed: ____________________
____
Dates employed: ____________________

Employers for Last Ten Years: Attach extra pages if necessary.
(A) Name, address, and telephone number: ____________________
____
Title and duties performed: ____________________
____
Dates employed: ____________________

(B) Name, address, and telephone number: ____________________

____

Title and duties performed: ______________________________

____

Dates employed: _______________________________________

(C) Name, address, and telephone number: ____________________

____

Title and duties performed: ______________________________

____

Dates employed: _______________________________________

Educational Information of Client:

High school graduate? ______________ Year: ___________________

Name of college attended: __________________________________

Years: __________________ Degree achieved: __________________

Name of college attended: __________________________________

Years: __________________ Degree achieved: __________________

Other Technical/Trade Training:

Describe:

Occupation at Time of Injury:

Client's Career Goals:

Describe:

Incident/Injury Information:

(A) Date of incident: ___________ Location: ____________________

(B) Description of incident:

(C) Witnesses' names, addresses, and telephone numbers:

1) ____

____

2) ____

____

3) ____

____

4) ____

____

Medical Treatment Information: Attach extra pages if necessary.

(A) Doctors, hospitals, clinics, etc., providing treatment for injuries:

1) Name and address: ______________________________

____

Approximate dates of treatment: ______________________________

Nature of treatment: ______________________________

____

2) Name and address: ______________________________

____

Approximate dates of treatment: ______________________________

Nature of treatment: ______________________________

____

3) Name and address: ______________________________

____

Approximate dates of treatment: ______________________________

Nature of treatment: ______________________________

____

(B) Medical insurance at time of injury:

Who is paying your bills? _ Auto/PIP _Workers' compensation

_ Your medical insurer _ Self _ Other

Name: ______________________________

Address: ______________________________

Policy number: __________ Telephone number: ______________

Witnesses to Client's Injuries, Suffering, or Damages:

(A) Name: ______________________________

Address: ______________________________

Telephone number: (H) ___________ (W) ______________

What the witness knows: ______________________________

____

(B) Name: ______________________________

Address: ______________________________

Telephone number: (H) ___________ (W) ______________

What the witness knows:________________________________

____

Describe Your Injuries/Damages:

Thank you for completing this information sheet. This information is needed to evaluate your case and to expedite the handling of your case. Please return it to:

(Name of attorney/firm)
(Address)
(Telephone number)

FORM 2
CLIENT DATA SHEET
(Wrongful Death Case)

Please Type or Print Neatly
Name of Deceased: ____________________
Last address: ____________________
Date of birth: __________ Birthplace: __________
Social Security Number: ____________________

Personal Representative (or Administrator) of Probate Estate:
Name: ____________________
Address: ____________________
Telephone number: ____________________
Date estate opened: _____ Court: _____ Action number: __________

Probate Attorney for the Estate (if any):
Name: ____________________
Address: ____________________
Telephone number: ____________________

Spouse of Deceased:
Name: ____________________
Address: ____________________
Telephone number: (H) __________ (W) __________
Social Security Number: ____________________
Date of birth: __________ Birthplace: __________
Date of marriage: __________ Place: __________
Was a divorce ever filed? ______ If so, when? __________
Spouse's employer's name and address: ____________________
____

Former Spouse's Name (if applicable): ____________________
Address: ____________________
Telephone number: (H) __________ (W) __________
Social Security Number: ____________________
Date of termination of marriage: __________ Where? __________

Divorce or death? ____

List All Natural Children of Deceased:
Attach extra pages if necessary.

(A) Name: ____
Address: ____
Telephone number: (H) ____________ (W) ____________________
Social Security Number: ____________________________________
Date of birth: ______________ Birthplace: ____________________
Other parent's name, address, and telephone number: __________
____

(B) Name: ____
Address: ____
Telephone number: (H) ____________ (W) ____________________
Social Security Number: ____________________________________
Date of birth: ______________ Birthplace: ____________________
Other parent's name, address, and telephone number: __________
____

(C) Name: ____
Address: ____
Telephone number: (H) ____________ (W) ____________________
Social Security Number: ____________________________________
Date of birth: ______________ Birthplace: ____________________
Other parent's name, address, and telephone number: __________
____

List Any Other Dependent Children of Deceased:
Attach extra pages if necessary.

(A) Name: ____
Address: ____
Telephone number: (H) ____________ (W) ____________________
Social Security Number: ____________________________________
Date of birth: ______________ Birthplace: ____________________
Natural parent's name, address, and telephone number: ________
____

(B) Name: ____
Address: ____
Telephone number: (H) ____________ (W) ____________________
Social Security Number: ____________________________________
Date of birth: ______________ Birthplace: ____________________

Natural parent's name, address, and telephone number: ______
______

Did Deceased Support Any Others Not Listed Above?

(A) Name: ______
Address: ______
Telephone number: (H) ______ (W) ______
Relationship to deceased: ______
What percentage or amount of deceased's income was provided to this person? ______

(B) Name: ______
Address: ______
Telephone number: (H) ______ (W) ______
Relationship to deceased: ______
What percentage or amount of deceased's income was provided to this person? ______

Deceased's Father's Name: ______
Address: ______
Telephone number: (H) ______ (W) ______
Date of birth: ______ Birthplace: ______
If deceased, state date of death: ______ Where? ______
Cause of death: ______

Deceased's Mother's Name: ______
Address: ______
Telephone number: (H) ______ (W) ______
Date of birth: ______ Birthplace: ______
If deceased, state date of death: ______ Where? ______
Cause of death: ______

Deceased's Brothers and Sisters (including half-brothers and half-sisters, if any): Attach extra pages if necessary.

(A) Name: ______
Address: ______
Telephone number: (H) ______ (W) ______
Date of birth: ______ Birthplace: ______
If deceased, state date of death: ______ Where? ______
Cause of death: ______

(B) Name: ______

Address: ____
Telephone number: (H) ____________ (W) ______________
Date of birth: ______________ Birthplace: ______________
If deceased, state date of death: ________ Where? ________
Cause of death: ____

(C) Name: ____
Address: ____
Telephone number: (H) ____________ (W) ______________
Date of birth: ______________ Birthplace: ______________
If deceased, state date of death: ________ Where? ________
Cause of death: ____

Economic Losses (Deceased's Annual Income for Last Five Years before Death):

19__ $______________________
19__ $______________________
19__ $______________________
19__ $______________________
19__ $______________________

Deceased's Employers for Last Ten Years:

(A) Name, address, and telephone number: ______________
____
Title and duties performed: ________________________
____
Dates employed: ______________________

(B) Name, address, and telephone number: ______________
____
Title and duties performed: ________________________
____
Dates employed: ______________________

(C) Name, address, and telephone number: ______________
____
Title and duties performed: ________________________
____
Dates employed: ______________________

Educational Information of Deceased:

High school graduate? ______________ Year: ______________
Name of college attended: ______________________________
Years: __________________ Degree achieved: ______________

Name of college attended: ___________________________
Years: ______________ Degree achieved: ______________

Other Technical/Trade Training of Deceased:
Describe:

Occupation at Time of Death:

Deceased's Career Goals:
Describe:

Accident/Death Information:
(A) Date of accident: __________ Location: ______________
(B) Description of accident:
(C) Witnesses' names, addresses, and telephone numbers:
1) ____
____
2) ____
____
3) ____
____
4) ____
____
(D) Was an autopsy performed? __________
If so, by whom? ______________________________

Burial/Funeral Expenses: $ __________
Name of funeral home: ___________________________
Attach funeral bill(s).

Medical Expenses (if any):
Facility: ______________________________ $ ________
Facility: ______________________________ $ ________
Workers' Compensation Benefits Received? Yes ____ No ____
Insurance company: ___________________________
Address: ___________________________________
Telephone number: ____________ Claim number: ____________

Witnesses to Deceased's Injuries, Suffering, or Damages:

(1) Name, address, and telephone number: ______________________

____

What the witness knows: ______________________________

____

(2) Name, address, and telephone number: ______________________

____

What the witness knows: ______________________________

____

(3) Name, address, and telephone number: ______________________

____

What the witness knows: ______________________________

____

Thank you for completing this information sheet. This information is needed to evaluate your case and to expedite the handling of your case. Please return it to:

(Name of attorney/firm)
(Address)
(Telephone number)

FORM 3
AUTHORITY TO INVESTIGATE

I/We have discussed a potential claim with (name of attorney/firm) arising out of the following incident:

____
Type of incident

____
Date Place

I/We have not employed (name of attorney/firm) to file suit or to represent me/us as my/our legal attorneys.

I/We authorize (name of attorney/firm) to conduct an investigation of this incident with the understanding that the results of such investigation remain the property of (name of attorney/firm).

Check one:

_ I/We agree to pay the costs incurred in the conduct of this investigation.

_ (Name of attorney/firm) agrees to advance the costs involved in the conduct of this investigation.

I/We have no further responsibility or obligation to (name of attorney/firm) [except to reimburse the costs of the investigation]. (Name of attorney/firm) has no further responsibility or obligation to me/us.

SIGNED this _______ day of _________________, 19___.

For the firm: Claimant(s):

______________________ 1. ______________________

Address: ______________________

____

Telephone: (H) ______________________

(W) ______________________

2. ______________________________
Address: ________________________
____
Telephone: (H) __________________
(W) __________________

FORM 4
CLIENT INFORMATION SHEET

(Name of attorney/firm)
(Address)
(Telephone number)

Your file number: ___________

TO OUR CLIENT:

We know that your case is important to you; we want you to know that it is also important to us and that we will do the best we can to represent your interests.

This pamphlet was written for two reasons:

FIRST, to give you some idea of what to expect in the future and

SECOND, to offer some suggestions about how you can help us prepare your case.

We hope this pamphlet answers some of your questions. It was not written to discourage you from calling us about other questions you may have—please feel free to call us any time you feel the need to do so.

WHEN WILL THE CASE BE FILED?

It is entirely possible that we have already filed the case. If you would like to confirm that, you need only call the secretary of the attorney handling your file. We may wait until we have completed a preliminary investigation of the matter before we file the case in court. In the event that our investigation leads us to the conclusion that we cannot by legal action truly assist you, we will contact you immediately.

WHAT HAPPENS AFTER THE SUIT IS FILED?

After the suit is filed, there will be two areas of activity.

First, we will continue to investigate and research your case. Depending on the requirements of the case, we may be assisted by professional investigators and research assistants. This investigation and research often takes weeks or even months, and during this time we may not need to contact you personally.

The second area of activity is called "discovery." Various statutes and court rules permit representatives from each side of the lawsuit to file papers in court requesting the other side to furnish information about the case. When either side files such papers in court, the other side must respond within a fairly short time—usually 30 days. There are various types of discovery devices that the law allows:

1. *Interrogatories*. These are a series of written questions that one side asks the other. Interrogatories must be answered in writing and under oath.
2. *Requests for production*. Each side may request the other to produce documents or things that might relate to the case.
3. *Depositions*. This is a procedure in which the lawyer for one side asks a witness questions orally. The witness is under oath and answers orally while a court reporter transcribes the proceedings.

We almost certainly will use one or more of these discovery devices. The other side is also likely to use them. If and when they do, we will need your help in filing our response in court promptly. If and when the other side files a paper requesting discovery, we will write to you immediately and give you specific instructions about what to do. We will also ask you to call and make an appointment to come into the office before we file our response to the court.

WHEN WILL THE CASE BE TRIED?

At the present time, cases are generally scheduled for trial about _____ months after they are filed. You can figure from the filing date of your case the approximate time when your case will be set for trial.

THE PRINTED DOCKET

All the cases that are set down to be tried in any calendar month appear in a printed docket that the court gives to the lawyers about 30 days in advance. For instance, on about the first of January we get a printed docket in which appear all the cases that are set for trial in February.

Furthermore, cases are tentatively set for trial in a particular week. All the cases the court hopes to try are set at the beginning of a particular week. Then during the week, as the trial judges become available, the cases are assigned one at a time to specific judges for trial. However, if a case does not come to trial during the week when it is set, it is continued to another printed docket and is usually set again several months later.

The cases are set in numerical order with perhaps 40 cases set on Monday and another 40 each set on Tuesday and Wednesday. The presiding judge assigns the cases to the trial judges in numerical order. If your case is set on a certain morning at nine o'clock but is numerically behind other cases, it may not be reached until later that day, later that week, or several months later.

WHEN WILL YOU BE NOTIFIED OF THE TRIAL?

As soon as we receive the printed docket, we will notify you that your case is set for trial. This will give you about a month's advance notice.

WHEN WILL YOU HEAR FROM US AFTER TODAY?

Except for meeting with you to respond to the other side's use of the discovery devices discussed above, several months may go by during which it is not necessary for us to contact you in order to do what we must do to prepare your case.

If we find that we need additional information from you about your case, we will write to you. If you learn information beyond what you have already given us—such as the names of other witnesses, developments in your physical condition resulting from your injury, or anything else—please communicate it to us so that we may serve you fully.

IF YOU MOVE OR CHANGE YOUR ADDRESS, PLEASE INFORM US. IT IS NECESSARY THAT WE BE ABLE TO REACH YOU AT ALL TIMES.

SUPPOSE YOU DO NOT HEAR FROM US FOR SEVERAL MONTHS?

It is possible that months will pass without our having any necessity or occasion to contact you. If this happens, don't get the impression that your case is not receiving our interest and attention. In some states it takes four or five years for a case to be set for trial. In __________ it takes about __________ for a case to be set. Sometimes, in spite of everything everybody can do, a case is postponed, and all we can do is be sure that we remain prepared so that the delay will not disadvantage you.

One difference between the work of doctors and that of lawyers is in the amount of contact between client and professional. You are present while a doctor works on your body and you can see what he or she is doing, but the pretrial work that a lawyer does for you is often done in your absence—in the office, at the courthouse, or elsewhere. For this reason, and because everyone justifiably feels that his or her case is important, we have sent you this informational pamphlet.

SETTLEMENT

After a case has been turned over to us, it is possible that a compromise settlement can be made. We cannot legally make a settlement, nor do we wish to make a settlement, unless you approve of and consent to it. If you are not satisfied with the settlement offer, you have a right to let the jury decide your case. By the same token, the defendant also has a right to a trial, and we cannot force the defendant to settle the case. Bear this in mind, because if you exhibit haste and eagerness in a settlement, you are likely to decrease the value of your case in the eyes of the defendant.

The intelligent evaluation and settlement of a case calls for just as high a degree of legal skill as the trial of a lawsuit and, if done properly, often takes just as much time.

THE TRIAL

If the case has to be tried, do not consider it an ordeal or a cause of fear or embarrassment. Your neighbors in this county or district will sit on the jury. If you testify, you will only be asked to tell the court what you know in a simple straightforward manner. Almost everybody who goes through a trial is pleasantly surprised that there is nothing bad about it.

WHAT HAPPENS AFTER THE TRIAL?

If you win your case, the defendant can either pay the verdict or make a motion for a new trial. If the motion for a new trial is overruled, the defendant can appeal. If you lose, you have the same choice: to accept the verdict or to challenge it. We naturally hope to win your case. We would not have accepted employment to bring your case if we did not think that you have a good case and that you are entitled to win.

MOTION FOR NEW TRIAL

A motion for a new trial gives the trial judge the same chance that an appeal gives the Supreme Court: the right to grant the losing side a new trial if the first trial was not fair or if the trial judge made legal mistakes that make it right to grant the loser a new trial.

Many people think that an appeal automatically entitles the loser to a second trial. This is not true.

In many years of representing plaintiffs, we have found that the information in this pamphlet is the information people usually want to have. If you have any questions, please let us hear from you.

PLEASE READ THE FOLLOWING INSTRUCTIONS CAREFULLY

1. TALK TO NO ONE—Please do not talk to anyone outside of your family about your case, unless one of the lawyers or investigators from our office is present. You should always require identification so that you are sure to whom you are talking. DO NOT talk to your insurance company, railroad claim agent, company representative, or any type of agent, attorney, or investigator without first notifying our office so we can have these statements taken with one of our lawyers or investigators present. If you have already given a statement of *any kind*, call us *NOW*!
2. YOUR DOCTOR—You should return to each of your doctors as often as they feel it is necessary. You should always report each of your symptoms to them. Do not minimize your ailments to your doctors: doctors must know these things in order to treat you properly. If you plan to see any additional doctors, please advise us before you see them and tell us their names and addresses.
3. RECORDS—Please keep accurate and detailed records of the following:
   a. lost time and wages or income of any sort;
   b. hospital, doctor, drug, and other medical bills;
   c. other losses directly resulting from your injury;
   d. notes or a diary reflecting the effect of your injury on your daily life (you only need to make entries once every week); and
   e. any insurance policy that might afford you coverage or protection.

   You should pay all your bills by check or else obtain and keep receipts. These records will be very helpful a year later when you are asked by the defense to recall your pain, difficulties, and expenses.
4. REPAIRS—Do not have anything that was involved in your accident (your automobile, boat, airplane, farm implement, piece of machinery, household item, or other object) repaired until we have had time to examine it, have it photographed, and have it examined by an expert or impounded as we feel necessary to preserve the evidence for your case. If your case involves a product or instrument not in your control, please try to see that

it is not repaired or disposed of until we have photographed it and, if necessary, had it examined by an expert.

5. OFFENSES, FINES, OR DISCIPLINARY ACTION—Do not appear or give statements before a traffic court, a coroner's inquest, a Federal Aviation Agency investigation board, a railroad investigation agency, a union investigation agency, a maritime investigation agency, or any other type of disciplinary board, panel, or other proceedings without first notifying this office so that we might have one of our attorneys accompany and represent you at such a hearing. We take this precaution to ensure that you do not prejudice yourself in the action in which we represent you.
6. WITNESSES—IMMEDIATELY furnish us with the correct names, addresses, and telephone numbers of any and all witnesses you may learn of. This includes people who know how your injury has affected you (such as friends, family, neighbors, fellow workers, or employees).

   If you have any reason to think that a witness may be moving from the area permanently, please call us so we can take a deposition if necessary.
7. EVIDENCE—Please get and give to us or tell us about any photographs pertaining to your case that were taken by you or any of your friends. If you are required to be in the hospital and are receiving a treatment like traction or physical therapy, please notify our office so that we can have you photographed by our investigator or one of the members of your family. If your injury requires a cast, a brace, traction, or any other appliance, save it for evidence in trial. You should notify us that you are keeping these items, and bring these items with you when the case is set for hearing.

   We will contact your insurance carrier or company for copies of all their photographs and investigations in your case.

   Please talk to us about *any evidence* you have or know of that may help us! Save any physical evidence and discuss it with your lawyer or investigator.
8. HOSPITAL AND DOCTOR BILLS—Have your own insurance carrier pay as many hospital and doctor bills as possible. You should also have your medical insurance, such as Blue Cross and Blue Shield, pay as much of your bills as possible. Doctors and hospitals are more cooperative when their bills are paid.

You should not expect them to wait to receive payment until after your case is tried or settled. You should therefore pay any balance as soon as possible. If any bill remains unpaid, please call us. We will try to get your creditors to hold off until the case is concluded. If you do not call us until they have hired a lawyer or started collection procedure, it may be too late for us to help.

9. YOUR ADDRESS—Be sure to keep us advised of any change in your address or telephone number.

We appreciate the privilege of representing you in your case.

(Name of attorney/firm)

By: ____________________

FORM 5
EMPLOYMENT AGREEMENT

_________________, 19____

I/We hereby retain and employ _________________ as my/our attorney(s) to represent me/us in my/our claim for damages against ____________________ or any others who may be liable on account of ________________________ on or about the _________________ day of _________________, 19___.

I/We agree to pay said attorneys' fees as follows (initial one):

____ ____ Contingency:

________ percent of whatever may be recovered from said claim, whether by suit, settlement, or any other manner;*

____ ____ Hourly:

$ _______ per hour for all legal services rendered in this matter.

I/We agree that associate counsel may be employed at the discretion and expense of my/our attorney(s), and that any attorney so employed may be designated to appear on my/our behalf or undertake my/our representation in this matter.

I/We further agree that in addition to the above attorneys' fees, all court costs, subpoena costs, photos, depositions, court reporter costs, reports, witness statements, and other out-of-pocket expenses directly incurred in investigating or litigating this claim shall be paid by the undersigned, and that said expenses and attorneys' fees may be deducted from the proceeds of any recovery.

I/We have received a copy of this contract.

____
Client

____
Client

The above employment is hereby accepted on the terms stated, and if on a percentage contingent fee basis, we agree to make no charge for services unless recovery is had in this matter. In addition, we agree to make no settlement without the written consent of the claimant.

BY ____________________
Attorney

*NOTE: Agreed-upon percentage may be governed by statute, case law, or local rule. The agreed-upon percentage may vary according to the case and the circumstances.

____ Copy of contract given to client.

FORM 6
ATTORNEY FEE AGREEMENT

I/We hereby retain and employ the law firm of (name of attorney/firm, address of attorney/firm) as my/our attorneys to prosecute or settle all claims for damages against any and all parties who shall be liable on account of ______________________ on or about__________________ . In consideration for services rendered and to be rendered, I/we agree to pay a fee equal to 33-1/3 percent of the recovery (before deduction and/or reimbursement of costs) received through suit, settlement, or any other manner.

In the event a structured settlement is reached, I/we agree to pay to my/our attorneys a fee equal to 33-1/3 percent of the present cash value of the settlement recovery, which fee shall be paid in full at the time of settlement or, at the attorney's option, in installments over a determined period of years.

If the client discharges the law firm of (name of attorney/firm) for other than just cause, the client agrees that (name of attorney/firm) will have a lien for services rendered in an amount equal to 33-1/3 percent of any outstanding settlement offer at that time.

It is further agreed that in addition to the above attorney fees, all costs directly incurred by investigating or litigating this claim shall be paid by the clients. In the event that the clients cannot pay the costs as they are incurred, the costs will be advanced by the attorneys and deducted from any settlement or compensation at the time it is received by the client(s). Included in the costs will be a charge of $ __________ per month for copy costs, long distance telephone charges, and telex/facsimile charges.

DATED this ____________ day of _________________ , 19___.

CLIENT: ___________________________
ADDRESS: ___________________________
____

(Name of attorney/firm) agrees to the above and agrees to make no charge for services unless recovery is achieved in the above claim and agree to make no settlement without consent of the client.
DATED this _____________ day of __________________ , 19___.

ATTORNEY: _________________________
(Name of attorney/firm)
(Address)

AMENDMENTS AND SUPPLEMENTS TO FEE AGREEMENT:

DATED this _____________ day of __________________ , 19___.

CLIENT: ____________________________

FORM 7
MEDICAL AUTHORIZATION

TO: ______________________________

This is to authorize and request you to permit the law firm of (name of attorney/firm) or any agent and/or representative of said law firm to examine and copy any and all records or reports which you may have concerning (patient's name) relating to treatment past, present, or future, including medical, psychological, psychiatric, and vocational tests, evaluations, reports, charts, X-rays, and other diagnostic imaging, and financial statements.

A photocopy of this medical authorization shall be as valid as the original.

____
Patient's Social Security Number

____
Patient's name

____
Signature

Dated: ______________________

FORM 8

AUTHORIZATION FOR RELEASE OF PERSONNEL/EMPLOYMENT RECORDS

TO: ______________________________

ADDRESS: ______________________________

RE: ______________________________

You are hereby authorized and directed to furnish and release to my attorneys, (name of attorney/firm), all information and records requested regarding any employment, personnel, evaluation, pay and/or training records, *and* information concerning salary, wage increases, pension or retirement benefits, health benefits, income tax, and other deductions of the person named above.

This release is restricted to my attorneys and shall remain in force until revoked by me in writing. A copy of this authorization shall be as valid as an original.

BY: ____________________

DATED: ____________________

FORM 9
LETTER TO DOCTOR

Client: ______________________________

Address: ______________________________

Date of incident: ______________________________

Dear Doctor:

This is to advise you that we represent the above-named patient for an action for personal injuries related to an incident on the indicated date. Please mark our firm's name on your records so that you know that we are bringing the case.

We will encourage our client to pay your bill personally or by insurance if possible, but in any event we will protect your bill out of any amounts received in trial or settlement. It will, therefore, be unnecessary for you to send this matter to a collection agency if the client is unable to pay the bill and you have to wait for termination of the litigation.

We are NOT at this time requesting any medical reports from you. Please do not send us any unless we specifically request them in writing.

Please note that the attached medical authorization revokes all prior medical authorizations that have been given by the above patient.

We wish to cooperate with you in every way. If you want to discuss the medical matters of this case with us at any time, we would welcome your communication.

In order to protect your bill, we will need to receive a copy of all your charges relating to this case. **Your bill should include your total charges for services without showing the source of payment.**

Cordially,

Enclosure

ANALYSIS OF THE CASE

Dale Haralson

During the investigation and preliminary preparation process, you must conduct a continuing analysis of the case:

- whether the evidence being developed supports an actionable claim;
- whether the damages, when considered in light of the probability of success and cost of litigation, justify proceeding;
- whether basic procedural requirements can be satisfied and procedural options properly evaluated; and
- what defenses should be anticipated.

These matters are considered in this chapter in a simple, general fashion, rather than through the details of a particular case. Use this chapter as a checklist. However, be sure to research and evaluate in detail each procedural and substantive issue that is or may be applicable to your fact situation.

Your analysis of the issues should begin before you consider filing. It is a mistake to postpone this analysis until after the complaint has been drafted, filed, and served, and the issues have been joined. Potential substantive and procedural pitfalls may be avoided by adopting this approach. Without early analysis, you may first learn that you do not have a case after you have invested substantial time and effort. Even more tragically, you may learn of some procedural or jurisdictional flaw too late to correct it.

This analysis should be a continuing process that begins with the initial interview and is never complete until the trial is over. Because of the commitment that you make to the client and your reputation as a trial lawyer when the complaint is filed, you should make a detailed and critical analysis immediately before filing. Tell the client that this analysis will be performed periodically and that if you conclude that the claim should not proceed further, you will immediately inform the client. Early and continued analysis of the case will always be in the best interests of you, your client, and the courts.

This chapter outlines the main substantive and procedural considerations that typically apply to personal injury actions. Obviously, a discussion of the law in each state is beyond the scope of this chapter. The review given here is only a starting point; it should stimulate you to think of additional remedies appropriate to your facts, of basic procedural requirements that must be met and decisions relating to the requirements that must be timely made, and of potential defenses that can best be overcome by early planning.

The materials in this chapter are grouped in four parts. The first part lists common theories of liability applicable in tort cases. This section is in turn divided under ten basic headings. Special attention is paid to statutes that give rise to tort cases or otherwise affect them. The second part approaches the question of liability by considering the basic fact situations you may encounter (for example, motor vehicle collisions, products liability, premises injuries). The third part of the chapter concerns the fundamental procedural requirements for initiating an action. The fourth section lists the commonly asserted defenses to tort actions.

ANALYSIS BY THEORIES OF LIABILITY

The grounds of legal recovery that may support a claim for personal injuries include, but are not limited to, the following ten categories. You should consider each of them when analyzing a potential case.

A. Negligence (Simple or Gross)

The usual elements of a negligence case are

1. a duty owed by the defendant;
2. a breach of that duty by the defendant's act or omission, creating an unreasonable risk of harm (i.e., a deviation from the reasonable standard of care); and
3. injury or damage to the plaintiff as a consequence of (or proximately caused by) the defendant's breach.

In negligence cases against professionals, the legal standard of care may be determined by reference to the activities of reasonably prudent like practitioners.

The legal definition of the causal relationship that must be shown to exist between the defendant's breach of duty and the plaintiff's damages varies from state to state.

You should be aware of possible derivative actions, for example, secondary injury to a person related to the plaintiff, such as a spouse's action for loss of consortium, a parent's action for medical expenses for an injured child, a loss of consortium claim for a severely disabled child, or a child's loss of consortium for a severely disabled parent. In identifying potential defendants consider the doctrines of *respondeat superior* (liability for acts of employees or agents), negligent entrustment, and imputed negligence.

In jurisdictions where legislation has abrogated joint and several liability with the result being some form of several liability, the jury will likely be instructed to attribute a percentage of fault to each responsible entity. Here, you must know the applicable law well and the importance of naming each potentially liable entity as a party defendant.

In determining the proof requirements of a negligence action, you should consider the application of the *res ipsa loquitur* doctrine, which is sometimes used as a substitute for proof of fault.

The defendant's duty may arise from

- the relationship between the parties;
- a contract;
- an undertaking on the defendant's part; or
- an applicable statute, regulation, or ordinance (see section J).

B. Willful or Wanton Misconduct

This may be an essential basis for actions under guest statutes and for punitive damage claims. Counsel should check recent statutes and court decisions for changes in the quantum of proof (clear and convincing as opposed to preponderance) or definition of conduct (evidence of an evil mind or actual malice or reckless disregard for human life), depending on the jurisdiction.

C. Nuisance
   1. Public
   2. Private

D. Breach of Warranty (U.S.C. and/or Common Law)
   1. Express
   2. Implied
      a. merchantability
      b. particular purpose
      c. habitability

E. Strict Liability
   1. Products liability
      a. strict tort, privity-free liability
      b. action for breach of express or implied warranty
      c. statutory modification of causes of action and defenses (for example, statutes of repose, successor liability)
   2. Ultrahazardous or abnormal activities (for example, water, fire, electricity, gas, pesticides, blasting, and nuclear explosions—the defendant's duty regarding such activities may be nondelegable)
   3. Animals (for example, dog bites)
   4. Admiralty
   5. Statutory duty

F. Defamation
   1. Libel
   2. Slander

G. Fraud, Deceit, and Misrepresentation
   1. Intentional
   2. Negligent
   3. Innocent [*see* Restatement (Second) of Torts §402B]

H. Other Intentional Acts
   1. Assault and battery
   2. False arrest and imprisonment
   3. Malicious prosecution
   4. Abuse of process

5. Alienation of affections, criminal conversation, and breach of promise (where not banned)
6. Invasion of the right of privacy
7. Intentional or reckless infliction of mental suffering
8. Trespassing
9. Outrage (prima facie tort, bad faith)
10. Sexual abuse (this tort gives rise to negligence causes of action, for example, negligent hiring, negligent supervision, and negligent retention)

I. Breach of Contract
   1. Direct beneficiary
   2. Third-party beneficiary
      The existence and requirements of a contract between the plaintiff and the defendant may be implied from the relationship between the parties and/or the circumstances.

J. Effect of a Statute, Regulation, or Ordinance
   Depending on the law of the forum, an applicable statute, regulation, or ordinance may have any of the following legal effects:
   1. It may give rise to or define the scope of the defendant's duty.
   2. Its violation may be merely admissible as evidence of "fault" or "liability."
   3. Its violation may constitute "negligence *per se*" or make out a prima facie case standing alone.
   4. It may create an independent cause of action. The following list identifies some of the possible causes of action created by statute.
      a. wrongful death statutes
      b. survival statutes (the personal injury action that survives the death of the injured party)
      c. workers' compensation acts (and occupational disease statutes)
      d. Death on High Seas Act, 46 U.S.C. App. §§761–768 (1988)
      e. Longshoremen's and Harbor Workers' Compensation Act, 33 U.S.C. §§901–905 (1988)
      f. Jones Act, 46 U.S.C. App. §688 (1988) (seamen)
      g. Federal Employers' Liability Act, 45 U.S.C. §§51–60 (1988) (railroad employees)
      h. Federal Safety Appliance Act, 45 U.S.C. §§1 *et seq.* (1988) (railroad employees)

i. Boiler Inspection Act, 45 U.S.C. §§22–23, 28–34 (1988) (railroad employees)
j. Federal Tort Claims Act, 28 U.S.C. §§1291, 1346, 1402, 1504, 2110, 2401, 2402, 2411, 2412, 2671 *et seq.*, and comparable state laws (claims against governmental units)
k. Federal Civil Rights Act, 42 U.S.C. §§1981–2000 (1988) and comparable state laws
l. dram shop acts (liability of tavern for acts of intoxicated patron)—also imposed by common law
m. safe place to work acts, scaffold acts, and other legislation for the benefit of workers
n. Consumer Product Warranty Act, 15 U.S.C. §2301–2312 (1988)
o. state consumer protection acts
p. direct action statutes (allowing suit directly against the defendant's liability insurance company)
q. state legislation dealing with professional negligence, products liability, and claims arising from automobile collisions (for example, no-fault statutes)

Regarding Third-Party Actions and Insurance Actions

Note that the term "third-party action" is used for a number of situations, including (1) the action that a worker who is eligible for workers' compensation from his employer can bring against a party other than his employer who contributed to the causing of his injuries or (2) the action by a defendant who has been held legally responsible against a party who he believes should bear all or a portion of the responsibility.

Third-party actions and insurance actions may involve the following:

- indemnity (total responsibility of another party to the defendant)—the right of indemnity may arise from an express or implied contract;
- contribution (sharing of liability based on proportionate share of fault or based on the number of defendants);
- subrogation (insurer's suit on insured's cause of action);
- actions by an insured under life, accident, health, and disability policies;

- insurer's liability for failure to inspect properly;
- liability of the defendant's insurance carrier for payment of judgments that exceed the limits of the defendant's coverage for failing to settle within the limits of the defendant's insurance coverage;
- uninsured motorist actions, underinsured motorist actions, and Unsatisfied Judgment Fund Act violations; or
- bad faith actions against an insurance carrier by an insured, arising out of the carrier's failure to pay PIP or other first-party benefits or failure to defend and/or pay a judgment.

ANALYSIS BY BASIC FACT SITUATION

Some of the common fact patterns encountered in a tort practice include the following:

A. Vehicles and Transportation
   1. Private vehicle cases—check for special problems with guest statutes
   2. Owners' and/or lessors' and/or employers' responsibilities for the acts of the operator
   3. Passengers and pedestrians
   4. Taxis, buses, and other common carriers
   5. Aircraft
      a. commercial
      b. general
      c. military
   6. Railroads
      a. passengers
      b. crossing accidents
      c. injured workers (statutes relating to workers considered in part J.4.h–j above)
   7. Motorcycles
   8. Bicycles
   9. Recreational vehicles, for example, ATVs
   10. Tractor-trailer truck combinations

B. Premises (Occupiers)
   1. Owner and occupier
      Historically, the defendant's duty will vary according to the

classification of the plaintiff's status on the property, viz., trespasser, licensee, or invitee. However, there seems to be somewhat of a trend to abandon distinctions in duties based on the plaintiff's status and to substitute a general duty to use reasonable care under the circumstances. Check for local statutes as they may alter or affect the common law liability of the occupier of land.

2. Landlord and tenant
   Local statutes may govern or affect the landlord's liability to the tenant for injuries arising from the condition or use of the premises.
3. Child trespassers
   a. "attractive nuisance" doctrine
   b. "dangerous instrumentality" doctrine
4. Special responsibilities to fire fighters and police as well as special defenses applicable to claims made by fire fighters and police
5. Injury to persons who have a "right of entry"
6. Special duties of innkeepers to provide adequate security for guests
7. Duties of hospitals, nursing homes, and other institutions to exercise ordinary care in caring for patients
8. Liability to abutting owners
9. Liability for conditions or activities conducted on premises that injure people off the premises

C. Contractors and Construction Cases
Local statutes, including but not limited to workers' compensation statutes, may alter or affect the defendant's liability in a construction case.

1. Owner's responsibilities
2. General and special contractors or subcontractors
3. Independent contractors
4. Responsibilities to workers and to the public, on and off premises
5. Design and construction of buildings, viz., the architect's and/or engineer's responsibilities
6. Statutes and common law requiring a safe place for workers

D. Products Liability
Federal and state statutes may alter or affect the common law

liability of a defendant in a products liability case. The following conduct includes both strict liability and negligence bases of liability.

1. Potentially culpable activity/omission
   a. design (including crashworthiness)
   b. manufacture/assembly/construction
   c. quality control, for example, inspection and/or testing
   d. packaging/labeling/shipping
   e. marketing or selling a dangerous product
   f. failure to warn
   g. instructions for use or maintenance
   h. guarantee of quality or performance
   i. violation of a statute, regulation, ordinance, or safety standard
   j. failure to recall/retrofit/warn subsequent to manufacture and sale
2. Potentially culpable defendants
   a. provider of design specifications
   b. designer of component or finished product
   c. supplier of raw materials
   d. manufacturer of basic materials, component part(s), or finished product
   e. seller of component part(s) or finished product
   f. assembler of component or finished product
   g. party responsible for testing and/or inspection
   h. party responsible for warning and/or instructions for use/maintenance
   i. author of advertising or marketing literature
   j. party responsible for certifying quality and/or performance
   k. party responsible for maintenance and/or repair
   l. the entire industry

E. Professional Negligence
   1. Doctors, lawyers, accountants, architects, psychologists, nurses, clergy, engineers
      Local statutes may alter or affect the defendant's liability in a professional negligence case
   2. Departure from the standard of care set by reasonably prudent like practitioners
   3. "Captain of the ship" doctrine; *respondeat superior*

4. Duty to obtain an informed consent
5. In legal negligence, proof of "case within a case"

F. Aviation Accidents
1. Domestic or international air transportation (Warsaw Convention)
2. Airline or general aviation (standard of care)
3. United States government's responsibility for air traffic control and certification of aircraft and crew
4. Product liability of aircraft and aircraft parts manufacturers
5. Responsibilities of airports and fixed base operators
6. Federal Aviation Act of 1958, 49 U.S.C. App. §§1301–1557 (1988)
   Many states have adopted similar acts.
7. Federal Aviation Regulations, 14 C.F.R. §1 *et seq.* (1991)
8. Manufacturers and suppliers of navigational charts, aids, and equipment

G. Admiralty
1. Jones Act, 46 U.S.C. §688 (1988) (injuries to seamen or members of crew; based on negligence or unseaworthiness)
2. Duty of maintenance and cure (common law duty to seamen)
3. Death on the High Seas Act, 46 U.S.C. App. §§761–768 (1988) (wrongful death action, in admiralty court)
4. Longshoremen's and Harbor Workers' Compensation Act, 33 U.S.C. §901–950 (1988)
5. Seaworthiness doctrine (common law responsibility in admiralty to longshoremen and persons doing traditional work of ship's crew)
6. "Twilight doctrine" (consequence of overlapping remedies)—see Admiralty Jurisdiction Act, 46 U.S.C. App. §740 (1988)
7. Ship disasters, collisions (for example, limitations of liability to value of hull)
8. Ports and Waterways Safety Act, 33 U.S.C. §§1221–1227; 46 U.S.C. §2101 (1988)

H. Sports and Athletic Suits
1. Actions by participants, spectators
2. Defenses based on assumption of risk, contributory fault
3. Liability of players for intentional torts to other players
4. Liability of manufacturers, and lessors of equipment

5. Liability of sports and recreation facility owners and/or operators
6. Liability of instructors, supervisors (including coaches, schools, and booster clubs), and tour guides for sport and recreational activities

I. Toxic Torts
1. Proof of exposure to and injury by (proximate cause) pollutants or other chemicals or radiation sources in the air, water, or land
   Exposure frequently results from using toxic substances in the work environment or improper discharge or disposal of toxic waste products. Check the numerous federal and state statutes in this area.
2. Latent appearance of injuries and their effect on the statute of limitations
3. Actions based on products liability, negligence, trespass, or nuisance

J. Governmental Entities
1. Federal, state, regional, municipal, or other political subdivisions; agencies and commissions; governmental-proprietary distinctions
   Special statutes may govern the defendant's liability and immunities, if any. States vary widely in the scope of applicable statutory immunities; consult the law of each jurisdiction before accepting any governmental entity case.
2. Schools, hospitals, waterworks, police and fire fighters, transportation, public transit, and streets and sidewalks
   These entities may legally be treated as political subdivisions and may be entitled to the same or similar defenses as well as to a notice of claim requirements.
3. Short period for filing notice of claim
   It is essential for you to determine which governmental body or office is responsible for the service of the notice of claim (for example, Office of Risk Management), what period applies for serving a notice of claim and subsequently starting suit, how the notice of claim is to be made and delivered, and what specific contents the notice of claim must contain in order for it to be legally effective.

4. Actions against the United States other than under the Federal Tort Claims Act, 28 U.S.C. §§1291, 1346, 1402, 1504, 2110, 2401, 2402, 2411, 2412, 2671 (1988)
5. Actions against individuals and/or governmental bodies that violate a plaintiff's constitutional rights, for example, after a work-release prison inmate walks away from a community center, he rapes a woman

K. Familial Torts and Responsibility
   1. Actions between spouses, between a child and a parent, or between other family relations
   2. Derivative action for loss of services, consortium, and medical expenses brought by a parent, child, or spouse
   3. Actions for violations of parental responsibility statutes

L. Special Plaintiffs
   1. Persons who suffered prenatal injuries or were the victims of preconception torts (mutagenic substances)
   2. Persons who suffer emotional injuries as a consequence of the injury or death of a member of their family
   3. Incompetent persons
   4. "You take your plaintiff the way you find him"—idiosyncratic, allergic, or suffering from aggravation or precipitation of diseases or pre-existent injury, whether active or dormant
   5. Wrongfully fired employees

ANALYSIS OF PROCEDURAL REQUIREMENTS

Before you can properly commence suit, you should give careful consideration to the procedural requirements of the case and make important choices as to theories of law, choice of law, parties, and forum.

A. Choice of Law
   1. Conflicts of laws rules of the state; place of wrong versus "contacts" or "center of gravity" test
   2. Substantive versus procedural characterization by court
   3. *Erie* rule in federal diversity cases

B. Jurisdiction
   1. Over the subject matter

In federal court, a $50,000 minimum jurisdictional amount in controversy and diversity of citizenship is essential, or a federal question, 28 U.S.C. §§1331–1332 (1988).

2. Over the "person," viz., proper service; long arm statutes; attachments; publication
3. Pendant jurisdiction theory in federal courts

C. Venue, *Forum Non Conveniens*
1. Federal venue requirements, 28 U.S.C. §1391–1412 (1988)
2. Dismissal on *forum non conveniens* (inconvenient forum in which to try a case) in state courts, or transfer within state
3. In federal courts, transfer by change of venue, 28 U.S.C. §1441 (1988)

D. Choice of Forum
1. Federal versus state
2. Defendant's right to remove case to federal court
3. Inferior court versus one of general jurisdiction
4. Factors in choosing between courts and states: applicable laws, periods of limitations, types of jurors, judges

E. Jury
1. Under federal rules, demand at time of filing complaint or removal, FED. R. CIV. P. 38
   State court rules vary as to time of making jury demand.
2. No jury in Federal Tort Claims Acts and admiralty cases
3. Federal courts require unanimous jury verdicts; many state courts do not

F. Prior Events in the Case
1. *Res judicata*
2. Collateral estoppel (mutuality not required)
3. "Law of the case" (prior legal decisions of rulings in same litigation)
4. Prior dismissals; "two dismissal rule" in federal courts, FED. R. CIV. P. 41; dismissal with or without prejudice
5. Survival and abatement of actions (effect of death of party)
6. Releases and covenants not to sue or not to execute
7. Subrogation and intervention

G. Statute of Limitations
1. Statute applicable to the cause or causes of action

2. Date the cause of action accrued or date on which the running of the statute was triggered
3. Tolling devices (extending the time for the running of the statute)
4. Delayed discovery devices or common law
5. Estoppel to assert
6. Saving statutes (refiling after dismissal)
7. Laches in cases in equity

H. Multiple Plaintiffs and Defendants
1. Class actions, FED. R. CIV. P. 23
2. Multidistrict Litigation (MDL), 28 U.S.C. §1407 (1988)
3. Collateral estoppel; enterprise liability
4. Consolidation within districts
5. Voluntary cooperation

ANALYSIS OF POTENTIAL DEFENSES

The following is a selective list of defenses that may be available to the defendant in a personal injury case. Check local case law and legislation for a more complete and accurate list of potential defenses.

A. Defenses that Negate the Plaintiff's Right of Recovery
1. The defendant is immune from liability.
   a. statute
   b. contract
   c. case law
2. The defendant has no duty.
3. The defendant did not breach her duty; for example, she
   a. exercised due or ordinary care;
   b. complied with custom;
   c. complied with the state-of-the-art; or
   d. complied with applicable statute, regulation, standard.
4. The defendant's acts or omissions did not cause the incident or the plaintiff's injury; for example,
   a. the incident was not foreseeable,
   b. there was a subsequent change in condition of the product or premises,
   c. there was an intervening and superseding cause,
   d. the incident was unavoidable or inevitable, or

e. the incident was an "Act of God."

B. Affirmative Defenses
1. Contributory or comparative "fault"
    a. the plaintiff's or decedent's own
    b. imputed
2. Assumption of risk
3. Open and obvious
4. Unforeseeable misuse
5. Fraud
6. Statute of limitations
7. Waiver
8. Duress
9. Special statutory or court rule defenses

C. Defenses to Damages
1. Liquidated/limited
2. The plaintiff's duty to mitigate
3. Apportionment
4. Contribution
5. Comparative fault
6. Release
7. Set-off/recoupment
8. Prepayment
9. Collateral source (if permitted in the jurisdiction)
10. Speculative
11. Not within contemplation of parties
12. Reduction to present value
13. Pre-existent condition
14. Subsequently occurring incident
15. Limited by case law
16. Limited by special legislation

CONCLUSION

Continuing pretrial analysis of your case is important because it may disclose a problem not previously considered. Early detection of a problem can help you effectively meet anticipated defenses or prevent you from incurring substantial costs. If, after preliminary investigation and discovery, your analysis prompts you to advise your client not to proceed with litigation, your client is better served than if he or she learns that the claim was without merit later—after spending thousands of dollars for court costs and suffering an adverse verdict.

DISCOVERY

Linda Miller Atkinson

INTRODUCTION

The discovery process is a fundamental part of the constitutionally protected right to a jury trial. Two critical rights rest on thorough and effective discovery: the right to cross-examine and the right to present evidence to a jury. Without these two elements of the search for truth, the right to a jury trial becomes a hollow charade.

The discovery process has expanded in scope and complexity in recent years, but modern technology has expanded even more. Though discovery tools have not kept pace with technology, the process is beginning to adapt to telephone, video, facsimile, and computer forms. The expansion of discovery's scope reflects the increasing depth and sophistication of trial lawyers as well as the growth of industrial techniques, procedures, institutions, multinational corporations, and international business departments and organizations.

In most states, the discovery process has been streamlined over the last 20 years to substantially reduce judicial involvement; indeed, the court usually intervenes only to resolve conflicts and enforce compliance. However, obstruction and overreaching bring discovery conflicts before the courts all too often. In their frustration, court and academic personnel call some of these conflicts "discovery abuse." The real discovery abuses are

- unreasonable refusal to cooperate in document production and deposition testimony,
- unreasonable obstruction of deposition discovery by groundless instructions not to answer questions,
- refusal of courts to enforce discovery rules and remedies,
- blanket discovery requests by lawyers who hope their opponents will prepare the case for them, and
- interference in the judicial process by legislators who limit the number of interrogatories or requests to admit—this forces counsel to use additional and more time-consuming discovery procedures or to consume court time by moving for permission to increase the limits.

Although most state courts have patterned their own rules after the Federal Rules of Civil Procedure, state court interpretations, decisional law, and evidentiary rules have expanded discovery beyond the rigidity of federal practice. With the "new federalism" developing among state courts[1] and the stronger provisions of state constitutions, tools are in place for reaffirming separation of powers, eliminating rigid limitations on interrogatories, compelling full answers on deposition, and imposing penalties of default and judgment for failure to respond in discovery.

Strategy and full implementation of all available discovery mechanisms require familiarity with both state and federal rules of procedure and rules of evidence. The following discussion will refer to the Federal Rules of Civil Procedure and consider tools of discovery conceptually, rather than attempting to catalog anomalies among states.

Purposes

Some writers have said the purposes of discovery are to eliminate surprise, limit issues, expedite litigation, or provide the trier of fact with a technique for ascertaining the facts. In a philosophical vein, John Kennelly, one of the most thoughtful writers on discovery,

[1] Wright, *In Praise of State Courts: Confessions of a Federal Judge*, 11 Hastings Const. L.Q. 165, 182-83 (1984).

has said that "what is forgotten and what should never be forgotten is that the purpose of discovery is to ascertain the truth."[2]

Conceptually, however, discovery is *the court-enforced process for translating facts into admissible evidence*. This process, triggered by the filing of the complaint, is not the beginning of the litigation process.

Before a complaint is filed, you should have done considerable investigation—identified persons, formulated theories, and collected witnesses' names, records, and evidence. You should have conducted technical investigation, and, in some instances such as products liability and professional negligence, consulted experts.

Discovery, then, does not substitute for investigation. Likewise, it is not actually a search for truth but a search for confirmation of truth already suspected. It is not a search for the "smoking gun" but for proof of what was known by the defendant. It is not a fishing expedition but a setting of hooks for the trial proofs.

Always remember that pretrial discovery is a double-edged sword. Just as the plaintiff can obtain valuable proofs from the defendant, so the defendant can obtain significant disclosures from the plaintiff.

Much modern litigation is complex factually, procedurally, or technically, regardless of the theory of recovery. Whether the complaint sounds in negligence or strict liability, the plaintiff has the burden of proving that the defendant is responsible for having created an unreasonable risk of harm. In each case, the plaintiff must discover and present proof in four main areas, in varying proportions:

- a factual standard of care—what constituted reasonable prudence at the time;
- causation, cause in fact, and proximate cause;
- intervening conduct of another that was foreseeable and therefore not a superseding cause; and
- victim conduct—lack of risk recognition, lack of risk acceptance.

2 Kennelly, *Discovery: Is Its Stated Laudable Purpose—To Ascertain the Truth—Being Thwarted by the Courts? Some Suggestions As To How Find the Facts*, 31 TRIAL LAW. GUIDE 137 (1987).

The evidence in these substantive areas not only involves technologies in special fields usually inhabited by the defendant but also involves factual information and raw data in the exclusive possession of the defendant. Discovery, then, is the disciplined and precise use of all procedural tools to translate facts into admissible evidence.

For these reasons the rules clearly intend that discovery should take place when either party requests discoverable information, except where some specific, convincingly persuasive cause mandates otherwise.

Policy

Rule 26(b) governs the scope of discovery in using each of the available tools, permitting discovery of "relevant" information that is "not privileged." However, in the discovery process, the test of relevance is not "evidentiary relevance" but a broader, less stringent yardstick. True evidentiary relevance cannot be determined until evidence is offered with a proper foundation, in the context of other evidence at trial. The courts have generally held that relevance in discovery "has very broad meaning" and that its application should be liberally construed.[3]

The discovery process under the rules is designed to operate extrajudicially, without the necessity of court permission to commence discovery proceedings. This policy is reflected in the trend favoring a discovery conference and requiring as a prerequisite to either a motion to compel or a discovery conference that the parties make every reasonable effort to resolve discovery conflicts. The drafters of Rule 26(f) considered this significant enough to expressly require all parties to participate in discovery in good faith.

With respect to the specific rules governing the tools of discovery (Rules 33, 34, 36, and 37), see Appendix A to this chapter.

TOOLS OF DISCOVERY

Though most states have adopted provisions similar to the federal rules, all have local variations that affect your overall discovery planning. Some states have yet to develop any understanding of the use of interrogatories and do not permit them. Some states use rule-

[3] Heathman v. United States Dist. Court, 503 F.2d 1032 (9th Cir. 1974); Bowman v. General Motors Corp., 64 F.R.D. 62 (E.D. Pa. 1974).

mandated uniform interrogatories but allow supplementation by nonuniform interrogatories particular to the facts of the case. Many states limit the maximum number of interrogatories, thus shifting the discovery to more expensive and time-consuming forms. Some states allow the parties to embark upon discovery as it suits the circumstances of the case; others require or allow scheduling conferences so that the court appears to manage the case. Some states do not require the expense of final pretrial orders, and some do not recognize the issue-resolving nature of requests to admit, and thus limit their number or use.

Local variations affect planning and strategy. Local discovery rules may deprive parties of evidence, unreasonably limit discovery efforts, or otherwise restrict the process, thus foreclosing cross-examination and the right to present evidence to a jury. Where these restrictions exist, you should work to challenge and expand the discovery process through appropriate motions and appeals. For ease of reference the various discovery tools are discussed separately in this chapter, but this does not mean that only one method may be pursued at a time. Some lawyers prefer to file a set of carefully drafted interrogatories along with a request for production; some follow depositions with precise requests to admit with interrogatories attached. Discovery is a dynamic process; depending on the facts, the jurisdiction, and the expense, several tools may be used simultaneously.

Two principles apply to the use of these tools. First, drafting effective discovery tools that the court will enforce is not a task for a word processor; it requires precision, research, and skill. Second, begin early! Discovery actually begins with investigation, before the filing of the complaint. Playing catch-up discovery with a well-financed opponent can be disastrous.

Complaint

Narrow the Issues

The complaint, besides notifying the defendant of the claims in either "code pleading" or "notice pleading," sets forth certain allegations to which admissions are sought. These allegations include the legal relationship of the parties that gives rise to the duty and the legal identity of the defendant as a corporation, partnership, or other entity. Therefore, the complaint is the first tool of formal discovery. Drafting the complaint allows you to include factual allegations, the admission or denial of which can shorten and sharpen subsequent investigations and discovery. See Appendices B and C for examples.

Include an Ex Parte Order to Preserve, Produce, and Impound

Sometimes the logical prefiling investigation is obstructed by a treating doctor who refuses to furnish records or an employer who refuses to grant access to the site of an accident. At other times, routine occurrences may frustrate an investigation: erasure of police dispatch log tapes in the ordinary course before they can be transcribed to record notice of highway conditions or a salvage yard anxious to sell a wrecked car. When prefiling investigation becomes stalled, include allegations foundational to an ex parte order in the complaint. An order to produce, impound, or preserve, or to allow inspection and photographing, should be drafted with the complaint; then, when the complaint is filed, the order can issue and be served, thus effecting the surrender or preservation of key evidence. In these instances, the complaint functions as a discovery device and a means of preserving potential evidence. A sample complaint and order appear at Appendix D.

Interrogatories

FED. R. CIV. P. 33 and similar state provisions require parties to answer written questions known as interrogatories. Answers to interrogatories may be read into evidence at trial and often make economical and effective evidence, especially on foundational elements. Local procedures may limit the number and scope of permissible inquiries through interrogatories; research whether or not such limitations apply in your jurisdiction.

Although interrogatories are a static device, they offer two advantages. First, they permit careful framing of the questions; and, second, if they are drafted carefully with the rules in mind, they can obviate the expense of motions to compel.

Interrogatories are devices limited to obtaining specific information. The overuse of interrogatories as substitutes for more appropriate forms of discovery has been the source of criticism, much of it warranted. Judge Milton Pollack of the Federal District Court for the Southern District of New York wrote,

> Interrogatories have become a prime offender in abusive, burdensome, unjustified, limitless, wasteful discovery.
>
> Interrogatories as commonly utilized today in nearly every instance are a device to shirk preparation of a case—they are more often than not "a lazy lawyer's way to obtain evasive answers." The use of the product of interrogatories at trial is virtually nil. How often has anyone read at trial an answer to an interrogatory? You will say—but what about the means to discovery? The answer is that there are quicker and better means—namely documentary disclosure and oral depositions.[4]

Of course, when cynical judges refuse to compel answers to interrogatories, or refuse to enter orders to compel answers against obstructionist parties refusing to answer, few answers are obtained that can be read at trial.

However, what the critics are telling trial lawyers is that interrogatories can only be used for preliminary, precise information and will only be enforced when clearly drafted. Interrogatories are not substitutes for depositions; at best they are a prelude, establishing foundational facts and areas for investigation. Interrogatories should be drafted with precision and clarity so that they and their answers can be read aloud at trial.

Interrogatories can effectively discover

- ► identity of witnesses;
- ► corporate or business identity;
- ► insurance coverage;
- ► custodians of records, documents, photos, things;
- ► existence (not content) of information gathered by attorney;
- ► existence of investigation;
- ► liability facts;
- ► identity and opinions of experts and grounds for the opinions;
- ► facts providing bases for affirmative defenses and denials in answering the complaint; and
- ► computer use, data, and storage.

4 Milton Pollack, *Discovery—Its Abuse and Correction*, 80 F.R.D. 219, 224 (1978).

An interrogatory may call for an opinion that requires application of law to fact. Such an interrogatory has been difficult to enforce, with courts attempting to shield parties from disclosure. The court may allow a defendant to delay responding to contention interrogatories, but after some discovery has proceeded, the court may order full responses to precisely drafted inquiries into the party's contentions.

Timing

Most state and federal rules allow interrogatories to be filed and served along with the complaint but extend the time for answering the interrogatories. Wherever permissible, interrogatories should be served with the complaint to confirm certain facts that may affect the statute of limitations, explore collectability of a judgment, and speed the scheduling of depositions.

Answering Interrogatories

Self-executing discovery processes require good faith in answering. Ethical, reasonable trial lawyers furnish full responses to fair interrogatories, rather than interposing evasions or objections merely to buy time or to avoid answering. The basic rule in discovery is you should answer as you would want your opponent to answer and inquire fairly as you would expect your opponent to inquire.

Supplementing Answers

Interrogatories are deemed to be continuing inquiry; where this is not specified by local rules, you should incorporate this specific requirement into the interrogatories. Rule 26(e) requires that answers be supplemented when additional information is received. Any additional information—such as the testimony of an additional witness or additional reports or documents—may be excluded from evidence if you fail to supplement answers to the interrogatories. A discovery plan must include reviewing answers given and supplementing before discovery closure. Be sure to serve your opponent with a formal request for supplementation under this rule.

Compelling Answers

The inquiring party bears the burden of enforcing the interrogatories and bringing objections to the court's attention. If the defendant objects to an interrogatory, the plaintiff, under Rule 37(a), must move to compel the answer. The burden of justifying the objection or answer is on the objecting party; as a practical matter, the moving party has the burden of supporting the inquiry. The topics of inquiry must be shown to be relevant, and the language of the question must be clear and fair. The court should enforce full and complete answers to fairly drawn interrogatories.

In addition, Rule 37(a)(4) provides for expenses on the motion to compel to be assessed against the losing party unless the objection had substantial justification. A party who answers frivolously or makes a careless objection and forces the opponent to bring the motion to compel can be ordered to pay costs on the motion. This is a serious consideration for the inquiring party as well; if the objection was justified, or the interrogatory impermissible, the moving party may be required to pay costs under this rule.

Ordering costs for motions to compel is a "band-aid" form of remedy. The extent of discontent with discovery conflict in the courts demonstrates that this remedy is ineffective and sporadically enforced. It has little deterrent effect on the obstructionist and some chilling effect on the one seeking a fair answer to a question. A more appropriate remedy is to strike the pleadings and enter default and judgment against the uncooperative party. This is consistent with the discovery process; the law recognizes failure to answer as admission.[5]

Scheduling Conference and Order

FED. R. CIV. P. 16(b) requires a scheduling conference and order within 120 days of filing and makes the initial scheduling order an integral part of the case management process. A party may also move for a scheduling conference and thus gain some advantage in the timing and posture of the case, including the direction of discovery. This subtle maneuver deserves much closer attention than it ordinarily gets, because the scheduling order (1) determines the time provided to prepare for the final pretrial conference and (2) forces the ordering of discovery priorities. As the court observed in *McCargo v. Hedrick*,[6]

5 Affanato v. Merrill Bros., 547 F.2d 138 (1st Cir. 1977); Insurance Corp. v. Compagnie des Bauxites, 456 U.S. 694 (1982); Annotation, *Judgment in Favor of Plaintiff in State Court Action for Defendant's Failure to Obey Request or Order to Answer Interrogatories or Other Discovery Questions*, 30 A.L.R. 4th 9 (1984).

6 545 F.2d 393, 401 (4th Cir. 1976).

> In our system lawyers worry about the whereabouts of witnesses. The court does not. Lawyers worry about proof. The court does not—except in the rare case of collusion. Lawyers get the case ready for trial. The court does not.

Thus, you should seek as much participation and control as possible in the scheduling phase. Strategies include

- serving interrogatories and requests to produce with the complaint as provided in FED. R. CIV. P. 33(a) to get preliminaries dispatched promptly and to identify witnesses for deposition early;
- requesting a scheduling conference as early as provided under Rule 16(b) so the court and counsel can tailor scheduling to any case complexity, such as multiple parties and distant witnesses, as contemplated by the Committee Comments to the 1983 amendments to the rule; and
- scheduling the final pretrial conference as close as possible to the trial date to maximize the conference's effectiveness, minimize stale issues, and facilitate trial preparation.

In *Identiseal Corp. v. Positive Identification Sys., Inc.*,[7] the court recognized that "the parties rather than the court should determine litigation strategy."

The federal rules for discovery as amended in 1983 necessitate a planned discovery strategy. Judge Pollack has explained,

> Case management, in the pretrial phase, planning and scheduling, is the overall contribution of the new proposals. The objectives of the proposed pretrial procedures are to enlist the judge's personal intervention practically from inception of the case and the undertaking of judicial management thereafter that shall embrace the entire pretrial phase, especially motions and discovery, as a means of reducing litigation expense and delay and to assure a better prepared product for a more efficient trial.[8]

7 560 F.2d 298, 302 (7th Cir. 1977).

8 Milton Pollack, *Cutting the Fat from Pretrial Proceedings*, 97 F.R.D. 319 (1982).

Since FED. R. CIV. P. 16(b) requires the scheduling conference and scheduling order to be completed within 120 days of filing, the discovery plan must be developed by the time the complaint is filed.

Requests to Inspect and Produce

FED. R. CIV. P. 34 and its state correlates require anyone, upon request, to produce documents and things, and to allow entry upon land for inspection and other purposes, such as photographing. An important aspect of Rule 34 is that it applies to nonparties. Thus, for example, a defective machine on an employer's premises in a third-party products liability case may be the subject of an inspection order under this rule. The same applies to medical or pharmacy records in a drug products liability case. The purpose of this rule is to make relevant and nonprivileged material available to the parties before trial, eliminating surprise and delay and simplifying the issues to be tried.

Requests for production should accompany interrogatories and specifically seek subject records, test protocols, and design files. Wherever handwritten or coded documents are sought, request typed transcriptions for clarity. Particularly in medical negligence cases, request typed verbatim transcriptions of pertinent records, history and physicals, discharge summaries, doctor's orders, and progress notes. See Appendix F for a sample request to produce.

As with interrogatories, the burden is on the trial lawyer to know the specific areas of information and the specific types of material sought from the opponent and to draft a request for production broad enough to encompass each type or category, yet specific enough to support a motion to compel. Such requests should always include a request for the index to each file or category of documents.

Rather than producing documents, a party may try to overwhelm the seeking party by offering to have the records available and to allow the lawyer to rummage through them. They then produce carts full of files, rooms full of notebooks, and shelves full of boxes. The unsuspecting lawyer thinks there must be some smoking gun in there somewhere and spends days fumbling through thousands of internal memos, cover letters, and routine correspondence.

Strategically, especially in products liability cases, it is more productive for the lawyer to inspect the documents personally at the defendant's headquarters, but only if the lawyer has investigated sufficiently beforehand to know what kind of information to look for and where to find it.

Material Generally Sought

Requests for production are effective discovery tools for evidence on issues such as the defendant's activities, knowledge, and investigation. These documents and items are usually in the custody of the defendant or someone under the defendant's control, and they may be inspected, copied, or photographed.

But the process does have limits. As one commentator has admonished,

> It is readily apparent that preservation of physical evidence is imperative, but obviously this is not feasible in many instances. There is an excess of rhetoric regarding this subject. Some writers offer oversimplified advice to the effect that "all the recoverable parts of the suspected product(s) should be obtained, sequestered and minutely examined." This advice sounds quite plausible, but is unattuned to reality. Economic facts must be considered.
>
> Thoroughness is not equatable with needless exposure of clients to enormous expenses. It is easy to have 20/20 hindsight and criticize lawyers for what they did not do or order to be done.[9]

Common sense and due consideration for economics have to govern the judgment of an attorney representing plaintiffs or defendants in regard to preservation of physical evidence.[10]

Which Tool—Requests for Production or Deposition Duces Tecum?

The overall discovery strategy should include using the request to produce to discover information or the often more fruitful and dynamic deposition duces tecum, which notifies a witness to bring files and documents in response to a notice or subpoena for deposition. The subpoena duces tecum not only brings about the production of documents, it also facilitates inquiry about the documents and their substance, thus effectively fulfilling several discovery goals. Because plaintiff's counsel does not have the luxury of using

[9] Kennelly, 31 TRIAL LAW. GUIDE at 141.

[10] *Id.*

the subpoenaed documents in preparing mechanical questions, part of planning for the deposition duces tecum requires you to (1) prepare conceptual questions anticipating the types of material to be produced and (2) deliberately take time during the deposition to review the material and frame questions directed to it.

The fact that documents or other things have been produced in response to a request for production satisfies the requirement of authenticity but not necessarily of admissibility. Documents, debris, disks, wreckage, photographs, blueprints, and other evidence must still be reviewed after production to determine strategies for foundation for their admission or use at trial. These strategies include

- ► eliciting, marking, and identifying foundational testimony in deposition and deposition transcripts;
- ► attaching the documents or other evidence to requests to admit and seeking admission to accuracy and knowledge; and
- ► seeking stipulations before or at pretrial conference.

Depositions

Rule 30 governs the procedure, scope, and enforcement of depositions—sworn testimony that may have the same effect at trial as if the witness were present. Depositions are the most effective discovery tool and can accelerate the discovery process, because they can be taken on short notice. There is no time lag between question and answer, and follow-up questions permit more complete coverage of a given subject.

But depositions are also the most expensive discovery tool. Therefore, you should prepare thoroughly and with the intent that the deposition be used at trial. Spending the client's money on a deposition can only be justified if the deposition is likely to result in evidence for trial. Some jurisdictions distinguish between so-called "discovery depositions" and "trial depositions," as if a witness's testimony under oath differs based on that distinction. Therefore, pay attention to drafting the notice or subpoena for the deposition so that the testimony can be used for all purposes at trial.

The most common uses of depositions are

- ► to discover information—to get the witness's or other party's versions of the facts,

- to commit a witness to specific testimony and to specific principles,
- to observe the demeanor and credibility of the witness,
- to serve as a basis for impeachment if a witness's testimony at trial is different,
- to explore and establish foundational facts and obtain admissions, and
- to preserve evidence and testimony.

Trial Purposes

Always take depositions with trial in mind, as if the jury were listening. Careful thought must be given to each question, with no meandering that might confuse the issues and admissions. A discovery strategy of taking all depositions for trial purposes imposes important discipline on the trial lawyer to prepare well—lay foundation for evidence; mark, identify, and clarify documents; prepare key documents and other exhibits for the deposition; mark and use demonstrative exhibits for clarity and emphasis; and use the tools of cross-examination wherever permissible.

Timing

Because of the expense and preparation involved in taking depositions, and because other devices provide answers and issues to be explored in deposition, taking depositions is usually deferred until after more preliminary discovery has begun. Some principles, however, mandate prompt scheduling of certain depositions.

When critical eyewitness testimony or the health of any witness is at issue, a deposition should be the first order of business. Promptly depose key witnesses whose testimony may identify other potential defendants. In addition, many lawyers advocate early depositions of hostile witnesses, for their recollections are fresher and less apt to be affected by "sandpapering" or suggestions of others. In medical negligence cases, the testimony of defendant physicians or nurses often affects consultation with experts and must be taken early in the case. Likewise, consider early deposition of eyewitnesses or investigators whose testimony is integral to accident reconstruction or identification of defect by experts.

The time for taking depositions may also be affected by rules of priority. In many jurisdictions where rebuttal is mistaken for defense, the defendant may take the plaintiff's deposition at any time, but the plaintiff must wait a set period of time after suit is filed. Timing may also be affected by rules concerning use of supplementary depositions and other devices. In some restrictive jurisdictions unaccustomed to liberal, self-executing discovery, serving one discovery device upon the defendant waives the use of other devices, that is, taking the deposition precludes any further discovery by interrogatory or further bill of particulars. In such jurisdictions, have a careful discovery plan, using such ancillary devices as the pretrial statement and conference, requests to admit, and outside investigation to develop the evidence.

Some practitioners advise that the first deponent be the party or the witness who has the most information or was the most involved in the events. That witness's testimony may be all that is needed or may indicate sources of other critical information, including key witnesses. After taking this deposition, other shorter ones may be all that are needed to complete the process.

Some counsel are also concerned that a dishonest witness or party can plan his or her testimony if given an opportunity to study the deposition testimony of others. Defense trial lawyer seminars advise lawyers to schedule the depositions of the plaintiff and plaintiff's witnesses well in advance of allowing depositions of any defense witnesses so that the plaintiff's transcripts can be studied. Some even suggest adjourning a deposition after plaintiff's counsel has examined the witness, claiming time problems or other excuses, to have the plaintiff's examination to study before examining the witness. This unethical conduct frustrates discovery and perpetuates the obstructionist game playing that damages the entire process. Conscientious courts and careful counsel can eliminate these schemes early with a proper scheduling order.

Scope of Inquiry

The rules support a broad examination. The deponent can be examined on any nonprivileged matter within the subject matter of the litigation, whether it relates to claims, defenses, other parties, or damages, or may lead to other evidence. The scope of the examination is not limited by the language of or the issues framed by the pleadings. A question that seeks to elicit testimony that might not be admissible at trial does not of itself provide a legitimate basis for counsel to obstruct inquiry by refusing to allow an answer. When an answer is refused to a question that is within the scope of inquiry, reserve the question for review by the court, and contrive inquiry on other matters without waiver of the right to obtain answers. If refusals to answer form a pattern that makes inquiry futile, adjourn the deposition, and move to compel answers to deposition questions.

In the same vein, the Federal Rules of Civil Procedure and the Code of Professional Responsibility prohibit harassment of, embarrassment of, and attacks on witnesses. Questions by or conduct of counsel that seek to intimidate or harass the witness should trigger objection; if the conduct persists, adjourn the deposition until the court intervenes and issues an order governing the completion of the deposition.

Objections

Most objections, except those as to form, are reserved until trial. Therefore, experienced attorneys recognize that depositions need not be interrupted by strings of objections and argument, since argument at deposition serves no purpose other than to increase the deposition's length and cost.

However, FED. R. CIV. P. 32(d)(3)(A) says that objections as to competency, relevancy, or materiality are waived "unless the ground of the objection is one which might have been obviated or removed if presented at that time."

Likewise, there is no legal or procedural basis other than privilege and the fifth amendment for instructing a party or witness not to answer a question. The remedy for any irrelevant, immaterial, or embarrassing information elicited is exclusion from evidence on proper motion at the time the testimony is offered. Rule 30(c) provides, "Evidence objected to *shall* be taken subject to the objection."[11]

Counseling the Deponent

Experienced lawyers advise thoroughly counseling the plaintiff-deponent about the deposition process and what to expect. The deponent needs the benefit of counsel's experience, familiarity with the issues and the case, and judgment to understand a relatively esoteric and formal process. The amount of time needed for this preparation varies with the complexity of the case and other factors,

[11] For a useful discussion about handling objections at deposition, see Thames, *Discovery Strategy*, For The Defense, 12-22, Jan. 1966.

including the passage of time since events occurred and the memory and fluency of the client. Any answers to interrogatories already furnished by the plaintiff form a good base for preparation.

The most important rule of deposition is to tell the truth. While this is obvious, and we hope all witnesses will be honest, always advise the plaintiff to tell the truth. This guides the plaintiff when questions are ambiguous and answers ambivalent. Also tell the plaintiff that

- she or he must answer all questions fairly. However, this is not the time to tell the story; this is the time to answer with the minimum commensurate with the truth, and not to volunteer what is not asked;
- the defendant knows or has resources to learn everything adverse to the case. Therefore candor is desirable;
- the defendant knows or has resources to learn many things considered private, which may or may not be involved in the case. Therefore, the plaintiff is warned not to be too sensitive;
- lying or exaggerating will make it difficult for plaintiff's attorney to continue representation and will certainly destroy the case;
- guessing, speculating, or acting like a know-it-all will damage credibility, so the plaintiff should listen thoughtfully before answering;
- rushing into an answer or guessing at the meaning of a vague question is dangerous; the witness has every right to request an explanation of any question, to ask the meaning of a term, or to ask that the question be repeated before answering;
- the defendant may try to anger, frighten, or embarrass the witness, but this is only a tactic to handicap the witness's reasoning powers. Anger, panic, and embarrassment have no place in the process; and
- if pain, anger, panic, or anxiety occurs and interferes with the witness's concentration, the witness can and should request an intermission and leave the room to regain composure.

The plaintiff deponent should review, in addition to interrogatory answers, any statements made to investigative agencies or police;

discrepancies with other testimony, in medical histories, or in other records should be explored. If numbers, dates, expense amounts, or other figures or facts are essential to the testimony and the witness lacks confidence in remembering them, you may counsel the plaintiff to write notes to ensure accuracy in the deposition.

Some practitioners obtain greater benefit from the predeposition conference if they send an instruction sheet describing the deposition procedure to the client ahead of time. Some lawyers have brochures describing deposition formalities, and some lawyers, as well as a few state bar associations (e.g., Wisconsin), use or market a predeposition video instruction tape for the client to watch at home or in the lawyer's office.

In preparation for the plaintiff's deposition, you must review factual intricacies and discrepancies. You must know every tax audit problem, domestic abuse arrest, drug charge, custody dispute, or aborted divorce proceeding lurking in the plaintiff's closet. While printed instructions and videotaped descriptions may help, adequate preparation requires healthy skepticism and hard, concentrated personal dialogue between you and your client, including cross-examination to uncover concealed matters. This will also dispel phony or unrealistic notions about the judicial process stemming from television, the press, or elsewhere.

Video and Telephone Depositions

Although the rules recognize that advances in video and telephone conferencing technologies provide additional flexibility to discovery and trial practice, these options have limitations and should only be used as a last resort.

Rule 30(b)(7) provides for telephone deposition with notice and agreement and specifies that, if court supervision is invoked, the supervising court will be the court located in the district where the witness is. While the rules do not specify requirements for location of counsel during a telephone deposition, some advantage is gained when one lawyer is with the witness and one attends by phone. It is important to have a court reporter transcribe the deposition at each end of the telephone to ensure accuracy.

Video depositions must be properly noticed under Rule 30(b)(4); they provide an opportunity to enliven testimony that must be given by deposition. Like telephone depositions, video depositions are subject to the limitations and reliability of the technology involved and are no substitute for the real thing. When they must be used, however, the same strategies apply as to depositions generally. Video depositions provide an opportunity to focus on demonstrative exhibits and record the witness's pointing, marking, or otherwise referring to the exhibit. Video transcription is so unreliable, however, that experienced counsel always schedule stenographic court reporting, as well, for accuracy and dependability. Then, if the video is unusable, the transcript can still be read.

Video and telephone testimony are controversial, and whether they're advisable in specific cases is beyond the scope of this discussion. However, these forms of deposition are available under the rules and may be accomplished by stipulation, motion, or right, in some jurisdictions. Video depositions are expensive and would ordinarily be done only when it is extremely important to convey a visual impression of the witness to the jury, such as a dying plaintiff whose appearance is relevant; an expert who must refer to charts and models; a highly technical witness; or a witness whose testimony includes demonstrations, testing, or field investigation.

Designated-Witness Rule 30(b)(6) Depositions

Before the 1970 revisions of the federal rules, discovery within such organizations as corporations, governmental agencies, and other associations often foundered on a "Catch-22:" because these organizations were faceless, you had to know the identities of witnesses beforehand to obtain discovery of witnesses and facts. Otherwise, depositions often wasted time and money as you hunted through corporate agents for the one witness with some knowledge.

The revision adding subsection (b)(6) to FED. R. CIV. P. 30 remedied this situation considerably. This addition was intended to curb the corporate agents' "bandying," where individual deponents disclaimed facts obviously known to someone in the organization and thus attributable to it. Additionally, the revision was meant to assist organizations whose agents were being unnecessarily and excessively deposed by counsel searching for a useful witness.[12]

Generally, the designated-witness deposition can obviate interrogatories that seek to identify agents with knowledge of organizational matters. Most significantly, the rule provides for depositions

12 Advisory Committee Notes to Rule 30(b)(6), 48 F.R.D. 487, 515.

of nonparty organizations as well as parties.[13] Since it applies to entities that are not subject to other discovery, Rule 30(b)(6) can also facilitate amendment and settlement. For these designated-witness depositions to be effective, a subpoena to the organization to be deposed is required, in addition to written notice to the parties. The subpoena must specify the area of inquiry so that the appropriate witness can be designated. This is critical: if the subpoena is too vague, the organization may designate an unproductive witness. If the subpoena is reasonably specific, the moving party at least has the foundation for further discovery and grounds for recovering costs and sanctions for the wrong or inept designee.

The 30(b)(6) subpoena must advise the organization of the duty to designate an agent-deponent to ensure that a subpoenaed non-party organization knows its duty even if it is not represented by counsel.

Some suggestions for effectively handling these depositions follow:

Seek designated-witness depositions of as many witnesses as there are issues requiring special knowledge, rather than chasing one designee for all purposes. Areas that are frequently a productive subject of these depositions include such specialties as design, safety, quality assurance, warnings, recalls, marketing, sales training, statutory compliance, testing, loss control, and computer storage.

Plan these depositions duces tecum so the witness will bring a curriculum vitae (where appropriate); a list of company incentive or safety awards; a bibliography of publications in which the deponent participated; and files concerned with design modifications, regulatory compliance, loss control statistics, testing data, and product complaints. Examine the witness about compliance with the subpoena and preparation for the deposition.

Take these depositions not in lawyers' offices, but at organizational headquarters—this is for witness convenience and for you to observe the environment, resources, and collectability. Taking depositions at the organization also prevents the deponent from avoiding either the production of materials or the checking of a particular fact.

Always prepare and take these depositions as if they were trial testimony—define goals, outline concepts and questions, investigate and collect materials, and refine theories, themes, and questions.

[13] Ghandi v. Police Dep't of Detroit, 74 F.R.D. 115, 121 (E.D. Mich. 1977).

You never know when a witness will be unavailable for trial, and, of course, party designees' deposition testimony can be used for any purpose under Rule 32(a)(2).

Where the organization sidesteps the rule and designates a functionary or executive who knows nothing substantive about the issues, proceed with the deposition anyway to show the designee's ignorance and the organization's bad faith. Then use the deposition to seek further discovery and sanctions. This type of deposition may also be useful at trial to show a party's ignorance and indifference.

The rules provide the same enforcement for noncompliance as with any other refusal to comply with proper discovery requests.

The designated-witness deposition under Rule 30(b)(6) streamlines discovery. When the rule is vigorously enforced, it is a most effective tool at trials.

Physical and Mental Examination

The "examination rule," FED. R. CIV. P. 35, has generally been considered a defendant's tool, but it can actually provide valuable evidence for a plaintiff as well. When, under Rule 35, the injured plaintiff is sent to be examined by a physician or psychologist who is selected and paid by the defendant, this is an adversary proceeding. Because of its nature, and to protect cross-examination, sophisticated courts recognize that these examinations are not "independent medicals" but "defense examinations." You should recognize these differences and take more than a routine look at this rule, with an eye toward using it affirmatively.

First, where the defendant seeks a court-ordered examination of the plaintiff, you can use Rule 35 to:

- limit the order to protect the client from invasive, painful, unnecessary, and cumulative or experimental diagnostic procedures;
- furnish relevant scientific or medical literature to the examining physician in advance, noting that the literature may be of *scientific* interest in the scope of the examination;
- furnish relevant records, reports, or excerpts of witness testimony to the examining physician in advance to assist in completing the *history* of the injury; and

- accompany the plaintiff to the examination to observe the length, scope, and conduct of the examination, but not to interfere or cue the plaintiff at all.

The first, second, and third measures are particularly useful in cases where historical indifference has prevented some medical specialties from recognizing the scope of the injury, as in the castration of women by IUD-induced pelvic inflammatory disease or by unnecessary or negligent hysterectomy, the disability and disfigurement wrought by amputation of a breast necessitated by delayed diagnosis, the full panoply of disabilities of chronic thrombophlebitis, or future career loss to a homemaker whose intellectual capacity has been damaged by delayed diagnosis of a brain tumor or by traumatic axonal injury from head impact. Some scientific documentation of the full scope of these injuries, furnished in advance, assists the examiner in conducting a fair examination.

Many experienced lawyers recommend meeting with the plaintiff before the examination to review medical history, check records, and dispel anxious questions.

The fourth step, accompanying the plaintiff to the examination, is an essential part of the representation of the plaintiff; it is also vital to plaintiff's right to cross-examine the examining physician when the physician's opinion is offered in the case. The right to cross-examine depends on your attendance and knowledge of the examination itself and observation of such facts as

- the lack of the examining physician's familiarity with the plaintiff's medical history;
- the distractions of phone calls and other patients;
- any limitations in the scope of the examination;
- the available tools of the examination including X-rays, lab work, and reference books;
- discrepancies between what was tested by the examiner and observed by counsel and what is detailed and discussed in the report by the examiner; and
- the brevity of the examination.

Cross-examination seeks to expose the examiner's lack of knowledge, lack of opportunity to observe, interest, bias or prejudice, and any exaggeration or perjury in the opinions. Your attendance at a

Rule 35 defense medical exam is necessary to fulfill this function.

The rule does not limit the party for whom the examination is ordered. In certain cases, you may want to seek a court-ordered examination of the defendant or the defendant's agent. In medical negligence cases, for example, where the defendant obstetrician appeared drunk at delivery, the infant suffered birth trauma, and inebriation is denied, examination of the defendant obstetrician by a neurologist and an addictionologist can prove helpful.

FED. R. CIV. P. 35 requires good cause and that the party's condition be "in controversy." The United States Supreme Court analyzed these elements as requiring more than "mere conclusory allegations;" instead, the rule requires an "affirmative showing by the movant that each condition . . . is really and genuinely in controversy and that good cause exists for ordering each examination." It does *not* require that the "movant must prove his case on the merits."[14]

This tool is particularly useful in employment discrimination or sexual harassment cases. Neuropsychological and psychological examination can document race and gender biases (mental condition) of such agents of the defendant as

- the personnel supervisor who has the responsibility for hiring or promotion;
- the foreperson responsible for job appraisal and assignment;
- the job supervisor responsible for assignment or training and promotion; and
- the officers responsible for hiring, the personnel manual, and company policy.

In *Schlagenhauf v. Holder*, the Court indicated that where allegations of mental or physical injury have been made, or mental or physical conditions asserted as a defense, the pleadings are sufficient to satisfy the "controversy" requirement.[15]

In *Brewster v. Martin Marietta Aluminum Sales, Inc.*,[16] an employment discrimination case where the requirements of Rule 35 were otherwise met, the Michigan Court of Appeals allowed the

[14] 379 U.S. 104, 118 (1964).

[15] *Id.* at 119-20.

[16] 107 Mich. Ct. App. 639, 309 N.W. 2d 687 (1981).

plaintiff's use of the analogous state rule, M.C.R. 2.311. In considering such a use of the rule's predecessor, G.C.R. 1963, 311.1, the court said:

> We note that the plain language of G.C.R. 1963, 311.1 does not preclude the rule's application to cases like that brought by the plaintiff. The availability of mental examinations is extended to any action in which a party's mental condition is in controversy. Once placed in controversy, a moving party need only show good cause to secure the petitioned for examination.[17]

Requests to Admit

It is a mistake to think of requests to admit as dry, perfunctory devices for dispensing with legal formalities sometime before the final pretrial. Technically, requests to admit are not discovery at all but vital tools used during the entire discovery process. An important use of requests to admit early in the case is to confirm a legal relationship, such as physician-patient, or a role or status, such as designer, manufacturer, agency, or successor corporation, for liability purposes. This allows discovery to proceed economically and correctly, and amendments to the complaint can be avoided.

Requests can be used to follow up answers to interrogatories and depositions. A party may change, explain, and contradict interrogatory answers and explain deposition testimony. Therefore, certain facts learned through interrogatory or deposition should be submitted as requests to admit because these admissions are then binding as true, under Rule 36(b).

Furthermore, requests to admit distill the significant concepts and facts from an otherwise meandering deposition, economizing proofs and emphasizing important issues. When digesting the deposition in requests to admit, indicate the page and line of the witness's transcript for the convenience of the answering party and the reviewing court, should enforcement by the court become necessary.

As technical investigation and discovery progress and legal and factual issues emerge, requests to admit can be used to establish

- foundational elements for admissibility of potentially disputed evidence,

[17] 107 Mich. Ct. App. at 645, 309 N.W. 2d at 690 (1981).

- concepts and principles applicable to standard of care and causation,
- stipulated facts for the joint pretrial order,
- concepts and principles to meet defenses, and
- issues for summary judgment.

Areas where dispute as to admissibility may be eliminated by requests to admit include

- technical or scientific literature;
- subsequent remedial measures or modifications by seeking admission as to control, knowledge, or feasibility;
- a presumption that if the evidence were produced it would support the plaintiff's case; and
- direct proof of the defendant's actual or constructive knowledge of scientific conferences, code committee recommendations, and journals of professional or technical societies concerning reasonable care, causation, and foreseeability, in particular.

Later in the case, requests to admit that seek to establish safety principles, design concepts, operative definitions, and principles of due care should be drawn both to simplify issues for trial and to provide the context of stipulated facts for the proposed joint pretrial order. Such requests have their foundation in all the facets of the case previously reviewed above—the investigation, discovery documents, technical and scientific research, and depositions.

Requests to admit require thorough investigation, vigorous discovery, expertise in the technical proofs, and detailed, precise knowledge of the entire case. The requests to admit are well worth the discipline and intensity required, for they provide leverage for settlement discussions, a handy index to the proofs available in the case, the stipulated facts required for the joint pretrial order, and possible bases for summary judgment on some aspects of the case.

One dramatic and under-recognized use of requests to admit is to read the admissions to the jury. Requests to admit provide an orderly, simplified, and lucid presentation of key facts that might otherwise enter the record buried in the fine print of a contract, a scientific journal, or a truncated deposition, where their significance might be overlooked. Rule 36(b) provides for admissibility of admissions; following the court's instruction as to the effect of requests to admit, reading the admissions can have substantial impact and save considerable time.

While this discussion suggests numerous applications for requests to admit to stimulate broader and more intense use of these issue-resolving devices, certain caveats are in order. As with any tool stipulated by the rules, requests to admit cannot be abused. They must not be carelessly drafted or used to substitute for other discovery. Requests must be used precisely and decisively, for as the Comments to the 1970 Amendment to Rule 36 indicate,

> Requests to Admit may be so voluminous and so framed that the answering party finds the task of identifying what is in dispute and what is not unduly burdensome. If so, the responding party may obtain a protective order under Rule 26(c). Some of the decisions sustaining objections on "disputability" grounds could have been justified by the burdensome character of the requests.[18]

Furthermore, where the requests concern technology or scientific principles, definitional preludes will likely be necessary to avoid confusion, delay, or objection.

Rule 36 provides specifically how requests to admit must be answered. The fact that a particular request to admit concerns an issue "in dispute" is not grounds for objection. The Comments to the 1970 Amendment Subdivision (a) make clear that the proper response to requests that the answering party claims are issues for trial is still an answer, not an objection.

As the comments make clear, the trend is toward requiring answers in compliance with the rule, that is, admission or denial, and toward deeming failure to answer in compliance with the rules to be an admission.

As the district court wrote in *Chess Music, Inc. v. Bowman*,[19] "[i]t is well settled that a failure to respond to requests for admission is deemed to be an admission of the matters set forth." Silence is tantamount to an admission.[20] And from *Luick v. Graybar Electric*

[18] *See, e.g.*, Syracuse Broadcasting Corp. v. Newhouse, 271 F.2d 910, 917 (2d Cir. 1959).

[19] 474 F. Supp. 184, 185 (D. Neb. 1979).

[20] *See also* Adventures in Good Eating, Inc. v. Best Places to Eat, Inc., 131 F.2d 809, 812 (7th Cir. 1942).

Co., "[u]nanswered requests for admission render the matter conclusively established for the purpose of that suit."[21]

Argumentative answers injecting theories of defense into matters in which there is no genuine or good faith dispute plainly constitute defective answers, under Rule 36.[22] Rather, "[t]he party asking for the admissions is entitled to a direct and unequivocal answer to his request in order to properly prepare his case."[23]

Because of the important functions of requests to admit, vigorous enforcement of Rule 36 is in order. Courts have not been reluctant to examine the sufficiency of a party's answers and deem requests admitted where answers have not been made in good faith in conformity with the rule.[24] Requests to admit should be used early, often, and precisely to serve their purpose. As comments to the federal rules observe,

> Rule 36 serves two vital purposes, both of which are designed to reduce trial time. Admissions are sought, first to facilitate proof with respect to issues that cannot be eliminated from the case, and second, to narrow the issues by eliminating those that can be.[25]

Skillful use of requests for admissions during case preparation and trial will narrow the case to the important issues and focus on the evidence necessary to decide those issues. Proper application and courageous enforcement of the rules concerning requests for admissions reduces judicial and courtroom delay, aids in resolving the case, and ensures economic use of pretrial and trial time.[26]

21 473 F.2d 1360, 1362 (8th Cir. 1973).

22 *See, e.g.*, United States Plywood Corp. v. Hudson Lumber Co., 127 F. Supp. 489, 498 (S.D.N.Y. 1954).

23 In re Independent Distillers of Kentucky, 34 F. Supp. 724, 729 (W.D. Ky. 1940).

24 *See, e.g.*, Farina v. Mission Inv. Trust, 615 F.2d 1068 (5th Cir. 1980); Chrapliwy v. Uniroyal, Inc., 17 Fed. R. Serv. 2d (Callaghan) 719 (N.D. Ind. 1973); Southern Ry. v. Crosby, 201 F.2d 878 (4th Cir. 1953); United States Plywood Corp. v. Hudson Lumber Co., 127 F. Supp. 489 (S.D.N.Y. 1954); and Princess Pat Ltd. v. National Carloading Corp., 223 F.2d 916 (7th Cir. 1955).

25 FED. R. CIV. P. 36, Comment 1970 Amendment.

26 For a helpful analysis of the use of requests to admit, see Finman, *The Request for Admissions in Federal Civil Procedure*, 71 YALE L.J. 371, 376 (1962).

Final Pretrial Conference and Order

Many states have adopted the federal pretrial scheme, with the final pretrial order controlling the ensuing phases of the case. FED. R. CIV. P. 16(d) and many of the local rules implementing it implicitly require joint participation in preparing the proposed order—a stage many lawyers perceive as onerous. From a strictly mechanical perspective, it is.

However, this rule does present yet another opportunity to propose facts and issues for stipulation, to narrow the issues to be tried, and to translate some facts into admissible evidence. FED. R. CIV. P. 16(c)(1), (3), and (9), the stipulations and admissions contained in the final joint pretrial order, are generally read to the jury as the facts are conclusively established. Some examples of these issues on which admission may be proposed in the proposed joint pretrial order, and even forced during the final pretrial conference, are

- the agency relationship;
- the physician-patient relationship;
- the successor or parent corporation;
- a de facto merger or other successor facts;
- the anticipated life expectancy by U.S. Census Life Tables; and
- the total amount of claimed medical and treatment expenses based upon summaries or copies of bills, especially where paid by a disinterested third party.

In effect, the pretrial conference influences the discovery strategy from the first filing through the trial, affecting scheduling, witnesses, theories, and proofs. So whether the case concerns drug-induced cerebral palsy, vaccine-induced encephalopathy, contraceptive-induced stroke, or death from seat belt failure, strategies for the pretrial conference really include three areas: (1) strategies of the scheduling conference (see "Scheduling Conference and Order" under "Tools of Discovery" above); (2) preparation of the proposed order; and (3) conduct of the final pretrial conference itself.

The final pretrial order controls all the subsequent conduct of the case;[27] its preparation really begins with drafting the complaint

[27] FED. R. CIV. P. 16(e).

to pose and resolve as many issues and areas of proof as early as possible. Strategies for this phase include

- using requests to admit comprehensively throughout the pretrial phase and then incorporating the admissions in the proposed order as stipulations of fact;[28]
- culling answers to interrogatories for stipulations of fact such as knowledge of design alternatives, acceptance of physician-patient relationship, and successor corporations;
- filing a request for supplementation[29] in anticipation of the pretrial conference to flush out incomplete discovery raised in the order for resolution at the pretrial conference;
- filing as part of the proposed order as contemplated by Rule 16(c)(9) any necessary motions that have not been determined—such as motions to strike, amend, or deem admitted—with briefing for determination at the conference; and
- anticipating trial questions, such as attorney voir dire and admissibility of tests or video films and other evidentiary issues, by raising these in the proposed order as motions *in limine* with briefing, as contemplated by Rule 16(c)(10).

Finally, attendance at the pretrial conference itself should be approached, not as a perfunctory session, but as yet another opportunity for discovery. Possible strategies for the conference follow.

- Regard the conference as an opportunity to secure further admissions, tie up loose ends in discovery,[30] obtain expert witness reports, and get a final assessment of witnesses, including new witnesses recently learned of or discovered.[31]
- Take videos, charts, photo enlargements of claims, sketches, and photographs for review to obviate later evidentiary problems.[32]
- Request and carefully examine the opponent's exhibits, documents, and demonstrative evidence for potential evidence to be introduced in the plaintiff's case.

28 FED. R. CIV. P. 16(c)(3).

29 FED. R. CIV. P. 26(e).

30 FED. R. CIV. P. 16(c)(3).

31 FED. R. CIV. P. 16(c)(5).

32 FED. R. CIV. P. 16(c)(3), (10), (11).

With the scope of and preparation for the pretrial conference, some strict constructionists have lost perspective. While the pretrial order and conference are intended to minimize surprise, they are not intended to rehearse or replace the trial, or to reduce it to a rote exercise. They are intended to facilitate the trial.[33]

For the court, the pretrial conference functions as a tool of case (and lawyer) management with the ultimate tool not being sanctions or exclusions, but the trial itself. After all, the purpose of the pretrial, like that of discovery, is the fair and just presentation of the case to the jury—a trial, not a docket or an empty courtroom at the expense of justice.[34]

CONCLUSION

The modern trial lawyer devotes significant time and strategy to the full use of discovery procedures. This is ethical and professional because thorough preparation for a case often effectuates settlement, thereby eliminating the time and expense of trial.

The careful lawyer assesses how much discovery is really necessary and whether discovery will support the plaintiff's case as much or more than the defendant's case. Beyond this initial assessment, the experienced lawyer weighs each discovery tool for economy, effectiveness, vulnerability, enforceability, and use at trial. Discovery initiated by the defendant can, in many circumstances, be more useful and effective for the plaintiff than if the plaintiff initiated that particular discovery. For example, consider the eyewitness or fact witness deposition. If noticed by the defendant, plaintiff's counsel retains the right to cross-examine and thus the opportunity to translate witness facts into more effective evidence through leading questions.

When trial lawyers employ discovery ethically and appropriately and courts enforce discovery rules, substantial savings in judicial time and court expense result. When the discovery process is fully and correctly implemented and courageously enforced, the truth is more likely to emerge and justice more likely to be served.

[33] Padovani v. Bruchhausen, 293 F.2d 546 (2d Cir. 1961); Flannery v. Carroll, 676 F.2d 126 (5th Cir. 1982).

[34] Laird v. Air Carrier Engine Service, Inc., 263 F.2d 948 (5th Cir. 1959).

APPENDIX A

Rule 33. Interrogatories to Parties.

(a) AVAILABILITY; PROCEDURES FOR USE. Any party may serve upon any other party written interrogatories to be answered by the party served or, if the party served is a public or private corporation or a partnership or association or governmental agency, by any officer or agent, who shall furnish such information as is available to the party. Interrogatories may, without leave of court, be served upon the plaintiff after commencement of the action and upon any other party with or after service of the summons and complaint upon that party.

Each interrogatory shall be answered separately and fully in writing under oath, unless it is objected to, in which event the reasons for objection shall be stated in lieu of an answer. The answers are to be signed by the person making them, and the objections signed by the attorney making them. The party upon whom the interrogatories have been served shall serve a copy of the answers, and objections if any, within 30 days after the service of the interrogatories, except that a defendant may serve answers or objections within 45 days after service of the summons and complaint upon that defendant. The court may allow a shorter or longer time. The party submitting the interrogatories may move for an order under Rule 37(a) with respect to any objection to or other failure to answer an interrogatory.

Rule 34. Production of Documents and Things and Entry Upon Land for Inspection and Other Purposes.

(b) PROCEDURE. The request may, without leave of court, be served upon the plaintiff after commencement of the action and upon any other party with or after service of the summons and complaint upon that party. The request shall set forth the items to be inspected either by individual item or by category, and describe each item and category with reasonable particularity. The request shall specify a reasonable time, place, and manner of making the inspection and performing the related acts.

The party upon whom the request is served shall serve a written response within 30 days after the service of the request, except that a defendant may serve a response within 45 days after service of the summons and complaint upon that defendant. The court may allow a shorter or longer time. The response shall state, with respect to each item or category, that inspection and related activities will be permitted as requested, unless the request is objected to, in which event the reasons for objection shall be stated. If objection is made to part of an item or category, the part shall be specified. The party submitting the request may move for an order under Rule 37(a) with respect to any objection to or other failure to respond to the request or any part thereof, or any failure to permit inspection as requested.

A party who produces documents for inspection shall produce them as they are kept in the usual course of business or shall organize and label them to correspond with the categories in the request.

Rule 36. Requests for Admission.

(a) REQUEST FOR ADMISSION. A party may serve upon any other party a written request for the admission, for purposes of the pending action only, of the truth of any matters within the scope of Rule 26(b) set forth in the request that relate to statements or opinions of fact or of the application of law to fact, including the genuineness of any documents described in the request. Copies of documents shall be served with the request unless they have been or are otherwise furnished or made available for inspection and copying. The request may, without leave of court, be served upon the plaintiff after commencement of the action and upon any other party with or after service of the summons and complaint upon that party.

Each matter of which an admission is requested shall be separately set forth. The matter is admitted unless, within 30 days after service of the request, or within such shorter or longer time as the court may allow, the party to whom the request is directed serves upon the party requesting the admission a written answer or objection addressed to the matter, signed by the party or by the party's attorney, but, unless the court shortens the time, a defendant shall not be required to serve answers or objections before the expiration of 45 days after service of the summons and complaint upon the defendant. If objection is made, the reasons therefore shall be stated. The answer shall specifically deny the matter or set forth in detail the reasons why the answering party cannot truthfully admit or deny the matter. A denial shall fairly meet the substance of the requested admission, and when good faith requires that a party qualify an answer or deny only a part of the matter of which an admission is requested, the party shall specify so much of it as is true and qualify or deny the remainder. An answering party may not give lack of information or knowledge as a reason for failure to admit or deny unless the party states that the party has made reasonable inquiry and that the information known or readily obtainable by the party is insufficient to enable the party to admit or deny. A party who considers that a matter of which an admission has been requested presents a genuine issue for trial may not, on that ground alone, object to the request; the party may, subject to the provisions of the Rules 37(c), deny the matter or set forth reasons why the party cannot admit or deny it.

The party who has requested the admissions may move to determine the sufficiency of the answers or objections. Unless the court determines that an objection is justified, it shall order that an answer be served. If the court determines that an answer does not comply with the requirements of this rule, it may order either that the matter is admitted or that an amended answer be served. The court may, in lieu of these orders, determine that final disposition of the request be made at a pretrial conference or at a designated time prior to trial. The provisions of Rule 37(a)(4) apply to the award of expenses incurred in relation to the motion.

Rule 37. Failure to Make or Cooperate in Discovery: Sanctions.

(a) MOTIONS FOR ORDER COMPELLING DISCOVERY. A party, upon reasonable notice to other parties and all persons affected thereby, may apply for an order compelling discovery as follows:

(1) *Appropriate Court.* An application for an order to a party may be made to the court in which the action is pending, or, on matters relating to a deposition, to the court in the district where the deposition is being taken. An application for an order to a deponent who is not a party shall be made to the court in the district where the deposition is being taken.

(2) *Motion.* If a deponent fails to answer a question propounded or submitted under Rules 30 or 31, or a corporation or other entity fails to make a designation under Rule 30(b)(6) or 31(a), or a party fails to answer an interrogatory submitted under Rule 33, or if a party, in response to a request for inspection submit-

ted under Rule 34, fails to respond that inspection will be permitted as requested or fails to permit inspection as requested, the discovering party may move for an order compelling an answer, or a designation, or an order compelling inspection in accordance with the request. When taking a deposition on oral examination, the proponent of the question may complete or adjourn the examination before applying for an order.

If the court denies the motion in whole or in part, it may make such protective order as it would have been empowered to make on a motion made pursuant to Rule 26(c).

(3) *Evasive or Incomplete Answer.* For purposes of this subdivision an evasive or incomplete answer is to be treated as a failure to answer.

(4) *Award of Expenses of Motion.* If the motion is granted, the court shall, after opportunity for hearing, require the party or deponent whose conduct necessitated the motion or the party or attorney advising such conduct or both of them to pay to the moving party the reasonable expenses incurred in obtaining the order, including attorney's fees, unless the court finds that the opposition to the motion was substantially justified or that other circumstances make an award of expenses unjust.

If the motion is denied, the court shall, after opportunity for hearing, require the moving party or the attorney advising the motion or both of them to pay to the party or deponent who opposed the motion the reasonable expenses incurred in opposing the motion, including attorney's fees, unless the court finds that the making of the motion was substantially justified or that other circumstances make an award of expenses unjust.

If the motion is granted in part and denied in part, the court may apportion the reasonable expenses incurred in relation to the motion among the parties and persons in a just manner.

APPENDIX B

Franklin Beyer, Plaintiff, v. Carlson Pools, Inc., an Indiana corporation; Blue Lagoon Pools, Inc., an Indiana corporation; Burton Enterprises, Inc., an Indiana corporation; John Doe Construction Company; and Whitton & Hatch Manufacturing Company, a Connecticut corporation, Defendants.	Amended and Substituted Petition at Law

NOW COMES the Plaintiff and hereby amends his Petition at Law to add the following named defendant: Whitton & Hatch Manufacturing Company, a Connecticut corporation, and hereby amends his Petition at Law as follows:

1. The Plaintiff is a quadriplegic citizen of Indiana, paralyzed on March 15, 1982, as a result of a diving injury sustained while he was a guest at the Allen Family Motel pool at 1680 Grant Street, Indianapolis, Indiana.
2. The Defendant Carlson Pools, Inc. is an Indiana corporation that in 1973 did the engineering design of the installation of the aforementioned pool.
3. The Defendant Blue Lagoon Pools, Inc. is an Indiana corporation that in 1973 was a franchiser of swimming pools and that undertook the engineering design of the aforementioned pool.
4. The Defendant Burton Enterprises, Inc., an Indiana corporation, was the owner and operator of the aforementioned pool at the time of the Plaintiff's injury.
5. The John Doe Construction Company is a fictitious name for the presently unknown construction company that built the aforementioned pool.

6. The Defendant Whitton & Hatch Engineering Company is a Connecticut corporation, doing business in Indiana, that was at all times material hereto a franchiser of swimming pools, and that undertook the engineering design of the aforementioned pool.

7. Each of the Defendants owed the Plaintiff the duty of due care.

8. Each of the Defendants violated its duty and was negligent as follows:

The Defendants Carlson Pools, Inc., Blue Lagoon Pools, Inc., and the John Doe Construction Company

- a. designed and built an unmarked underwater construction ledge that would cause diving from the side of the pool to be hazardous;
- b. designed and built an unmarked shallow section of the pool immediately adjacent to an area of the pool marked with a seven-foot depth;
- c. designed and built the pool so that the depth of the water adjacent to the seven-foot marker was much less than seven feet;
- d. failed to provide NO DIVING—SHALLOW END warnings as part of the pool design and construction; and
- e. failed to provide
  - (1) pool fencing or a pool cover,
  - (2) television monitoring or water sensors, and
  - (3) a spine board and directions for emergency treatment of spinal cord injury victims.

The Defendant Burton Enterprises, Inc.

- a. operated a swimming pool without an attendant for accident prevention purposes,
- b. maintained without pool lights an unfenced and uncovered pool in which guests were swimming at 10:20 p.m. with motel permission,
- c. misrepresented water depth to be seven feet adjacent to one side of the pool,
- d. failed to have a pool safety line separating the deep end from the shallow end,
- e. failed to monitor pool use by either television monitors or water sensors,

f. failed to mark dangerous underwater construction ledges,
g. failed to limit by warning signs the areas from which it was unsafe to dive,
h. failed to post emergency treatment guidelines for persons temporarily paralyzed in the water, and
i. failed to provide a spine board for immobilizing a temporarily paralyzed person in the pool.

The Defendant Whitton & Hatch Manufacturing Company

a. designed and prefabricated an unmarked underwater ledge that caused diving from the side of the pool to be hazardous;
b. designed and prefabricated an unmarked shallow section of the pool immediately adjacent to an area of the pool marked with a seven-foot depth;
c. designed and prefabricated the pool so that the depth of the water adjacent to the seven-foot marker was much less than seven feet;
d. failed to provide NO DIVING—SHALLOW END warnings as part of the pool design and prefabrication; and
e. failed to provide as part of the basic design or as part of their prefabricated materials kits
   (1) pool fencing or a pool cover,
   (2) television monitoring or water sensors, or
   (3) a spine board and directions for emergency treatment of spinal cord injury victims.

9. Each of the aforesaid acts of negligence was jointly and severally a proximate cause of the Plaintiff's injuries and damages.

10. The Plaintiff suffered cervical spine injuries that have made him a permanent quadriplegic. He has lost and will lose earnings and earning capacity. He has required and will require hospital, medical, drug, and rehabilitation care, as well as transportation for medical and nursing care. He has suffered pain and will continue to suffer pain throughout his life. He is disfigured and has suffered and will suffer embarrassment because of this disfigurement. He has lost enjoyment of life.

WHEREFORE, the Plaintiff seeks such damages as are fair, just, and reasonable in a sum not to exceed eight million dollars, together with interest from the date of this filing, and of this Amended and Substituted Petition and costs of this action.

APPENDIX C

Eileen Nolan and William Nolan,
Plaintiffs,
v.
Martin M. Brooks, M.D. and
Howard & McGeary, Inc., an Ohio
corporation, jointly and severally,
Defendants.

VERIFIED COMPLAINT AND JURY DEMAND

NOW COME the Plaintiffs, Eileen and William Nolan, by and through their attorneys, ________________ , and for their Complaint allege as follows:

Count One—Negligence

1. The Plaintiffs Eileen and William Nolan are wife and husband, and are and have been at all times material hereto citizens of the State of Washington and residents of the City of Redmond, in the County of King.

2. The Defendant Martin M. Brooks, M.D. is a physician licensed to practice medicine in the State of Washington, and is established and engaged in the practice of medicine in the City of Kirkland, County of King.

3. The Defendant Howard & McGeary, Inc. is an Ohio corporation having its principal place of business in a State other than Washington, but doing business in this judicial district.

4. The amount in controversy exceeds Ten Thousand Dollars ($10,000.00), exclusive of interest, costs, and attorneys' fees.

5. Prior to 1976, Defendant Brooks accepted Plaintiff Eileen Nolan as a patient and undertook to provide competent medical services.

6. During or prior to 1976 Defendant Brooks prescribed an oral contraceptive known as "Novo-D," which is designed, manufactured, marketed, and sold by Defendant Howard & McGeary, Inc., for

Plaintiff Eileen Nolan, and Plaintiff continued to take Novo-D as prescribed under the care and supervision of Defendant Brooks until on or about May 19, 1978.

7. On or about May 15 and 16, 1978, Plaintiff Eileen Nolan presented to Defendant Brooks complaints of severe leg cramping for which Defendant Brooks prescribed a course of drug therapy including calcium and steroids.

8. On or about May 23, 1978, Plaintiff Eileen Nolan was hospitalized with acute thrombophlebitis of both legs secondary to her prolonged ingestion of Novo-D, prescribed by Defendant Brooks.

9. The Plaintiffs believe that their injuries and damages are due to the negligence of Defendant Brooks and Defendant Howard & McGeary, Inc. and have requested copies of Plaintiff Eileen Nolan's medical records from Defendant Brooks, which request was refused.

10. Defendant Brooks owed the Plaintiffs the duty of due care and the exercise of that degree of diligence, knowledge, and skill ordinarily exercised and possessed by similarly trained and experienced members of the medical profession.

11. The accepted method of practice and Defendant Brooks's duties to the Plaintiff were

a. to be familiar with the current state of knowledge in the medical profession as to the risks, dangers, effects, and alternatives involved in any course of contraceptive counseling and treatment and other gynecological treatment;
b. to adequately inform patients as to the risks, dangers, effects, and alternatives involved in contraceptive and gynecological treatment;
c. to gather the appropriate patient and family history and to conduct the proper examinations, tests, and other procedures in order to properly assess the safest method of treatment for gynecologic conditions;
d. to prescribe the type of therapy and treatment that was the safest method available based on patient and family history and the patient's condition;
e. to adequately inform patients of the physical manifestation of all possible side effects associated with the use of the prescribed treatment;
f. to provide for necessary reevaluation of the patient's course of treatment during prolonged oral contraceptive use;

g. to consult with or refer to other physicians for competent medical examination and treatment for his patients when he is not able to adequately and properly treat his patients' conditions;
h. to refrain from prescribing oral contraceptives for non-indicated purposes; and
i. to examine, test, diagnose, and employ the proper procedures to do a differential diagnosis to adequately isolate the cause of the symptomatology exhibited by Plaintiff Eileen Nolan to avoid unnecessary and hazardous treatment and render the treatment required by the condition in a timely fashion.

12. The Plaintiffs believe that Defendant Brooks was negligent, breached the aforesaid duties, and deviated from the accepted practice and procedure as follows:

a. The Defendant failed to be familiar with the current state of knowledge in the medical profession as to the risks, dangers, effects, and alternatives involved in any course of contraceptive counseling and treatment; and in the use of oral contraceptives for treatment of gynecological disorders other than control of contraception.
b. The Defendant failed to adequately inform the Plaintiffs as to the risks, dangers, effects, and alternatives involved in oral contraceptive treatment.
c. The Defendant failed to gather the appropriate patient and family history and to conduct the proper examinations, tests, and other procedures in order to properly assess and prescribe the safest treatment for Plaintiff Eileen Nolan's gynecologic condition.
d. The Defendant failed to prescribe the type of treatment that was the safest available based upon patient and family history and the physical condition of Plaintiff Eileen Nolan.
e. The Defendant failed to adequately inform Plaintiff Eileen Nolan of the physical manifestations of all side effects associated with the use of the prescribed oral contraceptives.
f. The Defendant failed to provide for or conduct necessary examinations, tests, and procedures for monitoring and reevaluating Plaintiff Eileen Nolan's physical condition

and proper course of treatment during her prolonged oral contraceptive use.

g. The Defendant failed to refer Plaintiff Eileen Nolan to other physicians and failed to consult with other physicians regarding her condition when he knew or should have known that he was not capable of adequately diagnosing, treating, and advising as to Eileen Nolan's condition and complaints of leg cramps.

h. The Defendant prescribed the oral contraceptive Novo-D for purposes other than the indicated use of prevention of pregnancy.

i. The Defendant failed to examine, test, diagnose, and employ the proper procedure to do a differential diagnosis to adequately isolate the cause of Plaintiff Eileen Nolan's complaints and symptomatology, thereby misdiagnosing Plaintiff's condition and prescribing unnecessary and hazardous drug therapy, including calcium and steroids.

13. The Defendant Howard & McGeary, Inc. owed the Plaintiffs the duty of reasonable care.

14. The Defendant Howard & McGeary, Inc. was negligent and breached its duty as follows:

a. The Defendant undertook to provide physicians and users with warnings and information as to the dangerous propensities and serious complications that could foreseeably result from use of Novo-D, and those warnings that were provided were inadequate and were diluted by the Defendant's overpromotion of the product.

b. The Defendant undertook to provide users, including Plaintiff Eileen Nolan, with warnings and information as to the indications, contraindications, risks, side effects, and dangerous propensities of Novo-D, and those warnings and information that were provided were inadequate, incomplete, and not reasonably calculated to alert users to the dangers associated with use of the drug of which the Defendant was aware and users, including the Plaintiff, were unaware.

c. The Defendant failed to advise physicians and users of necessary diagnostic testing prior to prescribing and using its product Novo-D.

d. The Defendant undertook to perform testing of its product before and after initially marketing Novo-D for determining the efficacy and safety of its product, and the testing done has not been thorough or adequate.

e. The Defendant failed to adequately warn and inform physicians and users of the singular purpose for which Novo-D is indicated, when the Defendant knew or should have known that physicians and users were prescribing and using Novo-D for treatment of gynecologic conditions other than to prevent pregnancy.

15. The aforementioned negligence acts and omissions of the Defendants and each of them were a proximate cause of the injuries and damages sustained by the Plaintiffs.

16. The Plaintiff Eileen Nolan has, does now, and will in the future suffer physical and mental pain, loss of enjoyment of life, loss of wages and earning capacity, disfigurement, and embarrassment and has, does now, and will in the future require medical, hospital, nursing and drug therapy, care, and services, and incur medical expenses.

17. The Plaintiff William Nolan has, does now, and will in the future suffer the loss of services, support, companionship, society, and consortium of his wife, Eileen Nolan.

WHEREFORE, the Plaintiffs seek a judgment against the Defendants in the amount in which they are found to be entitled together with costs, interest, and attorneys' fees.

Count Two—Breach of Implied Warranty

18-25. The Plaintiffs reallege and incorporate herein fully Paragraphs 1 through 8 of Count One above.

26. The product, Novo-D, was defective when it left the control of Defendant Howard & McGeary, Inc. in that it was unfit and not safe for its reasonably foreseeable uses.

27. The aforesaid product when sold was defective in the following ways:

a. It lacked adequate warnings and instructions to physicians and users as to the dangerous propensities and serious complications that could foreseeably result from the use of Novo-D, and those warnings that were provided were diluted by the Defendant's overpromotion of the product.

b. It lacked adequate warnings, instructions, and information to users as to the indications, contraindications, risks, side effects, and dangerous propensities of Novo-D; and those warnings, instructions, and information given were diluted by the Defendant's overpromotion of the product.
c. It failed to adequately advise physicians and users of necessary diagnostic testing prior to prescribing and using Novo-D.
d. It was not adequately or thoroughly tested on animals and human beings either before or after initial marketing for the purposes of determining the efficacy and safety of the product and was in fact not safe.
e. It lacked adequate warnings and information alerting physicians and users as to the conditions and purpose for which Novo-D was indicated and those gynecologic conditions for which it was not indicated.

28. The Plaintiffs' losses and damages were jointly and severally caused by the defects in the product designed, manufactured, sold, and supplied by Defendant Howard & McGeary, Inc.

29-30. The Plaintiffs reallege and incorporate herein fully Paragraphs 16 and 17 of Count One above.

WHEREFORE, the Plaintiffs seek a judgment against the Defendants in the amount in which they are found to be entitled together with costs, interest, and attorneys' fees.

Count Three—Misrepresentation

31-38. Plaintiffs reallege and incorporate herein fully Paragraphs 1 through 8 of Count One above.

39. Defendant Howard & McGeary, Inc. misrepresented to Plaintiff Eileen Nolan material facts as to the safety of the product Novo-D, knowing its misrepresentations to be false, with the intent that the Plaintiff rely on these representations, which she did, with a right to do so, and in ignorance of their falsity.

40. If the Defendant was not aware of the falsity of its statements, it made such statements in negligent disregard of reports of the dangerous nature of Novo-D and information of the manner in which it was being used.

41. Defendant Howard & McGeary, Inc.'s misrepresentations, and each of them, were a proximate cause of the Plaintiffs' injuries and damages.

42-43. The Plaintiffs reallege and incorporate herein fully Paragraphs 16 and 17 of Count One above.

WHEREFORE, the Plaintiffs seek a judgment against the Defendants in the amount in which they are found to be entitled together with costs, interest, and attorneys' fees.

DATED THIS ____________ DAY OF _______________ 199 ___ .

____

[Name of Plaintiff's counsel]
[Law Firm of Plaintiff's counsel]

APPENDIX D

GARY WHEELER, Plaintiff, v. DONNELLY ENGINEERING & EQUIPMENT CO., a corporation, Defendant.	COMPLAINT FOR DAMAGES (Personal Injuries)

NOW COMES the Plaintiff, Gary Wheeler, and for cause of action against the Defendant, alleges as follows:

First Cause of Action

1. The Defendant, Donnelly Engineering & Equipment Co., is a foreign corporation licensed to do business in the County of Middlesex, State of New Jersey.

2. The Plaintiff is a resident of the City of Mesa in the County of Maricopa, State of Arizona.

3. On or about July 13, 1980, the Plaintiff's left arm was traumatically amputated by the unguarded, unmarked, free-spinning saw blade of the Hi-Blade model mill saw, serial number C2930, manufactured by Defendant Donnelly Engineering & Equipment Co. and in ordinary use at the Plaintiff's employment.

4. The Defendant owed the Plaintiff the duty of reasonable care and compliance with the law.

5. The Defendant breached said duties and was negligent in the design, manufacture, and sale of said mill saw, having knowledge, both actual and constructive, because of the Defendant's negligence as follows:

a. It failed to include as part of the basic design of its mill saw adequate warnings that the blade continued to spin when the machine was shut off, including dots or stripes on the blades to indicate blade movement.
b. It failed to equip the Hi-Blade mill saw with adequate point-of-operation guards to prevent contact with the spinning saw blades while the operator was cleaning or maintaining the machine.
c. It failed to equip the Hi-Blade mill saw with blade brakes, an electrical stop device, or another quick-stop device to prevent running on of the free-spinning blade after power shut-down.
d. It failed to equip its Hi-Blade model mill saw with sliding, removable debris trays or other adequate and safe methods or routes for removing sawdust and wood chips from under the blade without exposing the operator to the unguarded blades of the machine.

6. As a proximate result of the Defendant's negligence, the Plaintiff suffered serious and permanent injuries to his left arm and hand, causing great pain and suffering and injury to his body, disfigurement, mental and emotional suffering, all to his general damages in an amount in excess of the jurisdictional limits of the Court.

7. Prior to the events herein described, the Plaintiff was gainfully employed and by reason of the premises the Plaintiff has been unable to follow his usual occupation as a carpenter, resulting in a financial loss to the Plaintiff in an amount unknown to the Plaintiff at this time, and the Plaintiff prays leave to insert with appropriate allegations when the same has been ascertained.

8. The Plaintiff has incurred and will in the future incur expenses for surgery, microsurgery, therapy, medical care, and treatment in an amount that he does not know at this time, and the Plaintiff prays leave that when said amounts are ascertained, he may be permitted to amend his Complaint accordingly.

Second Cause of Action

1. The Plaintiff incorporates herein Paragraphs 1 through 6 of his First Cause of Action herein, as if the same were set forth in full verbatim.

2. Defendant Donnelly Engineering & Equipment Co. was at all times material hereto engaged in the business of designing, manufacturing, assembling, and selling industrial mill saws to and for use by people engaged in manufacturing, and as part of its business designed, manufactured, assembled, and sold the specific mill saw known as "Hi-Blade, serial number C2930," hereinafter referred to as "subject mill saw."

3. Defendant Donnelly Engineering & Equipment Co. intended that the subject mill saw above described—manufactured, designed, and assembled by them—was to be used for general manufacturing.

4. The Plaintiff is unaware of the date of manufacture or sale of the subject mill saw by the Defendant at its principal place of business in Middlesex County, New Jersey, and prays leave to amend his Complaint when such date is ascertained.

5. At the time the subject mill saw was manufactured, assembled, and left the Defendant's control, and at the time of the Plaintiff's employer's purchase, the mill saw was defective and unsafe for its reasonably foreseeable uses in that the saw as manufactured, designed, and supplied by the Defendant lacked

   a. adequate warnings, verbal and/or nonverbal, that the blade continued to spin for a long time after the power to the machine had been shut off;
   b. adequate point-of-operation guards to prevent inadvertent exposure to spinning saw blades by persons engaged in servicing the machine;
   c. blade brakes, electrical stop devices, or other safety devices to prevent the blades from running after the power had been shut down; and
   d. adequate components or devices to permit debris removal without exposing persons servicing the machine to the unguarded spinning saw blades.

6. The subject mill saw was not altered in any material way from the date of sale to the date the Plaintiff was injured.

7. The Plaintiff neither knew nor had reason to know at the time of his use of the mill saw, or at any time prior to the accident

hereinafter described, of the existence of the foregoing described defects.

8. On or about July 13, 1980, the Plaintiff was in the course of his employment working with the subject mill saw for one of its foreseeable and intended manufacturing uses, milling beams from rough lumber. During the course of said use, and as a proximate result of the defects hereinabove described, the free-spinning saw blade traumatically amputated the Plaintiff's left arm and hand.

9. As a further proximate result of these defects, the Plaintiff was required to and did employ physicians and surgeons to examine, treat, and care for him, and incurred additional medical expenses for hospital bills and other medical expenses in an amount that has not yet been fully ascertained, and the Plaintiff will ask for leave to amend his Complaint to insert the amount thereof when the same has been ascertained.

10. As a further proximate result of the defect and injuries hereinabove described, the Plaintiff was prevented from attending to his usual occupation, and thereby lost earnings in an amount that has not yet been fully ascertained, and the Plaintiff will ask leave to amend his Complaint to insert the amount thereof when the same has been ascertained. The Plaintiff is informed and believes and, upon such information and belief, alleges that he will be prevented from attending to his usual occupation for a period in the future that the Plaintiff cannot now ascertain, and will, thereby, sustain further loss of earnings; that the Plaintiff asks leave of Court to amend his Complaint to set forth the amount of such additional damages when ascertained.

WHEREFORE, the Plaintiff prays for Judgment against the Defendant as follows:

A. For General Damages in an amount in excess of the jurisdictional limits of the Court.

B. For medical and incidental expenses, according to proof.

C. For loss of earnings past, present, and future, according to proof.

D. For costs of suit incurred herein.

E. For such other and further relief as the Court may deem just in the premises.

Dated: ________________

GARY WHEELER,	)	
Petitioner,	)	
v.	)	PETITION FOR TEMPORARY INJUNCTIVE ORDER ENJOINING CONCEALMENT OF EVIDENCE AND ALLOWING ENTRY TO INSPECT AND PHOTOGRAPH MACHINE
HIGH TECH TOOLS, INC.,	)	
Defendant.	)	

NOW COMES Petitioner, Gary Wheeler, pursuant to Civil Practice Rules 4:18-1(c) and moves this Court as follows:

1. Plaintiff Gary Wheeler is and was at all times material hereto a resident of the County of Maricopa, State of Arizona.

2. Defendant High Tech Tools, Inc., is and was at all times material hereto a corporation engaged in manufacture and having its production plant at 120 Southern Avenue, in the city of Mesa in the County of Maricopa, State of Arizona.

3. On July 13, 1980, Gary Wheeler suffered injury during the course of his employment while working with a defective saw believed to have been manufactured by Donnelly Company supposedly of Edison, New Jersey.

4. The subject defective machine continues to be in use on the premises of High Tech Tools, Inc.

5. The Plaintiff has a cause of action against Donnelly for his injuries caused by the defective machine and requires inspection of said machine to preserve his rights in said cause.

6. The Plaintiff will suffer irreparable harm and loss if he and/or his representatives are denied inspection of said machine, and the Plaintiff has no plain, ordinary, speedy, or adequate remedy at law.

7. The Plaintiff's inspection requires only a view and photographs of said machine on the premises of High Tech Tools, Inc. to preserve necessary evidence identifying the defects and the particular machine.

8. The Plaintiff does not seek in any way to interfere with, disturb, or otherwise disrupt the business operation of Defendant High Tech Tools, Inc.

WHEREFORE, Petitioner prays that this Honorable Court shall issue a Temporary Injunctive Order immediately and without notice, enjoining High Tech Tools, Inc. and any of its agents, representatives, and employees from concealing the aforesaid machine and allowing the Plaintiff and Plaintiff's agents or attorneys to enter the plant on May 25, 1981, to inspect and photograph the defective Donnelly machine.

____

Gary Wheeler

Dated:

Subscribed and sworn to me before this 5th day of May 1981.

____

Notary Public

GARY WHEELER,	)	
Petitioner,	)	
v.	)	AFFIDAVIT OF ______
HIGH TECH TOOLS, INC.,	)	
Defendant.	)	

______, being first duly sworn, deposes and says,

1. that she is one of the attorneys for Petitioner herein, that she makes this Affidavit of his behalf, and that she is authorized to do so;

2. that she is familiar with the matter insofar as the information available to the Petitioner is concerned; and

3. that the information set forth in the within Petition for Temporary Injunctive Order Enjoining Concealment of Evidence and Allowing Entry to Inspect and Photograph Machine is true to the best of her knowledge and belief, and she believes the same to be true.

______

Subscribed and Sworn to Before
Me this 5th day of May 1981

______
Notary Public

GARY WHEELER,	)	
Petitioner,	)	
	)	ORDER ALLOWING PLAINTIFF'S
v.	)	ENTRY TO INSPECT AND
	)	PHOTOGRAPH MACHINE
HIGH TECH TOOLS, INC.,	)	
Defendant.	)	

PRESENT: HONORABLE ______________________
Superior Court Judge

Upon the reading and filing of Plaintiff's Petition for Temporary Injunctive Order and the Court being fully advised in the premises;

IT IS HEREBY ORDERED that High Tech Tools, Inc., its employees, servants, and representatives shall not conceal the defective machine, but shall allow Petitioner and/or his agents and attorneys to inspect and photograph said machine at the Defendant's plant located at 120 Southern Avenue, in the County of Maricopa, State of Arizona, on May 25, 1981.

____
Superior Court Judge

APPENDIX E

BRIAN TYLER and BARBARA TYLER,
Individually, and BARBARA TYLER as
Next Friend of their minor son,
BRANDON TYLER,
Plaintiffs,

v.

JAMES CLARK,
Defendant.

______________________________/

BRIAN TYLER and BARBARA TYLER,
Individually, and BARBARA TYLER as
Next Friend of their minor son,
BRANDON TYLER,
Plaintiffs,

v.

STATE OF PENNSYLVANIA, DEPARTMENT OF
TRANSPORTATION,
Defendant.

____

PLAINTIFFS' REQUESTS FOR PRODUCTION OF DOCUMENTS TO DEFENDANT

PLEASE TAKE NOTICE that pursuant to M.C.R. 2.310 you are hereby served with the following Requests for Production on behalf of the Defendant to be answered within twenty-eight (28) days from the date of service hereof, if answer or objection is to be made; otherwise, each of the documents requested herein shall be produced for the purposes of inspection and duplication.

PLEASE TAKE FURTHER NOTICE that for failure to respond to any request, or any part thereof, or for failure to permit inspection as requested, or with respect to any objection unwarranted in law or made for the purpose of hindrance or delay, the Plaintiffs shall seek sanctions against the Defendant pursuant to M.C.R. 2.313.

PLEASE TAKE FURTHER NOTICE that each of the following Requests for Production that requests the production of documents or memoranda is also a request for the production of complete and accurate documents or memoranda including, but not limited to, writings, drawings, graphs, charts, photographs, magnetic tapes or other mechanical recording device(s), and/or computer software, provided that any item of computer software shall be produced in a reasonable usable form, that is, printouts; and, further, that each Request for Production of documents and/or memoranda shall include all the parts, subparts, attachments, or riders thereto.

DEFENDANT IS REQUESTED TO PRODUCE THE FOLLOWING:

1. Any and all minutes of meetings, interoffice memos, interdepartmental memos, notations, correspondence, memos, reports, evaluations, studies, work orders, or any other written or recorded item that pertains to or discusses, in whole or in part,
    a. consideration of median structures for use on the subject highway at or near the site of injury,
    b. consideration of median treatment on the subject highway at or near the site of injury, or
    c. consideration of median safety on the subject highway at or near the site of injury.
2. Any and all minutes of meetings, interoffice memos, interdepartmental memos, notations, correspondence, memos, reports, evaluations, studies, work orders, or any other written or recorded item that pertains to or discusses, in whole or in part,
    a. consideration of signing to use on the subject highway at or near the site of injury regarding the hazard of ice, snow, or slipperiness;
    b. consideration of any other type of traffic control device for use on the subject highway at or near the site of injury regarding the hazard of ice, snow, or slipperiness.
3. Any and all highway maintenance manuals, policies, procedures, plans, guidelines, specifications, standards, notices, direc-

tives, or other written or recorded item that the Defendant

a. formulated for use by the Minnesota Department of Transportation ("PDOT") or any other agency for removal of snow and for salting and sanding or other methods of ice removal on

    (1) limited access freeways,
    (2) state trunk lines,
    (3) rural trunk lines,
    (4) bridges, and
    (5) the subject highway area

    from 1987 to the present;

b. required that the Carbon County Road Commission use or follow for removal of snow and for salting and sanding or other methods of ice removal on

    (1) limited access freeways,
    (2) state trunk lines,
    (3) rural trunk lines,
    (4) bridges, and
    (5) the subject highway area

    within Carbon County from 1987 to the present; and

c. recommended that the Carbon County Road Commission use or follow for removal of snow and for salting and sanding or other methods of ice removal on

    (1) limited access freeways,
    (2) state trunk lines,
    (3) rural trunk lines,
    (4) bridges, and
    (5) the subject highway area

    within Carbon County from 1987 to the present

4. A copy of the planning map, regional map, boundary layout sketch, route assignments, or other written or recorded item that illustrates the snowplowing and salting or ice control routes, boundaries, areas, schedules, and/or crew assignments that were in effect in 1985, 1986, 1987, 1988, and 1989

a. for the Carbon County Road Commission's responsibilities for Route 1,

b. for the PDOT's responsibilities for Route 1, and
c. for the Carbon County Road Commission's responsibilities within Carbon County.

5. Any and all PDOT standards, guidelines, criteria, plans, forms, policies, procedures, specifications, or other written or recorded item in effect in 1985 through the present that pertain to

a. prioritizing roads for snow removal and ice control;
b. the length, time, plow speed, spreader speed, and chemical or sand application of each trip for plowing routes or salting and sanding routes;
c. assigning equipment (type and size) to plowing routes and salting and sanding routes;
d. identification of trouble spots requiring ice control (such as bridges) and assignment of ice control equipment and scheduling of ice control for trouble spots; and
e. any forms, formulas, procedures, etc. for use in adjusting plowing and salting routes, schedules, and assignments in the event of special need (by way of example, but not limitation: extraordinary snowfall, snow drifting, or formation of ice trouble spots).

6. Each plowing and ice control or salting/chemical/abrasive plan in effect for Route 1 in Carbon County in 1985 through the present.

7. Any and all PDOT training guides that pertain to

a. planning chemical/salt/abrasive applications and/or snowplowing routes,
b. winter operations for highway maintenance and safety,
c. inspecting or monitoring bridge decks during winter weather, and
d. de-icing or ice control of bridge decks.

8. Any and all daily work sheets or assignments for the crews, employees, or operators responsible for snow and ice removal on the subject highway on February 2, 1989, including an explanation sheet for any codes used on the daily work sheets or assignments.

9. A copy of the contract with the meteorological center that provided

a. PDOT and
b. Carbon County Road Commission

with climatological data or weather service applicable to the subject highway on February 2, 1989.

10. Copies of all training films, training texts, training manuals, training videos, or other written or recorded training item or literature the Defendant has used for winter operations and safety training of the Defendant's employees or employees of county road commissions from 1985 to the present that pertain to snow or ice removal.

11. The daily storm tally sheet or other written record for February 2, 1989, that pertains to or tends to evidence

a. snowfall for the subject highway;
b. time, location, and/or method of snow or ice treatment for the subject highway; and
c. ice formation for the subject highway and/or overpass.

12. Any and all climatological or weather service records, reports, or other written information for February 2, 1989, that pertain to or tend to evidence

a. anticipated precipitation, temperature, and wind direction and velocity for the subject highway within the 24-hour period prior to 6:45 a.m. on February 2, 1989; and
b. actual precipitation, temperature, and wind direction and velocity for the subject highway within the same 24-hour period.

13. A copy of the following:

a. radio log or "base station log" required by the Federal Communications Commission used for communicating with the maintenance commission or crew, and
b. radio logs identified in the Defendant's Answer to Interrogatory Nos. 5 and 6 of the Plaintiffs' Second Set of Interrogatories dated February 2, 1990.

14. A copy of any and all documents possessed by the Defendant, or Defendant's agent, the Carbon County Road Commission, that evidence in whole or in part the following:

a. the number of total employees working on snow and ice winter road maintenance on the subject highway, at any time February 2, 1989, in Carbon County;
b. the identification, by number and by type, of any equipment, including, but not limited to, plows and spreaders, that was in operation or used February 2, 1989, on the subject highway in Carbon County for snow and ice maintenance on the roadways;
c. the actual time cards or other records that identify the

actual hours worked by each Carbon County Road Commission employee who performed snow and ice maintenance on the subject highway in Carbon County on February 2, 1989;

d. the actual time and/or amount of time charged to the State of Pennsylvania for ice and snow maintenance performed by Carbon County Road Commission employees on the subject highway in Carbon County on February 2, 1989;

e. the actual periods or hours during which any Carbon County Road Commission employee performed maintenance on the subject highway snow route or run in Carbon County on February 2, 1989, for purposes of

   (1) salting,
   (2) salting and plowing,
   (3) plowing,
   (4) monitoring or patrolling the run, and
   (5) any other purpose or reason;

f. the identity of the Carbon County Road Commission employees who were present during and/or participated in the rescue of Mr. Brian Tyler following his accident on February 2, 1989;

g. the total number of Carbon County Road Commission employees under the supervision of PDOT on February 2, 1989, whether or not actually working at any time that day, whose job responsibilities or duties included driving salt spreaders and/or plows for snow and ice removal on the subject highway in Carbon County;

h. the identification, by number and type, of all spreaders, plows, or other snow and ice removal trucks or equipment available for use and/or assigned for use on the subject highway in Carbon County during the 1988-1989 winter season; and

i. the actual amount of salt use charged to the State of Pennsylvania for the subject highway in Carbon County on February 2, 1989.

15. Any and all documents in the possession of the Defendant or of Defendant's agent, Carbon County Road Commission, that pertain to or evidence, in whole or in part, the following:

a. any complaints or problems regarding Route 1 in Carbon County near Four Mile Road in Hazleton, Pennsylvania
   (1) prior to February 2, 1989, and
   (2) since February 2, 1989;
b. any engineering analysis, modifications, changes, corrections, alterations, or recommendations regarding Route 1 in Carbon County, near Four Mile Road in Hazleton, Pennsylvania
   (1) prior to February 2, 1989, and
   (2) since February 2, 1989;
c. any complaints, problems, engineering analysis, recommendations, or discussions about the effectiveness or lack of effectiveness of salt use and/or brine, and/or sand on the control of ice or ice formation on Route 1 in Carbon County, near Four Mile Road in Hazleton, Pennsylvania
   (1) prior to February 2, 1989, and
   (2) since February 2, 1989; and
d. any response to citizens' complaints of ice and snow on Route 1 in Carbon County, near Four Mile Road in Hazleton, Pennsylvania
   (1) prior to February 2, 1989, and
   (2) since February 2, 1989.

16. A copy of any and all studies identified in the Defendant's Answer to Interrogatory No. 15 of the Plaintiffs' First Set of Interrogatories to the Defendant, dated August 29, 1989.

17. A copy of any and all contracts and/or agreements identified in the Defendant's Answer to Interrogatory No. 82 of the Plaintiffs' First Set of Interrogatories to the Defendant, dated August 29, 1989.

18. A copy of any and all photographs identified in the Defendant's Answer to Interrogatory No. 90 of the Plaintiffs' First Set of Interrogatories to the Defendant, dated August 29, 1989.

19. A copy of any and all articles, manuals, journals, or other written or recorded information (not in the public domain) identified in the Defendant's Answer to Interrogatory No. 96 of the Plaintiffs' First Set of Interrogatories to the Defendant, dated August 29, 1989, and identified in the Defendant's Answer to Interrogatory No. 1 of Plaintiffs' Second Set of Interrogatories dated February 2, 1990.

20. A copy of any and all in-house or PDOT guidelines, stan-

dards, specifications, warranting practices, or procedures identified in the Defendant's Answer to Interrogatory No. 97 of the Plaintiffs' First Set of Interrogatories to the Defendant, dated August 29, 1989.

21. A copy of any and all in-house or PDOT guidelines, standards, specifications, warranting practices, or procedures identified in the Defendant's Answer to Interrogatory No. 98 of the Plaintiffs' First Set of Interrogatories to the Defendant dated August 29, 1989.

22. A copy of the job description and educational requirements for the person(s) in the Defendant's employ identified in the Defendant's Answer to Interrogatory No. 3 of the Plaintiffs' Second Set of Interrogatories, dated February 2, 1990.

FORM 1

TOPICS FOR INTERROGATORIES

1. Ensure all the defendants are correctly named.
2. Identify other potential defendants.
3. Ensure allegations as to the defendant(s) are correct.
4. Establish relationships, such as agency, physician-patient relationship.
5. Establish facts of collision, explosion, incident, injury.
6. Establish successor corporation, merger, parent-sub.
7. Explore collectability.
8. Identify all witnesses and persons having knowledge about
   a. liability and
   b. damages.
9. Identify sources, types, and custodians of information:
   a. defendant files, procedures, guidelines and
   b. computer stored data—
      (1) system, form, format, and
      (2) persons responsible.
10. Identify foundations for evidence:
    a. professional and trade organizations;
    b. conferences, meetings, seminars;
    c. standard and code committees; and
    d. safety organizations.
11. Identify and explore investigation:
    a. all statements,
    b. photographs and measurements,
    c. reports in course of business, and
    d. testing.
12. Identify experts:
    a. liability and
    b. damages.
13. Identify defense contentions:
    a. facts in support of affirmative defenses,
    b. witnesses in support,
    c. liability, and
    d. damages.

FORM 2

TOPICS FOR PRODUCTION

1. Statements of the plaintiff.
2. Surveillance films of the plaintiff.
3. Statements of "witnesses."
4. Photographs and films of
   a. vehicles or product,
   b. scene or incident, and
   c. parties.
5. Liability insurance contracts.
6. Evidence of ownership/interest.
7. Evidence of vehicle or product maintenance or prior use.
8. Material regarding the plaintiff's injuries.
9. Typed translations of medical, hospital, design records.
10. Exemplars of product, packaging, or substance.
11. Files of the defendant, including
    a. research and development files,
    b. warning files,
    c. personnel files,
    d. sales and marketing files,
    e. test files,
    f. complaint files, and
    g. an index to the files.
12. Policies and procedures/guidelines.
13. Organizational charts.
14. Patents.
15. Catalogs and sales brochures.
16. Research and test data, including
    a. protocols,
    b. statistics and questionnaires,
    c. films, and
    d. printouts.
17. Copies of disks storing the above information in computer form.
18. Manuals, handbooks, and package inserts.

FORM 3

TOPICS FOR ADMISSIONS

1. Establish whether
   a. the plaintiff is named correctly (Attach documentary evidence of representative capacity as exhibit.);
   b. the defendants are named correctly;
   c. the service, jurisdiction, and venue are proper;
   d. the basic facts are correct;
   e. the agency, successorship, partnership, and subsidiary are admitted; and
   f. the legal relationship is admitted (such as the physician-patient relationship);
2. Describe the contract in effect, including
   a. the application of specific provisions and
   b. the duties specified in the contract.
3. List the plaintiff's expenses (attach documentary evidence as exhibit), including
   a. medically necessary services and
   b. amount fair and reasonable.
4. Establish authenticity of documents (attach as exhibit).
5. Establish truth of documents.
6. Establish conclusions and principles contained in documents.
7. Produce statements of principle, conclusion, or admission made in deposition.

FIGHTING PROTECTIVE AND SECRECY ORDERS

Nicole Schultheis and Arthur H. Bryant

For years, trial lawyers have been signing stipulated protective and secrecy orders under the mistaken belief that such orders were in their clients' best interests. In fact, protective and secrecy orders pose a real threat to injured victims, their lawyers, and the public at large. This chapter explains why and how litigators should oppose such requests for secrecy.

At the outset, it is important to recognize that some commercially valuable information—the formula for Coca-Cola, for example—truly deserves protection. That type of information is rarely involved in personal injury cases. Rather, the personal injury defendant that seeks a secrecy order wants to hide potentially damaging information from the public and other litigants. Plaintiffs' lawyers should oppose these efforts.

Four critical principles should guide the plaintiffs' lawyer. First, the public has a presumptive right of access to all court proceedings, files, and discovery in civil litigation, and plaintiffs have a presumptive right to share with the public what they have learned during such litigation. Second, the defendant has the burden of proving the need for secrecy for each piece of information for which secrecy is sought. Third, once a defendant proves that a piece of information deserves protection, the plaintiff retains the right to share that information with similarly situated victims and their counsel, as long as they agree to respect the need for secrecy. Fourth, plaintiffs should never agree to destroy or return documents when a case is over unless the defendant at least agrees to preserve them for access and use by other victims and their lawyers.

WHY DEFENDANTS SEEK PROTECTIVE ORDERS

Defendants in personal injury cases desire secrecy because information is power. Without information, plaintiffs' counsel, their clients, and the public are powerless to act. With information, plaintiffs' counsel can act to ensure that victims are fairly compensated and that future injuries are prevented.

Protective orders are routinely sought by defendants in personal injury cases, particularly products liability, toxic tort, and medical negligence litigation. While these cases occasionally involve discrete pieces of information that deserve protection, defendants rarely, if ever, limit their requests for secrecy to such data. Rather, defense counsel usually seek protective orders without analyzing whether the material actually contains trade secrets or sensitive commercial data.

Nothing makes this clearer than *Defendant's Primer* published by the Defense Research Institute, which urges defense counsel to routinely move for protective orders, regardless of the merits of the secrecy claim.[1] This primer's purpose is stated as follows:

> The purpose . . . is to suggest ways to minimize the chance that documents and other materials produced during discov-

[1] Kearney & Benson, *Preventing Non-Party Access to Discovery Materials in Products Liability Actions: A Defendant's Primer*, CURRENT ISSUES IN LAW AND MEDICINE 36, 37 (Defense Research Institute 1987).

ery will be distributed to, or shared with, nonparties such as plaintiff's counsel in other jurisdictions.

The primer goes on to instruct, "*Even where defense counsel can make no special claim of confidentiality*, he or she should *routinely* seek a protective order limiting the dissemination of discovery information."[2]

Besides the protection of genuine trade secrets, defendants in personal injury cases desire secrecy to

- prevent other victims from learning that the defendant is responsible for their injuries,
- segregate lawyers new to the litigation from experienced trial lawyers who have sued the defendant in the past,
- impede cooperative discovery efforts by members of a formal or ad hoc litigation group,
- keep plaintiffs' counsel from hiring knowledgeable experts,
- prolong the corporation's ability to make money selling dangerous and defective products to an unsuspecting public,
- elude community outrage or even boycott when the public learns the details of corporate misconduct,
- evade enforcement of state and federal regulations and law, and
- avoid the enactment of remedial legislation.

None of these motives constitutes legitimate grounds for a protective order, yet they often impel the holders of corporate purse strings to insist that litigation be conducted in secret. To many defendants, it is a matter of dollars and cents: maximize secrecy to maximize profits.

Do not agree to a protective order on the theory that it will expedite discovery and enable the defendant to give you everything you seek. Usually, entry of a protective order will simply enable the defendant to thwart your efforts to obtain complete discovery. If you fight a protective order, you will still get the documents you need, but there may be a delay if the defendant declines to produce the discovery before a ruling is made on the merits of its protective order claim. Such delaying tactics should be strenuously opposed. Unless the defendant can sustain its burden of showing that a need

2 *Id.* at 40 (emphasis added).

for secrecy exists and that any protective order entered will be properly limited, however, you should never agree to secrecy.

WHY SAY NO TO A PROTECTIVE ORDER?

Contrary to the Plaintiffs' Interests

Some reasons to resist protective orders are:

First, if a protective order is entered, it will be virtually impossible to determine whether the defendant's discovery responses are truthful. There is no reason to assume that the defendant, who is being sued for injuring or killing people, will now be honest and thorough in responding to discovery, even when represented by honorable defense counsel.

Second, signing a protective order will *not* enable full discovery to be obtained more quickly. The defendant will still avoid producing incriminating information. The protective order will simply make it harder to learn the truth.

Third, a protective order will limit your ability to fully investigate facts that could help you develop your case or rebut the defendant's case. Secrecy orders can prevent the review of materials by those who may be able to impeach the defendant's witnesses, such as former employees, subcontractors, consultants, and joint or subsequent tortfeasors who may not be parties in the case.

Fourth, protective orders effectively require every victim's lawyer to reinvent the wheel. They restrict the sharing of information and, therefore, restrict effective and efficient case preparation.

Fifth, the defendant and the defendant's insurer may lose their motivation to settle the claim expeditiously once a binding restrictive protective order has been entered.

Sixth, defendants generally draft protective orders in a way that requires plaintiffs to reveal the identity of consulting experts or other privileged work product. For example, the order might require you to list each person who will be permitted to see and review the protected documents, a list that could include consulting, nontestifying experts. If defense counsel gives a court such a proposed order, ask for a provision that requires the defendant to reveal the same information. If any disclosure is ultimately required, it may be limited to the court only.

Seventh, protective orders inhibit your ability to prepare fact witnesses for deposition and to refresh their recollection for trial. When defense counsel asks the doctor to admit he would have prescribed drug X even if the manufacturer had warned about its side effects, it is helpful for the doctor to know what the defendant knew about these risks, the availability of a safer drug, or other facts pertinent to the answer that a treating doctor is not likely to know unless the plaintiff is free to share information with him.

Eighth, an overly broad protective order has a chilling effect on the willingness of experts to assist the plaintiff. If the expert will be bound by the protective order's terms, he may be disqualified in other cases or, worse, held in contempt. Defendants in other cases will claim that the expert witness is not at liberty to disclose all of the information forming the grounds for his opinions and that he cannot be adequately cross-examined. Or they will challenge the expert's refusal to answer certain questions, then convince an unsophisticated discovery master to impose sanctions.

Contrary to Your Responsibilities as a Lawyer

Stipulated protective and secrecy orders may raise ethical questions. Check rules of professional responsibility, official comments, and ethics committee opinions of individual states. Rule 5.6 of the Model Rules of Professional Conduct provides,

> **Restrictions on right to practice.**
>
> A lawyer shall not participate in offering or making:
>
> . . . .
>
> (b) an agreement in which a restriction on the lawyer's right to practice is part of the settlement of a controversy between private parties.

Although typically interpreted to mean that a lawyer may not be asked or agree to forego representation of other plaintiffs as part of the settlement of a case, Model Rule 5.6 could well have broader implications. Discovery disputes are certainly "controversies" between the parties.

Since 1987, both the American Bar Association (ABA) and the Association of Trial Lawyers of America (ATLA) have adopted policies that discourage the imposition of unnecessary protective orders. Recommendations 10, 11, and 12 of the ABA Action Commission to Improve the Tort Liability System, as adopted by the ABA House of Delegates in February 1987, discourage secrecy of discovery that is relevant to other cases or indicates a risk of hazard to others, destruction of information at the end of a case, and agreements preventing counsel from representing future claimants. All three recommendations are reproduced in Appendix A to this chapter. The recommendations can be submitted to the court as an exhibit along with a response to an unfounded motion for a protective order; they are frequently cited to courts of appeal.

Far broader, the "Resolution Concerning Protective Orders," adopted by the ATLA Board of Governors at its Tampa, Florida, meeting on May 6, 1989, (1) urges judges to apply very strict criteria in evaluating requests for protective orders, (2) encourages courts to fashion orders that protect the public's right to know about product hazards and other information relating to public health and safety, (3) asks courts to look favorably on motions to modify or grant other relief from unnecessary protective orders, and (4) discourages attorneys from agreeing to secrecy agreements and encourages attorneys to resist secrecy orders that prevent disclosure of documents to attorneys handling similar cases or to public agencies. This resolution is reproduced in Appendix B. It can also be brought to the court's attention.

Contrary to the Public Interest

Unnecessary and overly broad protective orders are contrary to the public interest. They prevent victims from learning of previous claims and erect economic barriers by impeding preparation of a winning case when the cost of duplicating discovery is too high. Even those victims who learn of other claims and who can bear the expense of independent discovery suffer: the repetitive costs come out of their pockets. As taxpayers, moreover, all of us pay the increased costs that repetitive discovery imposes on the courts.

Secrecy has an extremely harmful effect on public health and safety. As documented in a superb series of articles in *The Washington Post*, protective and secrecy orders often prevent consumers from learning about unsafe products, toxic hazards, incompetent doctors, and other avoidable dangers.[3] Because the dangers are not

[3] Walsh & Weiser, *Public Courts, Private Justice*, (pts. 1-4), Washington Post, Oct. 23-26, 1988, at 1; Weiser, *Public Courts, Private Justice*, Washington Post, March 13, 1989, at 1.

known, the public, the press, and the government cannot act. Inevitably, there are more victims. Secrecy should always be fought to protect the public. Submit to the court copies of *The Washington Post's* series of articles and similar articles to stress the public interest issues at stake in the proposed secrecy order.

Finally, court secrecy damages the public's ability to evaluate and control the operation of the civil justice system. Under our democratic system, the public must decide whether the courts are working well, whether justice is being done, and whether the laws need to be changed. To make these decisions, the public needs to know the facts. Otherwise, defendants and others who hope to limit victims' rights can make claims that can never be verified or disproved.

Fortunately, in the federal courts and in most states, the ability to fight secrecy and preserve the public interest is fairly well protected. Existing law disfavors secrecy.

SEATTLE TIMES AND ITS PROGENY

Lawyers often report speedier and more successful claim resolution in cases where the plaintiffs actively encourage the courts to protect other litigants, to consider the public interest—pursuant to the exhortations of Federal Rules of Civil Procedure 1 and 5(d)—and to properly enforce the "good cause" requirement of Rule 26(c) before entering protective and secrecy orders. To understand why this is so, it is important to review several 1980s cases that shaped existing law.

Seattle Times

Seattle Times Co. v. Rhinehart[4] is the only United States Supreme Court case that analyzes the relationship of the first amendment to protective orders entered in civil cases. Its facts are unusual and important. The plaintiff, Rhinehart, was the spiritual leader of a religious group called the Aquarian Foundation. He and several members of his group sued *The Seattle Times* for libel. The *Times* sought discovery of the group's members and donors, stating its intention "to continue publishing articles" about Rhinehart and his

4 467 U.S. 20 (1984).

5 *Id.* at 25.

group and "to use information gained through discovery in future articles."[5]

Seeking a protective order, Rhinehart produced affidavits detailing

> a series of letters and telephone calls defaming the Foundation, its members, and Rhinehart—including several that threatened physical harm to those associated with the Foundation. The affiants also described incidents at the Foundation's headquarters involving attacks, threats, and assaults directed at Foundation members by anonymous individuals and groups. In general, the affidavits averred that public release of the donor lists would adversely affect Foundation membership and income and would subject its members to additional harassment and reprisals.[6]

Based on this evidence, the trial court entered a protective order prohibiting the newspaper from publishing the group's membership and donor information or using it for purposes other than preparing and trying the case. The newspaper appealed, claiming the order violated first amendment rights.

In an opinion written by Justice Powell, the Supreme Court affirmed. It noted that *The Seattle Times* had obtained the information at issue by virtue of the discovery process; no one was seeking to prevent it from disseminating information obtained through other means. The Court pointed out that discovery was not public at common law and did not usually take place in public. And, citing cases like *NAACP v. Button*,[7] which recognized constitutional interests in keeping membership and donor information secret, the Court expressed concern that discovery abuse could make others reluctant to use the courts to vindicate their important and constitutionally protected religious, associational, and privacy interests.

Summarizing the applicable criteria, the Court said that, under the first amendment, it had to decide (1) whether the practice in question furthered an important or substantial governmental interest unrelated to suppression, and (2) whether the limits placed on first amendment freedoms were no greater than necessary or essential to protect the particular governmental interest involved.[8] Based

6 *Id.* at 26.

7 371 U.S. 415 (1963).

on that standard, it held that "where . . . a protective order is entered on a showing of good cause as required by Rule 26(c), is limited to the context of pretrial civil discovery, and does not restrict the dissemination of the information if gained from other sources, it does not offend the first amendment."[9]

Concurring, Justice Brennan, joined by Justice Marshall, stressed that the Court was, in fact, holding that protective orders were subject to first amendment scrutiny. He noted that, in this case, the plaintiffs had produced evidence to support the lower court's finding that a protective order was required to protect "the first amendment rights of members and donors to privacy, freedom of religion, and freedom of association."[10] Given this fact, he agreed that the protective order was justified.

Defendants seeking protective orders frequently attempt to make more of *Seattle Times* than was intended. Ignoring its unique facts, they cite dicta out of context from the Court's opinion and assert that the Court held that the public has no right of access to discovery information and that plaintiffs have no right to share it. (A particular favorite of the defense bar is the sentence, "Liberal discovery is provided for the sole purpose of assisting in the preparation and trial, or the settlement, of litigated disputes."[11])

Seattle Times was not a case in which a defendant was attempting to keep secret a threat to the public health or safety. It was not a case in which a third party asserted a right of access to discovery information. Instead, a defendant, clearly seeking to abuse the discovery process, asserted a first amendment right to disseminate personal information relating to third parties. Even so, the Court upheld the protective order only because strong facts supported it, and there was no other way to protect extremely important constitutional interests. Properly read, the judgment demonstrates how difficult it is to obtain a protective order and the applicability of constitutional rights to protective orders.

After *Seattle Times*, the lower courts split on the question of precisely how the first amendment applied to protective order dis-

8 467 U.S. 20 at 32.

9 *Id.* at 37.

10 *Id.* at 38.

11 *Id.* at 34.

putes. Was the good cause requirement of the rules sufficient, or must the first amendment shape our interpretation of those rules? Was the Court saying that one must merely follow the rules, or that each protective order must be scrutinized to make sure it complies with the first amendment?

While different courts took different approaches, their main focus was on the requirements of Rule 26(c) and making sure those requirements were not given short shrift. Judges also started to reevaluate the burdens placed on the proponents and opponents of orders when modification is sought.

Later, two substantial series of opinions explored the various protective order issues in light of *Seattle Times*. The first involved the health of our citizens at home—the cigarette cases; the second concerned the health of our servicemen and women and their children—the Agent Orange litigation.

Cigarette Cases

Four reported opinions, commencing with *Cipollone v. Liggett Group, Inc.* ("*Cipollone I*"),[12] began to analyze what was required of defendants before protective orders would be entered. In *Cipollone I*, an appeal from the entry of a magistrate's umbrella protective order, United States District Court Judge H. Lee Sarokin held that the umbrella order prohibiting disclosure of all information obtained in discovery was not justified by good cause under Rule 26(c) and violated the first amendment. Further, defendants would have to show good cause for each of their confidentiality designations. Equally important, plaintiffs' counsel could use information obtained through discovery in their other cases.

In *Cipollone v. Liggett Group, Inc.* ("*Cipollone II*"),[13] the defendants appealed and also sought review by way of mandamus. The Third Circuit declined to address the appeal because of the collateral order doctrine. However, it granted mandamus because it found that Judge Sarokin had committed clear errors of law by misinterpreting language in the *Seattle Times* that seemed to require application of a first amendment "least restrictive means" test to the defendant's proposed order, rather than the good cause test set forth in the high Court's decision. The Third Circuit also agreed with the

[12] 106 F.R.D. 573 (D.N.J. 1985).

[13] 785 F.2d 1108 (3d Cir. 1986).

defendants that Judge Sarokin had clearly erred in reviewing the magistrate's order under an incorrect plenary review standard.

The Third Circuit went on to address two remaining issues for guidance on remand. First, it explained that broad allegations of harm, unsubstantiated by specific examples or articulated reasoning, do not satisfy the requirement that there be good cause to enter a protective order. Specifically, "embarrassment," where asserted as the basis for a protective order, must be demonstrated to be particularly serious—such that "would cause a significant harm to [the tobacco company's] competitive and financial position."[14] Second, the court approved of the concept of umbrella protective orders but warned that the burden of proving the need for continued protection of specified documents must remain with the party opposing dissemination.

On remand after mandamus issued,[15] Judge Sarokin held that, while the umbrella order permitting the defendants to make the initial designation of a document's confidential status was not clearly erroneous or contrary to law, the magistrate's finding of good cause to enter an order restricting the plaintiffs' use of nonconfidential materials *was*. Judge Sarokin went on to say that good cause required proof that financial and other embarrassment will be suffered by dissemination, that fairness at trial will be compromised, or that estoppel operates by virtue of counsel's prior agreement to confidentiality, and that none of these assertions had been proven. Moreover, "facilitating the discovery process" was not a justification that constituted good cause under Rule 26(c). In short, tobacco companies could not justify concealing their knowledge of the hazards of smoking and what they did about it.

The tobacco companies again sought mandamus, asking the Third Circuit to vacate Judge Sarokin's new order and to reassign the case to another judge.[16] This time, the appellate court held that the new order, which permitted use of discovery materials in all related and similar cases, did not warrant mandamus. The court declined to require Judge Sarokin's disqualification on the defendants' unsubstantiated claim of bias.

[14] *Id.* at 1121.

[15] Cipollone v. Liggett Group, Inc., 113 F.R.D. 86 (D.N.J. 1986) ("Cipollone III").

[16] Cipollone v. Liggett Group, Inc., 822 F.2d 335 (3d Cir. 1987) ("Cipollone IV").

Agent Orange

Meanwhile, a second group of cases was working its way through the courts, with veterans, plaintiffs' lawyers, and public interest groups seeking to lift restrictions placed on use of discovery materials in the Agent Orange litigation. In *In re "Agent Orange" Product Liability Litigation,*[17] the court required the defendants to make a showing of good cause to restrain the plaintiffs from disseminating the information previously obtained by discovery. Thereafter, in *In re "Agent Orange" Product Liability Litigation,*[18] the Second Circuit held that there was no abuse of discretion in modifying a sealing order to provide public access to discovery, despite defense contentions that (1) the modification improperly altered a term of the settlement between the parties, (2) the public had no right of access to discovery materials, and (3) the protective order could be modified only in exceptional circumstances.

In an extremely important opinion, the court reviewed the language and history of Rules 26(c) and 5(d) and held that, under the rules, "the public has a presumptive right of access to discovery materials."[19] It noted that the federal rules had originally provided for the filing of all discovery and that the public had routinely had access to it. It pointed out that when Rule 5(d) had been amended to allow courts to waive the filing requirement, the amendment was motivated solely by concerns for filing space, and the Advisory Committee explicitly stated its intention that "class action litigants and the general public be afforded access to discovery materials whenever possible":[20]

> [H]ad the district court not lifted the orders, we would be compelled to find that the orders had been improvidently granted because the district court never required appellants to make the requisite good cause showing. Appellants argue that the cost of poring through the voluminous discovery materials . . . would be prohibitive. However, appellants would have had to bear that cost during the pretrial stages of the litigation except for the protective orders. The orders

17 597 F. Supp. 740 (E.D.N.Y. 1984), *aff'd*, 818 F.2d 145 (2d Cir. 1987).

18 821 F.2d 139 (2d Cir. 1987).

19 *Id.* at 146.

20 *Id.*

merely delayed a document-by-document assessment; they did not obviate the need for such an assessment.[21]

One year later, in another cigarette case, the First Circuit agreed with the Second Circuit's *Agent Orange* analysis and held that "the public has a presumptive right of access to discovery materials."[22] The court said, "Rule 26(c)'s good cause requirement means that, [a]s a general proposition, pretrial discovery *must take place in the public* unless compelling reasons exist for denying the public access to the proceedings."[23]

NUTS AND BOLTS OF OPPOSING PROTECTIVE ORDERS

As the foregoing cases make clear, protective orders should be entered only in extremely limited circumstances. To make sure they are not improperly entered, you need to know the nuts and bolts of opposing protective orders under the rules.

Stress That the Defendant Has the Burden of Proof

Remember that it is the party bringing the motion for secrecy that has the burden of proving good cause.[24] This has been defined as a "heavy burden," requiring a showing that disclosure will work a "clearly defined and very serious injury."[25] The plaintiffs' willingness to agree to secrecy cannot satisfy the requirement that the defendant demonstrate good cause for imposition of the requested order.[26]

Stress That Proof Means PROOF

Broad allegations of harm, unsubstantiated by specific exam-

21 *Id.* at 148.

22 Public Citizen v. Liggett Group, Inc., 858 F.2d 775, 789 (1st Cir. 1988) (*quoting* In re "Agent Orange" Prod. Liab. Litig., 821 F.2d 139, 146 (1987)), *cert. denied*, 488 U.S. 1030 (1989).

23 *Id.* (citations omitted) (emphasis added).

24 *See, e.g.*, Smith v. Bic Corp., 869 F.2d 194 (3d Cir. 1989).

25 *See also*, Waelde v. Merck, Sharp & Dohme, 94 F.R.D. 27, 28 (E.D. Mich. 1981) (citations omitted); United States v. United Fruit Co., 410 F.2d 553, 557 (5th Cir. 1969), *cert. denied sub nom.* Standard Fruit & S.S. Co. v. United Fruit Co., 396 U.S. 820 (1969).

26 Vassiliades v. Israely, 714 F. Supp. 604 (D. Conn. 1989).

ples or unarticulated reasoning, do not satisfy the good cause test.[27] To sustain its burden, the party seeking secrecy must make "a particular and specific demonstration of fact, as distinguished from stereotyped and conclusory statements."[28]

Learn the Facts and Prove Them

It is essential to consult with experts on the need for a protective order. Expert consultants and fact witnesses may be able to explain why certain information is already in the public domain or otherwise fails to qualify for protected status. Professional groups, such as the Society of Automotive Engineers, can state whether the defendant's "confidential" procedures are in fact standard industry procedure. Once the expert or other witness is consulted, a detailed affidavit rebutting the defendant's assertions should be prepared, signed, and attached to the plaintiff's brief.

Contact lawyers handling cases involving the same or a similar product and those with cases involving a different product but the same defendant. Such inquiries frequently permit the plaintiffs to prove that the defendant has a history of producing incomplete or inconsistent responses to discovery, depending on the case. Also, consulting with other counsel may uncover cases where other courts declined to enter secrecy orders under similar circumstances. This has value as precedent and also helps disprove the defendant's claim that the information is secret: how can it be a secret if the same information is already in the public domain?

Sometimes unprotected deposition transcripts from other cases contain detailed discussions of the challenged documents, or perhaps the records were admitted into evidence at trial. The same subject matter may have been part of a public agency proceeding or a Senate subcommittee hearing. Sometimes, even in cases with protective orders, the parties ignore them and take depositions without asking the court reporter to keep the testimony secret. Often the secrecy claims can clearly be refuted. In one case, a

[27] Cipollone v. Liggett Group, Inc., 785 F.2d 1108 (3d Cir. 1986); Wilson v. American Motors, 759 F.2d 1568, 1570-72 n.4 (11th Cir. 1985); Joy v. North, 692 F.2d 880, 894 (2d Cir. 1982), *cert. denied sub nom.* Citytrust v. Joy, 460 U.S. 1051 (1983).

[28] General Dynamics Corp. v. Selb Mfr. Co., 481 F.2d 1204, 1212 (8th Cir. 1973) (*quoting* 8 S. C. WRIGHT & A. MILLER, FEDERAL PRACTICE AND PROCEDURE: CIVIL §2035 at 264 (1970)); Farnum v. G. D. Searle & Co., 339 N.W.2d 384, 389 (Iowa 1983) (same).

petrochemical company designated as confidential a long list of pleadings filed in other jurisdictions. In another case, the defendant claimed confidentiality for a consent decree entered by the Federal Trade Commission.

If the media have described a manufacturing process or the details of a business's operation that the defendant now claims is confidential, attach a copy of the article or transcript to the brief. On-line database services (Compuserve, DIALOG, NEXIS) can readily supply this sort of information. Articles that graphically describe reverse engineering (tearing down, analyzing, and testing a product), for example, have appeared in news magazines. In *Koval v. General Motors Corp.*,[29] the court denied a motion for a protective order after the plaintiffs produced samples of competitors' fuel system products that had been reverse engineered from General Motors (GM) products, along with a *Newsweek* article containing a photograph of GM's engineers themselves disassembling other manufacturers' products.

Consult local judicial conferences to determine whether the subject of protective orders has been discussed or a policy concerning them adopted, in light of the ABA and ATLA resolutions on this subject. If a policy has been adopted—it may be reflected in the official court reporter's notes—copies of the policy should accompany briefs.

Respond Effectively to Defendants' Arguments

Defendants have asserted a variety of grounds for imposition of protective orders. Some of the more popular ones are reviewed below.

Trade Secrets

"Trade secret" is a term of art growing out of common law tort cases in which companies sue one another for misappropriation of business information. Umbrella protective orders were designed to protect such secrets when disputes formed the basis of commercial litigation. To determine whether something is a trade secret, consult local law. Generally, though, six factors are considered important:

- the extent to which the information is known outside the company,

[29] No. 137016 (C.P. Cuyohoga County, Ohio, May 15, 1990).

- the extent to which the information is known by employees and by independent contractors involved with the company,
- the extent of measures taken by the company to guard the secrecy of the information,
- the value of the information to the company and to its competitors,
- the amount of effort or money spent in developing the information, and
- the ease or difficulty with which the information could be properly acquired or duplicated by others.[30]

The party moving for a protective order must show that each of these factors relates to the specific materials sought to be kept secret.[31]

Information concerning the hazardous nature of a product is *not* a trade secret.[32] Embarrassing information that details corporate mismanagement or the injuries occurring from a faulty product is not entitled to trade secret protection.[33] Under the Federal Food, Drug, and Cosmetic Act, trade secrets are privileged, but the definition of trade secrets does not include safety and effectiveness data, such as would be presented in a New Drug Application (NDA).[34]

For corporate information to qualify as a trade secret, it must have *competitive value*:

> We emphasize that the value of a trade secret lies in the competitive advantage it gives its owner over competitors.... If, however, a public disclosure of data reveals, for example, the harmful side effects of the submitter's product and causes the submitter to suffer a decline in the potential

30 United States v. IBM, 67 F.R.D. 40, 46-47 (S.D.N.Y. 1975); *accord* Turich v. Yamaha, 121 F.R.D. 32 (S.D.N.Y. 1988).

31 Waelde v. Merck, Sharp & Dohme, 94 F.R.D. 27, 28-29 (E.D. Mich. 1981); Reliance Ins. Co. v. Barron's, 428 F. Supp. 200, 202-03 (S.D.N.Y. 1977); Farnum v. G.D. Searle & Co., 339 N.W. 2d 384, 389 (Iowa 1983).

32 In re Upjohn Co. Antibiotic Cleocin Prod. Liab. Litig., 81 F.R.D. 482, 483-84 (E.D. Mich. 1979), *aff'd*, 664 F.2d 114 (6th Cir. 1981).

33 Joy v. North, 692 F.2d 880 (2d Cir. 1982), *cert. denied sub nom.* Citytrust v. Joy, 460 U.S. 1051 (1983).

34 *See* 21 U.S.C. §331(j)(1988); 21 C.F.R. §§20.61, 314.430. *See also* Anderson v. Department of Health and Human Services, 907 F.2d 936 (10th Cir. 1990).

> profits from sales of the product, that decline in profits stems from a decrease in the value of the pesticide to consumers, rather than from the destruction of an edge the submitter had over its competitors, and cannot constitute the taking of a trade secret.[35]

In addition, the competitive value of the information must be current. Obsolete information, such as data relating to a product that has long been off the market, is not likely to be commercially valuable or competitively harmful to the company if released.[36]

Where the materials concern matters of general knowledge within the industry, they are already in the public domain and are not "secrets." The same is true for information obtainable under the Freedom of Information Act (FOIA) or through inspection of public records or published journals. Accordingly, "[m]ethods of manufacture or design and details of construction which are matters of general scientific knowledge in the industry do not constitute trade secrets."[37] Similarly, the sale of a product defeats trade secret status for commercial information where the information is readily ascertainable from examining the product or from engaging in reverse engineering.[38]

Most of the cases that defendants cite to support trade secret claims are commercial cases, unrelated to the issues involved in personal injury actions. The defendant will be hard pressed to cite a single case to support its claim that documents concerning the dangers of its product, safety testing, or reports of injuries are trade secrets.

Public Embarrassment and Adverse Publicity

Where the defendant claims embarrassment as a reason for a protective order, the impact must be demonstrated to be particularly serious—such that it would cause significant harm to a com-

35 Ruckelshaus v. Monsanto Co., 467 U.S. 986, 1011 n.15 (1984).

36 *See, e.g.*, Deford v. Schmid Prod. Co., 120 F.R.D. 648, 653 (D. Md. 1987); Parsons v. General Motors Corp., 85 F.R.D. 724, 726 (N.D. Ga. 1980).

37 Midland-Ross Corp. v. Sunbeam Equip. Corp., 316 F. Supp. 171, 177-178 (W.D. Pa. 1970), (*citing* Cornell-Dublier Elec. Corp. v. Aerovox Corp., 71 U.S.P.C. 153, 154 (Mass. Sup. Ct. 1946), *aff'd*, 435 F.2d 159 (3d Cir. 1970).

38 Smith v. Bic Corp., 869 F.2d 194, 197 (3d Cir. 1989).

pany's competitive and financial position.[39] However, adverse publicity stemming from public reaction to the facts giving rise to liability does not qualify as good cause, even where the parties stipulate to entry of an order.[40]

Potential Discovery Sharing by Plaintiffs

Discovery sharing advances the just, efficient, and economical administration of justice, exhorted by Rule 1, while simultaneously reducing the time, effort, and expense involved in conducting discovery. *The Manual for Complex Litigation, Second Edition*, recognizes this, as do a number of courts.[41] The need for discovery sharing is a reason to *deny* entry of a protective order, not a reason to *grant* one.

Moreover, numerous courts have recognized that even when a defendant is able to prove that the information being discovered constitutes trade secret or truly confidential information, plaintiffs' lawyers still should be permitted to share the information, as long as they respect the need for confidentiality.[42] A protective order should never prohibit the sharing of discovery.

Other Protective Orders

If the defendant claims that the same information was previously prohibited from disclosure in another case and that, therefore, the present court ought not order its release, several steps may be taken.

First, study the order to verify that it prevents all parties—not just the plaintiffs—from releasing the materials. Find out whether the plaintiffs opposed entry of the order, whether the court was made aware of the existence of related cases, and whether there was

39 Cipollone v. Liggett Group, Inc., 785 F.2d 1108, 1121 (3d Cir. 1986).

40 Vassiliades v. Israely, 714 F. Supp. 604 (D. Conn. 1989).

41 *See, e.g.*, Graham v. Wyeth Laboratories, 118 F.R.D. 511 (D. Kan. 1988); Deford, 120 F.R.D. 648, 654; Ward v. Ford Motor Co., 93 F.R.D. 579, 580 (D. Colo. 1982); United States v. Hooker Chem. & Plastics Corp., 90 F.R.D. 421 (W.D.N.Y. 1981); Patterson v. Ford Motor Co., 85 F.R.D. 152, 153-54 (W.D. Tex. 1980); Williams v. Johnson & Johnson, 50 F.R.D. 31, 32 (S.D.N.Y. 1970); American Honda Motor Co. v. Dibrell, 736 S.W.2d 257, 258-59 (Tex. Ct. App. 1987).

42 *See, e.g.*, Wilk v. American Medical Ass'n, 635 F.2d 1295, 1301 (7th Cir. 1981); Kamp Implement Co. v. J. I. Case Co., 630 F. Supp. 218, 220-21 (D. Mont. 1986); Johnson Foils, Inc. v. Huyck Corp., 61 F.R.D. 405, 410-11 (N.D.N.Y. 1973); Garcia v. Peeples, 734 S.W.2d 343 (Tex. 1987).

an on-the-record finding of facts constituting good cause for entry of the order.

Second, urge the court to require the defendant to list the materials actually produced in the other case, subject to confidentiality. Then ask the defendant for proof that the confidential status of those documents was actually litigated.

Third, request that the court make the defendant seek modification of the order in the other case to permit discovery sharing.

Fourth, ask for an order setting forth the plaintiff's entitlement to the information free of restriction on its use, conditioned on modification of the prior court's order.

Fifth, move to intervene in the other case and seek modification or mandamus.

United States ex rel Woodard v. Tynan[43] reviews the procedure to be followed when two courts deal with records sealed by one of them. The case holds that a court may require the defendant, on the plaintiff's request, to apply to the court that had sealed the records to release them, so the defendant can respond to the plaintiff's discovery in the other case. The case dealt with state grand jury materials that were subsequently needed in a federal case.[44]

In *Anchorage School District v. Anchorage Daily News*,[45] the Alaska Supreme Court ruled that the terms of a confidential settlement were subject to disclosure, despite the existence of a U.S. District Court's sealing order, but delayed enforcement of the order until the federal court order had been vacated or modified. It was later reported that, once the federal court was apprised of the state court's order, it promptly removed the seal.[46]

Reliance on Promise of Secrecy

Typically, this argument is made when the defendant claims to have complied with overly broad discovery because it believed that the information would remain secret. Or, the defendant claims it

43 757 F.2d 1085 (10th Cir. 1985).

44 *See also* Douglas Oil Co. v. Petrol Stops Northwest, 441 U.S. 211 (1979), which discusses the relationship between two courts' exercise of jurisdiction over the same matter.

45 779 P.2d 1191 (Alaska 1989).

46 *See Asbestos Removal Pact Unsealed*, THE NEWS MEDIA AND THE LAW, Fall 1989, at 15.

would not have settled but for the promise of secrecy.

Numerous cases have held, however, that the defendant cannot and should not rely on the expectation of privacy, since the rules plainly permit nonparties to seek access to discovery and other materials, regardless of what the parties have promised. For example, in *United States v. Kentucky Utilities Co.*,[47] the court held that a newspaper had the right to obtain access to documents that the U.S. government had agreed to keep sealed in settling an antitrust suit.[48]

In addition, any protective order should, at a minimum, preserve the plaintiff's ability to challenge the designation of information as confidential. In *Litton Industries, Inc. v. Lehman Bros. Kuhn Loeb Inc.*,[49] the court held that a stipulated protective order that preserved this right did not create a reliance situation. The defendants still had the burden of proving confidentiality and were not entitled to rely on an assumption that the documents would remain secret.

Examples are legion. In *Anchorage School District v. Anchorage Daily News*,[50] discussed above, W. R. Grace claimed it had relied on secrecy in reaching settlement of an asbestos case; the argument was not persuasive. Grace knew or should have known that the state had an FOIA; the act's enforcement should not have surprised this sophisticated defendant.

Consider what *Mokhiber v. Davis*[51] says about the timeliness of a request for access:

> To the extent [that the right of access] exists, it exists today for the records of cases decided a hundred years ago as surely as it does for lawsuits now in the early stages of motions litigation. The fact that a suit has gone to judgment does not in any sense militate against the public's right to prosecute a substantiated right to see the records of a particular case.[52]

47 13 Fed. R. Serv. 3d (Callaghan) 545 (E.D. Ky. 1989).

48 *See also* Brown & Williamson Tobacco Corp. v. F.T.C., 710 F.2d 1165, 1180, *cert. denied*, 465 U.S. 1100 (1984); In re "Agent Orange" Prod. Liab. Litig., 821 F.2d 139, 144-48 (2d Cir. 1987).

49 122 F.R.D. 433 (S.D.N.Y. 1988).

50 779 P.2d 1191 (Alaska 1989).

51 537 A.2d 1100 (D.C. 1988).

52 *Id.* at 1105.

Defendants can hardly claim that the passage of time, in and of itself, gave them the right to rely on continued secrecy.

Plaintiffs' Stipulation to Secrecy

A stipulation does not satisfy the requirement that the defendant demonstrate good cause for imposition of a protective order.[53] The parties' agreement to a stipulated order does not relieve the court of its duty to require showing good cause.[54] And prior agreement of counsel to the entry of the order does not preclude its modification.[55]

Corporations' Alleged Right to Privacy

Individuals have the right of personal privacy deserving of protection in suitable cases. Corporations, however, enjoy no such right. The constitutionally protected right to privacy that we now recognize evolved from basic concepts of personhood and personal freedom, as expressed in *Griswold v. Connecticut*[56] and *Roe v. Wade*.[57] Corporations are artificial public entities and do not share in this entirely personal right.[58] The distinction is an important one, clarified in *In re Knoxville News-Sentinel Co.*[59]

Third Parties' Privacy and Scientific Research

The personal right to privacy of third parties was at issue in *Seattle Times* and can, of course, provide a valid ground for a limited protective order. Often, however, the disclosure of private data concerning third parties can be prevented by redacting names and

53 Vassiliades v. Israely, 714 F. Supp. 604 (D. Conn. 1989).

54 *See* Sharjan Inv. Co. (U.K.) Ltd. v. P.C. Telemart, Inc., 107 F.R.D. 81, 82-83 (S.D.N.Y. 1985); Broan Mfg. Co. v. Westinghouse Elec. Corp., 101 F.R.D. 773, 774 (E.D. Wis. 1984); Krekel Publications, Inc. v. Waukesha Freeman, Inc., 98 F.R.D. 745, 746 (E.D. Wis. 1983).

55 Wyeth Laboratories v. U.S. District Court for the District of Kansas, 851 F.2d 321, 322-23 (10th Cir. 1988); Litton Indus., Inc. v. Lehman Bros. Kuhn Loeb Inc., 122 F.R.D. 433 (S.D.N.Y. 1988).

56 381 U.S. 479 (1965).

57 410 U.S. 113 (1973).

58 *See* United States v. Morton Salt Co., 338 U.S. 632, 652 (1950).

59 723 F.2d 470, 477 (6th Cir. 1983). *See generally*, HARE, GILBERT & REMINE, CONFIDENTIALITY ORDERS, §7.9 at 199-200 (1988).

other identifying information from the challenged records, and if needed, substituting "A," "B," "C."[60]

Equally important, individuals participating in scientific research often have no reasonable basis for assuming that their contribution to a study will be kept a secret or otherwise private. These persons generally sign releases permitting the sponsor to publish their findings in a paper or otherwise make it available for use by the National Institutes of Health (NIH), the Centers for Disease Control (CDC), or others interested in the research. Often, the work product belongs not to them but to the institutions for whom they work, as can be shown in the institution's standard employment agreement. Other possibilities are that the research was in part publicly funded, by NIH, CDC, or a state agency, or that patients of public health clinics participated in the study, and the data are subject to release under FOIA (federal or state) because copies of it are maintained by the local department of health or by a federal agency.

Thus, you should always ask these questions:

- Who has custody or control of the data or copies of it?
- Who paid for the research?
- To whom do the researchers report, and by whom are they employed?
- Did any public entities participate?
- Has there been a public disclosure to peers?
- Is the research part of an Investigational New Drug Application or an NDA?
- Does a procedure exist that would permit public access?

Facilitate Discovery

"Making discovery easier" does not constitute good cause and does not obviate the defendant's burden of showing good cause under Rule 26(c).[61] This claim is often a veiled threat that the

[60] *See, e.g.*, Scott v. Washington Hosp. Center, Civil Action No. 11174-82 (Super. Ct. D.C., Memorandum Opinion and Order, March 14, 1990); Deford v. Schmid Prod. Co., 120 F.R.D. 648, 654 (D. Md. 1987).

[61] Cipollone III, 113 F.R.D. 86, 92-93.

defendant will refuse to produce discoverable information voluntarily unless the plaintiff agrees to secrecy or that the defendant will pursue baseless motions for protective orders as a way to forestall perfectly valid discovery sought by the plaintiff.[62] Both of these courses of action have ethical as well as Rule 11 implications.

Check Local Statutes and Rules

Most of the case law discussed thus far focuses on the Federal Rules of Civil Procedure and their state court counterparts. In many jurisdictions, however, local and state rules place far greater limits on secrecy than does federal law. Anti-secrecy and right-to-know legislation and court rules are being proposed more frequently all across the country. For example, Texas Rules of Civil Procedure, Rule 76(a) (effective September 1, 1990) provides the following:

1. *Standard for Sealing Court Records.* Court records may not be removed from court files except as permitted by statute or rule. No court order or opinion issued in the adjudication of a case may be sealed. Other court records, as defined in this rule, are presumed to be open to the general public and may be sealed only upon a showing of all of the following:

   (a) a specific, serious and substantial interest which clearly outweighs:

      (1) this presumption of openness;

      (2) any probable adverse effect that sealing will have upon general public health or safety;

   (b) no less restrictive means than sealing records will adequately and effectively protect the specific interest asserted.

2. *Court records.* For purposes of this rule, court records means:

   (a) all documents of any nature filed in connection with any matter before any civil court, except:

[62] *See, e.g.*, Ericson v. Ford Motor Co., 107 F.R.D. 92, 94 (E.D. Ark. 1985).

(1) documents filed with a court in camera, solely for the purpose of obtaining a ruling on the discoverability of such documents;

(2) documents in court files to which access is otherwise restricted by law;

(3) documents filed in an action originally arising under the Family Code.

(b) settlement agreements, not filed of record, excluding all reference to any monetary consideration, that seek to restrict disclosure of information concerning matters that have a probable adverse effect upon general public health or safety, or the administration of public office, or the operation of government;

(c) discovery, not filed of record, concerning matters that have a probable adverse effect upon the general public health or safety, or the administration of public office, or the operation of government, except discovery in cases originally initiated to preserve bona fide trade secrets or other intangible property rights.

Remaining sections of the new Texas rule require that hearings be held in open court, that notices of sealing motions be posted publicly, that *anyone* be permitted to intervene to argue for public access, that temporary sealing orders be granted only to prevent "immediate and irreparable injury," and that modification be liberally granted. The rule also provides for continuing jurisdiction over sealing orders and makes sealing orders "final judgments" for purposes of appeal.

Other states have taken a variety of actions. Florida has recently enacted legislation titled "Sunshine in Litigation; Concealment of Public Hazards Prohibited,"[63] which severely restricts secrecy in certain circumstances. North Carolina law prohibits public agencies, officials, and employees from entering into sealed settlements—the North Carolina "Act to Amend and Improve the North Carolina Public Records Law," S.B. 456, was ratified July 1, 1989.[64] And

63 FLA. STAT. §69.081 (Supp. 1990).

64 1989 Session Laws, c. 326; N.C.G.S. §132-1.3.

Virginia statutorily limits protective orders that prevent plaintiffs from sharing information, effective July 1, 1989.[65]

Furthermore, a number of states have FOIA-like statutes that govern access to court records. One interesting case, *Lemond v. McElroy*,[66] held that while Virginia's FOIA[67] exempts documents "compiled specifically for use in litigation," and the actual settlement agreement might be exempt from disclosure, the state's accounting records reflecting payment of the settlement would not be exempt.

Some state courts and state bar associations have adopted discovery guidelines to supplement the bare-bones language of the discovery rules. Sometimes state bar committees issue reports that are then acted on by the rules committees. Many courts now have written policies governing the televising of court proceedings; your local judicial conference's review of the competing interests at stake in the local TV-or-not-TV controversy may include language that can be drawn on in a brief filed in opposition to a proposed secrecy order. Every plaintiffs' attorney should read the local state's constitution in search of an open courts provision. Carefully review all aspects of local law and any available legislative history.

WORK WITH OTHERS

The information discussed above should help you to oppose and defeat unwarranted protective orders. It is important to recognize, however, that you are more likely to succeed when you work with others. As the following examples demonstrate, other lawyers, the press, and public interest groups can all be valuable allies in this battle.

Work with Other Lawyers

Garcia v. Peeples[68] both highlights and recognizes the value of lawyers working together. The case was brought by the survivor of an auto crash, who alleged that the design of his 1982 GM Buick's fuel system was defective and had caused him injury in the crash. At GM's request, the trial court entered a protective order prohibiting

65 VA. CODE ANN. §8.01-420.01 (1950 & Supp. 1990).

66 17 Media L. Rep. (BNA) 1749 (Va. Apr. 20, 1990).

67 VA. CODE ANN. §§2.1-346 (1950 & Supp. 1990).

68 734 S.W.2d 343 (Tex. 1987).

plaintiff's counsel from sharing information with lawyers representing similarly injured plaintiffs.

The plaintiff's lawyer sought mandamus, but he did not fight this battle alone. In a critically important move, the Attorneys' Information Exchange Group, a group of plaintiffs' lawyers, some of whom represent auto crash victims in similar cases, filed an *amicus* brief explaining why information sharing was so important to them and their clients.

Responding to these combined efforts, the Supreme Court of Texas issued a ringing decision extolling the virtues of discovery sharing. It held that, even where the manufacturer proves its records are confidential and of competitive value, it is an abuse of discretion for a trial court to prohibit discovery sharing by lawyers proceeding against the same defendant in similar cases. Other plaintiffs' counsel, the court noted, are not the defendant's competitors; their potential use of the information is not probative of a loss of competitive advantage claim.

Work with the Press

It can also be extremely helpful to work with the press. For example, in *Littlejohn v. Bic Corporation*,[69] the *Philadelphia Inquirer* intervened to gain access to allegedly confidential documents relating to the Bic lighter litigation. The Third Circuit held that the public gained a common law right of access to the materials on their admission into the record at trial.

While Bic asked the court to hold the plaintiff's attorney in contempt, charging that he had disclosed the documents in violation of a pretrial protective order, the court declined to permit contempt proceedings or further discovery on that issue. The court explained that although a court cannot compel parties to release materials not part of the official record, discovery documents admitted into evidence at trial and still in the custody of the court would be subject to public access. As to the materials otherwise protected, the court said that Bic's affidavit stating that the documents contained confidential trade secrets did not meet its burden of proof.

Later, in *Smith v. Bic Corporation*,[70] the court declined to enter a restrictive protective order regarding design information or data

[69] 851 F.2d 673 (3d Cir. 1988).

[70] 869 F.2d 194 (3d Cir. 1989).

concerning other complaints and accidents, in part on the basis that the information was already in the public domain or could be reconstructed using reverse engineering, and in part because Bic failed to meet its good cause burden by showing that the information provided it with a competitive advantage that would be lost by disclosure. Also, both the plaintiff and the *Philadelphia Inquirer* were gratified by an appellate ruling that upheld awards of counsel fees and costs.

Work with Public Interest Groups

One of the central goals of Trial Lawyers for Public Justice (TLPJ)'s Project ACCESS[71] is to help the public interest and trial lawyer communities work together to defeat unnecessary secrecy. The first Project ACCESS victory demonstrates the value of this approach.

In *Oberg v. Honda Motor Co.*,[72] a Portland jury awarded more than $5.5 million in May of 1989 to a man who suffered brain damage when his three-wheel all-terrain vehicle (ATV) overturned. The verdict was the first to include punitive damages against an ATV manufacturer for producing these dangerous machines.

Before trial, voluminous materials were produced in response to the plaintiff's discovery requests. Unfortunately for the plaintiff, however, these materials were produced subject to a court-imposed protective order. The order prohibited all parties from granting other litigants and nonparties access to confidential discovery materials produced or created during the case, and required return of all protected materials on conclusion of the litigation. (In another ATV case, *American Honda Motor Co. v. Dibrell*,[73] an order had been upheld that recognized plaintiffs' entitlement to share confidential discovery with other similarly situated claimants, following *Garcia v. Peeples*.[74])

In late 1989, TLPJ sought to intervene in *Oberg* on behalf of several public interest groups—Public Citizen, the Consumer Fed-

71 As part of Project ACCESS, its nationwide campaign against unnecessary secrecy in the courts, Trial Lawyers for Public Justice has gathered and prepared extensive materials—including model briefs, unpublished orders, compilations of the law, legislative materials, and a computerized index—to help plaintiffs oppose unjustified protective orders.

72 No. A8709-05897 (Cir. Ct., Multnomah County, Or., Feb. 21, 1990).

73 736 S.W.2d 257 (Tex. Ct. App. 1987).

74 734 S.W.2d 343 (Tex. 1987).

eration of America, the United States Public Interest Research Group (USPIRG), and the Oregon State Public Interest Research Group (OSPIRG)—as well as on behalf of representative class-action plaintiffs from related litigation. Armed with numerous affidavits and case law to support its position, the intervenors convinced the trial judge to lift the restrictions on public access. Today, important information concerning this unsafe product is available to the public as well as to other litigants.

PROTECTIVE ORDERS CAN BE DEFEATED

Protective orders can be defeated if they are steadfastly opposed. Extensive authority exists to help you and, as other Project ACCESS victories demonstrate, these battles can be won.

For example, in a major suit against the lead paint industry, *Santiago v. The Sherwin-Williams Co.*,[75] TLPJ successfully opposed the defendants' effort to keep their knowledge of lead paint's hazards secret. The court ruled that the defendants had failed to prove that secrecy was essential and permitted the plaintiffs to engage in discovery sharing. As a result, the victims of lead paint poisoning—possibly 25 percent of all children—will have access to what the industry already knows about lead poisoning in future cases.

An even larger victory was gained in the litigation over the Exxon Valdez oil spill in Alaska. In that case, TLPJ represented the National Wildlife Foundation, the Natural Resources Defense Council, and the Wildlife Federation of Alaska in an action to restore the Alaskan environment. Its suit was consolidated with more than 150 other cases for pretrial purposes. Exxon sought an umbrella protective order covering *all* the potential discovery in *all* the cases, claiming, among other things, that it was entitled to a protective order because a lack of one had contributed to the breakup of AT&T. Any showing of good cause was conspicuously absent.

Working together with the other plaintiffs and eventually the lawyers for four news organizations (Dow Jones, Inc.; Times Mirror Company; Associated Press; and the Anchorage Daily News), TLPJ convinced the courts that the imposition of umbrella secrecy was unnecessary, without foreclosing Exxon's ability to seek protected status for deserving materials at some later stage in the proceed-

[75] Civil No. 87-2799-T (D. Mass. Oct. 4, 1989).

ings.[76] However, the trial courts made it clear that they would carefully scrutinize the facts supporting all requests for confidentiality to ascertain whether the grounds asserted met the mandatory requirement of good cause. Significantly, the federal court was influenced by a close review of *Seattle Times*.

SEALED FILINGS AND SETTLEMENTS

Thus far, this chapter has primarily focused on protective orders relating to discovery materials—business records, for the most part—that have never been filed in court. However, when a court orders an entire court file or a settlement sealed, special problems and separate legal issues are presented.

The Law is Even Clearer That Secrecy is Disfavored

First and foremost, the court files in civil cases are presumptively subject to a common law as well as to the first amendment right of public access.[77] In addition, a constitutionally protected right of access to court records may exist under state law. And, in some cases, state or federal FOIA provisions may mandate access to court filings.

When a court is asked to determine the adequacy of a settlement or to seal a settlement agreement, or when public agencies seek to enter confidential settlements, rights of access may be directly implicated. Moreover, even private settlements are sometimes subject to mandatory disclosure, in appropriate circumstances.

This is a controversial topic. Not all plaintiffs or plaintiffs' counsel favor public access to the terms and conditions of settlements in all cases. There are circumstances, however, when the public's and other litigants' right to know the amount of settlement, to whom it is paid, and under what conditions, is extremely important.

This is especially true where settlement monies are contingent on destruction or return of discovery materials that provide evidence of corporate misconduct or facts that could lead to the imposition of fines or other penalties. How are litigants and lawmakers to evaluate cases or to see whether justice is being fairly administered? How else

76 In re Exxon Valdez, 17 Media L. Rep. (BNA) 1509 (D. Alaska Feb. 2, 1990); In re Exxon Valdez Oil Spill Litig., 17 Media L. Rep. (BNA) 1511 (Alaska Super. Ct., Feb. 2, 1990).

77 *See, e.g.*, Publicker Indus., Inc. v. Cohen, 733 F.2d 1059 (3d Cir. 1984).

can the potential recipients of monies produced from a limited fund know whether the fund is being justly distributed?

A case can be made for the proposition that secrecy provisions in settlement agreements are unenforceable as violative of public policy, within the contemplation of the RESTATEMENT (SECOND) OF CONTRACTS[78] or where such provisions could be deemed to constitute promises made in restraint of trade.[79] Question whether any settlement provision that prevents you from publicizing the result of litigation has either an "anticompetitive effect" or an "anticompetitive purpose."[80]

Courts Overturn Sealing Orders and Refuse to Enforce Confidentiality Provisions in Settlement Agreements

In *Anchorage School District v. Anchorage Daily News*,[81] the Supreme Court of Alaska ruled in favor of a newspaper that had filed an action in state court seeking the terms of a confidential settlement of an asbestos removal case against W. R. Grace & Co. brought by the school district in federal court. Grace, fearing the impact the news might have on its defense of a nationwide class action challenging the presence of asbestos in our children's schools, defended the state court-access case on behalf of the school district. The newspaper successfully argued that the state's open records statute[82] required the school district to release its settlement documents despite the secrecy agreement. The appellate court agreed but held that enforcement would be delayed.

While the case was on appeal, Grace returned to federal court and obtained a sealing order—without telling the federal court about the pre-existing state court order or its ongoing appeal and without notifying the newspaper, which was not a party in the federal case. The sealing order surfaced as an appendix to Grace's state court brief. The newspaper was then permitted to intervene in the federal case, and the sealing order was promptly lifted. Not

78 §§178-79.

79 §186.

80 *See generally*, Rieders, *A New Conspiracy of Silence*, (pts. 1 & 2), THE BARRISTER, Summer 1985, at 5, Fall 1985, at 8.

81 *Id.*

82 ALASKA STAT. §09.25.110-.120 (1990).

satisfied, Grace appealed, but it dropped the challenge once its $10-million-plus settlement was publicized.[83]

The *Anchorage Daily News* case highlights the complexity of seeking access to settlement data, even where public entities are involved. Yet, increasingly, the courts are realizing the harm that can be caused by permitting or encouraging settlements to take place in secret.

In *Little v. Abbott Laboratories*,[84] District Judge Robert J. Bryan declined to sign a proposed order approving confidentiality of settlement in a DES case, stating,

> If, for example, the desire for confidentiality is an attempt to avoid other cases, it would be poor practice for the court to endorse that move.[85]

The decision was in accord with *Wilson v. American Motors Corp.*,[86] in which the court ruled that the public enjoys a presumptive right of access to settlement agreements submitted to the court for approval.

One of the most powerful examples of the trend in favor of access is *Scott v. Washington Hospital Center.*[87] *Scott* began as an action for injunctive relief and declaratory judgment, seeking to prevent the defendant hospital from terminating the plaintiff physician's privileges to perform open-heart surgery. Shortly after it was filed, the trial court sealed the record, relying on plaintiffs' assertions that third-party privacy interests were at stake, along with plaintiffs' reputations, the preservation of which was stated to be the motivation for the lawsuit. The case was settled and voluntarily dismissed on November 12, 1982, but the sealing order remained in effect.

In late 1988, *The Washington Post* published a four-part series, "Public Courts, Private Justice,"[88] that, among other things, highlighted the fact that the sealed record in *Scott* precluded the District of Columbia medical authorities from determining whether Dr. Scott

83 *Asbestos Removal Pact Unsealed*, *supra*, note 46.

84 No. C87-668TB (W.D. Wash. Dec. 15, 1989).

85 Letter to counsel, Dec. 14, 1989.

86 759 F.2d 1568, 1570 (11th Cir. 1985).

87 Civil Action No. 11174-82 (Super. Ct. D.C., Memorandum Opinion and Order, March 14, 1990).

88 Walsh & Weiser, *supra*, note 3.

had acted improperly. The article said that the sealed file contained evidence that Dr. Scott's performance had played a key role in contributing to patients' deaths.

In 1989, the District of Columbia Department of Consumer and Regulatory Affairs and Board of Medicine moved to unseal the records in the case, citing regulatory mandates and duties and asserting that "at issue was the health and welfare of District of Columbia residents who are, or may become, patients of Dr. Scott."[89] The motion was granted, with some qualifications, under *Mokhiber v. Davis*.[90] *Mokhiber* holds that the presumptive right of public access to court records and documents cannot be overcome by the desire of the litigants to protect themselves from abstract harm. The court also relied on *Shenandoah Publishing House, Inc. v. Fanning*,[91] observing "that the public has a societal interest in learning whether compromise settlements are equitable and whether the courts are administering properly the powers conferred on them."[92] The decision in *Scott* and the authorities it cites weigh heavily against sealed settlements in cases affecting the public.

Do Not Unnecessarily Agree To Sealed Settlements

Usually, secrecy is sought because the defendant is afraid of the settlement's future repercussions. You and your client should consider carefully what the defendant is trying to avoid by entering into a secret settlement: Is it criminal penalties? Future claims? Administrative action? Larger settlements by the remaining litigants? Public outrage? Secret settlements and their motivators can thwart the public interest. Another consideration is how future plaintiffs will evaluate the sufficiency of proposed settlements when they are denied information about similar past settlements.

All of these considerations militate against voluntarily agreeing to secrecy as a condition of settlement. When there is no other choice, ask that the settlement be put on the record and that the confidentiality provision be passed on by the court. If defense counsel will not agree to this, you must, of course, consider the best interests of your client. Do not assume, however, that your client

89 Civil Action No. 11174-82, Memorandum Opinion and Order at 2.

90 537 A.2d 1100 (D.C. 1988).

91 368 S.E.2d 253, 255 (Va. 1988).

92 Civil Action No. 11174-82, Memorandum Opinion and Order at 6.

would prefer a secret settlement to continued litigation. And do not assume that the defendant will continue to insist on secrecy if your client firmly rejects it.

Educate Clients About Secrecy

In many cases, victims prefer justice to money. They know that money will never bring someone back to life or undo a harm. They want compensation, but they also want to make sure that others do not suffer similarly. Public access, of course, will not pay the rehabilitation bills, but secret settlements can deprive plaintiffs of the intellectual and emotional benefits of doing the right thing and seeing that justice is done.

Never assume that clients simply want the money, without regard to the conditions attached to it. Discuss the problems of secrecy with clients, and urge them to consider the public interest. Some plaintiffs' attorneys are too willing to trade money for their clients' right to speak freely about their experiences. It's easy to forget how hard the right of free speech was won. Clients respect their lawyers' advice; give them the best advice possible.

Inevitably, discussion of secrecy in settlements leads to the claim that attempting to resist confidentiality places plaintiffs' lawyers in conflict with their clients, who need and want to take the money, regardless of the strings attached by the defendant. But if clients are educated, those who want the settlement under any circumstances will become more the exception than the rule. You can avoid even these exceptions by placing a provision in your retainer agreement informing new clients that you will not agree to secret settlements. Many public interest law firms do just that.

Prepare for problems in advance. Discuss the pros and cons of a secret settlement with your client before negotiations begin. Your first duty is, of course, to your client, but your client's interests and the public interest will frequently be in accord.

CONCLUSION

Opposing unnecessary secrecy in personal injury litigation is not a simple matter. With carefully prepared and well-documented legal papers, knowledge of the public policy issues, and the assistance of others, you can, however, succeed. When you do, you, your clients, and the public interest will all be well served.

APPENDIX A

ACTION OF THE HOUSE OF DELEGATES FEBRUARY 16–17, 1987

Report #123
Action Commission to Improve the Tort Liability System

BE IT RESOLVED that the American Bar Association adopts the following recommendation:

F. *Secrecy and Coercive Agreements*

10. Where information obtained under secrecy agreements (a) indicates risk of hazards to other persons, or (b) reveals evidence relevant to claims based on such hazards, courts should ordinarily permit disclosure of such information, after hearing, to other plaintiffs or to government agencies who agree to be bound by appropriate agreements or court orders to protect the confidentiality of trade secrets and sensitive proprietary information.

11. No protective order should contain any provision that requires an attorney for a plaintiff in a tort action to destroy information or records furnished pursuant to such order, including the attorney's notes and other work product, unless the attorney for a plaintiff refuses to agree to be bound by the order after the case has been concluded. An attorney for plaintiff should only be required to return copies of documents obtained from the defendant on condition that defendant agrees not to destroy any such documents so that they will be available, under appropriate circumstances, to government agencies or to other litigants in future cases.

12. Any provision in a settlement or other agreement that prohibits an attorney from representing any other claimant in a similar action against the defendant should be void and of no effect. An attorney should not be permitted to sign such an agreement or request another attorney to do so.

APPENDIX B

RESOLUTION

ATLA BOARD OF GOVERNORS

MAY 6, 1989

TAMPA, FLORIDA

PROTECTIVE ORDERS

WHEREAS, current judicial interpretation often deviates prejudicially from the mandate of the established Rule FRCP 26(c) impeding an efficient, just, and speedy resolution of disputes; and,

WHEREAS, defendants in personal injury actions, as a condition to discovery or settlement, often demand the execution of an agreement ("Secrecy Agreement") or the entrance of an order ("Secrecy Order") which includes provisions, inter alia, (i) prohibiting the dissemination of discovery materials; (ii) precluding the disclosure of the contents of pleadings, motions and discovery requests; (iii) forbidding any communication concerning the terms of the ultimate resolution of a claim; (iv) enjoining plaintiff's counsel's participation in other similar cases; (v) insisting on the return and/or destruction not only of discovery materials but counsel's personal notes; and,

WHEREAS, Secrecy Agreements and Secrecy Orders which ignore the interest of individual victims, the courts and the public have harmful effects including: (i) they make it difficult if not impossible for plaintiff's counsel to fairly and properly prepare the victim's case; (ii) they guarantee an unfair advantage to defense counsel who retain full access to their collaborative mechanism; (iii) they inject collateral issues totally unrelated to the merits of the case; (iv) they greatly increase the time, effort and transactional costs associated with the preparation and presentation of a civil action; (v) they diminish the likelihood that the civil justice system will operate so as to secure the just, speedy and inexpensive determination of every action; (vi) they encourage the suppression and destruction of relevant documents by unscrupulous defendants and other discovery materials; (vii) they have a chilling effect on the right of persons to resort to the courts for redress of their grievances; and,

WHEREAS, the strong policy favoring openness in discovery, and public access to the materials which affect the decisions and the conduct of the civil justice system is based on recognition that the free flow of information is vital to the safety, health and general welfare of the public and to exposing unsafe products and activities for investigation and to the proper operation of the civil justice system, the governmental regulatory system, and the professional disciplinary system;

NOW, THEREFORE, BE IT RESOLVED that the Association of Trial Lawyers of America:

1. Encourages courts to refuse to enter any Secrecy Order and/or refuse to enforce any Secrecy Agreement in the absence of a finding based on a good cause showing supported by a particularized proof of the following: (a) that the proponent of the Agreement or Order possesses a cognizable legal interest entitled to the protection of secrecy; (b) that the subject materials meet the rigorous legal criteria applicable to trade secrets or privileged information or otherwise justify the court in exercising its judicial power to restrict the openness of discovery or public access to information; (c) that disclosure of the materials is, in fact, likely to result in a clearly defined and very serious harm.

2. Encourages courts in those rare instances in which a good cause showing supported by particularized proof would seem to justify the entrance of a Secrecy Order, to insist on the adoption of and the enforcement of such specific terms as are necessary and appropriate to protect such competing interest as the public's right to know, the rights of claimants involved in other similar actions, the public's concern for judicial economy, including: (a) provision for

limited disclosure to counsel representing plaintiffs in similar cases, to government agencies or to professional disciplinary bodies who agree to be bound by appropriate agreements or court orders against broader dissemination; (b) stringent safeguards surrounding any ordered return or destruction of documents to ensure that full and accurate copies of all documents will be available to the appropriate agencies or to other litigants in the future; (c) stringent safeguards that no Secrecy Agreement or Secrecy Order should prohibit an attorney from representing any other claimant in a similar action against the defendant or others; (d) stringent safeguards to the effect that no Secrecy Agreement or Secrecy Order should prohibit reporting to a governmental agency those facts reasonably necessary to prevent injuries to others.

3. Encourages courts to look favorably on and/or to freely grant petitions for modification which seek relief from Secrecy Agreements and/or Secrecy Orders which were entered into or obtained by a procedure which did not conform to the criteria stated in Resolution (1) above and/or which do not contain provisions similar to those contained in Resolution (2) above.

4. Discourages attorneys from agreeing to Secrecy Agreements and encourages attorneys to resist entry of Secrecy Orders that prevent disclosure of documents obtained during discovery to fellow attorneys handling similar cases, or to public agencies charged with enforcing safety.

VOIR DIRE EXAMINATION AND JURY SELECTION

Roxanne Barton Conlin

Most trial lawyers, even those with a great deal of experience, feel apprehensive when they first speak with prospective jurors. Such feelings are normal and even useful in this crucial part of every personal injury lawsuit. Heightened awareness can permit the trial lawyer to read nonverbal communication more accurately and to convey sincerity and commitment about the client's cause.

PURPOSES OF VOIR DIRE

The voir dire examination serves several purposes. It reveals whether panel members are statutorily qualified to serve, if and how they are biased, what their attitudes are about issues in the case, and which potential jurors are most likely to be fair with the plaintiff. Voir dire provides an opportunity to educate the jurors about the case and to obtain commitments on the issues from each juror. Voir dire also helps establish a rapport and credibility with the jury and begins the process of persuasion.

Do You Want a Jury Trial?

The first question is whether to seek a trial by jury. While the jury system generally works well to compensate victims of wrongful acts, there may be reasons for avoiding a jury trial. Each jurisdiction has laws governing when and whether a jury trial can be requested and whether it can be waived. Only the most unusual facts should cause a plaintiff's lawyer to give up the protection a jury trial provides.[1]

Types of Challenges Available Generally

Virtually every jurisdiction has statutes or rules that permit counsel to eliminate unfit or unqualified jurors. There are two basic types of challenges: challenges to the array and challenges to the polls.

Challenges to the array, which are very rare, are directed at the entire jury panel and question the validity of its makeup. They are based on claims of defects or irregularities in the selection of jurors from the jury lists or in the summoning of the jurors.

Challenges to the polls are addressed to individual jurors and consist of two types: (1) challenges for cause or for favor and (2) peremptory challenges.

One type of challenge for cause is based on a statutory disqualification in which case nothing is left to the discretion of the court, and the potential juror will be excused. A second type of challenge, which is usually called a challenge for cause but is technically a challenge "to the favor," is addressed to the discretion of the court. It is based on an allegation that the particular juror is biased in favor of or against one of the parties, in which case the court must exercise its discretion to rule on the challenge. There is no limit to the number of challenges for cause made by counsel.

The peremptory challenge, on the other hand, is limited, and need not be rationalized. Counsel's exercise of a peremptory challenge does not involve the trial judge's discretion and may be used to

1 For example, if the plaintiff is personally unpopular; if he or she is abrasive or obnoxious; or if evidence that might prejudice a juror is certain to be introduced, such as a felony conviction.

strike any panel member for any reason—or for no reason. Only a statutorily specified number of prospective jurors can be eliminated by each side.

PRETRIAL INVESTIGATION

As with every aspect of trial, preparation is the key to an organized presentation and a successful jury selection. Some preparation will begin at the time of the initial client interview, but most will be done immediately before the beginning of trial.

Investigation of the Community

Where will the lawsuit be tried? From what geographical area will jurors be drawn? To understand the general characteristics of the jurors, you must gather some intelligence about the community from which they come. You need to find out

- major neighborhoods or ethnic areas;
- important political parties, activist groups, churches, and business interests in the area;
- social and political issues of concern to the populace;
- employment patterns of different groups; and
- trends that have affected the composition of neighborhoods.

If you are trying the lawsuit in your home town, you will already be aware of most of these facts. If you are unfamiliar with the community, consult local attorneys and community leaders.

Public records contain easily accessible data. Counties keep information on their residents' income, education, and housing patterns in planning departments or the local chamber of commerce. Voting records indicate how different precincts voted on issues of special concern. Real estate boards keep interesting statistics on the movement of property and fluctuation of prices by neighborhood.

Investigation of Panel Members

Gathering information on the prospective jurors before voir dire is often useful. Some jurisdictions publish jury lists before the trial date. Where this is the case, you may investigate prospective jurors as long as you do not actually approach them.

Many sources of information concerning prospective jurors are available before trial. Official jury lists, usually published by the clerk of court, often contain the name, address, and occupation of each prospective juror. In some metropolitan areas, jury investigating services publish bulletins with information about prospective jurors. If you obtain the names of prospective jurors before trial, a private investigation may be conducted. Such a procedure is very expensive, though, and should be undertaken only in cases with very large damages potential. The investigator should be carefully cautioned not to contact the prospective jurors, either directly or indirectly.

Public records may provide you with valuable information concerning prospective jurors. Such records include city directories, court indexes, and police records. Credit bureaus can generally provide a great deal of financial information. In rural areas, where the population is small and stable, local politicians and officials may personally know the members of the prospective panel.

In jurisdictions where jurors hear more than one case in a court term, trial lawyers who have previously tried cases before members of the panel are a most valuable source. You will certainly want to contact those attorneys who have talked with jurors about their decisions and philosophy.

Conducting Voir Dire

The judge controls voir dire and, within statutory mandates, may set reasonable limits and guide the process. Practices differ from jurisdiction to jurisdiction and even within jurisdictions. Each judge is likely to have preferences.

Before appearing before a particular judge, attend a voir dire conducted in that judge's court, if possible. Ask other attorneys, the court attendant, the court reporter, or, if all else fails, ask the judge about voir dire preferences. However, most judges expect attorneys appearing in their courtrooms to be fully prepared for voir dire before beginning the process.

Before entering court, you must know the following:

- Who conducts voir dire? Is it the judge alone, the lawyers alone, or the law clerk?
- If the judge conducts voir dire, can the attorney supplement? Can the attorney submit written questions?

- Where is voir dire conducted? In the courtroom, jury room, or judge's chambers?
- Where are prospective jurors seated? In the jury box? In the spectator section?
- In what order are they seated?
- How many potential jurors does counsel address with questions to the panel? Four? Eight? Twelve? All?
- Is there a juror questionnaire? From whom is it available? When is it available?
- Are introductory remarks made by the judge? By the plaintiff's attorney?
- In what order will attorneys question prospective jurors?
- How many peremptory challenges does each side have? How many are permitted in multiple plaintiff or defendant cases?
- How and when are peremptory challenges exercised? In writing? Orally?
- Does the jurisdiction provide a pamphlet to potential jurors? Do they view a videotape?
- Under what circumstances are jurors excused for cause? Is the judge liberal or conservative in dealing with such challenges or granting excuses to potential jurors with conflicts or employment or health problems?
- Are objections made in front of the panel or at the bench?

USE OF SOCIAL SCIENCE TECHNIQUES

If you are handling a case that has had extensive pretrial publicity or involves a controversial issue, you may wish to use one or more social science procedure in jury selection and presentation of the case. Special assistance may also be needed when the judge conducts voir dire alone or when no voir dire is available, when a verdict may be perceived as having a direct effect on the jurors, or when the case has high potential value but involves complex strategy or legal issues. In each case, you will need to balance the benefit to be derived against the cost of the technique selected.

Community Attitude Assessment

Polling can be useful in constructing a profile of the "best" and "worst" juror, establishing the basis for a motion to change venue, or challenging the composition of the jury panel. If the polling is done before filing the lawsuit, results may be helpful in determining in which jurisdiction to bring the action. Particular trial strategy may also be explored.

Methods of community attitude assessment vary from hiring a professional pollster or social scientist specializing in forensic matters to "do-it-yourself" efforts. Many books and articles deal with this subject in depth and should be consulted.[2]

Mock Trial

Besides assisting in jury selection, a mock trial can help lawyers make appropriate choices for theory, argument, demonstrative evidence, experts, and other witnesses. What to test will depend on the problems in each case. The procedure is to gather a number of strangers, try an abbreviated case before them, listen to their deliberations and their decisions, and apply what has been learned to the actual trial.

Shadow juries can also be used in an appropriate case. These jurors, who closely match actual jurors, are hired to try the lawsuit. They come to court as spectators, listen to the evidence, and are debriefed at the end of each session. Their questions, observations, and conclusions are often useful in directing the course of the trial.

Jury Selection Expert

There are social scientists who specialize in assisting trial lawyers in jury selection. Use the same care in choosing such a person as you use in choosing any expert. The professional selector should certainly have a terminal degree in communications, psychology, or human behavior analysis and should be experienced in the areas needed for the case. Checking references is essential, as there are no "certifications" or other standards governing the practice of this profession.

Skilled social scientists can construct a jury profile to determine what kind of person would be most (and least) favorably disposed to

[2] V. STARR & M. MCCORMICK, JURY SELECTION (1985); NATIONAL JURY PROJECT, JURYWORK: SYSTEMATIC TECHNIQUES (2d ed. 1990).

the plaintiff's case; they can also assist in drafting voir dire questions aimed at exposing bias. During voir dire, selectors may observe nonverbal communication, watch potential jurors during questioning of other panel members, and provide coded notes advising the attorney on exercising peremptory challenges. Generally, selectors should sit in the spectator section and not at counsel table; if they are well-known, move *in limine* to prevent the opponent from commenting on their presence and duties.

SPECIAL STRATEGIES

Supplemental Juror Questionnaire

A set of written questions may be given to panel members either before voir dire or at the beginning of the process. Such questionnaires may be used either through court order or by agreement of counsel. Plaintiffs' attorneys must sometimes inquire into highly personal and potentially embarrassing areas, and offering jurors the possibility of privacy through questionnaires makes their revelations easier. Generally, jurors are more forthcoming with information when they write responses rather than say them in open court. In addition, a written questionnaire can permit inquiries into a potential juror's acceptance of such topics as insurance company propaganda on the "liability crisis" without poisoning the entire panel.

Courts are gradually becoming more amenable to supplemental juror questionnaires. If they are mailed to the panel members two weeks before trial with instructions to complete and return within a week, the supplemental juror questionnaire saves considerable trial time. It also gives counsel time to compile and analyze the responses.

Individual or Small Group Voir Dire

Individual or small group voir dire may be used in lieu of or in combination with a supplemental juror questionnaire. When highly personal questions must be asked, such as in third-party rape cases, a request to ask questions of individual panel members should be made. In the alternative, the court may permit groups of two or three panel members to be questioned separately from other panel members. Courts have recognized the power of group dynamics. In *Irvin v. Dowd*,[3] the Court said,

3 366 U.S. 717, 728 (1961).

> No doubt each juror was sincere when he said that he would be fair and impartial . . . but the psychological impact [of] requiring such a declaration before one's fellows is often its father.

In approving individual voir dire, the court in *United States v. Colabella*[4] said,

> [W]hen there is any foundation for concern about juror partiality . . . which . . . might affect other prospective jurors, the demands of the "most priceless" safeguard of individual liberty . . . justify the small expenditure of time [to question each juror separately if they express bias].

Note, however, *Press Enterprise Co. v. Superior Court*,[5] which requires that, except under compelling circumstances, voir dire be open to the press and public.

Motions *in Limine*

Consider whether any facts that harm the plaintiff's case are not admissible in evidence under the rules of the jurisdiction. Examples include the following:

- the plaintiff was operating a vehicle without a valid driver's license;
- the plaintiff was issued a traffic citation as a result of the collision;
- the plaintiff had a long record of traffic violations before the collision;
- the defendant was not issued a traffic citation;
- the plaintiff's medical bills or wages were paid by a collateral source;
- the plaintiff, before the collision, was convicted of a crime not involving moral turpitude;
- the plaintiff was arrested and charged with the commission of a crime;

4 448 F.2d 1299, 1304 (2d Cir. 1971), *cert. denied*, 405 U.S. 929 (1972).

5 464 U.S. 501, 509-10 (1984) (citing Globe Newspaper Co. v. Superior Court, 457 U.S. 596, 606-07 (1982)).

- the plaintiff had a prior claim involving injury to the same area of the body injured in the case on trial;
- the spouse prosecuting a death action is remarried;
- the plaintiff has had other accident claims or lawsuits;
- the financial status of either party; and
- the effect of any verdict on insurance rates.

In a medical negligence case, other matters may need to be addressed by way of motions *in limine* precluding any mention of

- the effect of the case on availability of health care or on the defendant's finances, reputation, or employment;
- the defendant's reputation before or after the incident in question; and
- the word "malpractice" because it is prejudicial to the plaintiff and not used in the court's charge.

Counsel should make the motion before voir dire. This motion may be called a "motion to suppress," "motion to quash," or "motion *in limine*," depending on local practice. File the motion in writing with a brief citing cases that support the proposition that the facts or matters specified are not admissible in evidence.

If prejudicial matters are brought before the jury, no amount of objection or judicial instruction can remove their harmful effect. The plaintiff is powerless unless he or she wants to forego this day in court and ask for a mistrial. Counsel should therefore state in the motion *in limine* that if the matter designated were brought to the attention of the jury, the plaintiff would be irreparably prejudiced, even if the court were to sustain an objection and instruct the jury to disregard the evidence. The purpose of the motion is thus to prevent a mistrial. Once the motion is granted, defense counsel is prohibited from making any reference to the stigmatizing facts during voir dire or opening statement or making any inquiry during examination of witnesses that might bring out the suppressed matter. Take care not to open the matter by statements or through the witnesses you call.

Limitations on Voir Dire

Federal Rule of Civil Procedure 47(a) governs voir dire in federal courts and gives judges broad discretion concerning its manner, scope, and length.[6] Each party in a civil lawsuit has three peremptory challenges; the court has discretion over the number granted when there are several plaintiffs or defendants.

It is common in federal and some state courts for the judge alone to question the panel. Certain judges will not even allow attorneys to submit questions for inclusion in the judges' voir dire, nor will they permit follow-up questions. This severely compromises the attorney's right to learn of any bias or prejudice held by those who will determine the outcome of the case. In *Leone v. Goodman*,[7] a defense verdict in a medical negligence case was set aside because the judge refused to ask any of the questions submitted by counsel or to permit either side to participate in voir dire. In *United States v. Ledee*,[8] the court stated

> . . . [W]e must acknowledge that voir dire examination in both civil and criminal cases has little meaning if it is not conducted by counsel for the parties.
>
> . . . [T]he real issue is whether the voir dire examination uncovers possible prejudice and bias of any juror so that a fair and impartial jury may be impaneled. Peremptory challenges are worthless if trial counsel is not afforded an opportunity to gain the necessary information on which to base such strikes.

In *United States v. Rucker*,[9] the court said

> A voir dire that has the effect of impairing the defendant's ability to exercise intelligently his challenges is ground for reversal, irrespective of prejudice.

Thus, even in federal court, voir dire may not be so limited as to prevent the intelligent exercise of peremptory challenges.[10]

If the trial judge shows signs of drastically curtailing the examination, file a written motion requesting the privilege of conducting

6 *See also* 28 U.S.C.A. §1870 (1966 & Supp. 1990).

7 773 P.2d 342 (Nev. 1989).

8 549 F.2d 990, 993 (5th Cir. 1977), *cert. denied*, 434 U.S. 902 (1977).

9 557 F.2d 1046, 1049 (4th Cir. 1977) (citing Swain v. Alabama, 380 U.S. 202, 219 (1965); United States v. Lewin, 467 F.2d 1132 (7th Cir. 1972)).

10 *See, e.g.*, Fietzer v. Ford Motor Co., 622 F.2d 281, 284 (7th Cir. 1980); Kiernan v. Van Schaik, 347 F.2d 775 (3d Cir. 1965).

voir dire examination. The motion may contain a list of the questions or topics you wish to cover, or it may request that the court make the necessary inquiries. File a brief citing supporting authorities for the position that a wide latitude of inquiry is permitted during voir dire examination. If at the time of the examination the court will not permit a full examination, take exception so that you will have a proper record for appellate review.

Even where the court permits voir dire, unrealistic time limits may be imposed. The only proper reason to curtail voir dire is to stop inexperienced or over-eager counsel from using the procedure to argue the case before the trial begins. Restricting voir dire to save time makes no more sense than limiting all trials to one day, closing arguments to ten minutes, or each side to one witness. There are many ways to shorten a trial, but justice should never be sacrificed for the sake of speed.

The exercise of peremptory challenges is a matter of right granted by statute and is inseparably related to the right to trial by an unbiased jury. You must be granted reasonable time to make inquiries of the prospective jurors under oath to intelligently strike potentially prejudiced panel members.

CONDUCTING VOIR DIRE

Mechanics

Many lawyers use a trial notebook to organize every part of the trial. Suggested tabs in the notebook for the voir dire are

- Rules of Court/Statutes,
- Case Law,
- Ideal Jury Profile,
- Questions to Be Asked, and
- Summaries of Questionnaires.

Whenever possible, the lawyer conducting the voir dire should *not* take notes. It is clumsy and unwieldy. Another lawyer, a communications specialist, a legal assistant, or a secretary can do the note-taking so you can concentrate on the selection process. Set up a chart with a box for each panel member. When a name is called, write it in the box, together with information gleaned from the questionnaire summaries.

An efficient way to conduct voir dire is to have each separate question written on a 3 x 5 card. Code questions to be asked of the entire panel and questions to be asked of each member; critical questions can also be marked or written in red so, if time limitations or your assessment of the panel's patience require, less important questions can be skipped.

Questioning with Sensitivity

It is essential that you display sensitivity toward women and minorities through your use of language and your attitudes. No attorney seeks to offend or stigmatize any member of the panel, but inappropriate language and stereotypical myths can creep into questioning. For example, while some adult women are flattered by being called "girl," most find it offensive. It is also important to use nonsexist job descriptions, such as flight attendant and mail carrier. Avoid using the so-called generic "man" or "he," or the word "mankind." While such language is widely used and acceptable to many people, some women perceive the user of gender-specific terms to be insensitive. Those women attuned to the connotations of such terms are very likely to be good plaintiffs' jurors but will not be favorably disposed to the attorney who has, however unintentionally, diminished them.

Certain questions can also betray sexist feelings. If you ask male jurors what they do for a living and then ask a female juror, "Do you work?", you will offend at least some panel members. Eliminate the phrase "just a housewife" from your vocabulary.

With respect to minorities, the currently acceptable term is either black or African-American—not Negro. Never refer to a black adult male as "boy." It is demeaning in the same way as the use of the word "girl," but it has additional racist connotations.

All belief systems contain some stereotypes. There are a myriad of such myths, and they infect our whole culture. If you are to be a truly competent trial attorney, you need to root out preconceived notions based on gender, race, sexual preference, ethnicity, and other characteristics. If you don't, those notions will spill out into the courtroom and make a mess. The ultimate effect of such insensitivity is serious harm to your client.

Relevant Factors in Jury Selection

Experts agree that the single most significant factor in establishing a person's mind-set is his or her occupation. Before commencing voir dire, consider which people in which occupations would most likely be sympathetic to the plaintiff's case. Educational background is important. Also consider the age range of the ideal person, the person's ethnicity, gender, and family status.

Do not be misled by stereotypes; careful observation and examination is essential to choosing fair jurors. Always be in place when the panel is called, and watch the members as they enter the courtroom. Observe how each of them walks, what they carry, how they are dressed. Request that the judge initially pronounce each panel member's name to save you from an embarrassing early misstep.

Introductory Questions

Either the judge or the plaintiff's counsel will introduce the parties. Prepare the client to acknowledge the introduction by saying "Good morning" to the panel. Even the most experienced counsel are likely to feel nervous when they first get up to address the jury panel, and some begin their presentation by acknowledging that the panel members may also be nervous. Such an opening can be disarming while giving the attorney an opportunity to explain the voir dire process.

If permitted to make introductory remarks, you should state the theme of the case in the very first sentence to take advantage of the principle of primacy. The theme should be short, simple, and imaginative. For example, "This is a case about worker safety and corporate irresponsibility," "This is a case about consumer safety," or "This is the case of the exploding pop bottle." Follow the theme statement by introducing yourself and explaining your role:

> I am ________________. I am an attorney, and I'm here to speak for Eddie M. This is his case, and I'm on his side. That's my privilege as a lawyer, and my duty to Eddie and to you.

An early test of whether individual prospective jurors are favorably disposed to you is to ask that they "lean back and relax." Those who do so are amenable to your suggestions. In addition, you may wish to say to the panel, "Raise your hand if you have ever heard a boring speech, lecture, or sermon." Because nearly everyone has had that experience, those who do not raise their hands may be resistant to you or your case. That is a useful thing to know.

As a part of the introduction, most attorneys explain the process and tell the panel that they must ask some personal questions solely to ascertain each panel member's qualifications to serve on the case and not to satisfy any personal curiosity. Some attorneys suggest that if any jurors are uncomfortable with any question, they should just say so and not feel compelled to answer because their "personal right to privacy is as important as any question" the attorney might ask. The refusal to answer certain questions may be as meaningful as an answer would be.

Form of Questions

Open-ended questions get more information. Ask potential jurors "how do you feel" or "what do you think" about particular issues and laws. Start questions with the words "what," "why," or "how." Closed questions are useful to clarify answers or to challenge panel members for cause. Avoid legalese, but do not talk down to potential jurors. Listen to the panel members, make eye contact, and respond to what they say. Wait for the person to complete the answer, and offer the potential juror an opportunity to explain, expand on the answer, and share knowledge with other panel members.

Evaluate, also, the *way* in which panel members answer. Vocal tone, inflection, pace, emphasis, and intensity are all more important than the words the potential juror uses. Watch jurors closely. Most people instinctively understand nonverbal communication. Indeed, more communication takes place through body movement and vocalization than through words.

For every question you ask, you should have a clear goal:

- Does the question provide information to challenge for cause or for favor?
- Does it provide information to determine the potential juror's mind-set or world view?
- Does it give jurors information about the case, the client, or the law?
- Does it secure commitments from jurors?
- Does it provide information useful for other phases of the trial?

Of course, avoid asking any question that will give the defense more information than it gives you.

No case is without problems, and these should be disclosed in voir dire. At that time, you can mention problems in the least harmful way and discuss them thoroughly with prospective jurors. Talking with potential jurors at the outset is better than having jurors focus on the plaintiff's problem areas in deliberations.

Stating problems in voir dire provides the opportunity to secure from each of the jurors assurance that the problem in itself will not affect the juror's judgment or prevent the juror from acting fairly and impartially. For example, suppose a key witness for the plaintiff is an ex-felon. The jury could be told the following:

> This collision was witnessed by John Doe. That is a fact over which ____________________ had no control. It could have happened in the presence of any citizen in this community. It is proper for you to know that earlier in his life Mr. Doe made a mistake for which he was imprisoned and for which he has paid his debt to society. That is also a fact over which the plaintiff had no control. Will you listen to Mr. Doe, who saw this collision, even though he has a criminal record?

Other problems that the plaintiff's counsel may wish to expose in voir dire include the following:

- the plaintiff was under the influence of alcohol or drugs at the time of injury;
- the defendant belongs to a profession held in high esteem;
- the plaintiff is suing a member of her or his family;
- the plaintiff is suing the driver of a car in which the plaintiff was a guest;
- the plaintiff was at one time convicted of a crime, if that fact will be admissible;
- the plaintiff has other lawsuits involving the same injury;
- the plaintiff has prior or subsequent injuries to the same part of the body that is the subject of the claim; and
- the plaintiff was riding a motorcycle.

Potential jurors bring the baggage of their life experiences to court with them. There are no "blank slates." It is foolish to try to dissuade potential jurors from their bias. You just need to know what those biases are. Do not ask a juror to "set aside" beliefs, except when you are trying to save a good, favorable potential juror from a challenge for cause. For example, ask sympathetic jurors follow-up questions to establish their objectivity:

"Mrs. Smith, when you came in this morning, you had no preconceived notions about this case, did you?"

"You will listen to the evidence, won't you?"

"Aside from a natural sympathy that we would all feel, you will not permit yourself to be unduly influenced by that sympathy, will you?"

"You will vote your convictions fairly and in accord with the law and based on the evidence?"

"You can, of course, set aside any natural feelings you have for the plaintiff and follow the law?"

Potential jurors should not be cross-examined or embarrassed. The lawyer who does so may offend other potential jurors.

Explain to jurors why objections are made, and secure from them a commitment not to react adversely to the attorney who makes objections to prevent confusing or improper evidence from coming before them. Many judges tell jurors that the attorneys and parties are not permitted to visit with them or even exchange pleasantries during the trial; make sure that the jury members know the reason you must ignore them in the hallways and the elevators. Otherwise, jurors may believe that you have purposefully snubbed them.

Commitments

Conclude the examination by obtaining a commitment from each potential juror to follow the law as stated by the judge and, if the evidence supports it, to award full and adequate damages. Such a commitment may be referred to during closing arguments. To get such a commitment, ask "will you," not "can you." They always can; the issue is whether they will.

Style

Every lawyer is an individual with a particular manner. Some general rules apply to every style, however. Do not walk and talk at the same time. Get everything out of your pocket that jingles. Use everyday words and common syntax. Never exaggerate.

Invariable Rule

One absolute rule applies to juror selection. If you do not like a prospective juror, that prospective juror does not like you and should be stricken. Whether it is body language, tone of voice, or something else not yet identified, animosity is usually mutual. This concept is supported by social science and trial experience. Follow it.

CONTENT OF VOIR DIRE

Each case is different; consequently, the content and conduct of each voir dire should be different. Exercise as much creativity and imagination in the planning and conduct of voir dire as you do in the presentation of your case in chief.

Areas of Inquiry

Biographical Information

Some of the information needed will be in even the most rudimentary jury questionnaire. Questions should include a person's address, length of residence, and whether the prospective juror rents or owns. Also, inquire as to birth date and place, marital status, occupation of spouse, number and ages of children, and occupation of grown children. The nature and extent of a person's formal education is also a proper subject of sensitive inquiry.

Occupational Status

Job title is far less significant than job duties and responsibilities. Questions such as "What do you like best and least about your job" can help establish rapport and provide important information. Occupational history and union membership should be established. Other possible inquiries include special skills in medical, legal, or technical fields; a juror with such training may become the expert to whom other jurors will turn for an evaluation of your evidence.

General Qualifications

Panel members may have physical conditions that would hamper their ability to serve. A person with a back problem may find it impossible to sit for long periods on a hard jury seat. However, try to make accommodations for them and also for persons with hearing or vision impairments. If the weather is likely to be harsh, inquire about the distance the panel members will have to travel each day and what transportation arrangements are available. Also important is whether any potential jurors have appointments or special occasions within the estimated time period of the trial that would cause great inconvenience or interfere with their ability to pay close attention. The parent whose child is getting married or the worker who has an interview for a promotion during the trial week(s) may not be excused for cause, but knowledge of these matters is essential nevertheless. If possible, strike such jurors, because they will be unable to focus on the lawsuit. They may blame the plaintiff who brought the lawsuit for interfering with their personal lives.

Nature of the Case

Once the jurors have been told what the case involves, they should be asked whether they have been involved in a situation similar to that of either the plaintiff or the defendant. Ask the jurors whether they or any members of their immediate families have been involved in any accidents that produced injury, have been a plaintiff or defendant in any lawsuit, or have had any injuries similar to those claimed by the plaintiff.

Explore the jurors' knowledge of the parties, witnesses, and lawyers. If one of the panel members is acquainted with one of the people involved, determine if the relationship is personal, social, professional, or casual. How often do they have contact? When was the last time? Have they discussed this case or any other legal matter? Assess how the relationship will affect the panel member's judgment. A potential juror who was briefly treated by the defendant doctor and who now goes to another doctor may have decided that the defendant was not very competent. A teacher who had the plaintiff's child in school may have had a bad experience with the child for which the teacher blames the parents. Direct questions rarely reveal this kind of view, but careful observation can give the attorney the necessary information.

Experience in Lawsuits

Has the potential juror been involved in any kind of lawsuit as a party or witness? Prior jury experience may also be an indicator of the juror's attitudes. A series of questions can be designed:

- What kind of a case—criminal or civil?
- What was it about?
- When was it tried?

- What was the verdict?
- How did you feel about the jury's deliberations?
- How did you feel about the jury system as a result of that experience?
- How do you now feel about the verdict in that case?
- Did anyone say anything to you about the case, i.e., judge, attorneys?
- Is there anything that occurred in that case that would influence your judgment about this entirely different case?
- Will you decide this case on its own facts regardless of the other case on which you sat in judgment?

Racial Bias

Never attempt to identify racial bias through direct questions. In addition to being useless, such questions can backfire and alienate your client and other panel members. Instead, ask general questions:

- What does racial discrimination mean to you?
- Has it been eliminated?
- What areas of life are/have been affected?
- What causes racism?
- What can be done?
- Have you worked with minorities? Did you attend school with minorities?
- Do any minorities live in your neighborhood?
- What is your feeling about affirmative action?
- Have you ever felt racial tension?

Jurors' World View

People are difficult to pigeonhole, but knowing that the panel members participate in certain activities is helpful in determining their general views of the world and philosophies of life. What TV programs do they watch; what newspapers and magazines do they read? What are their hobbies? What do the jurors do with leisure time? What do they read on the editorial page of the newspaper?

Have they ever written a "letter to the editor" or to a public official? Do they have any pets? What kind? What makes them angry? How do they feel about lawyers in general?

Legal Concepts

You cannot argue the law during voir dire. However, it is generally acceptable to state and define the important legal principles of the case and to ask jurors their view of those concepts.

If the case involves a claim of professional negligence, try to find out whether the jurors believe that professionals should be held to the standard of care required under the circumstances. Negligence is negligence, whether it is committed by a driver running a red light and injuring someone, a doctor leaving a surgical instrument in a patient's abdomen, or a lawyer letting a statute of limitations run. Standard of care should also be discussed.

If the case involves a claim that a defective product caused an injury, ascertain that the jurors have no quarrel with the applicable law on strict liability or breach of express or implied warranty.

An explanation of the civil burden of proof also needs to be provided, and each juror's understanding of the difference between "preponderance of the evidence" and "beyond a reasonable doubt" confirmed. In jurisdictions that have adopted comparative fault, find out if anyone feels that it is wrong for a person who was partially at fault to recover from others who caused or contributed to the harm. Proximate cause should also be discussed, and, in most instances, the jurors will need to be told that there can be more than one proximate cause. Where a claim for consortium is made, the term must be defined and close questioning done to assure acceptance of the idea that money can and should be awarded in a proper case to spouses and children for the loss of companionship and society. Some people have such strong adverse reactions to this element of damages, they can be challenged for cause.

Insurance Questions

Counsel for the plaintiff will generally ask the jurors whether they have ever been involved in the investigation or evaluation of claims and whether they have ever been employed by, held office in, or owned stock in an insurance company that writes casualty or liability insurance. Any question that relates to insurance or the insurance industry must be preceded by a careful check on the jurisdiction's law to determine what is permissible. If at all in doubt, clear potential questions pertaining to insurance with the judge.

Material for Closing Argument

- Do you know anyone with a brain-damaged child? What is life like for such children and their families?
- Do you know any people who are deaf? What effect has deafness had on these people and their families?
- What do you feel are the most important features of a trial by jury? What do you most appreciate about our system of justice?

Nominating the Foreperson

A sympathetic juror can, with great care, be nominated to be foreperson. Use tact and diplomacy. Highlight any special leadership qualities or capabilities the juror may possess. In preparation, ask this juror the following questions:

- Will you deliberate with your fellow jurors and let them freely exchange ideas?
- Do you agree that your fellow jurors are entitled to be listened to carefully?
- Do you agree with the jury system that allows six/eight/twelve people to decide a dispute of the type involved in this case?
- Will you participate in a democratic way with your fellow jurors so that all can share their viewpoints on your journey toward deciding this case?

DAMAGES

A panel member's understanding of the civil justice system and the award of money for intangible losses must be thoroughly explored. Most people have no idea of the role the award of damages plays in our society. The concept of paying dollars for pain and suffering, physical impairment, or lost consortium seems foreign to many and raises suspicions and discomfort. A brief explanation of the rationale for such damages is a good way to begin the questioning on damages.

The recent media campaign launched by various organizations to destroy the civil justice system diverts attention from human suffering and dignity and focuses on "desirable" levels of death and injury. Because of it, many potential jurors will come to court with a mind-set adverse to the plaintiff. You cannot ignore it—but you also want to avoid contamination of the panel and violation of your jurisdiction's laws and rules.

An aggressive motion practice may be helpful, including motions for individual voir dire and supplemental jury questionnaires. Alert the court by motion when you want an expanded voir dire into topics that will include references to the insurance industry.[11] Use poll data, newspaper articles, and advertisements to bolster your motion.

One approach is to ask general questions.

- Are you aware of controversy about so-called insurance crises or tort reform or liability crisis? Where did you read it, hear it, see it?
- Do you know it has two sides—maybe there isn't any such thing as an insurance crisis?
- Have you formed any opinions?
- Would those opinions cause you to favor one side?
- Do you realize each case is different and must stand on its own facts as developed from the evidence?
- Can you disregard what you have heard outside of court and decide this matter on evidence alone?

Another approach is open pursuit of the subject with individual panel members, but it is important to avoid arguing with those jurors whose views are antagonistic to the plaintiff's. A voir dire should combine an exploration of knowledge about the litigation crisis and attitudes about damages. The following are questions you can ask of individual panel members:

[11] Helpful cases include Borkoski v. Yost, 594 P.2d 688, 694-95 (Mont. 1979) (initial inquiry must be directed to jurors' exposure to adverse publicity—you can't show ads to jurors); Graham v. Waite, 257 N.Y.S. 2d 629, 630 (App. Div. 1965) (it is appropriate to mention news reports on impact of jury verdicts on insurance costs); King v. Westlake, 572 S.W.2d 841, 843-44 (Ark. 1978) (it is appropriate to ask a juror if he thought his verdict would have an impact on his insurance premiums). *See, contra*, Speet v. Bacaj, 377 S.E.2d 397 (Va. 1989).

- What are your general feelings about courts?
- How do you feel about the jury system? Do you think it works? Why? Why not?
- How do you feel about jurors being asked to decide cases involving large amounts of money?
- Do you ever think that people are getting millions of dollars for small injuries? Why does this happen? Who is responsible?
- How do you think insurance companies are doing financially? Are too many people suing each other?
- Have you read any articles or advertisements or heard anything about jury verdicts in this country?
- Where have you read or heard it?
- Have you ever attended a meeting at which this topic was discussed? Have you ever discussed it with family or friends?
- Have you heard of a verdict that you felt was excessive?
- Have you followed the controversy about caps on damages?
- How do you feel about lawyers?
- Based on what you have heard so far, are you open-minded on the subject of appropriate compensation for the plaintiff?
- Do you believe that you would in any way be influenced by what you may have heard or seen on TV or read in the paper about other cases of this kind, or will you decide based solely on the evidence in this case?
- Do any of you, for whatever reason, feel that you do not believe in large verdicts and would be reluctant to return one even if the evidence shows the plaintiff is entitled to it?
- Is there any reason why you would be embarrassed to return a large verdict?
- Do you believe people should not sue for their injuries but should endure their suffering?
- The only form of compensation recognized by the law is dollars. It is the only compensation we can seek. We cannot ask you to restore Connie to health, to fix her neck, to make her headaches go away, or ask you to restore her to her family as she was without her physical problems. You will hear all about her injuries and losses from the evidence.

What Connie and her family and I need to know now, if you are going to sit in judgment, is how you feel about awarding money damages in general. Is pain and suffering worth less than purely financial loss?

- Do you understand that no witness will get on the stand and say that the plaintiff should get *x* amount of dollars for her injuries? Do you understand that *you* will have to answer that based on the evidence we present on each of the elements of damages?
- Do you understand that it will be your duty to appraise Connie's suffering and losses and only you will do this? Do you understand that we ask people to do this and not machines because machines can't suffer or hope or dream—only real people do, and only real people can appraise other real people's losses?
- Sympathy has no place in this lawsuit. Can you set it aside?
- Just because we bring an action does not mean that we automatically recover damages. There must be evidence presented. Will you keep an open mind during the course of the trial?
- Does each of you understand that this is a once-in-a-lifetime verdict for the Moores and that it is necessary that you render a full and fair verdict for all the severe and permanent losses suffered by them in the past and those that will be suffered by them in the future?
- If we prove by a preponderance of evidence that a fair amount to compensate Connie and Jim would be $1 million, how would you feel about awarding that large a sum? How about $5 million or $10 million?

Concluding Questions

No matter how meticulous the questioning or how long it lasts, you cannot cover every possible issue. The standard concluding questions should underline your concern, sincerity, and desire to have a fair jury who will follow the law:

- Have you had any personal experiences we haven't touched on that would influence your vote—that would make you lean even slightly in favor of one side before the trial starts?

In asking this question, we rely on you to be sincere and honest and to tell us of any such personal experiences and their effect on you.

- Do you have any essential beliefs—religious, moral, political, or personal—that would interfere with your following the court's instructions on the law?
- If you were (*plaintiff's name*), would you want someone in your frame of mind sitting in judgment on you?
- When you take your oath as jurors, you promise to follow the law as given you by the judge. Will you also promise that you will listen and decide this case based on the evidence, and if the evidence shows that (*plaintiff's name*) is entitled to damages, that you will render a full and adequate verdict in an amount that will fully and fairly compensate the plaintiff for losses?

EXERCISING CHALLENGES

Challenges for Cause

Persons with statutory disqualifications are usually eliminated from the panel in advance. Nonetheless, some person who is not a citizen or who has a criminal record may be called. It is more frequent, however, to find on the panel persons related by blood or marriage to the parties, witnesses, or attorneys. Those who are disqualified by statute are easily identified, and the court must excuse them. The more common "challenge for cause" is based on bias or prejudice of the panel member.

If voir dire examination indicates that there is any matter that would probably affect the juror's attitude and influence the decision so that the juror would not be objective and impartial, a challenge for cause is indicated.

Since the number of peremptory challenges is limited, challenges for cause are important. Not infrequently, the juror will ask to be excused. This does not mean that you should ask jurors directly whether they would be prejudiced against the plaintiff. Such an inquiry will invariably be denied. But jurors will frequently admit that they have certain feelings and preconceived notions that may influence their judgment.

Common reasons for challenges for cause include the following:

- the juror knows one of the parties, lawyers, or key witnesses;
- the juror cannot follow applicable law, for example, the law regarding damages for pain and suffering;
- the juror has been a party in a similar lawsuit; and
- the juror has negative feelings about damage claims, large awards, or juries.

To permit a potential juror with bias to excuse himself or herself without embarrassment, the lawyer must establish an atmosphere of openness and acceptance of diverse opinions.

Start with open-ended questions. If the juror reveals information indicating bias, such as employment by the defendant, counsel should ask, "*How* would that affect your attitude?", not "*Would* that affect your attitude?" Reassure panel members who admit to some bias, "Your attitude is common—thanks for your candor." Then, solidify the admission of bias with leading questions: "Is it fair to say that you would tend to be wary of damages claims? Would you agree that you would make a better juror in some other kind of case? Would it be a fair statement that even if you tried your best, you might still be influenced by your distrust of damages claims generally?" Prepare for attempts at rehabilitation by opposing counsel or the judge by such questions as "How long have you had this attitude?", "Is it likely to change in a few days?", or "Would it be better if you didn't sit on this particular case?"

Peremptory Challenges

Hard and fast rules simply do not exist for the exercise of peremptory challenges. Ask everyone on the trial team, including your client, for input. Rank the challenges in descending order, starting with the person who absolutely should not sit on the jury. Where challenges are exercised consecutively, leave for last any person who the defendants may also want to strike. If you are permitted four challenges, prepare a list of six or eight, so if the defendants exercise a peremptory strike against a potential juror, you can simply move down the list to another less desirable juror without delay.

The manner of exercising peremptory challenges varies from jurisdiction to jurisdiction. In some courts, counsel rises and states the name or number of the juror whom he or she wishes to excuse. In others, peremptory challenges are exercised in writing so that the juror stricken and the remaining jurors do not know which lawyer is striking which jurors.

Be careful when using all peremptory challenges; the replacements could be less desirable than those initially challenged. Thus, before you use your peremptory challenges, try to analyze the relative desirability of the potential juror who will replace the challenged juror.

CONCLUSION

Voir dire is the only opportunity for counsel and the jury to talk with one another. Its primary objectives should include establishing rapport and enhancing your credibility. Once the jury is selected, you should appear confident and satisfied that the jury is the best possible jury to decide your client's lawsuit.

OPENING STATEMENT

David B. Baum

Well begun is half done.

– HORACE

IMPORTANCE OF OPENING STATEMENT

Experienced advocates know that a good opening statement can win the case. Some have heard jurors admit after the trial that the case was over once the openings were completed. The opening is presented when jurors are fresh and eager to hear the case and before they have reacted to the parties, the evidence, or the frustrations of the trial itself. By final argument, the jurors have listened to the evidence and either arrived at their conclusions or become thoroughly confused. The opening, therefore, is the best time to reach an open mind.

The opening was not always given so much importance. It was often considered a preliminary to the evidence, and lawyers commonly waived the opening statement, particularly in nonjury trials. Better lawyers, however, recognized its significance. Erskine, the great barrister, let his juniors make the final argument but handled the opening himself. He knew that the opening was a unique opportunity to establish rapport with the jury, provide a clear understanding of the case, simplify the issues, set the trial's tone, and motivate the jury to decide in his client's favor.

A University of Chicago study often cited on significance of the opening statement showed that 80 percent of jurors surveyed decided liability after the opening statements and never changed their minds. Experience leads to the same conclusion—the opening is critical to success.

Seize Primacy

Plaintiff's counsel has a potent weapon in the opening statement: the principle of primacy. Psychologists theorize that people tend to believe most deeply that which they learn first about a subject and resist altering that idea from then on. Primacy is an important advantage for the plaintiff; it means jurors will often make up their minds on the liability issue based on the opening statements alone.

Identify with Your Client

Another psychological principle, identification with the client, is also important. You can describe the plaintiff as a neighbor, a member of the community, or a co-worker, so the jury can identify with the client. People appreciate a trusted employee, a skilled worker, a family provider—someone like themselves.

To help the jurors identify with the plaintiff, you must learn everything there is to know about your client. Review the family photograph albums and scrapbooks, and talk with neighbors, co-workers, teachers, and friends of your client to develop a command of all pertinent facts for use in the opening.

Make a Good First Impression

The opening statement calls for more subtle forms of persuasion than does the final argument. The jury should accept that the plaintiff has a winning case and deserves adequate compensation. They should trust you as a spokesperson. A persuasive presentation will create interest and belief in your case, and your fairness and sincerity will establish rapport with the jury immediately from the very beginning.

Always be aware of courtroom etiquette. Before addressing the jury, say to the court, "May it please the court." Your manner is important to the jury; courtesy will gain the jurors' respect and help them identify with your client.

GUIDELINES FOR OPENING

Simplify the Case

Be aware of the jury's discomfort and confusion during the trial. The courtroom environment is particularly foreign and intimidating at the start of the case, when the jurors first hear your version of the case. Therefore, it is paramount that your opening statement be clear and simple. A poorly prepared opening will be rambling, disorganized, and confusing, and the jury will immediately lose faith in you and your case.

How much information should be in the opening statement? On the one hand, you want to present a complete picture of the case with all its ramifications and details. On the other, a jury unfamiliar with the case will be confused by an opening loaded with details. Dates, names, and places will mean little to new listeners, and excessive detail will lose the jurors, rather than win them over.

Give the jury enough information to know the parties, understand the case, and appreciate the plaintiff's position. Any more than this may be too much for the standard opening. However, the right balance is difficult to achieve. It requires careful preparation. Remember the familiar complaint, "If I had more time, I could have written a shorter letter." Follow this philosophy—consider the critical features of the case, review your file for details, and then decide what you will leave out.

Once your content is streamlined, simplify sentences and language—use fewer words. Avoid the natural fascination that we all have with our own words, and pare down the opening.

Focus the Issues

During the opening lawyers tend to concentrate attention on the disputed issues in the trial and ignore evidence on the rest of the case as superfluous. This is because attorneys are specialists. They presume that rear-end auto collisions are always the defendant's fault and so assume that there need be little discussion of this issue. The jurors, however, may not know that rear-end collisions are "always the defendant's fault"—an incorrect presumption to begin with. The effective advocate tries to clarify and simplify the issues so that the jurors will clearly understand what they are being asked to do. A careful analysis of the case will determine how to accomplish this.

Most cases have a critical jugular vein; focusing attention on it in the opening may win the battle, thereby carrying the war. Convert this advantage into a decision for the plaintiff on all issues.

The opening should not and cannot cover every detail in the case. Many facts may be left out, because (a) they are not critical, (b) their impact (or shock value) will be greater during the trial, (c) the jury can be kept in suspense on a dramatic point, or (d) there is a potential trap for the opposition.

Whether you should cover a subject or make a particular reference in the opening depends on whether it truly helps your case. If it doesn't, omit it.

Outline the Opening

An outline is invaluable for organizing your opening and preparing the flow of the facts to cover. A helpful technique is to highlight or underline points to emphasize. Once you develop a personal outline system, it will become second nature. You will use it constantly to flag critical points, organize your thoughts, and memorize presentations. Whether or not you actually use the outline in court, it is a great preparatory aid.

Develop Themes

Every case should have a theme or themes to which the jury can relate. The theme is introduced in the opening statement and reaffirmed throughout the trial. It is usually inherent in the factual setting of the case; you should give considerable thought to creating the theme in a single sentence that is catchy without being cute and effective without being confusing. General topics for your theme might be individual against giant corporation; consumer against manufacturer; safety in our homes, streets, or workplaces; redress for the victim; or the underdog fights back. Themes must be subtly invoked in the opening statement. A heavy-handed approach by the plaintiff in a bid for sympathy will be ineffective and lambasted by the defense.

Tell the Story

Everyone loves a good story. An opening statement that tells a gripping and dramatic story will hold the jury's interest and make the case compelling—but it requires planning and preparation to be effective. Like any good story, the opening should answer the traditional questions of who, what, when, where, how, and why (who are the parties, what happened to them, how and why did this happen).

The narrative should usually unfold in chronological order, though there are other techniques for fact presentation. The flashback, for instance, starts with the end result and then works backwards to the cause. This is particularly suitable for the major injury case, where the ending, a graphic description of the life of the quadriplegic plaintiff or the scene of an individual in a coma, serves as a vivid introduction to the case.

The parallel-actions technique is another dramatic device. Here the parties start out at the same time from different places. The actions of each are followed separately until the time of the accident or event that brings the parties together. A common example is a vehicular collision, with the protagonists proceeding toward the collision from different points.

Use a Grabber

The creative lawyer seeks a way to grab the jurors' attention. The traditional opening, which begins with the purposes of an opening or discusses procedural matters, will lose the jury at the outset. Get the jury's attention as soon as possible by using a dramatic device to present the case in a nutshell. It can be a slogan, a catchword, or a sentence that captures the case succinctly and embodies your theme.

This "grabber" or "hook" starts the opening by focusing the jurors' interest on the plaintiff's version of the case. Consider the following from actual cases:

> "This is the case of a baby crib that was sold with a headboard that strangled babies."
>
> "On April 4, 1984, the Hunter's Point Industrial Park in San Francisco exploded, killing nine people and injuring 30 more, because the owners permitted the illegal manufacture of fireworks inside the building."
>
> "On November 4, 1988, this young athlete entered University Hospital for minor foot surgery and left in a coma, which caused his death one week later. How that could happen is what this case is all about."

Rehearse the Opening

Trial lawyers often spend time preparing and rehearsing their final arguments but neglect the opening. This is a mistake; you can better assess your opening after rehearsing it alone or before colleagues, staff, or friends. Rehearsing any speech makes the presenter more comfortable with the flow and gives a sense of what is natural and what won't work. Until you rehearse the opening, you won't know if it feels right or falls flat. The rehearsal takes effort. I often quote Samuel Johnson as having said, "What is easy is seldom excellent." Repeated practice frequently triggers creative thoughts that strengthen the opening and give you (and ultimately the jury) insights that would not occur but for rehearsals.

Rehearsal before others provides feedback. Reactions and comments will help you refine your strategy and improve your presentation. The ideal reaction is indignation on hearing the defendant's conduct. In a serious injury or death case, does the opening arouse empathy for the plaintiff? Does the typical listener understand the technology described in a complex case, or must it be further simplified?

Determine the Length of the Opening

The court frequently restricts the time for final argument but rarely imposes time limits on the opening. As a result, *you* must determine the proper length of the opening.

This can't be arbitrarily fixed. It depends on the complexity of the case, the attitude of the court, and the style of the speaker. A general rule is that an opening should not exceed 30 minutes in a minor case or one and a half hours in a major case.

There are exceptions for cases involving extremely complex issues, such as medical negligence, products liability, governmental liability, and commercial or securities lawsuits, which require more time for fact presentation and for technical explanations to the jury. Even here, however, remember that it is difficult for any jury to absorb information beyond a certain length of time.

USE OF LANGUAGE

Use Positive Language

The opening is a positive statement of your case, so use words that create a forceful impact. There are great distinctions in the power of words, and the trial lawyer must be sensitive to the nuances of language. "Collision" or "crash" says more than "accident," which connotes unavoidability. Active verbs such as "raced," "careened," "accelerated," or "sped" communicate movement and force and convey the effects of trauma on the body. Consult a thesaurus for the right shade of meaning.

Certain buzz words or phrases trigger emotion. "Three Mile Island," "Watergate," "The Holocaust," and "Chernobyl" are examples of strong images used commonly and repeatedly as metaphors and symbols in our society.

Avoid Legalese

Lawyers use legal shorthand on a daily basis and sometimes continue using it before the jury. For example, they say, "this is a rear-ender," "this is a strict liability case," or "this is a medical negligence action." Counsel and the court understand these terms, but the jurors may not, and they may not attach the same connotations to the words as lawyers do. Using legalese often conveys arrogance or betrays a lack of preparation.

Sometimes, use of legalese stems from counsel's nervousness before an audience or jury. An inexperienced lawyer may freeze up completely. Nervousness brings on formality, which produces technical terms or lawyer talk. Such regression into technical or legal lingo removes spontaneity from the case and makes the presentation dry and boring. It also reaffirms the layperson's impression of the legal system as complex and foreign. Make every effort to avoid this by using simple lay language. Heed the words of an old German philosopher: "We hear only what we understand."

Because the jury is resistant to legal language, be careful to support your case by other than legal conclusions. A layperson is not as impressed by the failure to obey a particular law as by a departure from sensible and reasonable behavior. The opening should focus on a driver's failing to pay attention to traffic, driving too fast, or following too closely, rather than on a technical violation of a vehicle code section. In most cases, the jurors won't recognize the provisions of law by name but will know the common sense rules for daily living. It is appropriate to refer to the legal principle, but in the opening the emphasis should always be on the defendant's conduct, rather than a technical violation of law.

STRUCTURE OF THE OPENING

Each case is different, so always using the same format suggests a lack of creativity and preparation. The opening should vary with the case, with a flexible order of topics as follows:

- a brief statement of the plaintiff's claim (the grabber),
- an introduction to the opening,
- the role of the jury in the case,
- the order of events in the trial and burden of proof,
- an introduction of the parties,
- the facts of liability,
- the elements of damages, and
- the wrap-up.

Introduce the Opening

Many lawyers have a stock beginning for their opening statement. It may be to talk about the lawyer's duty as an officer of the court, to explain how the opening fits into the trial, or to give some analogy of the opening statement as a road map, an airplane view, or the picture on the box of a jigsaw puzzle. Such introductions have become common and are almost traditional, but that does not mean they are particularly effective; in recent years, the standard introduction has fallen into disfavor. Jurors may have heard it before in other cases, and to them a stock approach will seem stilted and outdated. An introduction takes up time that could be more effectively spent on instructively persuading the jury.

Sometimes the court usurps the introduction, and that permits counsel to launch right into the substance of the opening without a prologue. Even without this introduction by the judge, you may prefer to skip the preliminaries and start off with a dramatic statement (see "The Grabber," *supra*).

Say that the opening is not an argument to convince—it is an overview or outline of the respective claims to assist the jury in understanding the case. Comment about potential problems with the availability of witnesses and the need to vary the chronological order of the trial. Anticipated interruptions during the trial may justify an overview to serve as a guide to the jury.

Describe the Role of the Jury

Explain the role of the jury in the trial process. It is important to elevate the jurors' notion of their function and to show them as judges of the facts. If this is done properly, jurors will understand that their job is important and that the case before them is significant and requires thoughtful and careful attention; fawning over the jurors or otherwise insulting their intelligence won't accomplish this. You must make sure during the opening that the jurors truly understand their function and appreciate the solemn and serious nature of their task in rendering judgment.

Give the Order of Events and Burden of Proof

It helps to give the jury, particularly an inexperienced panel, the schedule of events in the trial—who presents evidence first, what follows, and how the case concludes (again, be careful not to waste valuable persuasion time). The jury should appreciate that the order of events, in which the plaintiff goes first, is based on the burden of proof. Jurors today are misinformed because of television's depictions of trials. They have repeatedly heard the "beyond a reasonable doubt" standard, and you will need to explain the distinction between the civil and criminal burdens of proof. At this point you also have a chance to explain that you do not seek the defendant's punishment (in the usual civil case) but only fair compensation.

Liability is typically discussed first and damages last in the opening. In some cases, however, the order may be varied, depending on the facts and circumstances of the case. Is liability strong or weak? Is liability aggravated to the point where the jury will be incensed? Are the damages so overwhelming that they need not be detailed during the opening? Are the damages so powerful that they will carry a weak case on liability? These are all considerations when you are determining the order of presentation.

In very serious cases, plaintiff's counsel may choose to summarize damages first, then proceed to liability, and finally return for more damage-specific details.

Introduce the Players

A brief introduction of the parties should be part of every opening. Introduce each of the parties and their counsel, and explain their respective roles in the case. If it hasn't already been mentioned, discuss the role of the judge in ruling on legal matters and instructing the jury. These introductions and explanations are proper etiquette and help the jury understand who's who.

Recite the Facts of Liability

Your recitation of the facts of liability should be selective. Jurors must be given a clear understanding of the case, but your opening cannot be bogged down by the multitude of details. If you attempt to cover every detail of the case, your opening will be long, ponderous, and ineffective. It is easy to become immersed in details and not let the jury see the forest for the trees. While preparing the opening, remember your time limits, sift through the facts and details, and decide what the jury needs to know.

Regardless of the kind of case—automobile collision, construction injury, professional negligence, or products liability—the jury should understand the basics of liability. The factual setting, the parties, and what went wrong are what count—not every detail or the testimony of every witness.

One exception is when a particular witness or key document will be a focus of your case. The jury certainly should hear about this in the opening. The significance of the testimony or the exhibit need not be revealed, but the stage should be set so that the jury will pay particularly close attention to that point in the trial. For example, "You are going to hear about an important letter from this manufacturer dated July 15, 1988. You will want to read that letter carefully, listen to the evidence about it, and see for yourself whether or not the manufacturer was, in fact, aware of this problem."

If the case involves conflicts in testimony, the jury must understand that there will be such conflicts. It should also know why the evidence will support the plaintiff's version. It's a mistake to present your side of an event or issue and suggest that that is the only version, when you know there will be conflicting evidence presented by defendant's counsel. It is far better to beat the opposition to the punch in the opening and condition the jury to deciding in favor of the plaintiff. Anticipate the opposing party's defenses, and discuss them during your opening. This will defuse the impact of those defenses when they are brought up during the defendant's case.

Present the Elements of Damages

Care must be given to the factual presentation of damages in the opening statement. If the damages are catastrophic, they will speak for themselves and require little embellishment in the statement. The testimony in the trial will be far more dramatic than the words of counsel. For the opening, just tell the jury that the full evidence is forthcoming without revealing all the details.

In cases involving less serious injuries, a detailed treatment of damages in the opening is preferred. The jury must fully understand the nature of the injury and the resulting problems for the plaintiff, described in an interesting and understandable way. Without counsel's elaboration, jurors might categorize the injury or damages as insignificant. Providing an explanation of damages can help the jurors better understand a plaintiff's loss.

A strong opening statement on the issue of damages may prompt further settlement negotiations. However, you never want to overtry a case in the hopes of settlement: if the desired settlement does not result, your chances of winning the case and obtaining a good verdict will have been seriously hurt.

The presentation of general damages, including pain and suffering, disability, and impairment of earning capacity, must be handled carefully. A good method for presenting damages is to outline the proof about each of the plaintiff's problems and losses, such as physical pain, mental suffering, depression, embarrassment, anxiety, and loss of independence. Sometimes, however, it is more effective to select the plaintiff's most serious loss and provide evidence on that only. For example, a permanently disabled construction worker who cannot return to the job may experience a loss of self-esteem, dignity, and independence because of inability to provide for the family or to continue working. You may want to dwell on this aspect of the case and spend less time on other damages.

The panoply of available damages should be covered in the opening. A jury should be told of the plaintiff's right to recover lost earnings to date; medical expenses, both past and present; compensation for diminished earning capacity in the future; and compensation for general damages sustained by the plaintiff. Similarly, the elements of economic and noneconomic losses in a wrongful death action should be explained. This groundwork paves the way for the jurors' understanding of the evidence and appreciation of the variety and magnitude of the plaintiff's loss. Conversion of these losses into dollar amounts may be left until argument, but listing the elements of damages or separate amounts of special damages is appropriate during the opening.

Wrap It Up

The conclusion of the opening should cement your rapport with the jurors, emphasize their role in the case, and summarize your position.

A technique frequently used to establish a bond with the jurors is to state that all the promises you made in the opening will be fulfilled during the trial. Another option is to explain that you will have a final opportunity to clarify the evidence for them in the summation or to express appreciation for their patience in listening to your opening and to the evidence that will follow.

Your conclusion should leave the jury with a strong feeling that you have been fair, that you have confidence in the case, and that you expect the jury will decide in your favor.

DELIVERY OF THE OPENING

Be Aware of Your Style and Manner

An effective opening statement depends on sincerity of delivery. All lawyers differ—in abilities, appearance, voice, and manner—so the time-honored guideline to be yourself is absolutely valid. Any lawyer who tries to imitate another will usually fail, sounding contrived and insincere. Style and manner in the courtroom must be individual and honest. Master technique, then adapt what you've learned to who you are.

In former days, the expected style in court was for a lawyer to orate in a forceful and grand manner. The modern era, with its television portrayals of lawyers, has brought new sophistication to the public; jurors now appreciate a conversational tone, without the histrionics of a bygone era. When strong emphasis or emotion is needed, raise or lower your voice, use facial expressions, or change your rate of delivery or your tone of voice; however, nothing should be forced.

Most jurors react unfavorably to counsel's hostility or anger, unless there is good reason for the anger. There is a tendency among lawyers to attack the opposition at every opportunity, but the lawyer who constantly attacks, insults, or baits an adversary invites jury resentment and sympathy for the opponent. There is room for courtesy and civility in all litigation, and good manners are always appreciated by both judge and jury. This is particularly true in the opening statement because there has been little foundation for the case put before the jury, and a sharp attack on opposing counsel is seldom justified. Leave your personal disagreements with or opinion of opposing counsel outside the courtroom—the jurors should be privy to nothing that is not happening in front of them.

Many lawyers adopt distracting mannerisms or gestures when they speak to a jury. Some jangle money or keys in their pockets; others fuss with their face or hair, cover their mouths, or scratch themselves. Some lawyers gesticulate too vigorously, while others remain wooden and expressionless. Be aware of your physical mannerisms; your movements should be compatible with the tone of your opening and with your style. Avoid folding your arms, slouching, or using overly repetitive motions. Tell your story naturally.

Be Spontaneous

An apparently spontaneous, albeit well-rehearsed, presentation is by far the most effective opening. Despite your nervousness or stage fright, avoid reading your opening to a judge or jury. Reading the opening severs jury rapport and prevents the eye-to-eye contact with the jury that is critical to the projection of sincerity.

Don't worry about perfect syntax or remembering every word or phrase you planned to use; concentrate on conveying sincere belief in your cause. The speaker who extemporaneously expresses a strong view projects the sincerity that is the *sine qua non* of the trial lawyer. What counts is that the advocate really believes in the case and shows that belief. If you don't believe in the case, someone else should try it.

Don't Race Through

With an increasing emphasis by many courts on assembly-line justice, the perceived need for a quick trial and a correspondingly brief opening statement can be detrimental to your case. The opening will suffer if it is too sketchy, and it is a mistake to abbreviate it by sacrificing facts and nuances necessary for persuasion.

Even though relatively few judges limit counsel's time for the opening, lawyers nevertheless worry about the court's emphasis on efficiency and may cut the opening short to accomodate the court. In the absence of a direct time restriction imposed by the court, allow your opening the time you think it needs.

Consider Your Staging

Many lawyers like the safe haven of a lectern. They station themselves at their post and remain fixed throughout the opening statement. This technique should be avoided unless it is required by the rules of court. Though the podium may lend you the aura of a learned professor, it imposes a barrier to communication with the jury that outweighs any practical advantage.

Psychological studies show that all people subconsciously establish barriers to preserve their space and have a need for others to remain outside. Therefore, avoid getting too close to the jury, leaning on the jury rail, or violating the jury's personal area within the jury box. Television and film portrayals to the contrary, a safety zone of three to four feet from the jury is about right.

Another form of intrusion is by voice or manner, so avoid speaking too loudly or gesturing too vigorously. Also, the nervous pacing adopted by some lawyers, who are never still and are always moving about the courtroom, will likely annoy some jurors.

Maintain Eye Contact

It is important to maintain eye contact with the jury. Many people believe that the eyes reveal true feelings; the jurors size up your sincerity, consciously or unconsciously, by whether you make eye contact with them during the opening.

The reaction of jurors, revealed by their eye contact, is also important. Jurors cannot speak, but their eyes, body language, and facial expressions signal the advocate. A grimace when the opening covers a key point of the defendant's conduct or the reaction in their eyes when your claim for damages is discussed sends you a strong message. Be careful not to misinterpret these reactions, as the trial lawyer never really knows what a juror is thinking.

During opening, plaintiffs' lawyers tend to concentrate on jurors who appear sympathetic to the plaintiff's case. This can alienate other members of the panel who are not receiving eye contact, particularly if an attractive juror is singled out, and other members (particularly of the same sex) resent the attention given. If a juror seems sympathetic to your side, direct your attention to those not yet convinced who still need to be persuaded.

Inexperienced lawyers often react to distractions in the courtroom, glance at the courtroom clock, or turn to watch any activity in court. Counsel should be oblivious to anything other than the presentation and the jurors. If you cannot resist such distractions, neither will the jurors.

Use Voice Control

The tone of the opening need not be argumentative or contentious, and considerable impact may be made by a low voice volume and gentle manner. This approach rarely draws an objection, even when the content and language of the opening are forceful and aggressive. The days of the bombastic, overly aggressive advocate are past, and a low-key, intelligent presentation is in favor.

Jurors sometimes have difficulty hearing lawyers and witnesses in the courtroom. Some lawyers, out of nervousness or inexperience, drop their voice level at the start of a trial, and particularly in the opening. Your speaking voice should be moderate in volume and clearly audible.

It is not necessary to be the greatest orator of the day to win a case. Many effective trial lawyers are not spectacular speakers but successfully communicate their causes through thorough preparation and sincere delivery.

Use Emotion and Drama

There may be greater opportunities to express emotion in final argument, but it is a mistake to assume that strong feelings should be eliminated from the opening statement. Controlled indignation, anger, or compassion should be shown either for clients or against the defendant in the course of an opening. Emotion, an important part of any speech, is conveyed by counsel's appropriate language, sincere delivery, and intensity. It should never be forced.

Avoid Objections

The most common objections to the opening statement are that counsel is

- making an argument, rather than overviewing the evidence;
- referring to inadmissible evidence;
- instructing the jury on principles of law; and
- referring to irrelevant and prejudicial matters.

Should the opening slide into any of these areas, objections often result. A highly prejudicial comment could even be the basis for a mistrial, if the comment is particularly flagrant and the court cannot correct the error by an admonition or instruction.

A properly prepared opening will draw few objections that interrupt the rhythm and flow of the opening with sidebar conferences or wrangling with opposing counsel. Your purpose should be to preserve the atmosphere you are trying to create; objections frustrate that purpose. Even though you may win the minor legal skirmishes triggered by the objections, the presentation of your case will have been disrupted.

Do not argue or quarrel with the court if it sustains an objection to the opening. Courtroom etiquette throughout the trial requires this. More importantly, jurors do not like counsel to argue with the judge and may well react with negative feelings toward the arguing lawyer. In the opening, you can simply drop the subject and hint that it will be revisited later. For example, say "Very well, Your Honor, we can leave that until the evidence" or "We can return to that later."

Be wary of drawing objections for comments that fall within prohibited areas. Examples include the financial circumstances of the parties (or their families); prior acts of misconduct; appeals to race, nationality, or religion of a party; the personal beliefs of counsel; the wealth or poverty of a litigant; the presence or absence of liability insurance; or evidence that will not be admissible and is highly prejudicial. Though these topics may later become relevant, it is wise to avoid them in the opening.

Repeated objections to an adversary's opening may offend the judge or jury or provoke objections to the plaintiff's case, particularly if the grounds are that the statement is argumentative or that counsel refers to the law, as these points are easily handled by defense counsel. More serious is a prejudicial reference, which calls for objection, admonition, or a motion for mistrial.

If your case has been seriously hurt by opposing counsel's errors, do not hesitate to move for a mistrial. A formal motion is necessary to establish a record for appeal, as well as to make the judge sensitive to the plaintiff's feelings on the issue. Many lawyers do not preserve their record in the opening and should do so.

Give thought in advance to how you will handle potential objections. If the basis for the objection is argument, and the court rules in your favor, you may repeat the statement or place it in context, since it has been approved by the court. If the court rules against you, use curative language, such as "the evidence will show . . . ," "we will establish that . . . ," or "the evidence will prove. . . ." Many judges will then allow the identical statement that drew the objection, because the preliminary statement has made it unobjectionable.

This technique, however, is frequently overused and can generate a negative reaction. Jurors may resent this form of game playing and become irked if you repeat a pattern of magic words throughout the opening statement to get argumentative or borderline statements before the jury.

COMMON ERRORS

Keep in mind the old Japanese proverb: "He who makes the first bad move always loses the game." A weak opening can set the stage for loss of the case. Some problems in the opening have been discussed; additional common errors are mentioned below.

Avoid Argumentative Openings

The common rule is that argument is not permitted in the opening statement. However, the opening *is* argument and an inherent part of the process of persuasion during the trial.

The most frequent objection to the opening is that counsel is "arguing". Cases provide little guidance as to what constitutes argument, but a rule of thumb is that an interpretation or characterization of the facts will be sustained as "argumentative". Judges often draw a distinction between presenting the facts, which is permissible, and presenting *your theory* of the facts, which is not.

The opening should be given in an effectively persuasive manner, against which no technical objection can be sustained. This can be accomplished by careful word selection, a subdued manner, and proper volume level. When the opening is quiet and rational, it often escapes objection.

Don't Overstate Your Case

A dangerous error in the opening statement is exaggeration or overstatement. It can destroy a good case, turn the jury off, or diminish the damages.

Plaintiff's counsel, having the burden of proof, must be particularly careful about breaking any promises made in the opening. Rest assured that defense counsel will raise any breach during argument. Don't make statements you can't support with evidence. Some lawyers go beyond the anticipated testimony to make grandiose predictions about the case. If your promised evidence does not materialize during trial, you will suffer a severe loss of credibility.

Such a failure to support predictions usually occurs with damages, but it can also happen with liability. For example, claiming that the defendant (whether a truck driver in an auto case or a doctor in a professional negligence case) was not just negligent but criminally negligent places a greater burden on the plaintiff than the law does. A good case may wind up with a hung jury or a defense verdict because the lawyer's opening set out a standard of proof greater than that required for a favorable verdict. Overstating your case, on either the liability or damage issue, is dangerous.

Avoid Weakeners

Many judges routinely explain to the jury before the opening that counsel's remarks are not evidence. Nevertheless, counsel will often repeat and, in fact, stress this fact during the opening. It is a prime example of how lawyers are drawn to "weakeners" that serve to deprecate their case. Often, plaintiff's counsel begins by telling the jury that the opening must not be accepted if it is not supported by the evidence, thus suggesting that the plaintiff's version of the case may be inaccurate. You cannot convey conviction in your case if you undermine your own knowledge of the facts. Jurors might well conclude that the lawyer who is not sure of the case is not worth their attention. It is far more impressive for you to display an air of confidence and to use positive statements, demonstrating that you are certain of the case and the evidence.

Instruct on the Law

The handling of applicable law in the opening is troublesome. Counsel who blithely enter into a discussion of the law governing the case generally draw an immediate objection that will probably be sustained. Judges are quick to rule that instructions on the law are the province of the court and not counsel. Yet it is often appropriate and sometimes essential to cover the legal principles that govern the case.

How can this problem be solved? Practice varies from jurisdiction to jurisdiction, but most judges permit reference to legal principles if the reference is brief and accurate. Once the factual conduct of a party is discussed, it is then appropriate to comment that this conduct violated a particular law or regulation. For example, "You will learn that this omission by the defendant violated the law requiring a contractor to provide a safe place to work." In another case, fair comment might be "The driver failed to come to a full stop and look before entering the intersection, as required by our state vehicle code." The court will usually accept a statement that the defendant failed to act in accordance with the law and that the specifics of that law will be discussed later by counsel (in argument), as well as by the court (in instructions).

It benefits counsel to set the stage and point out that matters of law are handled by the judge, who will provide a full explanation of the law at the conclusion of the evidence. If you make it clear that your reference to the law will be a brief statement to help the jurors understand the issues, you lessen the chance of interruption or admonition by the court. If no reference is made to the law of the case, the jury will remain unaware of the applicable requirements of law and the significant effect of the acts or omissions of the defendant.

SELECTED ASPECTS OF THE OPENING

Exclude Witnesses When Necessary

One decision deserving special consideration is whether to exclude witnesses from the courtroom when critical testimony is described during the opening statement. If you consult with the court before the opening, most judges will grant a motion to exclude when there is a valid reason for doing so.

It may be a good strategy to have prospective witnesses wait outside the courtroom during the opening to impress upon the jury that their testimony is spontaneous and not prompted by the script of the opening. Alternatively, your witnesses may gain confidence in your position and see where their testimony fits into the overall picture if they hear the opening statement. The strategy you use will depend on the case and the individual witnesses.

Preserve the Record

The opening statement should be transcribed as a safeguard. Though some courts do not routinely have the court reporter report the opening since it is not evidence, a specific request will generally be granted. The transcript keeps the defendant's lawyer in line, preserves the plaintiff's record for appeal, and provides an important basis for argument.

If opposing counsel misstates the evidence or makes a claim that is not established during trial, excerpts from the transcript can be powerful tools in final argument.

Use Visual Aids

Studies show that more than 50 percent of the total persuasion message in court is nonverbal, with less than 10 percent being purely verbal or limited to the content of the words being spoken. Nonverbal communication dominates, and visual aids along with spoken words make a far deeper impression than words alone. Visual aids should be used throughout the trial, particularly during the opening statement, to assist the jury in grasping and understanding the case.

Practice varies markedly in different courts or jurisdictions as to the use of visual aids in the opening. Most judges require that they give approval before you may use a prepared exhibit in the opening.

Using an unapproved exhibit on the assumption that it will be admitted into evidence later can trigger an objection from counsel and a ruling from the court that disrupts the presentation. If a particular exhibit is critical and considered necessary for the opening, advance approval by the trial judge or stipulation by counsel will smooth the process.

Using a blackboard or a paper pad in the opening avoids the need to obtain permission from the court. You can use the pad or blackboard in a variety of ways during the opening: to draw a diagram of the parties in a multiparty lawsuit, renditions of collision scenes, or diagrams of physiology; or to list technical and medical definitions, key words, or damages.

You may choose to postpone using an exhibit until later in the trial or to leave the full exposition of damages to the argument. Any diagram or sketch you make during opening can be used in the final argument if it is later admitted into evidence or used for illustrative purposes.

Make every effort in the opening to use exhibits that will be presented during the case in chief. Some judges will permit exhibits not yet admitted into evidence to be shown during the opening, while others are rigidly against this. Key physical evidence such as photographs, models, skeletons, and parts of cars or machinery should be shown to the jury during the opening statement, if possible.

Meet the Defense

A well-prepared opening, besides reciting the facts vital to the plaintiff's case, will anticipate the important defenses and meet them. In an auto case, a claim of contributory negligence based on the plaintiff's speed, failure to stop, insufficient braking, or violation of right-of-way must be recognized and refuted in the opening. Counsel should factually describe the plaintiff's conduct as being reasonable and free of fault. A jury likes to see problems acknowledged and logically resolved during the opening.

Do not place weak defense positions in your opening statement. The thrust of the opening must be on the positive side of your case; focusing on minimal defenses may dilute the opening's impact.

Pull Bad Teeth

Every case has sensitive areas that can affect the outcome. Damaging admissions, inconsistent statements, prior bad conduct, drug or alcohol abuse, or a criminal record can be addressed in the summation, but by then it may be too late to defuse the effects of such evidence. When you handle these issues in the opening statement, you pull the tooth before it infects the case during trial.

In the opening statement, consider addressing any negative aspects of your case that might be fair game for opposing counsel. If your client wasn't wearing a seat belt or had a pre-existing medical problem, you can beat the defense to the punch by covering the issue in your opening. The subject can be presented your way, with your perspective. For example, if the plaintiff had a prior injury that may be admissible in trial, the question will arise whether you should bring this out in the opening, wait for the evidence, or rely on argument. Most experienced lawyers feel such issues should be met head-on in the opening. The plaintiff's lawyer might say, "You will hear that Frank had a neck injury ten years earlier. It was fairly minor, compared with this one. He saw a doctor for two weeks, recovered, and was never troubled again. We are sure you will place it in perspective and not let an injury long since recovered from divert you from the issues of this case."

Humanize the Plaintiff

For jurors to appreciate the injuries and damages of the plaintiff, they must understand how the plaintiff has been affected. The plaintiff's normal recreational and daily activities, capacity to earn a living, and ability to enjoy life all become relevant, and the jury must be able to identify with the plaintiff's problems. Once jurors empathize with the plaintiff's plight from the opening statement, they may continue to empathize during the rest of the trial.

The plaintiff should be introduced during the opening, be present in the courtroom (depending on the case and your strategy), and be addressed by name rather than by "plaintiff". Provide background and personal information: describe the plaintiff's goals and aspirations, as well as achievements, abilities, and contributions to family, friends, work, or community. The plaintiff is thus *humanized* and made more appealing and acceptable to the jurors—a person to whom they can relate.

Should You Mention the Amount You're Seeking?

A dilemma faced by the plaintiff's lawyer in the opening is whether to mention the amount of compensation sought. There is no set solution to this problem.

Some lawyers believe in preconditioning the jurors at the earliest opportunity to help them understand how much money is involved. Others feel it is disadvantageous to discuss dollar amounts in the opening statement, since no foundation has yet been laid. Some jurors may be turned off. The latter school saves the translation of damages into dollars for the argument, after the jurors have heard the entire case.

This decision, like other opening statement strategies, will depend on the jurisdiction, the case being tried, your experience, and above all, your individual style.

CONCLUSION

Prepare your opening carefully; rehearse it aloud many times in front of others and alone. Its impact will remain with the jurors throughout the trial. It will be carried with them into their deliberations and reflected in their verdict.

CASE IN CHIEF

Paul N. Luvera

INTRODUCTION

The phrase "case in chief" refers to that portion of the trial in which the plaintiff's attorney presents witnesses and evidence to support the claim asserted. The phrase is apt because this part of the trial obviously is important.

The plaintiff must carry the burden of proof with sufficient evidence to avoid an involuntary dismissal of the case. Apart from this legal requirement, the plaintiff, using principles of psychology, must capture the jurors' minds and persuade them of the righteousness of the claim or, in all probability, lose the case. You would be foolish to think the case will be won on cross-examination of the defendant's witnesses or evidence withheld until after the defendant's case is presented.

Every attorney prepares and presents a personal injury case differently, depending on style and thought process. Many factors can influence you, including the size and location of your practice and the nature of the case. This chapter will identify areas that you ought to consider in processing a personal injury case for a plaintiff. It is impossible in one chapter to adequately detail all the ways to handle such a case. Nor is there a "right way" or an only way to prepare and try a case.

In addition, because of space constraints, it is not possible to describe the different approaches to use depending on the type of case involved. For example, a medical negligence case is not handled the same way as an automobile collision case. Therefore, these materials discuss fundamentals and principles of preparing and trying a general negligence case.

PLAN THE TRIAL

You should be formulating a trial plan for the case from the time the client first comes into the office until the moment the trial begins. It is important to identify the issues in the case and express them in very straightforward, simple language. You should develop the theme of the case early as well. It should be a simple statement that most people already accept as true that can be applied to the case.

To develop the trial plan, it is essential to have a grasp of the facts. With a clear understanding of the facts, you should be able to focus on the important issues and concepts.

It helps to talk to lay people and fellow attorneys to get other views. Examination of a file of a similar case handled by another attorney may be helpful.

Another source of information is a "focus group." Videotaped, written, or oral presentations outlining the salient facts in your case are given to a group of six to eight people, with a request for their reactions.

Reactions can be given in a general discussion or in the form of written answers to questions submitted after the presentation. Frequently, a group will quickly identify issues, some of which you may not have recognized initially. Such a discussion may also refine themes.

You can facilitate the focus group on an informal basis or hire a person trained in this kind of study to conduct the group more scientifically.

Variations of the focus group concept include the "mock trial." In that setting, portions of the plaintiff's and defendant's cases are presented in a mini-trial format to a jury of objective people. Usually, this presentation involves brief opening statements about the main issues, followed by short presentations of evidence, either by actual witnesses or persons serving that role, and concludes with a short summation. The jury then deliberates, as would a regular jury, in arriving at a verdict. By studying the deliberation process, you can get valuable information about the case. This type of presentation can also be done informally by you or formally by a trained professional.

Another way to get case information is through surveys, such as a telephone survey in which a simple issue is identified and a person's reaction is requested. A variation is a written survey distributed to a group of people who answer specific questions about the case. Both approaches can be done formally or informally.

It is important that the plaintiff's claims in a tort case be reduced to a minimum number of easily understood, simply expressed statements. For example, claims in a suit involving a negligently designed highway can be defined as follows:

- The state knew that a hazardous curbing had been installed along the edge of the highway that trapped the tires of cars, but the state failed to either remove the curbing or erect a guardrail.
- The state knew that the design of the highway caused water to accumulate, making driving hazardous, but failed to correct the problem or warn drivers of the hazard.
- The state knew this was a hazardous location for drivers but failed to warn or protect the driving public.

There might be several variations on a theme for such a case. For example,

- When it comes to safety, one should not be penny wise and pound foolish.
- When it comes to the safety of the public, an ounce of prevention is worth a pound of cure.

The contentions of both sides and the themes of the case should be written on a sheet of paper and kept in front of you at all times so that you can focus on the theme and the issues throughout the trial. Clear, simple contentions should be emphasized, and the plaintiff's themes should be repeated.

ORGANIZE FOR TRIAL

Preparation for the trial in chief requires some thought as to how best to organize the documents and other materials so that they are easily available throughout the trial. You must enter the courtroom with an organized system for quickly locating exhibits, examination outlines for witnesses, and anything else that will be needed to show the judge and jury that you are prepared. Judges and juries tend to perceive a well-organized lawyer as well prepared and knowledgeable. The attorney who can keep track of what is happening in the courtroom and locate material quickly stands out.

Most attorneys in trial still make notes on yellow pads surrounded by loose papers spread over counsel's table. Should a question arise as to what a witness said, or should some information be needed immediately, the attorney will frantically flip the pages of the yellow tablets or search through the papers scattered about, while the jury and judge look on impatiently.

Experienced trial lawyers avoid this confusion by using a trial notebook—a simple, inexpensive, but extremely effective system for organizing information during trial. A trial notebook requires these materials:

- a three-ring, letter-size notebook with a three-inch spine;
- ten blank dividers to which tabs may be attached;
- small overlapping dividers imprinted with the numbers one to thirty-one, originally designed for bookkeeping purposes, to represent the days of the month;
- dividers imprinted with the letters of the alphabet; and
- lined, three-hole punched notebook paper, for taking notes during the trial.

These materials, plus the forms presented in this article, are the basic ingredients of a trial notebook.

The trial notebook should be separated into sections by dividers labeled as follows:

(1) Things To Do During Trial
(2) Trial Outline
(3) Jury
(4) Opening Statements
(5) Witnesses
(6) Exhibits and Motions
(7) Rebuttal
(8) Instructions
(9) Argument
(10) Law

Internally, the notebook should be organized as follows:

Things To Do During Trial

Many matters that come up during a trial will remind you of things to be done, witnesses to be called, and laws to be briefed. It is important to have a single place where you can keep notes of these matters to prevent them from being overlooked. Therefore, this section should come first in the notebook.

Trial Outline

The divider marked "Trial Outline" should be used to designate a form that lists the names of witnesses in the order in which they probably will be called. Spaces are provided for noting the approximate time when the witnesses will be called and how long their testimony will probably take. When completely filled, this form provides an approximate schedule for the conduct of the trial.

Each witness listed for the plaintiff should be identified by a number corresponding to one of the 31 numerical dividers. Each of the defendant's witnesses should be identified by a letter corresponding to one of the alphabetical dividers. The trial outline immediately locates the dividers under which material about a witness can be found. This is particularly helpful in a case calling for many witnesses.

The Jury

The contents of the "Jury" section should depend on jurisdiction procedure. Typically, it should consist of a form with boxes corresponding to the number of jurors in the jury box.

The portion for jury challenges by attorneys provides a permanent record of that information. Voir dire questions to prospective jurors should also be kept behind this divider.

Opening Statements

The substance of the opening statements by each party should be outlined in the section marked "Opening Statements." The major assertions made by opposing counsel can be noted with comments. A separate sheet should contain the outline of your opening statement.

Witnesses

All material about your first witness should be placed behind divider 1, if you are the plaintiff's counsel, or divider A, if you are the defendant's counsel. The following witnesses should be assigned subsequent numbers or letters. Although the order in which opposing counsel will present witnesses cannot be predetermined, their names can be discovered. They can then be assigned numbers or letters.

All witness sections should include

- a summary of testimony,
- any exhibits that will be introduced through the witness,
- questions that should be asked,
- deposition testimony,
- oral and/or written statements, and
- other relevant information or documents.

At the end of each section, notebook paper should be inserted for additional comments about the witnesses.

Exhibits and Motions

Offered exhibits and trial motions should be noted on forms under the heading of "Exhibits and Motions".

As an exhibit is introduced, a record should be made of

- the name of the party offering the exhibit,
- the exhibit number,
- a description of the exhibit, and
- the court's ruling on admissibility.

This section should also contain pertinent information about trial motions, indicating

- the nature of the motion,
- its grounds,
- by whom it was made, and
- whether it was granted.

This material will be especially significant should counsel move for a new trial.

Rebuttal

Information about witnesses to be called in rebuttal and the substance of their testimony should be kept under this heading. Ideas for rebuttal should also be filed here.

Instructions

Exceptions taken by both parties to the instructions of the court should be recorded under this section. This material will also be helpful if a motion for a new trial is filed.

Argument

Ideas and materials gathered for final argument, as well as the outline prepared for that part of the trial, should be filed here.

Law

Legal memoranda written in anticipation of trial, briefs filed in the case, and citations of decisions that may become relevant should be collected in this final section.

The trial notebook is inexpensive to put together and easy to use. The advantages are substantial. By merely flipping a divider, you can immediately find necessary material. Such information is always literally at your fingertips.

OUTLINE PROOF

No trial moves according to plan; every case has unexpected interruptions and problems. Nevertheless, you should never enter the courtroom without a plan for trial.

To develop this kind of plan, the various aspects of the case in chief must be reviewed. The following is an example of a checklist for preparing a trial plan or schedule.

MAIN THEME OF CASE: ______________________

A. Proof of Damages

1. Hospital Records
   - 1.1 medical records administrator needed
   - 1.2 collateral source removed

2. Medical Bills
   - 2.1 witnesses identified
   - 2.2 collateral source removed

3. Wage Loss
   - 3.1 witness to identify

4. Auto Repair Bill
    4.1 witness to identify

5. Injury Exhibits
    5.1 medical illustrations
    5.2 X rays; positive prints
    5.3 photos—cars
    5.4 photos—scene
    5.5 photos—client
    5.6 model

6. Expert Witnesses
    6.1 physician
    6.2 chiropractor
    6.3 physical therapist
    6.4 economist

7. Nonexpert Witnesses
    7.1 client and spouse

8. Damages Witnesses (see above)
    8.1 before and after
    8.2 other
    8.3 conferences arranged

B. Liability Evidence

1. Photos at Scene
    1.1 diagram
    1.2 officers' notebooks
    1.3 models
    1.4 video
    1.5 others

2. Expert Witnesses
    2.1 police
    2.2 accident reconstructionist
    2.3 vocational rehabilitation counselor
    2.4 human factors expert

3. Nonexpert Witnesses
    3.1 eyewitnesses
    3.2 client

3.3 lay witnesses
3.4 other
3.5 conferences arranged

C. Trial

1. Issuances
   1.1 subpoenas
   1.2 notices of attendance issued

2. Motions *in Limine*

3. Depositions Summaries

4. Jury
   4.1 instructions
   4.2 panel investigated

5. Briefs
   5.1 trial
   5.2 special evidence

6. Opening Statement

7. Outlines
   7.1 direct examination
   7.2 cross-examination
   7.3 summation

8. Exhibits

9. Other

Depending on the complexity of the case, a more detailed overall outline may be necessary. Some checklist or plan of action should, however, be used in every case.

DETERMINE ORDER OF PROOF

Organization of the witnesses and the proof to be introduced at trial is important. Determine which exhibits will be necessary. Next, identify the witnesses who will authenticate those exhibits or with whom the exhibits will be used.

Review the discovery material to make sure that all relevant exhibits are ready for use at trial. The material should be organized and filed so that it can be easily located; an expansion file with individual file folders labeled as to the contents may help. The expansion file can be divided into categories such as trial exhibits, damages, and liability. When you need the material, that file can be pulled.

A trial outline, as previously discussed, is an effective organizing technique. The outline approximates when the various witnesses will be called and the overall length of the trial. In this way, you have a script for the trial and can better coordinate witnesses' attendance at trial. The more complex the case, the more complex the outline. A simple trial outline form appears in the appendix to this chapter.

OUTLINE WITNESS EXAMINATION

You should have an outline for each witness to be called at trial. This outline should identify the witness and indicate whether a subpoena has been issued, whether a deposition has been taken, what questions should be asked, and what exhibits need be discussed with the witness. You should create a form for this purpose and place it in the trial notebook; the witness's deposition, statements, and other material relating to that witness as well as an outline for further examination should be put behind the form.

This is the place to make notes about the witness as the trial progresses. Important matters and issues that come up through other testimony about which the witness should be questioned can be noted here. An example of a witness examination outline sheet is in the appendix to this chapter.

SCHEDULE THE WITNESSES

The order of calling witnesses differs for all cases. In some cases, the order will be determined by witness availability. This often occurs with experts.

The basic rule is to try to begin and end with strong witnesses. The same principle applies to each day of trial. The first and last witnesses should be strong whenever possible; follow the psychological laws of primacy and recency.

Scheduling witnesses will be determined, in part, by whether you are following the traditional procedure of first proving liability and then damages. There are cases where liability is weak and damages exceedingly strong; then, damages might be proved first. In a multiplaintiff automobile case, a traditional liability-first approach might be as follows:

- *The investigating officer.* The officer sets the scene, establishes liability issues, identifies diagrams and photographs, and describes injuries observed at the scene.
- *Eyewitnesses.* The eyewitnesses substantiate the officer's testimony or testify about their own observations of the collision.
- *Expert liability witnesses.* Experts on accident reconstruction or other liability-related areas are often called as the last liability witnesses since they are generally regarded as strong witnesses.
- *Medical records witnesses.* If necessary, these witnesses introduce into evidence documentation such as hospital records and medical bills.
- *Treating health care providers.* The physicians, chiropractors, physical therapists, and any other care providers relate their medical treatment of the plaintiffs.
- *Damage witnesses.* Witnesses establish wage losses or other claimed damages, including damage to the vehicle.
- *Lay witnesses.* Witnesses who knew the plaintiffs before and after the accident or who know about the effect of the injuries on them would be called to complete the picture.
- *The spouses.* If the plaintiffs are married, the spouses testify to the effect of injuries on their relationship.
- *The plaintiffs.* Usually, the plaintiffs are the last witnesses called, particularly if they will be exceptionally good.

Avoid repetitive witnesses. For example, lay witnesses testifying to the effect of injury on the plaintiffs should not all cover the same matters. Each should have a different story to tell and give different insight as to the effect of the injuries.

DETERMINE EVIDENCE TO BE INTRODUCED AND SEQUENCE OF PRESENTATION

The evidence or proof introduced as well as the sequence of introducing it will depend on the availability of witnesses, the complexity and nature of the case, and your style. In an automobile case, however, consider some other areas of proof.

Get the client's medical history to distinguish two facts. First, if no medical condition existed before the accident, this uneventful history must be established through testimony or documentary evidence. Second, where a medical condition existed before the accident, the condition may have been aggravated. All substantiating medical charts and records should be organized and ready for introduction into evidence.

The health care treatment received is also important. Prepare a list of medications, prescription numbers, dates prescribed and taken, prices, numbers of pills, and the purpose of each medication. Some attorneys have their clients keep the medicine bottles, and they introduce a sack of empty bottles to show the quantity of medication required. The pharmacist might be called to identify the purposes of the medication and to emphasize the amount of medication required for these injuries.

Consider calling the plaintiff's physical therapist. Frequently, in a soft-tissue neck injury case, the physical therapist has seen the client more often than the physician. The therapist can describe the muscle spasms and the patient's pain and suffering better than the doctor.

If an ambulance was involved, the ambulance driver may be called to testify regarding the injuries and impact. Where there was some damage to the vehicles, the tow truck driver can talk about the vehicle damage. The auto mechanic might be a witness—to identify the repair bill and to discuss the nature and extent of the property damage.

Experts, such as reconstruction experts or physicists, are available to talk about physical forces involved in automobile accidents.

Lay witnesses frequently are the most important witnesses in injury cases. Jurors relate better to such witnesses and identify more with them than with other witnesses, particularly experts. Prepare lay witnesses to testify to their personal observations of the extent of the plaintiff's injury.

Limit the testimony of this type of witness to one example or one subject. You might say to such a witness, "Were you at a picnic on June 3, 1982, where you observed the plaintiff?" People on your client's Christmas card list, her hairdresser, the supermarket clerk, church friends, fellow workers, and other people might substantiate your client's disabling injuries. Again, remember to avoid witnesses who repeat each other.

Sometimes the best way to prepare such witnesses is to hold a group meeting attended by all of them. Often, one witness's story may refresh the memory of another witness at such a meeting. Also, you can select the best witnesses from the group.

Photographs or videos of the client taken before the accident may demonstrate the client's preinjury physical fitness and ability to do activities. Some lawyers go to the plaintiff's workplace and videotape others doing the work the plaintiff can no longer do.

You must help the jury understand the anatomy and physiology involved in the plaintiff's injury. This can be accomplished through demonstrative aids such as medical illustrations that graphically show key areas such as muscles, ligaments, tendons, nerves, and blood supply. Only when the jurors fully appreciate the many injuries possible in a collision will they accept the extent of injury claimed by the plaintiff.

Generally, the case should be presented clearly and simply. It should be interesting and not tedious. Repetition is a persuasive technique, but it can backfire if overused.

PREPARE DEMONSTRATIVE EVIDENCE

An important part of the case in chief is demonstrative evidence. Many lawyers do not know the basics of using demonstrative evidence and the foundations needed to introduce such material into evidence. Many publications that deal with those subjects are available.

The importance of demonstrative evidence to persuade people is beyond dispute; numerous psychological studies demonstrate that when people hear statements, they do not remember as well as when they both see and hear statements. A photograph, model, or illustration will enhance the jurors' retention of important information.

Therefore, drawings or illustrations explaining oral testimony are essential for the jury to completely understand the facts in any trial. These may be schematic drawings by a police officer or other witnesses or illustrations specifically prepared for trial use.

Professional illustrators can prepare accurate drawings or illustrations. Maps, graphs, engineering diagrams, and other similar real evidence are often used.

The standard for the introduction of illustrations is (1) will the illustration assist the jury in understanding the facts of the case or (2) will the illustration assist the witness on the stand in testifying.

Whether the illustrative drawing was prepared before or during trial, it must be marked by the clerk for identification as an exhibit.

For many years, trial lawyers have submitted photographs and X rays to assist the jury in understanding the facts of the case. Courts have long favored the use of such evidence. Positive prints and transparencies from X-ray film projected onto a screen can be very persuasive.

Models can be prepared and used at trial as illustrations or accurate scale models. The authentication requirement is the same for a model as for other exhibits.

To lay a proper foundation for the introduction of a model, establish (1) the qualifications of the person who prepared the model; (2) the method used in preparing the model; (3) the knowledge of the person who prepared the model regarding the facts about the object shown; (4) the comparison in accuracy between the model and the object represented; (5) an explanation of what the model shows; and (6) whether the use of the model is material, relevant, and useful in connection with the case.

Objects reasonably similar to or illustrative of a matter involved in a lawsuit may also be introduced. Examples are anatomical skeletons or a grinding wheel such as the one that has exploded and is no longer available.

Real evidence, such as a murder weapon in a criminal case, requires identification to establish that the exhibit being introduced is, in fact, the original weapon, in the same condition as it was at the time of the alleged crime. The introduction of such exhibits is discretionary with the court.

In a personal injury case, hospital and/or medical records are usually introduced into evidence. Authenticated records must comply with the Uniform Business Records as Evidence Act, where adopted. Otherwise, the Best Evidence rule applies, and the foundation must be laid for the introduction of such documents.

When such records are offered, examine them carefully in advance to determine if they should be admitted and whether there is objectionable material (e.g., opinions or conclusions of the physician) in the records that should be deleted before admission into evidence. You can get inexpensive publications to help you understand the contents of hospital and medical records.

It might be appropriate to exhibit the body of the injured plaintiff in a personal injury case to prove the nature and extent of the plaintiff's injuries.

Experiments or tests can be used as evidence in a trial. They can be done beforehand and offered during trial, or they can be made in the courtroom itself.

Experiment or test results are generally admissible if the tests were conducted under conditions substantially or reasonably similar to conditions that are the subject matter of the case on trial. Whether such similarity of conditions exists is a matter for the trial court's discretion. To introduce evidence of such experiments, you must lay an extensive foundation to establish the similarity of conditions. The results must not mislead or confuse the jury. Generally, expert knowledge is necessary to conduct an experiment or test; the expert then must testify concerning the experiment.

Experiments done in the courtroom pose considerable risk since results cannot be controlled. To justify admission, the experiment must accurately reproduce the original event and should help the jury understand the subject matter in dispute. The opposing side may request that the demonstration or experiment first be done outside the jury's presence. All of this falls within the court's discretion.

Viewing the place where an injury has occurred has been approved in civil cases, subject to the court's discretion. Where there have been changes in the condition and appearance of the scene, the court should advise the jury of such changes. You should carefully evaluate whether such a view is advantageous to your case.

An evidentiary object may be brought to the courthouse area for the jury to view. For example, a wrecked automobile or an object too large to get into the courtroom could be brought to the parking lot. In such a case, you must get the court's permission, and witnesses must lay a proper foundation as to the object sought to be viewed.

Many possible demonstrative aids can be used in an injury case. Numerous books have been written on using such evidence.

Using Videotape

In 1927, a speech by President Herbert Hoover was telecast as an experiment from Washington, D.C., to New York City. Since that time, television has become a major medium of mass communication. For years the technology of television remained complex and expensive. Recent advances in video recording, however, have replaced cumbersome, costly stationary equipment with relatively inexpensive portable videotape recorders and videotape cameras.

Videotapes are useful to show the jury objects that are too big to bring to the courtroom or that provide access problems. Videotapes are also used to record, among other things, depositions, the taking of statements from witnesses, and views of an injured plaintiff as a demonstration in the courtroom.

Using an Overhead Projector

The overhead projector allows you to use physical exhibits effectively in the courtroom. The basic operating principle of all projectors is the same: A transparent sheet of film (containing the material to be exhibited) is laid horizontally on a glass plate, which is specially ground for even distribution of the light source underneath. The light shines through the transparency to a mirror-and-lens system suspended by an arm directly overhead, which projects the image horizontally onto a screen.

While the projector can be used in a variety of courtroom situations, it is especially well suited to opening statement, the presentation of documentary and oral evidence, and final argument. For example, rather than draw the accident scene on a blackboard or use a prepared diagram, you could project the scene onto a large screen during opening statement. The issues in controversy can then be clear to all in the courtroom. Anything permitted by the court to assist in opening and that might otherwise be demonstrated on a blackboard can be more easily and quickly shown to the jury using the projector.

After documentary evidence has been introduced, a transparency can be placed on the overhead projector and shown to the jury. Transparencies of anatomy can be used to illustrate expert testimony. The doctor can highlight for the jury the specific area of injury. Not only is this an effective method of presentation, but it assists the jury in understanding the testimony. Other witnesses can also directly mark on the transparency to supplement their testimony.

A grease pencil, colored felt-tip pen, or colored transparency material can be used, immediately projecting color effects onto the screen and highlighting important information. Overlays permit you to present final argument step by step by flipping one transparency on top of another.

Anything that can be photocopied can be prepared for use with an overhead projector. Special transparencies are used in the copy machine instead of paper.

Be aware that, generally, photographs do not copy well onto a transparency using a copy machine. They should be prepared by a photographer who will print the photograph directly onto the transparency. Photographic transparencies reproduce well on the screen.

There are several important benefits in using an overhead projector. It is a convenient, simple, and inexpensive way to assist the jury in visualizing the occurrence and to reinforce your oral presentation. It results in increased jury understanding and a more persuasive legal argument.

While writing on a blackboard or paper, your back is usually turned to the jury or judge, blocking somebody's view of the writing. The overhead projector, on the other hand, permits you to face the jury while projecting the image onto a screen. Eye contact is not lost.

Further, light is an attention getter. From the time the projector is turned on, the jury's attention will be riveted to the material shown on the screen. You can control this attention very simply by turning off the projector when you want the audience to pay attention to you. Therefore, the overhead projector offers the advantage of obtaining immediate interest and attention but always giving you complete control of this attention.

Importantly, the projector saves time by allowing everyone in the courtroom to see the same thing at the same time. Instead of passing exhibits from opposing counsel, the judge, and juror to juror, you can show a transparency on the screen, resulting in immediate and simultaneous viewing.

Lastly, by using the projector, you can carry all exhibits to the courtroom in a briefcase. Instead of bulky, enlarged photographs, maps, or other documents, only letter-size transparencies are required. The projector itself can be lightweight and portable.

PREPARE DIRECT EXAMINATION OF NONEXPERT WITNESSES

Direct examination of the witness must focus the jurors' attention on the witness. Questions should be short, direct, and to the point. Only relevant issues should be discussed; time spent on nonissues is wasted. There should be a story to tell or a game plan to follow. Proceed from a logical starting point to a logical conclusion.

Direct examination questions should be proper to avoid objections from opposing counsel to leading questions or other improper questions. Your opponent's objections will interrupt the jurors' train of thought.

Your choice of words is important. While the witness should be under control at all times, it is proper and, in some cases, a good idea to invite the witness to tell the story in her own words. However, don't allow the witness to exasperate the judge or cause the jury to lose interest.

Every topic to be discussed with the witness should be raised on direct. Don't omit some point on direct to bring it out on redirect. Not only does that violate principles of psychology, but you may lose your opportunity or even have an issue dismissed because information was not elicited at the proper time.

Always listen carefully to and concentrate on the witness's answer. Do not become preoccupied with what you are going to ask. Do not assume the role of alternate court reporter. Your notes should be brief, if made at all. Always ask "How is the jury hearing this testimony?" If the witness uses large words that need to be clarified, do it immediately.

Direct examination of each witness should end on a high point. If you know your adversary is going to raise certain points, raise them first yourself. It will soften their effect later. Rules of persuasion indicate that if the jurors hear negative facts for the first time on cross-examination, they may believe that the evidence was concealed. You will have greater credibility if you raise these points first.

Be aware of the judge, the jury, and the clock. The judge's facial expression and demeanor can convey information to counsel, the witness, and the jury. The jury's reaction to testimony is something that you must be aware of; demonstrative evidence or a change of pace may be necessary to retain the jury's attention. Watch the clock to measure the length of the testimony and to know how close recess is. Major points should be timed for just before recess.

Pretrial efforts should include a careful preparation of the specific questions to ask the witness at trial. Presentations should be lively and interesting. Complex terminology must be explained. A well-timed pause following a particular point may help emphasize it in the jurors' minds.

Nonexpert witnesses have to be prepared just as expert witnesses are prepared. Many written brochures exist that contain suggestions on how to be a good witness.

Instructions for Witnesses

The following are instructions and suggestions that I give witnesses during trial preparation. They are time-proven hints and aids that help make the testimony more effective:

As a witness in a lawsuit, you have a very important job. For a jury to make a proper decision, it must have all the evidence put before it truthfully.

You must take an oath in court to tell nothing but the truth. But here are two ways to tell the truth: one is in a halting, stumbling, hesitant manner, which makes the jury doubt that you are telling all the facts in a truthful way; the other is confidently and straightforwardly, which makes the jury have faith in what you are saying. You help yourself, the party for whom you are testifying, the judge, and the jury by giving your testimony this last way.

- ► As a witness to an accident, try to visit the scene before the trial. Stand on all corners and become familiar with the place. Close your eyes and try to picture the scene, the objects, and the distances.
- ► Before you testify, visit a courtroom and listen to other witnesses. This will familiarize you with a court and help you to understand what will happen when you give your testimony.
- ► Wear clean clothes in court. Dress conservatively.
- ► Do not chew gum while testifying or taking the oath.
- ► Stand upright when taking the oath. Pay attention and say "I do" clearly.
- ► Don't memorize what you are going to say.
- ► Be serious at all times. Avoid laughing and talking about the case in the halls, rest rooms, or other places in the courthouse.
- ► Talk to the members of the jury. Look at them most of the time and speak to them frankly and openly as you would to any friend or neighbor. Do not cover your mouth with your hand. Speak clearly and loudly enough so that the juror sitting farthest away can hear you easily.
- ► Listen carefully to the questions asked of you. No matter how nice the other attorney may seem on cross-examination,

he may be trying to hurt you as a witness. Understand the question. Have it repeated if necessary; then give a thoughtful, considered answer. Do not offer a snap answer without thinking. Don't be rushed into answering, although it may look bad to take so much time on each question that the jury would think you were making up an answer.

- Explain your answers if necessary. This is better than a simple "Yes" or "No." Give an answer in your own words. If a question can't be answered truthfully with a "Yes" or "No," you have a right to explain the answer.
- Answer directly and simply only the question asked, and then stop. Do not volunteer information not specifically asked.
- If your answer is wrong, correct it immediately.
- If your answer is not clear, clarify it immediately.
- The court and jury only want facts, not hearsay or your conclusions or opinions. You usually can't testify about what someone else told you.
- Don't say, "That's all I remember happening." Sometimes after more thought or another question, you will remember something important.
- Be polite always, even to the other attorney.
- Don't be a smart aleck or a cocky witness! The judge and jury will lose respect for you.
- You are sworn to tell the truth. Tell it. Every material truth should be readily admitted, even if it is not to the advantage of the party for whom you testify. Do not stop to figure out whether your answer will help or hurt that party. Just answer the questions to the best of your memory.
- Do not exaggerate to make your point.
- Stop instantly when the judge interrupts you or when the other attorney objects to what you say. Do not try to sneak your answer in.
- Give positive, definite answers when at all possible. Avoid saying "I think," "I believe," "In my opinion." If you don't know, say so; don't make up an answer. You can be positive about the important things that you naturally would re-

member. If asked about little details that a person might not remember naturally, it is best just to say that you don't remember. But don't let the cross-examiner get you in a trap of answering question after question with "I don't know."

- Don't act nervous. Avoid mannerisms that will make the jury think you are scared or not telling the complete truth.
- Above all—this is important—do not lose your temper. Testifying for a length of time is tiring. It causes fatigue. You will recognize fatigue by certain symptoms: (a) tiredness, (b) crossness, (c) nervousness, (d) anger, (e) careless answers, and (f) the willingness to say anything or answer any question to leave the witness stand. When you feel these symptoms, recognize them and strive to overcome fatigue. Remember that some attorneys on a cross-examination will try to wear you out until you lose your temper and say things that are incorrect or that will hurt you or your testimony. Do not let this happen.
- If you do not want to answer a question, do not ask the judge whether you must answer it. If it is an improper question, the attorney calling you will take it up with the judge for you. Don't ask the judge for advice.
- Don't look at the attorney calling you or the judge for help in answering a question. You are on your own. If the question is improper, the attorney will object. If the judge then says to answer it, do so.
- Don't "hedge" or argue with the other attorney.
- Don't nod your head for a "Yes" or "No" answer. Speak out clearly. The jury, judge, and court reporter must hear you.
- If the question is about distances, speed, or time and your answer is only an estimate, be sure that you say it is only an estimate. Be sure to think about speeds, distances, and intervals of time before testifying, and discuss the matter with the attorney calling you.
- When you leave the witness stand after testifying, wear a confident expression, not a downcast one.
- There are several "trick questions." If you answer them the way the cross-examining attorney hopes you will, your answer can sound bad to the jury. Here are two such questions:

(a) "Have you talked to anybody about this case?" If you say "No," the jury knows this is not right because a good lawyer always talks to witnesses before they testify. If you say "Yes," the lawyer may try to infer that you were told what to say. The best thing to say is that you talked to whomever you have—lawyer, party to suit, police—and you were asked to state the facts and to tell the truth.

(b) "Are you getting paid to testify in this case?" The lawyer asking this hopes your answer will be "Yes," thereby inferring that you are being paid to say what your side wants. Your answer should be something like, "No, I am not getting paid to testify. I am only getting compensation for my time off from work, and the expense (if any) it is costing me."

- Except in a few situations, an insurance company cannot be joined as a defendant. If anything is said that lets the jury know that an insurance company is actually defending the case, the judge will declare a mistrial; the jury will be discharged, and the case will start over. Therefore, be careful not to mention insurance.
- Go back, now, and reread these suggestions so you will have them firmly in your mind. I hope they won't confuse you. I hope they will help. They aren't to be memorized. Ask me about anything you don't understand. You will find there is really no reason why you should be nervous while testifying. If you relax and think that you are just talking to some neighbors on the jury, you will get along fine.

Nonexpert Witness Examination Outline

There are any number of publications that assist in outlining a direct examination for a nonexpert witness. Most attorneys use a checklist or an outline to ensure that they have covered all the important points with the witness. Samples of such lists appear in the appendix to this chapter.

CONCLUSION

Presenting the case in chief requires careful preparation. It is important to decide what you are claiming as to fault and damages.

If you are able to relate this in a few sentences, you have thought the case out thoroughly. Today people expect instant information. Jurors want us to make our points quickly and simply. The case in chief should be planned so as to satisfy these expectations. Keep in mind the overall components involved. Broadly divide the trial into the following groupings:

- motions to exclude evidence (Motions *in Limine*)
- trial brief and evidence or motion memorandum
- jury selection
- opening statements
- direct examination
- cross-examination
- jury instructions
- summation

Creating an outline will allow you to plan what witness(es) or exhibit(s) will be used in presenting evidence to prove your case.

In organizing the liability portion of the case, think about such types of witnesses as (1) experts, (2) liability lay witnesses, and (3) clients. Plan how to prepare these witnesses and the order in which they are called. Whenever possible, call the witnesses in an order that makes a good strong first impression. Sandwich less helpful witnesses between strong helpful witnesses, and start and end the day with the strong witnesses.

Carefully think about your exhibits, both the required exhibits to prove fault and damages as well as the exhibits intended to illustrate the facts. Illustrative exhibits should be simple and easily understandable. Think about television advertising, which must capture and hold your attention to get a message across in 30 seconds. Billboards are also designed to do this. Create exhibits based on the same concept.

Planning the case in chief is not unlike the work done by a director of a play. The overall picture must be kept in mind at all stages of planning. Psychologists tell us a trial is a battle of impression and not logic. Plan the case in chief in a way that will make the best possible impression of your client's case.

APPENDIX

TRIAL OUTLINE

1. Motion *in Limine* 9:30 to 9:45
2. Selection of Jury 9:45 to ______
3. Opening Statements (______ to ______)
4. Plaintiff's Witnesses (________________________________)
   (1) ________________________________ ______ to ______
   (2) ________________________________ ______ to ______
   (3) ________________________________ ______ to ______
   (4) ________________________________ ______ to ______
   (5) ________________________________ ______ to ______
   (6) ________________________________ ______ to ______
5. Defendant's Witnesses (________________________________)
   (1) ________________________________ ______ to ______
   (2) ________________________________ ______ to ______
   (3) ________________________________ ______ to ______
   (4) ________________________________ ______ to ______
   (5) ________________________________ ______ to ______
6. Rebuttal (________________________________)
   (1) ________________________________ ______ to ______
   (2) ________________________________ ______ to ______
   (3) ________________________________ ______ to ______
7. Motions–Instructions ____________________ (______ to ______)
8. Argument ____________________________ (______ to ______)

WITNESS EXAMINATION OUTLINE

Name ____

Spouse ____

Street ____

City ______________________ State ____ Zip Code ________

Employer ____

Work Phone ______________ Home Phone ______________

Date of Appearance __________ Time to Appear __________

Place ____

Subpoenaed ( ) Yes ( ) No   Deposition Taken ( ) Yes ( ) No

Nature of Witness ______________________________

A. Questions To Be Asked of Witness

B. Exhibits To Be Used with Witness

Eyewitness—Auto Case

A. Background Information
   1. What are your name and address? How long have you lived in this county?
   2. Are you married? Do you have children? How many?
   3. What is your occupation? What are your duties? Where are you employed? How long have you worked there?
   4. Were you subpoenaed by me to come to court?
   5. Do you know either party to the lawsuit? If so, explain.

B. Description of Scene and Weather
   1. Were you in the area when the collision occurred on ______?
   2. Where did the collision take place (include names of roads)?
   3. What was the approximate time of the collision?
   4. Describe the light conditions (sunny, dark, etc.).
   5. Describe the weather conditions.
   6. Describe the road surface conditions.
   7. Describe the type of road surface (blacktop, gravel, etc.).
   8. How many lanes were there?
   9. Describe the road character (straight, curved, level, etc.).

C. Traffic and Traffic Controls
   1. Describe the extent of traffic at the time of the collision (what direction, how much, etc.).
   2. Describe the traffic controls (stop signs, lights, etc.).

D. Location of Witness and Vehicles
   1. Where were you when you first became aware of either vehicle?
   2. How far away from that vehicle were you when you first saw it?
   3. What direction was your vehicle going at that time?
   4. What direction was the plaintiff's vehicle going at that time?
   5. What direction was the defendant's vehicle going at that time?
   6. Was your view obstructed? If so, explain.

E. The Collision

Describe in your own words what you saw happen:

1. What were the approximate speeds of the vehicles?
2. What were the signals given?
3. Did the drivers use their horns?
4. Did you see the drivers take evasive action?

F. After Collision

1. Where did the vehicles stop after the collision?
2. Did you stop?
3. Did you get out of your car and go over?

G. Damage to Vehicles

1. Plaintiff's car
   (a) Did you observe damage to the plaintiff's car?
   (b) Where did you observe the damaged car?
   (c) What was the extent of damage?
   (d) Describe any damage to property (pole, etc.) that you observed.
   (e) How did the plaintiff's car leave the scene of the collision?
2. Defendant's car
   (a) Describe any damage to the defendant's car that you observed.
   (b) How did the defendant's car leave the scene?

H. Conversations

Did you have or overhear any conversations with the plaintiff/defendant/passengers/police?

1. Plaintiff
   (a) When was the conversation? Where?
   (b) What was said?
2. Defendant
   (a) When was the conversation? Where?
   (b) What was said?
3. Passengers
   (a) Which car were the passengers in?
   (b) What are the passengers' names?
   (c) When was the conversation? Where?
   (d) What was said?

4. Police officer
    (a) When was the conversation? Where?
    (b) What was said?

I. Drinking
1. Was there any indication that either the plaintiff or defendant had been drinking?
2. Describe the plaintiff's and defendant's behavior.
3. Did either seem intoxicated?

J. Injuries to the Plaintiff
1. Where was the plaintiff when you arrived at the scene?
2. Did you observe any injuries to the plaintiff?
3. Did you hear the plaintiff complain of pain?
4. Describe the plaintiff's injuries.
5. Was first aid administered? What was done? By whom?
6. How did the plaintiff leave the scene of the collision?

Lay Witnesses

A. Background
1. What are your name and address?
2. What is your occupation?
3. Are you married? What are your spouse's name and occupation?
4. Do you have children? How many?

B. Knowledge Regarding the Plaintiff
1. How long have you known the plaintiff?
2. Are you related to the plaintiff? What is the nature of that relationship?
3. What is the nature of your knowledge of the plaintiff? Are you a neighbor, friend, fellow worker?
4. How often did you/do you spend time around/with the plaintiff?

C. Activities Before
1. Describe the plaintiff's work or activities before the injuries.
2. Describe fully: Did the plaintiff have any physical disabilities before the collision?

D. Health Before
   1. Describe the plaintiff's physical condition and general health before the collision.
   2. Did the plaintiff have any ailments? Use drugs?

E. Activities and Health Afterwards
   1. How frequently did you see the plaintiff after the injuries? Over what period of time?
   2. What were the circumstances of your seeing the plaintiff? Were you helping at the plaintiff's house, visiting, working?
   3. What problems did you notice regarding the plaintiff's activities/work?
   4. Describe the plaintiff's general health after the injuries.
   5. What was the most significant change you noted?

F. Present Condition and Health
   1. Do you have occasion to observe the plaintiff now? Under what circumstances?
   2. What do you observe about the plaintiff's present activities?
   3. Describe the plaintiff's current general health.
   4. Compare the plaintiff's present condition with that before injuries.

Spouse of Injured Plaintiff

A. Background
   1. What are your name and address?
      What is your spouse's name?
   2. How long have you and your spouse been married?
   3. Do you have children? What are their names and ages?
   4. What is your occupation? Give details.

B. Knowledge Regarding the Occurrence
   1. If you were present at time of the collision, describe the events.
   2. When did you learn of your spouse's injury? How? Describe the injuries.

C. Injuries When First Seen
   1. When and where did you first see your spouse after the collision? Describe your spouse's injuries/complaints.
   2. Describe the treatment given to your spouse.

D. General Problems Afterwards
   1. Describe the treatment received/problems.
   2. What are your spouse's complaints regarding sleep/pain/irritability?

E. Family Activities (Before v. After)
   1. Describe the effect of your spouse's injuries on family activities/recreational activities?
   2. Describe the effect of the injuries on your children/playing.
   3. Describe the effect of the injuries on the spouse relationship (consortium).
   4. Describe the change in your family life since your spouse was injured.

F. Changes in Health
   Describe any changes that you have noted in your spouse's health/physical condition since the collision.

G. Present Time
   1. Describe present-time family activities/marriage relationship/family life.
   2. Describe your spouse's current general health.
   3. Describe changes in your spouse's lifestyle/recreational activities/home life/personality.
   4. What was the most noticeable change?

Plaintiff—Auto Case

A. Background
   1. What are your name and address?
   2. Are you married? Do you have children?
   3. What's your birth date? What's your age?

B. Employment
   1. Describe your employment. How long have you worked for your current employer?
   2. Describe your spouse's employment.

C. Trip
   1. Where were you going?
   2. Where did you start?
   3. Who was with you?

D. Vehicles
   1. Describe the vehicles that were involved.
   2. Who owned the vehicles?

E. Scene and Weather
   1. Describe the time, weather, and light at the scene of the collision.
   2. Describe the place where the collision was. How familiar were you with the location?
   3. What was your direction of travel?
   4. Describe the traffic controls.

F. Description of Collision
   1. How did it happen?
   2. What was the force of impact?

G. Damage to Vehicles
   Describe.

H. After the Collision
   1. Where did you end up?
   2. What was your condition at that time?
   3. Did you talk to the defendant?

4. How did you leave the scene?
5. How did your car leave the scene?

I. Medical Treatment
  1. Were you hospitalized? For how long? What was done?
  2. How did you get along at the hospital?
  3. When you returned home, how did you get along?
  4. What injuries did you sustain?
  5. Describe the medical treatment you received after your hospital stay.

J. Losses
  1. Describe the damage to your car.
  2. Describe your medical bills.
  3. What was your wage loss?
  4. Were there other losses?

K. Present Condition
  1. Describe your health before the collision.
  2. What are your problems now?
  3. What is the effect of those problems on your normal activities/work?
  4. What treatment are you receiving now?
  5. What is different about your medical condition now compared with before the collision?

DIRECT EXAMINATION

Deanne C. Siemer

Direct examination is the heart of a case, whether for the plaintiff or the defendant. The jury must understand and be persuaded by the witnesses who present the plaintiff's side of the story. Good direct examination sounds like a straightforward discussion in which the witness responds to simple questions from the lawyer and tells what occurred. A considerable amount of preparation usually is required to make this happen.

This chapter covers the fundamentals of how to conduct a good direct examination of fact witnesses. The first section includes a discussion of the basic technical requirements; the second section provides a checklist for lawyer preparation, including techniques for examination; the third section sets out some suggestions for witness preparation; and the fourth section describes the important courtroom techniques for direct examination. The fifth section sets out methods for dealing with special circumstances that may arise during direct examination, including refreshing recollection and past recollection recorded, using depositions, examining adverse witnesses, and impeaching witnesses. The sixth section deals with the objections that can be raised during direct examination. The final section discusses redirect examination.

THE BASICS

The first order of business in undertaking any direct examination is to meet the basic requirements. These include the technical requirements of the rules, the presentation requirements, and the legal requirements of the case.

Technical Requirements

The Federal Rules of Evidence and most state rules impose two general requirements on witness testimony: First, the witness must be competent to offer the testimony. Second, the testimony to be offered must be relevant to the issues in the case.

Competence

Rule 601 of the Federal Rules of Evidence provides a general rule of competence: "Every person is competent to be a witness except as otherwise provided in these rules." In the federal system, this eliminates objections to witness testimony that are based on religious beliefs, conviction of a crime, connection to the litigation, spousal relationship, or connection to dead persons.

Rule 602 provides the general limitation:

> A witness may not testify to a matter unless evidence is introduced sufficient to support a finding that the witness has personal knowledge of the matter. Evidence to prove personal knowledge may, but need not, consist of the witness' own testimony.

A witness has personal knowledge if the witness has personally seen, heard, felt or handled, smelled, or tasted the matter about which testimony will be offered. Once some element of personal knowledge is demonstrated, the witness is competent to testify. The amount of the witness's knowledge goes to the weight of the evidence, not to its admissibility. As the competence of the witness is a fundamental requirement, testimony satisfying this requirement should be elicited from each witness at the earliest possible point.

The determination of the competence of a witness is left to the court under Federal Rule of Evidence 104(a). In making its determination, the court is not bound by the rules of evidence. The competence of expert witnesses is subject to the provision of Rule 703, which exempts the expert from the requirement of firsthand knowledge.

Relevance

Rule 401 defines relevant evidence as

> . . . evidence having any tendency to make the existence of any fact that is of consequence to the determination of the action more probable or less probable than it would be without the evidence.

This is also known as the test of probative value. If the evidence would help in any way to decide the case, then the evidence is relevant. Relevance is also described in terms of a logical connection between the evidence offered and the determination that the trier of fact must make. If the logical connection is too remote or speculative, then the evidence may be rejected by the court.

The lawyer presenting the direct examination should prepare a short defense of the relevance of each area of testimony to be offered by the witness just in case an objection is raised. For example,

> Your Honor, the objection to relevance is not well taken. This witness arrived at the scene of the collision minutes after it occurred. Although she did not observe the actual impact, she did observe the actions of the state police in making measurements. The care with which they performed this task is information that satisfies the requirement of having any tendency to make the existence of any fact more or less probable.

Testimony that is relevant to one of a number of issues in a case should not be excluded because it is irrelevant or inadmissible as to some other issue. The appropriate remedy is for the jury to be given a limiting instruction directing that the testimony be considered only for the proper purpose.

Presentation Requirements

Testimony must be understandable, believable, and persuasive. A brief summary of these requirements for effective presentation of direct testimony is set out here. Techniques for meeting these requirements are included in the sections that follow.

Understandable Testimony

For your presentation of direct testimony to be effective, the testimony must be understandable. Consider whether the explanation you plan to present would be readily understood by an average

15 year old. Jurors, particularly after sitting for a few days, have some of the same lack of patience and focus that teenagers have.

In preparing testimony, look carefully for technical words. Avoid them if possible; explain them thoroughly if you must use them. Use illustrative exhibits where appropriate. Directions north and south are much easier to understand with a diagram; events that flow from one to another benefit from a flow chart; working parts can be appreciated better with a model.

Organized testimony is also easier to understand. Descriptions that move from beginning to middle to end are easier to understand than accounts that skip from one time period to another.

Believable Testimony

Whether the jurors will believe a witness's testimony depends on two factors: how credible the witness is, and how well the testimony given agrees with the jurors' own life experiences. (The third section of this chapter provides more detailed information about establishing the credibility of witnesses.) Considerable thought should also be given to whether the information itself is counterintuitive. If it is information that the average person would not expect from his or her own experience, such as "water flows uphill," then a detailed explanation needs to be given to permit jurors to depart from their commonsense understandings and accept the evidence. A mock jury trial is a good test for finding any "water flows uphill" facts in your presentation.

Persuasive Testimony

Information that is understandable and believable may still fail to persuade a jury to decide in your client's favor. The persuasiveness of direct testimony generally depends on how well it fits into the logical pattern you are developing for the jury. Testimony that is concretely linked to other testimony and that leads inexorably to a conclusion will be persuasive.

The opening statement and closing argument provide the platform for persuasiveness. If you can explain how each piece of testimony to be offered by the witnesses on direct examination will lead to (for the opening statement) or has supported (for the closing argument) a conclusion in your client's favor, your understandable and believable direct testimony will probably also be persuasive.

Legal Sufficiency Requirements

Taken as a whole, the testimony offered in direct examination must establish the cause of action (or the affirmative defense), or the claim will be stricken. Every cause of action has specific elements that must be proved. These elements are contained in the jury instructions.

If your jurisdiction has pattern jury instructions for the cause of action you are asserting, you should analyze them before preparing direct examination.

If no pattern instructions exist, you should create proposed jury instructions based on your legal research about your causes of action. You need to analyze the requirements carefully and make sure that the proposed direct examination covers every necessary element.

One way to make sure that all legal requirements are covered is to construct a proof checklist. Break down the elements of each cause of action into their simplest component parts. List these components down the left side of a spreadsheet. Horizontally across the top put the categories witness, exhibit, stipulation, and judicial notice. Once the spreadsheet (or database, for extensive information) is constructed, for each component of the elements of the causes of action, indicate whether that component will be supplied by the testimony of a witness, an exhibit, a stipulation with opposing counsel, or judicial notice. Fill in the names of the witnesses and the document number or other designation of the exhibits. Make sure that every detail is covered.

As witnesses testify, you can check off the points that they were expected to make. If a witness fails to cover a required point adequately, you can bring the witness back or add that area to the testimony of a subsequent witness. If a motion for a directed verdict is made at the end of trial, you can pull out your proof checklist and explain exactly how every element of the cause of action has been proved.

LAWYER PREPARATION

Substantial background work is required before the first witness can be prepared for direct examination. There are three general parts to lawyer preparation for direct: the witness plan, the testimony plan, and the testimony draft. This preparation for direct begins after information has been assembled through interviews, investigation, examination of documents, and discovery, and after most of the legal research has been completed.

Witness Plan

Direct examination should be choreographed carefully. The witness plan sets out the selection, placement, and timing elements with respect to the direct examination as a whole.

Selection

In some cases, there are no choices with respect to the witnesses who will be used. There are only a few people who know the facts, and all of them will have to testify to present all necessary evidence. Most often, however, some selection of witnesses will need to take place.

Brevity and simplicity are the general rules for construction of the witness plan. Not every witness who saw something or knows something should testify. Cases are won by having the *best* witnesses, not the *most* witnesses; jurors may be confused if they hear too many witnesses. If a severe injury is at issue, hearing about it from many points of view may desensitize jurors to the horrible consequences the plaintiff has suffered. More serious, having several witnesses testify about the same thing may introduce contradictions your opponent can exploit.

Select only those witnesses necessary to make the points required to establish the elements of your causes of action. Then select the strongest witness for each point. The witness's strength is generally derived from the extent of firsthand knowledge. Occasionally a witness may, by force of personality, be the best person to present a particular part of the story. Avoid duplicating testimony. If one witness has said it well, consider carefully whether you gain anything by having another witness repeat it.

Placement

After the witnesses are selected, they must be put into "batting order." One practical way to approach these decisions is first to identify the key elements in the case, then to decide the order in which the key elements need to be proved to make the presentation logical and easy to follow, and finally to arrange the witnesses so that the testimony can be presented in this general order. If the witnesses have a chronological sequence, however, that should be considered as an alternative.

There are two exceptions to these ordering mechanisms that need to be evaluated. The first is whether the strongest witness should go first. Though the proof that the strongest witness offers might be out of order, either in elements to be proved or in chronology, it may be beneficial to start strongly. What a jury sees and hears first affects its view of the rest of the direct testimony. If a very strong witness testifies first, the jury's overall perception of the plaintiff's case may be improved.

The second consideration is whether the plaintiff should testify first. Jurors are always curious to see the actual parties and may form a more favorable impression of the plaintiff at the outset of the case.

Timing

When deciding the tentative order of the witnesses, it is necessary to take into consideration how long the witness will be on the stand and whether it is advantageous to finish examining a witness early enough in the day so that the cross-examiner will not get an overnight break to prepare. Thus, an important witness might be put on in the afternoon to cover preliminary matters, qualifications, and other background information that is relatively noncontroversial. The heart of the testimony might be put on first thing the following morning, when the witness is fresh, so that the testimony could finish up in time to allow the cross to be completed during the remainder of the morning and the afternoon sessions.

Testimony Plan

After the witnesses have been selected and a tentative order has been established, the plan for each individual witness must be set. As Pat Hazel, a talented trial advocacy professor from the University of Texas, puts it, like everything else in life, good direct examination has a beginning, a middle, and an end. There are some tactical choices about what testimony to put in the beginning, middle, and end of each witness's presentation.

Beginning

A good direct examination will begin with three things: introducing the witness to the jury, explaining why the witness is there, and accrediting the witness. Jurors are very attentive when a witness first takes the stand, so it is important to get to the good stuff quickly and not to spend too much time on the preliminaries.

Lawyers need to remember to introduce important witnesses to the jury in the opening statement. This introduction should give the jurors a context for key witnesses and let them know generally what information the witness will supply.

How to open with a witness on the stand is a perennial question. Most lawyers start with something like "State your name for the record." This is a very cold and formal opening. It fails to establish rapport. You might substitute "Tell us your name" or "Let's begin by asking your name and address."

Accrediting the witness is the process of asking a few background questions to let the jurors see who this witness is. Sample questions are "Where do you work?"; "Are you married?"; and "How many children do you have?". Every fact witness needs to be humanized to show the jury what is interesting about this person. This is the same process that occurs at the beginning of conversations between strangers: "Where are you from? What kind of work do you do?" Accreditation also eases the witness's tension because the questions asked are noncontroversial, and the answers will not be challenged.

Middle

The principal decision to be made regarding the middle portion of the testimony is whether to proceed chronologically or topically. A chronological account is the easiest for the jury to follow. It's also the easiest for the lawyer to extract: "Tell us what happened next?" and so forth. But a topic-by-topic presentation may be the most effective, because it allows you to get the most important topic up front and to proceed chronologically within that topic. Even if you decide to proceed chronologically, it may be useful to move a few topical questions up front on important matters. One traditional pattern proceeds as follows:

Q. Now, Mr. Smith, tell us where you were on October 9, 1989, at about 3:00 p.m.

A. I was planting trees at the Seven Oaks subdivision.

Q. What happened at that time?

A. My backhoe struck some metal. We dug around and found a bunch of barrels with greenish stuff oozing out of them.

Q. I'd like you to go back, if you will, and describe for the jury the arrangements that you made with respect to the job at the Seven Oaks subdivision.

A. Well, in early September 1989 I met with Mr. Jones. He wanted to have some trees planted before winter set in . . .

You can use transition sentences to shift from one topic to another. Keeping the chronology confined to one topic may also help the witness give you a complete account without prompting.

The middle portion of the testimony is also the place to anticipate cross. Unless you think that the cross-examiner will miss some lines of attack, you are better off raising troublesome issues on direct when the witness can deal with them in a nonconfrontational context. When you discuss unfavorable issues with your witness on direct, it helps indicate to the jury that the witness is a forthright and honest person.

Unfavorable testimony generally should be bracketed by favorable testimony. Lead up to the difficult point with a strong area of testimony. Move quickly and easily to the anticipation of cross, then shift back quickly to another area that is strong for the witness.

End

The end of a witness's direct testimony needs to be strong. Cross will follow immediately, so direct should end on a point that cannot be attacked easily and is not repetitive or cumulative—this is not the place to sum up. Also, avoid making your ending question something to which your opponent can object successfully. Direct should never end with an objection that has been sustained. To help avoid this kind of final objection, don't signal your opponent that you are about to end. Try not to say, "Now I'd like to ask you one last thing, Mr. Jones."

Testimony Draft

You have put together a coherent plan as to which witnesses are going to be called and what points each of them will make; now it is time to draft the testimony. Detailed preparation at this stage will allow the direct examination to proceed smoothly, without significant objection. There are a number of ways to prepare for direct examination and various methods to fit individual styles.

One method that is effective for both beginners and experienced lawyers faced with difficult direct examination is to prepare the testimony in three stages. First, draft each question and the preferred answer and work with the witness to see if the questions you have prepared will actually get the answers you want. Second, after your witness preparation is complete and you have worked over every point with the witness, reduce the detailed draft to an outline. Third, after you have mastered the outline, reduce it further to key words that remind you of the points you want to make.

Reading questions at trial from a prepared script adversely affects your ability to listen to answers and to be flexible in effectively eliciting testimony when the witness turns in an unexpected direction. However, writing out a question-by-question examination can increase your effectiveness at trial by forcing you to prepare completely. Your list of key words will provide reminders of the points to be covered. If the witness digresses, you can go back to your outline. If you run into trouble with an objection or a problem with a witness, you can go back another step to your question-by-question draft. This is particularly useful with foundation for exhibits or qualifying for an exemption from the hearsay rules. If you have written a question-by-question approach to the problem, and you know it works, you can always go back to it when an objection is raised, and then explain to the judge why the questions you have just asked are sufficient for the purpose at issue.

To master your materials, color code your notes. The sections of your detailed draft, your outline, and your key words that relate to a particular point all will be noted by the same color. Indicate which exhibits need to be introduced with each point in the margins of the draft, outline, and key words documents.

One reason to write out the questions and answers is to do self-editing to ensure that all questions on direct are nonleading. Leading questions are permitted for preliminary matters, and some opponents rarely object to leading questions even on nonpreliminary matters. Still, you should avoid leading questions for two reasons. First, an objection can throw you and the witness off a good pace. Second, the jury may perceive that you are spoon-feeding the witness, and believability or persuasion will be affected adversely.

Written questions should begin with

- who,
- what,
- where,

- when,
- why,
- how,
- describe, and
- explain.

Every question structured this way should withstand a leading question objection.

Each question should be a simple question. Compound questions are objectionable. Simple questions are easy to follow. Compound questions may not be. If the witness does not answer the whole question, jurors may be left wondering about the unanswered portion, and on appeal you may be left without a record on a key fact.

Scrub each question to eliminate "lawyer talk." Make sure your words are simple and direct. Avoid legalese if at all possible. Are you talking about a "vehicle" when you could refer to a "car"? Have you referred to "extenuating circumstances" when you could say "reasons why you decided not to do this"? Edit out phrases like "what, if anything" and "did there come a time." Change "prior" and "subsequent" to "before" and "after." Rigorously root out the pompous phrases lawyers become accustomed to using.

Finally, examine each question to determine whether it really needs to be asked. On direct examination, you are trying to impart information as efficiently as possible. The longer a jury has to listen to a particular witness, the less effective the witness's overall message will be.

WITNESS PREPARATION

Witnesses need to know the fundamentals of testifying. Most have only seen testimony given on television and have an artificial notion about the process. Some witnesses even believe that preparation with a lawyer is somehow sneaky and underhanded. Reassure them that preparation is proper and expected.

Every witness should be prepared by the lawyer who will be doing the direct examination. Each witness's fears, limitations, and personal quirks must be considered to make the witness's testimony as effective as possible. This can be done well only if the lawyer has worked with and understands the witness thoroughly.

There are two principal objectives in witness preparation: first, maximizing witness confidence so that the witness presents information as effectively as possible; and second, maximizing the witness's credibility so that the jury will find the information believable and persuasive.

Confidence

Every fact and lay witness is nervous. Stage fright is normal for anyone appearing in front of any audience—even a small audience. This fear is compounded by the witness's worries about cross-examination and about being found credible by the jury.

You need to develop a rapport and a comfortable working relationship with your witness. The first step is to put the witness's task in context; describe the trial format and how the witness's testimony fits into the plan for presenting the case on direct. Explain that there is no perfect way to present testimony and that everyone has stage fright.

Next, enlist the witness's help in finding the clearest and most interesting way to explain what the witness knows about the events at issue in the case. Explain why oral testimony is hard for jurors to follow, and suggest that the witness think about how this information would be presented to his or her children in a way that would keep their attention.

Explain how your outline of the witness's testimony works. Describe the method of presenting an overview first and then developing specifics. Be careful to abide by the witness preparation rules in your jurisdiction. In the federal system and some states, any document shown to a witness during preparation for testimony is discoverable; this includes your notes.

Try out each question in your script. See whether it elicits the answer you thought it would. At this stage it is *much* better to change the question than to try to teach the witness to answer as planned. Show the witness how you will move smoothly from topic to topic using introductory sentences. For example:

Q. Now, Ms. Weller, I would like to turn to the company's procedures for inspecting gear parts before the product is shipped. Explain for us how that is done.

A. (series of questions and answers on inspection procedures)

Q. Would you focus now on the company's procedures for responding to complaints when they are received from customers? How does that work?

A. (series of questions and answers on customer complaints)

This will demonstrate to the witness that you will move the testimony along by asking more specific questions. The witness does not have to worry about remembering to put everything into the answer to the first question.

As you work through the questions you have prepared, show the witness how you will interrupt if the answer rambles.

Q. Could I just stop you there and ask what specific role you had in responding to customer complaints?

Being interrupted is jarring to a witness and may cause a temporary loss of composure unless there is some practicing before the in-court appearance.

Familiarize the witness with the litany for providing a foundation for any exhibits the witness may use. The usual formulations are unfamiliar to a fact or lay witness.

Explain how objections work—what they are for and why they are made. The witness must understand the etiquette of objections. A witness should wait until the judge has ruled and respect the ruling. If the judge sustains an objection, the witness should not try to load the information into the next answer.

It is important to explain the hearsay objection. In everyday life, reporting what someone else told you is entirely appropriate. It is very hard for some witnesses to understand that they cannot do that in the courtroom. It is particularly difficult for fact and lay witnesses to understand why this exchange is perfectly appropriate—

Q. What happened next?

A. The veterinarian began to explore to see whether there was a broken bone.

while a similar exchange is not—

Q. What happened next?

A. The veterinarian said that it might be a broken bone.

and may draw an objection.

You must also explain how the assertions of privilege work. These may come up in the context of an inquiry by opposing counsel as to whether the witness has worked with the lawyer in preparing for testimony at trial. You need to explain that the opposing lawyer can inquire about whether such meetings took place but not about the substance of the discussions at those meetings.

When preparing a witness in your office, simulate a courtroom setting by having the witness sit in a chair isolated from other furniture and at some distance from you. This removes the witness from familiar items such as desks that may foster a sense of security that will not be present in the courtroom.

Sometime before trial, have any witness who has not seen a live trial in your jurisdiction go to the courtroom and observe for a few hours. If possible, take the witness to an empty courtroom for a short practice with the witness actually sitting in the witness chair answering questions. It will also help to practice a small, but very important, detail: how to leave the witness stand confidently. If the witness steps down after cross and there is no need for redirect, the witness's demeanor should convey that everything went well.

Credibility

Witness credibility starts with a careful investigation of the facts. Examine every possible hole in a witness's testimony. Just because your best witness says something doesn't make it so. Witnesses are anxious to please and may exaggerate slightly to meet your expectations. In this respect, discovery is no substitute for good investigation. The witness who is testifying about an observation should return to the scene to refresh recollection. If it would be useful, the witness should talk to others about what she or he saw. Make sure to explain that this is perfectly acceptable preparation and that any question on cross-examination should be answered forthrightly.

Witness credibility is affected by personal characteristics, handicaps, and body language. The best way to help a witness understand the impact of these personal traits is to use videotape preparation. Run through direct examination with the witness in front of a video camera. Playing back the videotape will give the witness a much better understanding of these personal factors than will your exhortations and explanations. Prepare the witness for the fact that most people think they look bad on television—you don't want a witness to be even more nervous and ill at ease after the videotape preparation.

The witness should look directly at you when you are posing questions and when answering you. The same holds true for responding to cross-examination. It will seem unnatural to a jury if a questioner and a respondent don't have good eye contact.

The witness should have a serious demeanor and should be polite to the judge and to opposing counsel.

Watch body language. Some witnesses adopt a defensive or "closed" posture by wrapping their arms around themselves or putting their hands near or around their mouths. An "open" position with hands in the lap or on the knees is much better.

Focus on speech habits. Does the witness speak loudly enough? Most lay witnesses are accustomed to communicating primarily through face-to-face conversation, which doesn't require much volume or projection. Have the witness try talking to you from a distance of 20 to 30 feet. Are the witness's hands around the mouth in a way that makes what is being said inaudible?

Think carefully about the special cases: the handicapped, blind, elderly, very young, disfigured, or culturally different witness. Care also needs to be given to witnesses with accents, foreign language problems, or speech defects. You need to decide, in consultation with the witness, how to explain and overcome these problems. Some jurors will assume that a handicapped person is incompetent in other ways. Or a handicap may be so distracting that jurors do not pay attention to the testimony. You need to be open with the jury about the disability. Explain it, and then set it aside.

Off-the-stand behavior can affect witness credibility. Explain that the jurors will be looking at all the people in the courtroom. Witnesses should not chew gum, read the newspaper, or fidget nervously while waiting to testify. Similarly, they should not talk about the case in the halls, the rest rooms, or anywhere else in the courthouse.

Witness credibility can also be affected by the witness's dress. Most lawyers have a good feel for appropriate courtroom attire. Enforce those instincts and clarify what the witness should wear. Clothes should be suitable, clean, and neat.

Advise the witness to tell the truth. It is astounding how many otherwise sensible people think this is not what is expected.

COURTROOM APPEARANCE

Good, solid preparation leaves very little to chance. The courtroom appearance will go smoothly. Only a few pointers remain to ensure a successful direct examination.

Decide where you will stand during the direct examination. Some jurisdictions will confine you to your table or a podium. If you can move freely, consider starting out rather close to the witness to give confidence and support. Then move away from the witness as you come to the critical parts of the testimony, so the jury does not get the impression that the witness is relying on you. While some commentators suggest standing at the far end of the jury box, juror reactions to this are mixed. In this situation, the witness is looking at both the lawyer and the jury. This may disturb the jurors. They are used to looking at both sides of a conversation, and if the lawyer stands at the end of the jury box, the jurors can see only one of the participants at a time. This may make it more difficult for the jurors to concentrate.

Focus on the witness, not on your notes. Look at the witness as you ask the question and as the answer is given. Don't look down until the answer is over. If you look at your notes while the witness is talking, you signal that the answer is unimportant to you. And what's even more troubling, you can't listen to the answer. You need to catch every word of the answer to be sure that it is what you expected and that it is understandable to the jury. If you need your notes for help with the next question, look at them after the witness answers.

Don't interrupt your witness unless the interruption is absolutely necessary. You are aiming for a flowing dialogue, and interruptions may disrupt the concentration or rattle the confidence of the witness. Remember to prepare the witness in advance for possible interruptions.

Keep up your energy level even if the witness is soft-spoken or reticent. Use pauses. Move around. Sound interested.

Sensitive subjects need to be handled carefully. Give a reasonably long lead-in so the witness knows what is coming and is not surprised. Let the jury know there may be some emotion in the responses. For example,

> Q. I know the next subject is going to be difficult for you to discuss. I need to ask you about what happened after Mr. Degenerate, the defendant, held a knife to your throat. It is necessary for the jury to know all the details. We will understand if you have to stop for a moment.

The witness has now had some time to get collected for the launch into the lurid details.

SPECIAL CIRCUMSTANCES

Trial rules provide for the special circumstances of refreshing your witness's recollection during direct examination, using deposition testimony instead of a live witness on direct, using one of your opponent's witnesses as an adverse witness on direct, and impeaching your own witness on direct. The following are suggestions with respect to these special circumstances.

Refreshing Recollection and Past Recollection Recorded

If a witness forgets something because of the stress of testifying or a temporary lapse of memory, you may use a document to assist the witness in providing the jury information on this point. There are two ways to do this: refreshing recollection and past recollection recorded.

Refreshing Recollection

To lay a foundation for using a document to refresh the witness's recollection, the attorney must elicit testimony that there is some matter the witness cannot now remember, that a document would help refresh the witness's memory, and that after reviewing the document, the witness now recalls the matter and can testify about it.

Any document used for this purpose must be submitted to opposing counsel before the examination to refresh recollection begins. The document itself is not introduced into evidence because the evidence is the witness's own recollection.

Past Recollection Recorded

The foundation for using a document in substitution for the witness's own memory is different. In this instance, the witness once knew the information but now does not recall it, even with the assistance of the document.

In this case, the direct examination must establish that the witness previously knew about the matter, that the witness prepared a record of the matter, that the record was prepared while the matter was still fresh in the witness's mind, and that the record was accurate when it was prepared. The document itself is introduced into evidence with this foundation.

Direct Examination Through Deposition Testimony

There are four situations where deposition transcripts help to present direct testimony at trial because the witness is not going to appear at all. These occur when (1) the witness is busy and would prefer not to appear as a matter of convenience; (2) the witness refuses to appear; (3) the witness is dead, incapacitated, or ill, and therefore cannot appear; or (4) the witness is adverse, and you would prefer that the witness did not appear as part of your case because of the risk involved. In each of these situations, portions of the deposition transcript can be used at trial. If the deposition transcript to be used at trial will require more than ten minutes to read, consider videotaping the deposition. It is difficult to read from a deposition transcript for more than ten minutes, and a video will sustain the jurors' attention.

If your witness is busy and would prefer not to appear at trial, and if the witness is located more than one hundred miles from the place of trial, you are entitled as a matter of right under the federal rules to use the deposition.[1] If the witness is closer than one hundred miles, and opposing counsel will not stipulate to the use of the deposition at trial, under federal procedure you must move for permission to use the deposition in place of live testimony.[2] This method is often used for expert testimony from doctors or other specialists who are needed for emergencies or other special commitments that could not be interrupted for testifying.

If a witness refuses to appear, the federal system allows you to issue a subpoena for the attendance of the witness. You are entitled to use the deposition if the witness fails to respond to the subpoena.[3]

If the witness is unable to appear because of illness or incapacitation, or if the intended witness is dead, you can use a deposition after providing a foundation, usually by affidavit, as to the circumstances causing the unavailability of the witness.[4] An affidavit may be used because the availability of the witness is a preliminary question, and the rules of evidence do not apply.[5]

1 FED. R. CIV. P. 32(a)(3)(B).

2 FED. R. CIV. P. 32(a)(3)(E).

3 FED. R. CIV. P. 32(a)(3)(D) and FED. R. EVID. 804(b)(1), (5).

4 FED. R. CIV. P. 32(a)(3)(A), (C) and FED. R. EVID. 804(a)(4).

5 FED. R. EVID. 104(a).

If you do not want to call a witness during your direct case because the witness is adverse, but you need some specific facts to prove the elements of your cause of action, you can use a deposition if the witness is a party or managing agent of a party.[6] Generally, these aspects of foundation are established during discovery.

If long portions of a deposition transcript must be put into evidence, an alternative technique is to prepare a deposition summary. In the federal system, this practice is governed by FED. R. EVID. 1006. The summary reads like a narrative and shortens the presentation while preserving the necessary details. Normally the narrative is submitted to opposing counsel during pretrial proceedings for additions or corrections. Any unresolved disputes are decided by the judge at the pretrial conference.

Deposition testimony is dull for the jury. In planning the direct examination, put deposition testimony somewhere in the middle of the direct, bracketed by more interesting testimony.

Direct Examination of an Adverse Witness

Calling one of your opponent's witnesses during your direct case is a risky, but sometimes rewarding, tactic. Because the witness is adverse, you may ask leading questions. You can extract the good parts of the witness's testimony without waiting until cross-examination during your opponent's case and without risking that your opponent will decide not to call the witness at all. Often you can catch the other side off guard, and you may be able to inflict damage on your opponent's case. The witness may be unprepared for this examination because opposing counsel was planning to prepare the witness for direct examination at some later date. But the risks are real. An adverse witness will try to load testimony with damaging facts, and you may appear defensive as you try to keep the testimony on track.

An adverse witness should be placed somewhere in the middle of the witness lineup. If the adverse witness does harm, the bad testimony will be followed by good testimony from your own witnesses. In fact, it may be useful to save a very strong witness to clean up any harmful testimony that the adverse witness unloads. It may also be a good strategy to question a favorable, noncontroversial witness immediately before the adverse witness. You will be able to

6 FED. R. CIV. P. 32(a)(2).

elicit your witness's information with simple, straightforward questions and answers. This kind of witness will be a good example of a how a witness should behave and will compare favorably with the adverse witness, who will likely fight your questions.

Impeachment on Direct Examination

Traditionally, courts have significantly limited the use of impeachment during direct examination. The underlying theory was that when a party calls a witness, that party vouches for the credibility of the witness. Therefore, if a witness unexpectedly gave testimony contrary to the interests of the party presenting the witness, that party was not permitted to impeach the testimony.

Today, in the federal system and in states that follow the Federal Rules of Evidence, parties are no longer required to make any showing before they can impeach their own witnesses.[7] Prior inconsistent statements given under oath are admissible for any witness.[8]

Even under restrictive state systems, if a party calls a witness who has reputation flaws, the party may expose those flaws to preempt cross-examination. A party is also entitled to introduce other substantive evidence, through other witnesses, that discredits a turncoat witness.

OBJECTIONS

Six principal objections may be raised as to testimony from a witness on direct examination:

- objections to the qualification of the witness or the testimony—competence and relevance objections;
- objections to the form of the question—leading and compound question objections;
- objections to hearsay;
- objections to opinion testimony from a nonexpert witness;
- objections to narrative answers; and
- policy objections to testimony that confuses, misleads, wastes time, or is needlessly cumulative.

7 FED. R. EVID. 607.

8 FED. R. EVID. 801(d)(1)(A).

There are additional objections that may be raised to exhibits used with direct examination, including the best evidence rule that requires that if you want to introduce testimony to prove the content of a document or other exhibit, you must put the document itself into evidence before testimony about it will be admissible.

Competence and Relevance Objections

Objections to the fundamental requirements of witness competence and subject matter relevance generally go to the thoroughness of preparation and the care with which the testimony has been assembled. The requirements are straightforward, and it should be readily apparent during the lawyer's and witness's preparations whether a witness can qualify to present specific facts. Under the federal rules, the test of relevance is extremely broad and should rarely cause a problem.

Leading and Compound Questions

Except during examination on preliminary matters, leading questions may be objected to at any time during direct examination.[9] Preliminary matters are background information not directly at issue. A leading question is any question that suggests to the witness the desired answer; in practical terms, it may be defined as any question that does *not* begin with who, what, where, when, why, how, describe, or explain.

Compound questions may be objected to as unfair to the opponent and as producing an unclear record. A compound question includes two or more questions, for example, "What did you do, and how did you know what to do?" The witness may describe actions and then launch into a response containing hearsay in answer to the "how" part of the question. Or the witness may respond to the "what" part of the question and never reach the "how" part.

Hearsay Objections

Hearsay is an objection to foundation. If a statement was made out of court, its trustworthiness is not sufficient to qualify it as evidence unless the requirements of one of the exceptions set out in the rules or in the common law can be met.[10]

9 Rule 611(c) of the Federal Rules of Evidence is typical in this regard.

10 In the federal system, there are 25 exceptions set out in Rules 803 and 804, FED. R. EVID.

Most hearsay problems are easily resolved, as the requirements of the rules are straightforward. The proponent of the evidence should have in his or her notes a reference to the hearsay exception applicable to the evidence being elicited or a clear explanation why the evidence is not hearsay. Hearsay objections can lead to reversal, so judges are more careful in analyzing hearsay objections than they are in some other aspects of the trial where greater judicial discretion is recognized.

Opinion Testimony

Opinion testimony may be given only by an expert who is duly qualified by in-court testimony that can be tested by cross-examination. The federal system allows some leeway for opinion testimony from lay witnesses. It provides,

> If the witness is not testifying as an expert, the witness' testimony in the form of opinions or inferences is limited to those opinions or inferences which are (a) rationally based on the perception of the witness and (b) helpful to a clear understanding of the witness' testimony or the determination of a fact in issue.[11]

Under this rule, lay witnesses are permitted to testify, for example, that a person appeared to be drunk or that a car appeared to be going more than 30 miles per hour. You can assume a lay witness has the perceptive capabilities to make these kinds of everyday determinations.

Narrative Answers

Narrative answers arguably deprive the cross-examiner of the opportunity to object when the testimony strays from acceptable subject matter. The witness may include information in the narrative answer that is inadmissible but, because the cross-examiner did not have an opportunity to consider a question seeking to elicit this information, the testimony is out and before the jury before the cross-examiner has a chance to object.

FED. R. EVID. 611(a) provides,

> The court shall exercise reasonable control over the mode and order of interrogating witnesses and presenting evi-

[11] Rule 701, FED. R. EVID.

> dence so as to (1) make the interrogation and presentation effective for the ascertainment of the truth . . . .

A lawyer may seek protection against narrative answers under this rule.

Policy Objections

Four basic policy objections may be raised on direct examination. Evidence may be excluded for policy reasons even if it has been qualified properly as to competence and relevance. In the federal system, FED. R. EVID. 403 provides,

> Although relevant, evidence may be excluded if its probative value is substantially outweighed by the danger of unfair prejudice, confusion of the issues, or misleading the jury, or by considerations of undue delay, waste of time, or needless presentation of cumulative evidence.

Rule 403 includes most of the policy objections available under state law. Its balancing mechanism is important. For an objection to be sustained, the probative value must be substantially outweighed by the policy reasons for exclusion. The first argument, therefore, will be about the probative value of the testimony to be offered. If the probative value is high—the testimony is directly connected to an important issue—then the balance will be harder to tip against admission. The second aspect of the argument will be defining "substantially." If the probative value supporting the admission of the testimony and the policy reasons for excluding it are nearly in balance, then the judge should exercise discretion to allow the evidence because the "substantial" imbalance test is not met.

Unfair Prejudice

An objection based on unfair prejudice generally is directed at testimony that arouses emotion to an extent that rational thought processes may be overcome. The emotions aroused may be sympathy, resentment, revulsion, indignation, anger, or anything else that would bias a jury unfairly.

In the federal system, FED. R. EVID. 407 through 412 legislate certain kinds of evidence into the unfair prejudice category. These rules exclude evidence of subsequent remedial measures, settlement offers, payment of medical expenses, the existence of liability insurance, and, in rape cases, the victim's past behavior. Testimony that touches on any of these matters could be excluded by reference to the rules.

Confusion / Misleading

Although the federal rule points to "confusion of the issues" and "misleading the jury" as two separate bases for an objection to evidence that meets the fundamental requirements for admissibility, these two concepts are very close, if not identical. A principal concern is that certain evidence may create a side issue that will distract the jury from the main issues or that the manner of presentation may affect the jury's consideration unduly. Evidence that will require lengthy jury instruction as to its proper and limited uses may also be excluded on this ground.

Undue Delay / Waste of Time

Rule 403 sets out "undue delay" and "waste of time" as separate bases for objections, but these two concepts probably are intended to avoid the same potential abuse. Evidence that may draw an extended, detailed rebuttal may be excluded on this ground if it appears likely that, after all the evidence and rebuttal are in, there will be little gain in probative value. Evidence that draws a justifiable request for a continuance to prepare a rebuttal adequately also may be excluded on this ground.

Needless Cumulative Evidence

Cumulative evidence can be entirely relevant and presented with a totally proper foundation. Indeed, the primary purpose of direct examination is to pile one bit of evidence on top of another until the sum is persuasive. The objection to needless cumulative evidence is related both to misleading the jury and wasting time. If the evidence on a particular point has already cumulated so that the point may be fairly assumed to be established, further evidence on the same point may mislead the jury on the relative importance of the evidence and waste time, because the additional probative value is slight.

REDIRECT

The basic procedural rule on redirect examination is that it must be limited to matters raised within the scope of the cross-examination that preceded it.

There are a number of tactical considerations in redirect. First, prepare for redirect. Don't leave it to chance. Prepare a plan that accounts for both the direct and the expected cross.

Second, redirect is intended to repair damage done on cross. When the cross-examiner has unfairly limited the witness to a yes or no answer, redirect gives the witness a chance to explain. When cross-examination has suggested a limitation, redirect allows the witness to enlarge the explanation. Repair work, however, should be done only when really needed. It is not necessary to rebut on redirect every small insult made during cross. The jury will grow tired of the repetition.

Third, redirect examination is also an opportunity to reemphasize points made on direct and not touched during cross. Most judges tolerate repetition as long as you do not telegraph your intent by introducing your questions with phrases like “once again,” “tell us again,” or “repeat for us.”

Fourth, redirect examination, like direct examination, should end strong. Do not spend the entire redirect patching up things said on cross; it makes the witness sound too defensive.

Fifth, redirect can be very effective if some interesting part of the direct examination is left to redirect. There is a real risk in this approach, however, because your opponent may not open up the subject on cross and that will leave you subject to an objection that your redirect is not within the scope of the cross.

One aspect of redirect that is subject to debate and different practice among jurisdictions is whether it is appropriate for a lawyer to talk to a witness between the cross and redirect. The redirect may come after a break, an overnight recess, or some other opportunity for consultation. While the witness will want to discuss redirect, some judges, believing that any consultation would interfere with spontaneous testimony, might hold the lawyer in contempt. Other judges believe consultation is perfectly proper, as it is before direct, and expect it. Find out about the judge's view before planning to consult with the witness.

CONCLUSION

Good direct examination presents a coherent explanation of why your client should prevail. This explanation should be in a form that jurors find informative and easy to understand. The witnesses produce information with which they are very familiar and the import of which they understand. Like a good television interview that leaves the viewer with the impression of a well-informed questioner dealing with an equally well-informed interviewee, the in-court presentation of direct examination should flow easily from question to question with the principal focus always on the witness.

CROSS-EXAMINATION

Howard L. Nations

No skill of the trial advocate epitomizes adversarial confrontation as dramatically or significantly as that of cross-examination. An ancient legal maxim states that there is never an outcome of a cause contested that is not mainly dependent on the advocate's skill in cross-examination.

Over the centuries of testing the veracity of witnesses by cross-examination, from Socrates' masterful questioning of his accuser Miletus through the trials that fill courtrooms today, the skills required of the advocate have developed into principles that can be learned, practiced, and mastered by the diligent advocate. The timeless nature of the adversarial skills required of the cross-examiner was recognized by the eminent New York trial lawyer, Francis Wellman, 90 years ago in his excellent treatise on the *Art of Cross-Examination*:

> It requires the greatest ingenuity; a habit of logical thought; clearness of perception in general; infinite patience and self-

> control; power to read men's minds intuitively, to judge of their characters by their faces, to appreciate their motives; ability to act with force and precision; a masterful knowledge of the subject matter itself; an extreme caution; and, above all, the *instinct to discover the weak point* in the witness under examination.[1]

Consequently, cross-examination is the most difficult of the adversarial skills to acquire. Once mastered, however, it is also the most significant skill, since it is from the crucible of cross-examination that truth most often emerges. As with all significant skills, mastery of the basic principles and techniques must combine with hard-earned experience to mold the neophyte into a seasoned cross-examiner. The purpose of this chapter is to present an overview of several principles and techniques of cross-examination that have been passed to our generation from the master advocates who have preceded us.

SILENT CROSS-EXAMINATION

There are many instances when the most brilliant cross-examination consists of "Thank you, your Honor, but it is not necessary to cross-examine this witness." A skilled advocate will recognize those instances and overcome the compulsion to cross-examine every witness. The categories you should carefully consider for the silent cross-examination technique include the scope of cross-examination permitted under the rules, the harmless witness, the unimpeachable witness, avoidance of the baited trap, avoidance of unnecessary reiteration, and avoidance of improper motives to cross-examine.

Scope

The seminal point in preparing and conducting cross-examination is a clear understanding of the rules controlling the scope of permissible cross-examination in the particular court in which the case is to be tried. A significant disparity exists between the restrictive federal rule and the common law rule regarding the scope of permissible cross-examination. The common law rule, which is retained in many state courts, regards cross-examination as the acid test of the truth and affords the parties a wide latitude in the cross-

1 FRANCIS L. WELLMAN, THE ART OF CROSS-EXAMINATION 22-23 (1904).

examination of an adverse witness. This rule permits counsel to question the witness on any subject relevant to the dispute and does not restrict the scope of cross-examination to matters on which the witness was questioned on direct.

The restrictive rule, usually referred to as the federal rule, greatly reduces the effectiveness of cross-examination as an adversarial weapon by limiting the scope of cross-examination to the same subject matter as the direct examination and matters relating to the witness's credibility. This rule requires the cross-examiner to call the witness as part of his own case if he wants to range further afield. The resulting loss of the right to ask leading questions on the new subject matter greatly reduces counsel's opportunity for an in-depth cross-examination in the professed search for "the whole truth and nothing but the truth." As adopted, Federal Rule of Evidence 611(b) provides:

> Scope of Cross-Examination.
>
> Cross-examination should be limited to the subject matter of the direct examination and matters affecting the credibility of the witness. The Court may, in the exercise of discretion, permit inquiry into additional matters as if on direct examination.

Additionally, Federal Rule of Evidence 611(a) gives the court wide latitude in controlling the mode and order of interrogating witnesses and presenting evidence "so as to (1) make the interrogation and presentation effective for the ascertainment of the truth, (2) avoid needless consumption of time, and (3) protect witnesses from harassment or undue embarrassment."

The restrictive federal rule requires the cross-examiner to assess the damage done by opposing counsel during direct examination and weigh even more carefully the critical decision of whether to cross-examine. A cross-examiner confined by the restrictive rule risks re-emphasizing the harmful effects of the direct examination without the opportunity for a collateral attack to discredit or impeach the witness.

Harmless Witness

When a witness has not hurt your case, there is little to be gained and potentially much to be lost by cross-examining that witness. The witness who was ineffective during direct testimony may recoup during cross-examination and offer testimony that is even more damaging to your case because it emerges on cross-examination. Additionally, by cross-examining, you give opposing counsel the opportunity to redirect, rehabilitate the witness, and elicit adverse testimony. The potential for scoring points during cross must be weighed against the potential for losing points on redirect. And when you consider that opposing counsel on redirect will be dealing with a cooperative witness, cross-examination of the harmless witness becomes an option to avoid.

Unimpeachable Witness

You will encounter witnesses who are totally unimpeachable, who are giving factual accounts and honest testimony, and who are not subject to any legitimate cross-examination. If you can elicit no evidence on cross-examination either to bolster the plaintiff's case or hinder the defendant's case, do not give the unimpeachable witness the opportunity to reiterate the damaging testimony, either on cross or redirect.

Baited Trap

When an opposing witness fails to testify on direct examination to a known, important fact that is detrimental to your case, you should be alert to the possibility of a baited trap. Opposing counsel may have chosen not to elicit the evidence on direct examination to allow the testimony to emerge during cross-examination, thereby giving it more impact and allowing the witness to score points against you. The theory is that such evidence, emerging adversely to the cross-examiner, will have a greater impact on the minds of the jurors than if elicited during direct examination.

You can deny your opponent this planned impact by either (1) avoiding the subject matter or (2) if otherwise appropriate, choosing not to cross-examine, thereby also denying opposing counsel the opportunity to elicit the evidence on redirect.

Unnecessary Reiteration

If, on examination by opposing counsel, a witness has testified unfavorably to your opponent, you will be strongly tempted to elicit the same testimony on cross-examination to reiterate it for the jury. This should be avoided since such cross-examination allows the witness to explain and thereby reduce or eliminate the effect of the adverse testimony. This is particularly true if there has been a recess between direct and cross-examination during which opposing counsel can tell the witness how to explain away the adverse testimony. Such repetitive cross-examination is wholly unnecessary—and precarious. The jury has heard the evidence; the testimony is in the record and can be typed by the court reporter and read to the jury during summation with the full impact and sanctity of "sworn testimony reduced to writing." Don't attempt a reiteration: it has minimal value, and you risk having the valuable summation material nullified by the witness's explanation. While it is true that opposing counsel may try to elicit an explanation on redirect, this effort will appear contrived and will not have the same ring of truth as the witness extricating herself on cross-examination.

Improper Motives for Cross-Examination

Avoid deciding to cross-examine to please your client, to attack a witness, or to maintain your aggressive posture in the eyes of the jury. Examination without a proper motive will justifiably rebound against you and will often alienate the judge and jury, all to the detriment of your client's case. Make your decisions on cross-examination tactically, based on a positive decision that testimony can be elicited from this witness that will either bolster your client's case, diminish the opponent's case, or predicate summation. If these goals are not well served, you should seriously consider silent cross-examination, that is, "It is not necessary to question this witness, your Honor."

GOALS OF CROSS-EXAMINATION

During direct examination, you must listen carefully to fully comprehend the substance of the adverse witness's testimony, watch the witness closely—particularly the eyes—and listen to the way the witness expresses himself. Attention to detail during direct examination is often the key to successful cross-examination.

If, during direct examination, you determine that cross-examination is necessary, conduct a quick damage assessment from the perspective of the jury—keeping clearly in focus that the jurors are the sole judges of factual disputes, the credibility of the witnesses, and the amount of damages to be awarded. Approach cross-examination with three principal goals: to prejudice the opponent's case, to bolster your case, and to predicate your summation.

Prejudice the Opponent's Case

Three primary approaches to prejudicing the opponent's case on cross-examination are to discredit the witness, to highlight error or confusion in the witness's story, and to bolster your case.

Demonstrate Bias of the Witness

As part of the preparation for trial, you should investigate the background of every potential witness to discover information that may be useful to mitigate the impact of the witness's testimony. Depending on the veracity and integrity of the witness, your attack may range from demonstrating a bias of the witness to total impeachment. In most jurisdictions, pretrial discovery of information with which to reduce or destroy the credibility of potential adverse witnesses is permissible. Under these procedures, surprise witnesses should be a relic of the past. However, you should directly attack the character of a witness only when the evidence is conclusive, and then only as a last resort. An attack on character is, by far, the most dangerous form of impeachment. The backlash resulting from a failed impeachment attempt can damage your case.

A less dangerous way to discredit the witness is to elicit facts that demonstrate bias or prejudice, for example, if the witness is a relative, close friend, co-worker, or professional colleague of the defendant. Establishing any type of pecuniary interest in the outcome of the litigation will diminish the witness's credibility in direct proportion to the amount and type of the witness's financial interest. Simply stated, seek to elicit anything that casts doubt on the witness's objectivity.

Questioning a witness about bias is a double-edged sword. A grueling examination on the witness's relationship to the opposing party that fails to establish bias may augment, rather than diminish, the witness's credibility. You must seek a balance between timidity and reckless aggression during cross-examination, being mindful that most of the wounds you can suffer during cross-examination are self-inflicted.

Highlight Error or Confusion

The most common objective of cross-examination is to diminish the witness's reliability by highlighting errors or confusion in the testimony. You can accomplish this objective by emphasizing inherent improbabilities in the testimony, conflicts with common sense, internal conflict and confusion within the testimony, the witness's limited access to the facts, and, most importantly, prior inconsistent statements or testimony given by the witness.

At no point in cross-examination is your preparation more important than when you attempt to impeach a witness by bringing out prior inconsistent statements. Most modern rules of civil procedure provide ample opportunity to discover statements such as depositions, signed statements, sworn statements, sworn answers to interrogatories, and prior testimony in other proceedings. Before the trial, you must personally read all prior statements of the witness and cross-index every deposition by name and evidentiary topic. Thus prepared, you can listen very attentively during direct examination of the witness and readily recognize conflicts in testimony when they occur.

When the witness is passed for cross-examination, carefully consider the most auspicious time for impeachment. Then take the witness back over the testimony given during direct to fix the point of impeachment clearly in the minds of the jurors. Ask the witness whether he has ever testified any differently. The witness may then respond with "yes," "no," or "I don't remember." If the witness says yes, you may ask the witness about the time and place of the testimony and its nature (for example, sworn testimony has the same effect as testimony in open court, and it is given under the same oath the witness took before testifying inconsistently on direct examination).

At this point you must carefully consider the relationship between the witness and the jury. With a witness who has made a mistake and freely admits it, your object should be to discredit rather than to destroy. Your attempt to pounce on the witness with such questions as "You were sworn to tell the truth both times and you gave different testimony, so you've lied under oath, haven't you?" may result in disaster. Americans love an underdog, and so do American juries. Jurors occupy a position in court much more closely aligned to that of the witness than to that of the attorney, and they will forgive the witness for what appears to be an honest and admitted mistake. Your unsuccessful "attack" on the witness will invariably lead the jury to side with the witness at great expense to your client and case.

Consider first that opposing counsel is aware of the prior sworn testimony and should have prepared the witness to respond to the cross-examination. This will explain a witness's open admission of having testified differently. In this situation, the witness and counsel have probably prepared an acceptable reason as to why the witness is testifying differently: "Since I testified on deposition, I have learned additional factors that cause me to testify differently here today. These factors include . . . ." At this point, since you asked the open-ended question of whether the witness lied under oath, the witness may detail all of the reasons why she changed her testimony.

It is essential to learn to distinguish between discrediting and impeaching a witness. It is part of the art of cross-examination to determine how far to go in attacking a witness who has given inconsistent testimony. A few factors that you must consider include the overall effect the witness has had on the jury; whether the witness is a party, a hired expert, a partisan, or a neutral observer; and the significance of the evidentiary point on which the witness is being discredited. Common sense dictates that an impeaching statement must be on a matter of substance. The court and jury have little patience with a lawyer who attempts to discredit a witness by bringing up immaterial, minor inconsistencies. The rule is "impeach; don't quibble."

The technique of cross-examining through prior inconsistent statements is particularly valuable when confronting opposing experts, especially hired guns or in-house experts in products liability cases who travel the country testifying similarly in case after case. Before trial, you should make every effort to gather all prior testimony of such an expert, as well as all books and articles authored by the expert. Once you have accumulated this material, you must read it all thoroughly. Successful cross-examination of an expert using the expert's own articles or prior sworn testimony as weapons is another of the art forms of the skill of cross-examination.

Impeach the Witness

If the witness, confronted with your question "Have you ever testified any differently?" answers "no," the stage is set for the most interesting and dramatic aspect of the trial: the verbal jousting between you and the witness as you attempt to impeach the witness. However, unless you handle the situation properly, the witness may escape impeachment and leave you looking foolish in the eyes of the jury, thereby damaging your client's case. Your absolute control over the questioning is essential to impeachment. The complete avoidance of open-ended questions is crucial. In the ideal scenario, you will control the witness through a series of carefully crafted questions that, as the jury watches, lead inescapably to the lie emerging from the witness's lips.

When the witness responds "no" to the inquiry as to whether he has ever testified any differently, you must meet the predicate for impeachment by identifying the time, place, and circumstances of the prior inconsistent statement. At this point, you should approach the witness and stand next to the witness box so as to cause the witness to turn and directly face the jury. Then inquire, "Mr. Jones, on this previous sworn testimony I asked you the following question, 'What color was the light as you entered the intersection?' Please read to the jury your answer under oath at that time." Hold the deposition in front of the witness so that the witness is looking down to read the answer, and the jury has the opportunity to look directly into the witness's eyes as he repeats the prior sworn inconsistent testimony. You must retain control at this point by allowing the witness to read only the specific answer from the deposition and not give any further explanation.

If this is done properly, the jury is now fully aware that the witness has given prior inconsistent sworn testimony, and the witness is successfully impeached. At this point, many impeachments are lost by counsel asking one question too many: an open-ended question or an attempt to reiterate the impeachment material, either of which may allow the witness to explain the inconsistencies and nullify the impeachment.

One impeachment, on a major point, is all that is needed to destroy the witness's credibility in the eyes of the jury. After the witness has read the impeaching material from the deposition, you should remove the deposition, leaving the impeached witness directly facing the jury. You should pause and look further at the deposition as if reviewing the material; leave the witness for as long a pause as possible after the impeachment with the jury looking directly into the witness's eyes. Then return slowly to counsel table and retrieve other materials for questioning, taking as long as possible before the next question, possibly inquiring of the court, "May I have a moment, your Honor?" Judges resent witnesses who lie under oath in their courts and will generally be very cooperative at this point. This leaves the impeached witness on the hot seat under the intense scrutiny of the judge and jury with no place to hide.

The entire courtroom is now focused for your next question of this impeached witness. The pause after impeachment, in addition to allowing the jurors to fully appreciate the significance of what they have observed, piques their interest as to the next line of inquiry. It is absolutely essential, to maintain control of the witness and to protect the impeachment that has occurred, that two things occur in the next line of questioning: (1) you should move completely away from the topic on which the witness was just impeached, and (2) you should maximize the witness's loss of credibility before the jury by cross-examining the witness on the most important outcome-determinative issues in the case.

The reason for moving away from the subject of impeachment is so that the witness has absolutely no opportunity in subsequent questions to regroup and explain away the basis of the impeachment. The reason for moving to the most outcome-determinative issues in the case on which this witness is able to testify is that the jury's interest is at a peak and the witness's credibility is in a valley. Therefore, you should be able to maximize the effect of impeachment by controlling the further examination of the impeached witness and eliciting favorable testimony on the outcome-determinative disputes. The witness may testify more favorably on the outcome-determinative issues for fear of being impeached again. If the witness refuses to cooperate with you and shades the testimony in favor of your opponent, the jury will not accept the testimony since the witness was just impeached.

Total impeachment of a witness is rare. Therefore, the lesser goals of discrediting the witness, highlighting confusion, and showing bias or the inability of the witness to testify accurately may be the small victories that cumulatively weaken the jury's faith in the witness. While total impeachment is desirable, do not overlook the cumulative effect of numerous small disparities, as long as they are directly relevant to material issues in the case.

Bolstering the Plaintiff's Case

Not all cross-examination is directed toward discrediting or impeaching a witness. As you prepare for the cross-examination of each witness, carefully consider every evidentiary subject on which the witness is qualified to testify that will materially bolster the plaintiff's case. You must view adverse witnesses not only as objects of confrontation and impeachment but also as potential ratifiers of important aspects of the plaintiff's case. At the outset of the cross-examination you should, whenever possible, secure positive agreements, enhance the credibility of the plaintiff's witness, and verify the plaintiff's theory of the case through adverse witnesses.

Secure Positive Agreements

Frequently there are many strong points in the plaintiff's case that cannot be denied by the opposing side. When preparing for cross-examination of each adverse witness, include each line of questioning that clearly bolsters the plaintiff's case and that cannot be denied by the defendant's witnesses. For example, if the plaintiff has a catastrophic injury, such as a paraplegic, the witnesses for the defendant (the defendant doctor in a medical negligence case) cannot deny the nature, extent, and permanence of the injury; the plaintiff's physical pain and suffering, mental anguish, physical disability, loss of consortium, loss of society and companionship; or the extensive future lifetime disability the plaintiff will suffer.

In a common law jurisdiction, or if opposing counsel raises the subject on direct in a restrictive or federal jurisdiction, each witness called by the defense may become a damages witness for the plaintiff. For example, a defendant doctor called on the medical causation or negligence issue in a medical negligence case can become a powerful witness for the plaintiff on each of these damages issues. The more reluctance the doctor demonstrates in offering such favorable testimony, the more impact the testimony will have on the jury. This type of cross-examination, besides bolstering the plaintiff's case, predicates a persuasive argument in summation: "Even the defendant's witnesses cannot deny the devastating nature of the permanent injuries suffered by the plaintiff."

This is where the distinction between the restrictive federal rule and permissive common law cross-examination becomes highly significant. The foregoing cross would not be allowed under the federal rules unless the doctor testified regarding plaintiff's damages on direct. Therefore, you must listen attentively during direct examination for the opponent to "open the door" for areas of cross.

Under the common law rule, the witness may be examined on any issue relevant to the case. Many lawyers believe that the common law rule leads the witness closer to "the truth, the whole truth, and nothing but the truth." The common law rule can provide a no-lose situation for the cross-examiner: either the adverse witness ratifies the strengths of the plaintiff's case on cross-examination, or the witness denies those matters that can easily be proven and reduces her own credibility in the eyes of the jury.

Enhance the Plaintiff's Witnesses

Consider whether adverse witnesses can be used effectively during cross-examination to enhance the qualifications, integrity, and credibility of the plaintiff's witnesses. For example, if in an orthopedic-injury case the defendant's medical witness is a non-board-certified general practitioner and the plaintiff's medical witness is a board-certified orthopedic surgeon, the defendant's general practitioner will of necessity acknowledge that the board-certified orthopedic specialist is more qualified both to treat and to testify about the plaintiff's treatment.

The general practitioner can be called on to give a thorough explanation of board certification: how it is acquired, how it is a recognition by a body of medical peers as to the skill and expertise of the orthopedic surgeon, how it represents a level of skill far greater than the mere designation of medical doctor, and how this is the particular area of medical expertise that is required for the treatment of the plaintiff. If the fact has been established on deposition before trial, the general practitioner may also testify as to the orthopedic surgeon's high standing and general reputation in the medical community as an outstanding specialist in the treatment of the particular type of injury with which the plaintiff is afflicted. This type of enhancement of the plaintiff's witnesses through effective cross-examination of the opposing expert sets up a very effective summation: you will be able to compare the conflicting testimony and qualifications of the two doctors.

If the general practitioner refuses to acknowledge that a board-certified orthopedic surgeon is more qualified to treat an orthopedic injury than a general practitioner, the jury will view this response as indicating bias and will doubt the credibility of the general practitioner. Properly utilized, this can be a win-win line of questioning for the plaintiff.

Verify the Plaintiff's Theory as a Reasonable Alternative

Another cross-examination technique used to bolster the plaintiff's case is having the opposing experts acknowledge that the plaintiff's theory is a reasonable alternative theory. It is not necessary that the experts admit that the plaintiff's theory applies to this case as long as they will acknowledge that the plaintiff's theory is viable. The plaintiff's experts then provide the testimony that the plaintiff's theory is the correct theory in the case, and the plaintiff's summation is once again enhanced by admissions from opposing witnesses.

Predicate the Plaintiff's Summation

Eloquent summations are the progeny of diligent preparation and effective witness examination. No jewel shines more brilliantly in summation than the diamond that emerges successfully during cross-examination from the black coal of adversarial confrontation.

You must plan the examination of witnesses with the understanding that testimony elicited on cross-examination is more memorable to the jury and carries more weight than direct testimony. Jurors will cling more diligently to the conclusions they reach on their own than to those that were spoon-fed to them on direct. Therefore, given the choice between proving an important fact on direct examination of a plaintiff's witness or allowing it to emerge during cross-examination of the opponent's witnesses, consider that the jurors are more attentive during cross because of its adversarial nature and will give more weight to such testimony. You may then reiterate the evidence through direct examination of your own witnesses and remind the jury on summation that the evidence was elicited first from the adverse witness. It is extremely effective on summation to remind the jury that several defense witnesses gave various testimony that bolstered the plaintiff's case, recognized the qualifications and integrity of the plaintiff's witnesses, and verified the plaintiff's theory as a viable alternative theory in the case.

PLANNING AND PREPARATION OF CROSS-EXAMINATION

Extemporaneous brilliance on cross-examination increases in direct proportion to extreme diligence in planning and preparation. A good cross-examination is seldom the result of chance. The more spontaneous a cross-examination seems, the more likely it is that counsel carefully planned the examination well in advance of trial.

Cross-examination of a witness generally falls into two categories: offensive and defensive. In an offensive cross-examination, you can establish salient points that advance your client's case. A defensive cross-examination is usually directed at blunting the effect of adverse testimony and at diminishing the opponent's case.

One technique of cross-examination is to write out every question in advance. This may be a worthwhile tool to give self-confidence to the neophyte, but, with experience, a more flexible approach is to select the subject matter to be covered and the points to be made under each subject and to use them as a checklist. The totally scripted cross-examination appears stilted and makes it more difficult to immediately accommodate the information derived from the witness during the examination. The ability to assimilate the line of questioning to maximize use of information received in answers is a vital skill of the master cross-examiner that derives from careful planning and experience under fire.

As part of your preparation of the offensive cross-examination, prepare a complete list of subjects about which the witness cannot avoid giving favorable testimony for the plaintiff. These might include, in a serious injury case, acknowledgement of the nature and extent of the plaintiff's injury and acknowledgement of the extensive damages suffered by the plaintiff.

The offensive cross-examination serves several major purposes. It bolsters the plaintiff's case through the use of defense witnesses, breaks the rhythm of the favorable testimony with which defendant's counsel probably concluded the direct examination, and catches the defendant's witness—who is expecting a hostile cross-examination—off guard by beginning with areas in which the examiner and the witness are in agreement. Also, by beginning with a series of admissions by the defense witness, you attain a big opening on cross-examination and immediately gain control of the witness and the courtroom. This is consistent with the rule of primacy.

CONDUCTING THE EXAMINATION

The three most important aspects of conducting cross-examination are control, control, and control: of the witness, the evidence, and the entire scenario in the courtroom. The rules of primacy and recency state respectively that the jury will believe the credible testimony they hear first and remember the longest that which they hear last. Therefore it is essential in planning cross-examination to ensure a strong opening and finish on the strongest point possible. Technique is crucial. Open-ended questions such as "why" or "please explain," which allow the witness to gain control of the answer, must be avoided. Reiteration of the witness's testimony on direct is disastrous and should also be avoided. Repetition of each answer as a preface to the next question breaks the rhythm of the cross, and you must be careful not to fall into such habits as beginning each question with "Now, let me ask you this question . . . ."

Primacy—Use a Strong Opening

Consistent with the rule of primacy, you should seek a strong opening in your cross-examination; that is, you should begin cross-examination with a point on which you are certain you can score. You may accomplish this by eliciting testimony to bolster your case from the list of points with which the witness must agree, as discussed above. Beginning cross-examination of the witness on the last matter covered in direct is generally weak and inefficient. This subject matter is clearest in the witness's mind, most logically related to the body of the witness's testimony, and, if mishandled, will merely appear as a continuation of the direct examination rather than as the dramatic change the cross-examiner should seek to achieve. If there is a line of questioning with which you can obtain several agreements from the witness to bolster your case, pursue this line before discrediting or impeaching the witness. It is a quantum leap to ask the jurors to reject the witness's testimony that is favorable to the defendant because the witness has been discredited and then to ask them to accept the witness's testimony that bolsters the plaintiff's case.

Use Signposts

Ideally, in preparing cross-examination, you should frame the individual questions in the context of their relationship to a specific dispute or issue that the jury will be called on to resolve. You may establish the context of the question with the jury by using signposts during cross-examination to indicate the issues to which questions relate. A signpost is an indicator at the beginning of a question or series of questions that shows the jury the direction you are taking and the issue to which the question relates, such as the following:

> "Doctor, with respect to the physical pain suffered by Mr. Jones, the muscle spasm that you felt in Mr. Jones's back is an objective sign of the presence of pain, isn't it?"

The signpost "with respect to the physical pain suffered by Mr. Jones" alerts the jurors that the following question will relate to their duty to assess the amount of damages to be awarded to compensate Mr. Jones for the physical pain arising from the injury. During voir dire examination and opening statement, the jurors will have been educated that their role in the trial includes assessing damages for physical pain and suffering. The signpost provides the jury with a framework for understanding the significance of the question and answer. Signposts are particularly useful in helping the jury follow the flow of the testimony when you shift from one subject to another.

Obviously, if it would be advantageous to you for the witness not to follow shifts in direction of the cross-examination, signposts should be avoided.

Be Brief

Numerous legal maxims have evolved through the ages that lead to one overall proposition: brevity in cross-examination is important. Ask no unimportant questions on cross-examination. A question that does not advance your case hinders it. As cross-examination begins, you have the renewed attention of the jurors, who are hoping for an interesting confrontation. However, being granted the gift of a hopeful jury's attention, you must retain that attention by asking poignant, significant, and relevant questions, and by scoring points consistently during the examination. A cross-examiner is only as good as her last series of questions. The jury will not remember a great deal of the testimony of any one witness. The typical personal injury lawsuit lasts several days, and jurors remember only the high spots of the testimony of any witness. Therefore the cross-examiner should, if possible, limit cross to those few points or areas that are critical.

Some cross-examiners hide the key questions by presenting them in the midst of a lengthy cross-examination. They hope to camouflage important questions in the midst of many unimportant questions.

While you may surprise the witness with this tactic, the value of the admission may be lost on the jurors, who by the end of cross-examination will have become confused, bored, or totally anesthetized.

Under some circumstances, you have no choice but to conduct a seemingly endless cross-examination in an effort to elicit significant admissions. When this occurs, if you believe that significant admissions went over the head of the jury, have the court reporter transcribe the pertinent portions of the testimony. With this transcript, you can convert the seemingly insignificant admissions into a weapon during summation. This way there can be no question in the minds of the jurors as to what was actually said by the witness.

Recency—Time the Examination Properly

Recency, the principle that the jurors will remember longest that which they hear last, has multiple applications during trial. You should end each cross-examination on a very strong point. However, it is also important to finish each prerecess testimony, each day's testimony, and the case as a whole with very significant points. Thus, you must be constantly aware not only of the content of cross-examination but also of the timing of the questioning. It is imperative that you not end the cross-examination lamely on a matter of little concern. At all cost, avoid closing cross with the witness in control and you discomfited. If you reach a climactic point—such as impeachment of the witness or the witness's admission of a vital point—weigh the significance of the remaining material against the importance of an immediate strong finish, with the clock as one factor in the equation.

MAINTAINING CONTROL

Use Leading Questions

The leading question is the primary weapon in the arsenal with which the cross-examiner controls the witness. Since witness control in the sine qua non of successful cross-examination, effective use of the leading question is a vital skill. The leading question allows you to couch each question in terms of your theory of the lawsuit and, when properly framed, limits the response of the witness.

Avoid Overuse

Avoid overusing leading questions. If you use too many, the

jurors may get the impression that you are testifying rather than the witness. Also avoid the appearance that, because you will not allow the witness to fully answer the question, the witness is being treated unfairly. Explain to the witness that his counsel can permit him to fully explain his answer during redirect examination but that it is important on cross-examination to follow the rules and simply affirm or deny your questions.

Elicit "Yes" or "No"

The leading question contains within itself the answer that the examiner seeks, thus requiring only a ratification from the witness. Leading questions should be couched in terms of the examiner's theory of the lawsuit so that an affirmative answer advances the plaintiff's cause. For example, the leading question, "as you approached the intersection the signal light was red, wasn't it, Mr. Jones?" contains the answer that the questioner seeks, that the light was red. Mr. Jones need answer only yes or no with no necessity to expound further on the answer.

More significantly, the question is also couched in terms of the plaintiff's theory of the lawsuit, that Mr. Jones was negligent in running a red light and in causing the accident and resulting injuries to the plaintiff.

Skillful phrasing of leading questions, carefully couched in terms of the plaintiff's theory of the case, is essential to several aspects of cross-examination: the witness is limited to yes or no answers, the testimony of the witness is controlled through avoidance of lengthy answers, the plaintiff's case is advanced through affirmative responses to leading questions, and tightly controlled leading questions are of extreme importance in maintaining control while discrediting or impeaching a witness.

Avoid Open-Ended Questions

The open-ended question is one that allows the witness to explain fully and often at length the answer to the examiner's question. The classic example of the catastrophically open-ended question is asking an expert, "How can you possibly have arrived at such an opinion?" In answering this question, the expert may testify at length as to every factor that played a part in forming the opinion. Such a recitation can only be disastrous to the cross-examiner's case. While there are no universal rules of witness examination, inquiries such as "why," "how," or "please explain" are almost invariably to be avoided.

Allow Renarration or Repetition Rarely

You may permit the witness to renarrate or repeat an answer given on direct when you are trying to demonstrate that the witness has memorized the story and will tell the same story two, three, or more times in precisely the same words. Normally, a witness will not repeat a story verbatim unless it is memorized. However, few counsel will leave their witnesses open to this type of cross-examination. Another situation in which a witness may be encouraged on cross-examination to renarrate is when the witness has told a story on direct that is so vulnerable that it can be totally destroyed. It must be emphasized, however, that such an approach is rarely indicated or justified.

Limit the Talkative or Evasive Witness

The cross-examiner frequently encounters witnesses who will not respond yes or no to leading questions but either insist on explaining every answer or evade answering the questions. Dealing with such witnesses creates problems, and there are two basic approaches to handling them. First, the cross-examiner can seek to enlist the aid of the judge in limiting the talkativeness or evasiveness of the witness. Faced with an unresponsive answer, the cross-examiner may move to strike the answer and request the court to admonish the witness to respond directly to the question.

When examining a witness who seeks to explain every answer, you may request the court to instruct the witness to limit answers during cross-examination to responses to the questions posed by the examiner and to further instruct that defense counsel, during redirect examination, will have a chance to bring out explanations.

The second approach is to allow the witness to duck, dodge, and explain, within certain limits. If the witness gives an unresponsive answer, ask the question again; if the answer is again unresponsive, ask the same question a third time. Then ask the "explainer" to limit answers to yes or no; explain that the witness will have a chance during redirect examination to explain the answers. Those examiners who do not seek to enlist the aid of the court in dealing with the problem witness and allow the witness to be unresponsive or evasive believe that the jurors will be able to detect the witness's lack of cooperation and candor and will draw their own adverse conclusions about the witness.

The choice between the two methods—invoking the power of the court or allowing the witness to appear evasive to the jury—should be decided based on your perception of the witness's relationship with the jury and the court and the significance of the subject matter of the testimony.

STYLE OF EXAMINATION

"Watch" the Case

One major premise on which master cross-examiners, past and present, agree is the importance of "watching" the case, particularly the witness. Counsel, with her face buried in a legal pad taking notes during direct examination of the opponent's witness, is missing many important elements of the case, including the witness's demeanor, opposing counsel's histrionics, the judge's body language, and the jury's reactions to the entire scenario. Never underestimate the importance of the trial judge, who is being closely observed by the jury and whose facial expression and body language can send vital and powerful messages to both the jury and counsel.

During cross-examination, it is crucial to watch the witness closely to determine the line of questioning that causes nervous responses, avoidance of eye contact, and changes in demeanor indicating a lack of confidence in the answers. It is often as essential for the cross-examiner to decipher the witness's body language as to hear the verbal answers. For example, if an expert witness is testifying confidently and with strong body language indicating a self-assured or arrogant attitude, you may decide that this is the proper point at which to impeach the witness—to increase the length of the witness's fall from the heights of arrogance to the pits of impeachment.

Listen to the Answers

It seems axiomatic to state that the cross-examiner should listen carefully to the answers from the witness. However, jurists and other observers of courtroom behavior advise that one of the most frequent mistakes of the cross-examiner is asking a well-planned question and immediately moving on to the next question while ignoring the witness's answer. Being so wrapped up in the questioning as to miss the effect, nuances, innuendos, and manner of delivery of the answer is a self-imposed trap for the inobservant cross-examiner. The ability to assimilate the questioning to the answers is one of the hallmarks of a master cross-examiner.

Control Your Anger

One clear axiom for the cross-examiner is to hold your own temper while you lead the witness to lose his. Our precursors in ancient Greece were taught: "He whom the Gods will destroy, first make angry." The concept that the cross-examiner must maintain control has broad applications, for example, control of the witness, the testimony, the atmosphere of the case, the theme development, and your own temper and demeanor.

Avoid Animosity

Fictional characterizations of cross-examination portray the lawyer as a relentless prober who storms about the courtroom pointing a finger at the terrified witness. In actual practice, the most effective cross-examination is usually conducted in a courteous and conciliatory manner. The witness is more likely to admit error to the courteous examiner with a friendly approach than to the hard-driving examiner who firms up the witness's opposition. Further, as the jurors look on cross-examination as an unequal contest—with the advantage on the side of the lawyer—the aggressive cross-examiner risks having the jurors disregard an admission because they feel that the examiner violated the rules of fair play in securing it. This is not to say that you should overlook or excuse conflicts; to the contrary, you must be tenacious in the pursuit of inaccuracies. You should merely seek to do your job without creating animosity between yourself and the witness. If the witness is caught in a lie, there is no need to emphasize that point to the jury during cross-examination by calling the witness a liar.

Never underestimate the collective wisdom of the jury to fully comprehend the impeachment; the jurors will give more weight and cling tenaciously to discoveries they make on their own. Unless the impeachment is unequivocal and directly on a point that is highly relevant, the jury may sympathize with the witness whom they regard as being unduly berated on cross-examination by an overbearing attorney.

Cross-examination is most likely to be effective when it is conducted in a calm, rational, and unemotional manner, although righteous indignation, even controlled rage, may be indicated—and effective—in certain circumstances. While many hard-driving, savage cross-examiners have been successful, those who attempt to mimic this technique must exercise caution, for the technique can carry penalties. The quiet, calm, soft-spoken, yet confident and forceful examiner has an equal if not greater chance of being successful and does not risk alienating the jury.

Give Deference to the Court

You must treat the court with due deference at all times. If you convey animosity toward the court, the jury will be aware that you and the judge are in disagreement. The jurors will almost invariably assume that the judge is correct and that you are wrong, and your position will thereby be weakened in their all-important eyes. Additionally, the mandates of professionalism, which dictate the demeanor of the bench and bar, require you to pay due respect to the bench and those who occupy it.

However, deference to the court should not result in your failure to vigorously prosecute your client's claim to the fullest extent of the law. An advocate who allows the court to abuse its power to the detriment of her client's rights is flagrantly violating the duty to fully represent the client. It is essential to know the rules of court and fully exercise all your rights under those rules. In the event you disagree with the court, handle the conflict in a dignified and professional manner, such as "I appreciate that your Honor is performing your role as you perceive it, and I trust that the court will afford me the same courtesy as I proceed to represent my client's interests fully, within the parameters of the rules." Never be in the position of the counsel of whom the court inquired "Are you trying to show your contempt for this court?" and who replied "No, your Honor, I am doing my very best to conceal it."

Give Deference to the Witness

There is a vital distinction between discrediting the testimony and discrediting the witness. Unless the witness is a perjurer who can be clearly demonstrated to the jury as such, wise counsel will begin cross-examination by treating the witness deferentially. Only after careful probing demonstrates bias, lack of qualification, or other aspects that diminish the testimony of the witness are you free to directly attack the witness. At the outset of examination, the sympathies of the jury are invariably on the side of the witness, and jurors are quick to resent any unfounded discourtesy.

Jurors love the confrontation of advocate and witness when truth is tested in the crucible of cross-examination. Jurors are never more attentive than during a well-planned and executed cross-examination that draws from the witness a story or theory different from that which was given on direct examination. However, counsel takes no greater loss in the eyes of the jury than when, having viciously attacked a witness, the attack fails or when, having failed to successfully elicit favorable testimony, counsel places a false construction on the words of the witness to claim the victory that eluded him.

Country Bumpkin Versus Lawyer Expert

It is a matter of style for each individual lawyer to determine the appropriate persona to adopt in cross-examining each witness. The persona may vary from witness to witness or within the examination of the same witness. In a cross-examination of an annuity expert on deposition, you may appear to be totally ignorant of the subject matter and thereby lead the witness into overstating her position on direct examination at trial. Then, when you are suddenly sophisticated during cross-examination at trial, the witness is surprised and subject to dismantling because of her overstatements on direct examination.

If the witness did not overstate her position on direct, you may proceed with the poor-old-country-bumpkin routine during early cross-examination and lead the witness into overstating her position. You then shift into the lawyer-expert persona with full knowledge and fluid use of the technical terms of art for the purpose of discrediting or impeaching the witness. This technique is particularly useful with medical witnesses who virtually never perceive that the cross-examiner may be even more knowledgeable in certain areas of medicine than themselves.

Your adoption of a persona depends to a large extent on the makeup of the jury, the venue, the witness being cross-examined, and the personality and style with which you are most comfortable.

Respect the Jury

A fascination with law pervades our society, and jurors enter the courtroom with preconceived notions of a trial derived from television, film, and theater dramas based on trials. In these versions of trial, the high point of confrontation and drama almost always occurs during cross-examination, and jurors watch cross-examination with an anticipation of high drama, or at least a few sparks. If you disappoint jurors with boring, repetitious, and meaningless cross-examination, you will find that the jury will respond in kind with a disappointing result for you and your client.

Jurors—who are captives in the jury box, unable to speak or express themselves—have nothing to do with their time but observe the most minute aspects of the protagonists in the drama that is unfolding before them and of which they are an integral part.

Long before the advent of television, Francis Wellman described the role of counsel and the relationship to the jury:

> It is the love of combat which every man possesses that fastens the attention of the jury upon the progress of the trial. The counsel who has a pleasant personality; who speaks with apparent frankness; who appears to be an earnest searcher after truth; who is courteous to those who testify against him; who avoids delaying constantly the progress of the trial by innumerable objections and exceptions to perhaps incompetent but harmless evidence; who seems to know what he is about and sits down when he has accomplished it, exhibiting a spirit of fair play on all occasions—he it is who creates an atmosphere in favor of the side which he represents, a powerful though unconscious influence with the jury in arriving at their verdict. Even if, owing to the weight of testimony, the verdict is against him, yet the amount will be far less than the client had schooled himself to expect.
>
> On the other hand, the lawyer who wearies the court and the jury with endless and pointless cross-examination; who is constantly losing his temper and showing his teeth to the witnesses; who wears a sour, anxious expression; who possesses a monotonous, rasping, penetrating voice; who presents a slovenly, unkempt personal appearance; who is prone to take unfair advantage of witness or counsel, and seems determined to win at all hazards—soon prejudices a jury against himself and the client he represents, entirely irrespective of the sworn testimony in the case.[2]

[2] Wellman at 30-31.

HANDLING OBJECTIONS

If during the course of cross-examination the court sustains opposing counsel's objection to some aspect of your cross-examination, you must proceed confidently and undeterred, without demonstrating the slightest sign of distress or anger. It is particularly crucial that you not demonstrate any hostility to the court, since the jury will almost invariably side with the court in matters involving disputes between the judge and counsel.

You may effectively exercise damage control after having an objection sustained to a question on cross-examination by replying, "Thank you, your Honor, I'll rephrase the question." This conveys to the jury the understanding that the problem was the manner in which the question was phrased rather than the substantive content you are attempting to elicit.

CROSS TO COMPETENCE OF WITNESS

An essential skill for the cross-examiner is the ability to question the witness's legal competence either to testify as a lay witness or to render opinions as an expert.

Voir Dire Examination

The procedural mechanism for testing the competence of the witness to testify is to conduct a voir dire examination of the witness in the absence of the jury before the rendering of adverse testimony by the witness. While it is possible to get the judge to advise the jury to disregard testimony that the witness has just given and not to consider it during deliberations, the practical effect of this is only to highlight such testimony. Therefore, you must examine each witness first in terms of whether the witness meets the legal requirements to qualify as a witness.

Legal Competence—Layperson

Age

There is no specified age at which an individual becomes competent to testify as a witness in a lawsuit. This is a matter purely within the discretion of the trial court, to be decided on a witness-by-witness basis. The underlying test generally applied is whether the court is satisfied that the witness is old enough to understand the oath and the significance of sworn testimony.

Non Compos Mentis

In certain types of cases, particularly closed-head injury traumas, there may be a question as to whether the plaintiff is too disabled to testify. This disability is based on the mental incapacity of the witness to understand the oath or to factually and accurately relate information to the jury. Or it may be due to a memory deficit that renders the plaintiff's testimony unreliable.

Qualifications—Expert

The competence and qualification of a witness to render an opinion in a case is predicated on the seminal finding by the court that the witness has expertise greater than that of the jury on a given subject and will aid the jury in rendering its decision in the case. Determining whether an individual is an expert is a matter within the discretion of the trial court. The threshold of expertise is generally very low, and the court will generally rule that attacks on the competence to render an opinion go to the weight to be given the testimony rather than to its admissibility.

Direct Attack

Fallacies of Testimony

Effective cross-examination begins with the understanding that not every witness testifying for the opposition is automatically committing perjury. There are many witnesses who believe their testimony to be the truth and who testify with an honesty and sincerity which is impressive and persuasive to the jury. This can be very frustrating to counsel, armed with vast knowledge of the case, who believes that the witness is not testifying truthfully. However, it is essential in preparing to cross-examine such a witness to understand why the witness is testifying in this manner and to seek out the fallacies in the testimony.

The witness is testifying from personal knowledge of the facts. However, knowledge is the impression in the witness's mind and not the fact itself. You must understand that the witness is testifying from data acquired from two distinct sources: (1) the witness's sensory perceptions of sight, sound, touch, smell, and taste, and (2) the witness's conscious impressions based on personal experiences, bias, financial considerations, pride, motivation, loyalty, and personal character. It is for these reasons that two persons can witness the same event, experience the same sensory perceptions, testify completely differently regarding the events, and both feel that they are telling the truth.

Assume for example that the beating of a black teenager by a white police officer is witnessed by the mother of the teenager and the partner of the police officer. Each witness will have experienced the same unconscious sense perceptions, that is, the same sounds, sights, and smells. But when called on to describe the scene and events, the mother and the police officer would give considerably different accounts of the events, despite the fact that both would be testifying to what they perceive to be the truth.

The sensations they experienced would be the same. However, superimposed on these sensations would be their own personal biases, motives, experiences, and self-interests that, when applied to interpreting the sensations each witnessed, create the perceptions in each individual mind that form the bases of the testimony. Therefore, in cross-examining either of these witnesses, you must first understand and then probe deeply into each conscious motivation or bias that the witness applied to the unconscious sensory perceptions to arrive at the perceptions that form the basis of the testimony.

In addition to the conscious interpretation of the perceived sensations, you should inquire into the state of the attention level with which the witness focused on the facts. Undoubtedly, the attention level of the mother would be complete and undivided because of her personal interests in the matter she was witnessing. However, a passerby in a vehicle who also had to attend to driving would not be nearly as perceptive a witness because of a far lesser degree of interest in the events and a preoccupation with driving.

Desire is another fallacy of testimony that requires your examination. Witnesses who have a personal interest in the matters about which they are testifying are extremely prone to see what they wish to see. Additionally, the more they are called upon to repeat the story, the more likely they are to believe that they did, in fact, witness the events they have recalled.

Demonstrating extraordinary perception, Francis Wellman discerned that perhaps the most subtle and prolific of all of the fallacies of testimony arises out of unconscious partisanship. The witness will frequently feel complimented by the confidence of the party calling her as a witness and mold her testimony unconsciously so as to prove worthy of the confidence. Some witnesses derive a tremendous sense of power from being the center of attention in the witness chair with the ability to sway the verdict of a jury in one direction or the other. You should never overlook the desire to win that can color the testimony of a witness to the point that the witness leans in the direction of the one who called her as a crucial part of the case.

Therefore, when you are confronted with a witness who is unshakable in his apparent veracity, it is essential that you examine closely the witness's biases that are shading the testimony.

Probabilities

In evaluating the testimony of a witness, you should analyze whether the testimony comports with probabilities based on human knowledge and experience. Aristotle stated that "probability is never detected during false testimony." Therefore, one area of analysis and examination when preparing the cross-examination is to determine whether the evidence proffered by the witness comports more with probability or improbability.

Common Sense

While evaluating the testimony offered by the opposing witness in terms of probabilities, you should also examine the testimony in light of common sense. One of the great strengths of our jury system is that the collective common sense of the jury is a highly effective testing ground for evidence. This is more true now than ever before, since so much of current litigation is predicated on the testimony of dueling experts: experts hired by each side offer highly sophisticated and technical testimony on which the theory of the case or defense is predicated. Frequently, an appeal to the collective common sense of the jury during cross-examination of such an expert will serve as an extremely valuable tool in disarming the hired gun, since a commonsense argument is much easier for a jury to accept than highly technical theories.

Collateral Attack

It is very difficult to attack expert witnesses directly within their area of expertise. For example, attempting to cross-examine Dr. Michael DeBakey on the techniques of heart surgery will lead to catastrophic results except at the hands of the most experienced and highly skilled master cross-examiners.

However, in this age of narrow specialties, the cross-examiner, by moving slightly out of the expert's area of expertise, can often conduct devastating cross-examination of an expert witness through collateral attack. For example, an orthopedic surgeon who testifies as a defense witness in a case in which a tomographic examination of the plaintiff is very important may be cross-examined successfully by the plaintiff's attorney. Tomography is a topic with which the orthopedic surgeon has only surface knowledge, and the cross-examiner, thoroughly self-educated about tomography before cross-examination, can often effectively decimate the credibility of the opposing expert by moving slightly out of the expert's area of expertise.

Another way to attack collaterally involves avoiding direct confrontation with the expert on his opinions within his narrow area of expertise while collaterally attacking the underlying assumptions on which the opinions are based.

For example, when electromyography was a new diagnostic tool about which few doctors and no lawyers had any knowledge, a certain polished doctor was considered to be a highly dangerous witness for the plaintiff. In numerous cases, juries had accepted this doctor's testimony and returned defense verdicts.

Finally, in a confrontation with a master cross-examiner, the doctor gave his usual, seemingly unimpeachable testimony regarding electromyography and his interpretation of the results of his electromyographic test on the plaintiff. On cross-examination, counsel inquired first about the extreme importance of an accurate medical history. The doctor agreed that the medical history was important; that the medical history plays an important role as a tool of differential diagnosis; that if the patient had experienced a previous back injury that the doctor was not told about during the medical history, this could be fatal to the diagnosis; and that without knowledge of the complete medical history, a doctor's diagnosis could be wrong, even when using the new magical electromyograph.

The doctor agreed with each of these propositions rather hastily as he anticipated moving on to his favorite discussion of the wonders of electromyography. However, counsel then surprised the doctor with "No further questions of this witness, your Honor." After the doctor was excused, counsel subsequently proved that the plaintiff had a prior back injury that she had not related to the doctor during the medical history. During summation, counsel was able to advise the jury that the doctor, in his own words, had stated that if the medical history was incomplete in such an important matter as omitting the prior back injury, the diagnosis would be totally inaccurate. The jury returned a verdict in direct contravention of the doctor's medical testimony on direct examination. This is a classic example of a successful use of the collateral attack technique.

LEARNED TREATISES AS CROSS-EXAMINATION TOOLS

In virtually every jurisdiction, where an expert witness has specifically relied on a treatise or text as supporting her opinion given in direct examination, she may be cross-examined from other portions of that treatise to show that the treatise does not in fact support her position. If the witness is to be cross-examined from the contents of some other treatise, some states require either independent authentication (e.g., from the plaintiff's own expert) or an admission by the witness that the text is regarded as authoritative. Some jurisdictions permit learned treatises or technical works to be used in the cross-examination of an expert witness—to test the witness's competence or qualifications—without imposing any specific requirement that the witness has relied on or recognized the authoritative status of the work.

The Federal Rules of Evidence have adopted the following exception to the hearsay rule:

> Learned Treatises. To the extent called to the attention of an expert witness upon cross-examination or relied upon by the expert witness in direct examination, statements contained in published treatises, periodicals, or pamphlets on a subject of history, medicine, or other science or art, established as a reliable authority by the testimony or admission of the witness or by other expert testimony or by judicial notice. If admitted, the statements may be read into evidence but may not be received as exhibits.[3]

[3] FED. R. EVID. 803(18).

In using this technique of cross-examination, you must establish—by an independent expert witness, admission by the expert being cross-examined, judicial notice by the trial court, or request for admissions—that the authorities you intend to use are indeed authoritative in the field.

No examiner should ever attempt this technique without engaging in exhaustive preparation, as you will often find yourself playing on the expert's home field, where the expert is quite familiar and comfortable. Do not attempt to use isolated spot references from the treatise that may be completely repudiated or explained away elsewhere in the text.

CROSS-EXAMINING THE DEFENDANT'S MEDICAL EXPERT

During the trial, you as counsel for the plaintiff frequently will be faced with the problem of cross-examining a medical doctor who has testified for the defendant and cast serious doubts on the plaintiff's case. It will be your job to do what you can to mitigate the detrimental effect of the testimony and, if possible, to bolster your own case.

Again, you should not cross-examine at all unless your client's case has been hurt by the defense doctor's testimony, and you believe you can mitigate the damage by cross-examination or can bolster the plaintiff's case.

However, if the defense calls a medical expert, the expert's direct testimony is probably going to be damaging. There are many areas in which a judicious cross-examination of a medical expert can prove beneficial to the plaintiff. Attorneys must realize that medicine is far from an exact science. Doctors are human beings; each doctor has biases, prejudices, preconceptions, and predilections. There are many medical questions about which equally competent and honest physicians hold diametrically opposed views. Recognizing this, it becomes clear that cross-examination of even the most prestigious physician can be of value.

Qualifications

Almost invariably, the defense doctor will be a highly qualified physician. Therefore, an attack on qualifications should rarely be employed; however, situations can occur where such an attack may be indicated. Where you have determined that the expert is not board-certified in a specialty, this point may be brought out during cross-examination. Organized medicine created specialty boards during the 1930s to elevate the standards of practice in the various specialties; a doctor may be certified by a board only after pursuing a prescribed course of study and passing prescribed examinations, demonstrating competency in a particular specialty. Thus, board certification indicates special achievement.

Further, when a qualified specialist is called to testify in an area outside of his specialty, this should be brought to the attention of the jury during cross-examination; that is, the witness may be a qualified expert in his own field, but not specifically qualified to render an accurate medical opinion concerning the medical issue in the case. For example, if the defense doctor, an orthopedic surgeon, renders an opinion concerning the relationship of a coronary occlusion to trauma, you should attempt to point out by cross-examination that the particular problem is highly complex and falls outside the specialty of orthopedics.

You should only attack the basic qualifications of the defense expert or the expert's qualifications to testify concerning the particular medical problem in the case when you are certain that such an attack is well founded. Further, when such cross-examination is indicated, it should be employed gently. You should make it clear that you are not seeking to embarrass the doctor but rather to make the record clear concerning the extent of the doctor's qualifications to testify in a particular case. You can obtain information about the defense doctor's qualifications through several sources: interrogatories, depositions, and prior trial transcripts. You should also become conversant with the reference work *Directory of Medical Specialists* because it lists all the board-certified physicians in the country, as well as their areas of certification.

When preparing to cross-examine an important medical witness, obtain the curriculum vitae of the witness as far in advance of trial as possible. Peruse the curriculum vitae and investigate the accomplishments claimed therein. Most doctors regard the curriculum vitae as an important reflection of their professional status, and many will exaggerate their claims of accomplishments such as education, internships and residencies, certifications, and even licensure to practice. Also, in pretrial, ask a non-board-certified doctor whether he has ever taken the boards and failed them. Ask a board-certified specialist if she failed the boards before finally passing them. Jurors can readily decide that medical witnesses who have been exposed as exaggerating their qualifications and accomplishments are also exaggerating their testimony.

Opinions

Frequently, you can attack neither the basic qualifications of the defense expert nor the expert's qualifications to testify in a particular case; nevertheless, you may be able to attack the expert's medical opinions. The more you know in advance of the trial what the defense doctor's testimony is likely to be, the better prepared you will be to employ this technique. Where court rules permit, you should obtain the expert's reports. Where there is no such rule, make every attempt to persuade defense counsel to turn over copies of the reports; you could suggest that all reports of experts be exchanged. Where discovery procedures permit you to make direct inquiries of the defense expert, either by interrogatory or deposition, use such procedures fully.

Once you have informed yourself as fully as possible before the trial about the defense doctor's opinions, weigh and evaluate the doctor's position. A conference with the plaintiff's physician can be extremely valuable. Go over the defense doctor's reports with the plaintiff's doctor to determine in what respect the defense doctor's opinions are vulnerable. Read the defense doctor's report as much for what is not in it as for what is in it. Even if you are unable, because of local discovery rules, to obtain the doctor's report or depose the doctor, a conference with the plaintiff's doctor may still be valuable. The plaintiff's doctor may know the physician testifying for the defense and may be able to predict the general position the defense doctor will take and the concessions he will make during cross-examination.

In preparation for the trial, gather and read all books, articles, and speeches authored by the defense doctor. The text *Index Medicus* contains an index of medical publications by subject and author and is a valuable source for much of this information. Further, since many defense experts testify frequently, you should try to gather transcripts of prior testimony. Cross-examination of a defense expert by means of her own published or spoken words is a devastating tool of advocacy.

Notes and Reports

Doctors frequently testify from their notes and reports, so it is important for you to obtain all reports and records used by the doctor to refresh his recollection for his direct testimony. During cross-examination, have the doctor admit that he has virtually no independent recollection of this examination because he sees many patients over the course of a year. Once it has been established that the doctor has no independent recollection of this particular examination and is testifying on the basis of his notes, the doctor is thereafter tied to his notes and report. If the notes fail to mention any of the classic medical tests indicated by the plaintiff's complaints, this fact should be brought out on cross-examination. If there is no indication in the notes and records that the doctor gave a particular test, he may have trouble convincing the jury that he distinctly remembers giving that test.

Financial Bias

A frequent and often effective line of inquiry relates to the financial bias of the defense doctor. Every metropolitan community has a group of doctors whose services are frequently used by the insurance industry and the defense bar. Examinations of claimants can be a lucrative aspect of a medical practice. For a typical case, a defense physician conducts an examination, prepares a report, confers with defense counsel if trial appears imminent, and testifies in court if the case is not settled. Some doctors conduct one or more of these examinations each day and derive a substantial portion of their income from them. The jury may be interested in the financial stake the defense doctor has in performing defense examinations. Cross-examination that brings out the fact that the doctor conducts these examinations often or that the doctor frequently and typically testifies for the defense may greatly impair the witness's credibility.

But before you attempt to establish such a picture through cross-examination, make certain that such an attack is indicated. Make every attempt before trial to determine how frequently the doctor testifies, how frequently the doctor examines, and how frequently the doctor is retained by the defense firm involved in the case. It is a mistake to assume that simply because the doctor was called by the defendant, this line of attack will be worth following. Never go on a fishing expedition during the trial and never use this line of attack unless your success is assured by pretrial preparation and discovery.

Information concerning the financial stake of the defense doctor in medical-legal practice can be derived from several sources; for example, the transcript of the defense doctor's testimony in prior cases may be valuable, as may be arranging a conference with experienced lawyers in the community.

Where pretrial deposition of the defense doctor is available, this line of inquiry should be pursued fully. Ask the doctor on deposition the number of times per week she is called by defense law firms, insurance companies, or adjusting agencies to conduct examinations of claimants. Also ask the charge for each examination, the charge for each report, the charge for pretrial conferences with defense counsel, the charge for deposition testimony, and the charge for courtroom testimony. During deposition you also should determine the number of times in the preceding year the doctor was requested to make examinations of a claimant, testify on behalf of a defendant, and testify on behalf of a plaintiff.

Medical Books

Frequently, you will seek to challenge the validity of the defense expert's medical opinion. Before undertaking such a confrontation, attempt to know more than the doctor knows about the medical questions involved. Again, a conference with the plaintiff's doctor will be invaluable in educating you as to the inaccuracies, if any, of the defense physician's position and about the authoritative sources that can be used to point out these inaccuracies.

The use of medical books as a means of cross-examining the defense doctor may be effective, particularly with a doctor who does not have experience in giving expert testimony. Generally, before you may use such a book or article to attack the opinion of the defense doctor, the doctor must first admit that the particular work is authoritative and that he recognizes it as such.

Where deposition of the defense doctor is available, try to determine what books the doctor considers authoritative, the names of the teachers under whom the doctor studied, the leaders in the doctor's field, the basic medical texts on the question involved, and the names of any publications that the doctor may have authored in this area. Some jurisdictions have taken the position that if the plaintiff's doctor states that the medical text in question is generally considered authoritative, the plaintiff's lawyer may use the text to cross-examine even though the defense doctor will not admit to personally considering it as such.

Frequency and Length of Medical Exam

The defense doctor is not a treating physician, and she has normally seen the plaintiff only once. Apprise the jury of this fact at the beginning of cross-examination. During cross-examination, you may also wish to point out that the single examination conducted by the defense doctor was a brief one. Find out precisely how much time the doctor spent in the hands-on examination of the plaintiff. Frequently the patient will have been in the doctor's office for more than an hour but actually in the presence of the doctor for less than five minutes with only two or three minutes devoted to the examination. Often, the medical history is filled out by the patient and completed by a nurse.

Finally, ask the doctor to whom she reported her findings after completing the examination of the plaintiff. Did she treat the plaintiff as a patient and give him medical advice, prescribe medication, refer him to another specialist, or schedule a return visit? Did the doctor discuss her findings, diagnosis, and prognosis with the plaintiff as she normally would with her own patients? When the doctor reported back to the defense lawyer who hired her, did she send a copy of her medical report to the patient? When you carry this line of questioning out to its logical conclusion, it becomes obvious to the jury that the doctor is the defense lawyer's hired gun, not a treating physician of the plaintiff, and should be rejected by the jury as a credible medical witness in the case.

Collateral Legal Attack

Defense medical doctors are accustomed to the type of cross-examination discussed here and will frequently be hired because of their ability to withstand cross-examination. However, one effective means of cross-examination for which the defense medical doctor is seldom properly prepared is the collateral attack based on the legal predicates controlling the plaintiff's damages. For example, instead of cross-examining the doctor on the medical aspects of the case, cross-examine as to the physical effects that the plaintiff will suffer from his injury. Doctors are generally not aware that the disability of the plaintiff is determined by his inability to perform usual tasks. Therefore, if you can secure admissions from the doctor that the plaintiff is unable to perform certain physical functions, this can later be translated to the jury as damages to wage-earning capacity.

In a case involving a rotator-cuff injury to a private pilot, the examining doctor for the defense determined that the plaintiff had only five percent general disability to the body as a whole. However, when questioned about the ability of the pilot to reach directly overhead and backwards with the injured arm and, more importantly, about the plaintiff's ability to lift with the arm extended backwards at a 45-degree angle, the doctor verified that the plaintiff would be totally unable to perform these functions, that this physical restriction was permanent, and that the condition would worsen as the plaintiff aged. Through other witnesses, including the plaintiff, it was established that these are precisely the functions a pilot would have to perform with the injured shoulder to manually lower the emergency landing gear on the plane. The doctor, who had admitted these disabilities of the plaintiff on deposition, testified on cross-examination at trial that under no circumstances would he ride as a passenger with a pilot who had no strength to operate overhead controls or lower the emergency landing gear. Thus, the five percent medical disability to the body as a whole was effectively translated into a permanent inability of the pilot to perform his usual work, thereby greatly damaging his wage-earning capacity. Through this collateral attack, the defendant's medical expert became the most valuable witness in the case for the plaintiff on the issue of permanent damage to wage-earning capacity.

Concessions

You can frequently secure sufficient concessions from the defense doctor to cast doubt on the witness's testimony. These concessions can be used in argument to the benefit of the plaintiff. Examples of these concessions follow:

- The defendant's physician will frequently admit that she has not treated the plaintiff and that she examined him only for the purposes of rendering an opinion to the defendant's lawyer and testifying in court. She will generally concede that she does not know the plaintiff as well as the plaintiff's physician does and that the plaintiff's doctor is in a better position to give a complete picture of the extent and nature of the injury because of familiarity and the continuing nature of the treatment.

- The doctor will frequently concede that he cannot say that the plaintiff does not feel pain. He should admit, also, that a physician cannot see pain and that he has no medical basis to reject the validity of the plaintiff's description of his own personal experience, even though the doctor cannot demonstrate correlative objective symptoms.
- The doctor will generally concede that she treats many of her own patients on their subjective reports of pain—even when no objective signs of injury are present—and that certain injuries are likely to produce pain without producing objective symptomology.
- The doctor will frequently concede that he does not regard the claimant as a malingerer or that he has no basis to support the charge that the plaintiff is malingering.
- You can often secure a concession that much of the practice of medicine involves a difference of opinion among physicians and that the conflict between herself and the plaintiff's doctor is not unusual. The defense doctor will generally concede that she cannot say with certainty that the plaintiff's doctor is wrong.
- The doctor will generally concede that the course of recovery for most injuries is marked by periods of remission and exacerbation and that he has no way of knowing whether, during his one particular examination, the plaintiff was in a period of remission.
- Frequently, the doctor will admit that she did not determine whether the plaintiff had taken pain relief drugs or muscle relaxants before the examination. Once this concession is gained, the doctor can be asked whether such medications could affect the validity of the examination by masking the symptoms of injury. Frequently, the doctor will concede such drugs could have masked symptoms of injury.
- The doctor will generally admit that in his own practice, after initial examination, he forms a tentative diagnosis and

that, sometimes, he subsequently decides that his tentative diagnosis was wrong. One examination is generally not as good as a complete series of examinations, and occasionally he must revise and change his opinions.

- The doctor may admit that she has no idea of the severity of the initial trauma that gave rise to the plaintiff's injuries.
- If the plaintiff's treating physicians are well-qualified doctors, the plaintiff's lawyers will generally have little trouble gaining a concession from the defense doctor that these doctors are skilled, well-trained physicians.
- Frequently, the defense doctor will concede having little knowledge of the plaintiff's work requirements and leisure activities.
- In a trauma case where the defense is pre-existing arthritis of the spine, you should attempt to have the defense doctor concede that arthritis of the spine is present in many individuals over age 40 and that the condition frequently causes absolutely no pain or disability. The doctor may also concede that such a condition makes the affected person more prone to injury as the result of trauma and serves to delay the healing process.
- As discussed, the defense doctor may frequently concede that the plaintiff, despite a small percentage of medical disability to the body as a whole, has physical impairments that will render the plaintiff unable to perform the usual tasks of a worker, thereby reducing wage-earning capacity.

Re-emphasizing the Plaintiff's Case

Cross-examination of the defendant's doctor gives you an excellent opportunity to re-emphasize your own medical case. With leading questions, you can cover the basics of the plaintiff's injury so as to highlight the significance of the injury. If the plaintiff's doctor testified that there was a muscle spasm, you should ask the defense doctor if it is not true that muscle spasm is an involuntary reaction of the muscles, that this involuntary reaction is the body's means of splinting an injured area, that this is a defensive mechanism by which the body protects an injured area, and that a muscle spasm is an objective sign of injury.

Likewise, if the plaintiff's doctor has testified that the plaintiff's muscles or ligaments were torn, the defense doctor can be asked to affirm that torn muscles heal with scar tissue, that scar tissue is permanent, that scar tissue is less elastic than normal tissue, and that the plaintiff will be permanently scarred with the result of loss of motion in the area. Generally, if you stick to well-accepted medical propositions, you will be able to gain positive concessions when you cross-examine, and you will help make the plaintiff's injury and disability more vivid.

Style

During cross-examination of the defense doctor, you should be polite and courteous, yet firm; recognize that as a general rule the jury identifies with the witness more than with the lawyer. This problem may be compounded when the witness is a doctor, for most physicians are highly esteemed by the public, but this does not mean that you should hesitate to cross-examine the defense doctor. It does indicate that you should be careful before undertaking a direct attack on the doctor.

Attacking Damaging Opinions

If the doctor renders damaging opinions, do not be reluctant to point out to the jury that the doctor's opinions are at odds with other recognized authorities in the field, that the doctor has made prior inconsistent statements, or that there were defects in the doctor's capacity to observe and gather information that reflect on the validity of her opinion.

CONCLUSION

The consummate cross-examiner's skill emerges from many individual traits that must be developed and honed before the cross-examiner masters the craft of testing witnesses' competence and veracity in the ultimate search for truth. The cross-examiner must be a logician in analyzing facts, opinions, documents, and law; a psychoanalyst in reading minds, observing body language, and discerning weaknesses; a master detective in sifting through the clues in the prosecution of the wrongdoer; and a skillful surgeon in probing the body of proffered evidence, swiftly excising cancerous perjury, and closing with only the truth intact.

Of all the skills required of the advocate, cross-examination is the most complex and the most crucial. Fortunately, the skills can be acquired through study, preparation, focus, and practice. Study the great cross-examinations of the past, read transcripts of current trials, and study the numerous treatises that analyze techniques; obtain assistance from others by attending a trial advocacy college, such as the programs presented by the National College of Advocacy. Prepare for cross-examination with extraordinary diligence and attention to detail. Focus on the specific goals you need to accomplish during cross-examination. Carefully analyze the character, motivations, bias, jury appeal, and areas of vulnerability of each witness whom you will cross-examine. Know precisely what you wish to achieve, and when you achieve your goal—STOP.

Finally, practice the various techniques, particularly during deposition, until you have mastered several different approaches to cross-examination and have learned to adapt your style and techniques to the immediate situations that confront you.

One of the fascinating aspects of trial advocacy is that no one ever truly masters its skills because its challenges are always changing. The education of the master advocate is perpetual. There are no universal rules that apply to every cross-examination situation, but there are guidelines, as discussed in this chapter, that are time-tested and that you, as a skilled advocate, must possess.

The following guidelines for cross-examination, which were written 150 years ago by David Paul Jones, a British barrister, demonstrate the timeless nature of cross-examination skills. They serve those of us who labor in the vineyards of litigation today as well as they have served the barristers and attorneys who followed them in the past:

- Except in indifferent matters, never take your eye from that of the witness; this is a channel of communication from mind to mind, the loss of which nothing can compensate. "Truth, falsehood, hatred, anger, scorn, despair, and all the passions —all the soul—is there."

- Be not regardless, either, of the *voice* of the witness; next to the eye this is perhaps the best interpreter of his mind . . . [T]he mental reservation of the witness . . . is often manifested in the tone or accent or emphasis of the voice.

- Be mild with the mild; shrewd with the crafty; confiding with the honest; merciful to the young, the frail, or the fearful; rough to the ruffian; and a thunderbolt to the liar. But in all this, never be unmindful of your own dignity. Bring to bear all the powers of your mind, not that you may shine, but that virtue may triumph, and your cause may prosper.
- An equivocal question is almost as much to be avoided and condemned as an equivocal answer; and it always leads to, or excuses, an equivocal answer. Singleness of purpose, clearly expressed is the best trait in the examination of witnesses, whether they be honest or the reverse. Falsehood is not detected by cunning, but by the light of truth.
- But in any result, be careful that you do not lose your temper; anger is always either the precursor or evidence of assured defeat in every intellectual conflict.
- Like a skilful chess-player, in every move, fix your mind upon the combinations and relations of the game—partial and temporary success may otherwise end in total and remediless defeat.
- Never undervalue your adversary, but stand steadily upon your guard; a random blow may be just as fatal as though it were directed by the most consummate skill; the negligence of one often cures, and sometimes renders effective, the blunders of another.
- Be respectful to the court and to the jury; kind to your colleague; civil to your antagonist; but never sacrifice the slightest principle of duty to an overweening deference toward either.[4]

Thus, as you rise to cross-examine a witness, you should be armed with the skill to adopt the style required for this particular witness and jury, the technique to search out the truth, the knowledge of guidelines that have developed over the centuries, and, most important, the wisdom to discern the proper combination of style and technique you need to serve well the consummate role of the cross-examiner—the truth giver.

4 Wellman at 400-03.

EXPERT TESTIMONY

Peter Perlman

Rule 702 of the Federal Rules of Evidence sets forth the guidelines for admissibility of expert testimony:

> If scientific, technical, or other specialized knowledge will assist the trier of fact to understand the evidence or to determine a fact in issue, a witness qualified as an expert by knowledge, skill, experience, training, or education, may testify thereto in the form of an opinion or otherwise.[1]

The rule gives the trial judge great discretion, and the criteria for determining an expert's qualifications are broad. The trial judge should not rely on labels but must investigate the competence that a particular witness would bring to the issues and whether that expertise would aid the trier of fact in reaching its decision.[2] One leading case states the test as follows:

> Under the Federal Rules of Evidence, the only thing a court should be concerned with in determining the qualifications

1 Most states have adopted provisions that parallel the federal rules.

2 WEINSTEIN & BERGER, 3 WEINSTEIN'S EVIDENCE, (MB) ¶ 702 [04] (1990).

of an expert is whether the expert's knowledge of the subject matter is such that his opinion will likely assist the trier of fact in arriving at the truth. The weight of the expert's testimony must be for the trier of fact.[3]

SOURCES OF EXPERT WITNESSES

The Roman philosopher and poet Virgil is credited with advising "Experto credite," or "believe an expert." In our complex society the need for a well-qualified expert has taken on an increasing significance in almost all aspects of trial practice. It is almost unheard of to try anything but a simple case without an expert.

There are many sources of expert witnesses. These include universities and academic institutions, present and former industry employees, and former employees of the federal government. Frequently, a present or former member of a safety or industry committee or the author of a technical article or treatise may be able to function as an expert. An excellent directory of experts is the *Lawyers Desk Reference*.[4]

An expert's name can also be obtained from the records of similar litigation. The names of lawyers who have handled litigation in specific areas and the experts who have assisted them can be obtained from The Exchange, a research database service of the Association of Trial Lawyers of America.[5]

BASES OF OPINION TESTIMONY

Most states follow the Federal Rules of Evidence with regard to the bases of opinion testimony by experts. Rule 703 of the Federal Rules of Evidence provides

> The facts or data in the particular case upon which an expert bases an opinion or inference may be those perceived by or made known to the expert at or before the hearing. If of a type reasonably relied upon by experts in the particular

3 Mannino v. International Mfg. Co., 650 F.2d 846, 851 (6th Cir. 1981).

4 PHILO, LAWYERS DESK REFERENCE (7th ed. 1987).

5 The Exchange services are available from the Association of Trial Lawyers of America, 1050 31st St., NW, Washington, DC 20007.

> field in forming opinions or inferences upon the subject, the facts or data need not be admissible in evidence.

In other words, an expert may testify concerning any information presented, even though the facts or data may have been outside of court and the expert's personal observation, as long as such information is of the type reasonably relied on by experts in that field in forming opinions. The underlying evidence need not be admissible in itself.

An illustrative case is *Mannino v. International Manufacturing Co.*[6] In that case, a small child was injured in an automobile collision, allegedly due to a defect in the infant car seat. The seat was disposed of after the collision and was not available for examination by any expert witness. The trial court rejected a biomechanical engineer's testimony that the seat had been improperly designed and tested. On appeal, the trial court's decision was reversed. In its opinion, the Sixth Circuit stated that Rule 703 of the Federal Rules of Evidence should be broadly interpreted, and an expert may have a broad foundation for his testimony. The court further stated

> The purpose of Rule 703 is to make available to the expert all of the kinds of things that an expert would normally rely upon in forming an opinion, without requiring that these be admissible in evidence. Under the Rule, the expert is free to give his opinion relying upon the types of data an expert would normally use in forming an opinion in his area of expertise. In short, through Rule 703, the law is catching up with the realities of professional life.[7]

The court held that there was an adequate basis for the expert's opinion within the meaning of Rule 703. The witness had based his opinion on his experience with biomechanics, various studies in the field, personal experience in dynamic testing, attendance at specialized seminars, and literature and information furnished by the plaintiff's attorney. The court observed that the fact that much of this information was hearsay, and probably would have been inadmissible, was not relevant to the issue of whether it could form the basis of the expert's opinion. The question was whether it was the

6 650 F.2d 846 (6th Cir. 1981).

7 650 F.2d at 851.

type of material on which an expert would rely, and there was no showing that it was not.

The court further addressed the respective responsibilities of the trial judge and the jury:

> The trial judge misconceived his responsibilities under Rule 703. Great liberality is allowed the expert in determining the basis of his opinions under Rule 703. Whether an opinion should be accepted is not for the trial judge. That is for the finder of fact. Here the trial judge substituted himself for the finder of fact by finding that the witness did not have an adequate basis for his opinion. There is sufficient evidence in this record to find that the expert did have an adequate basis for his opinion. The trial judge erred in excluding the testimony.[8]

Despite the language in *Mannino* that broadly interprets the scope of Rule 703, you should never assume that all expert opinion is admissible. For example, in a products liability case, an expert witness was precluded from expressing an opinion where there was no showing that the opinion was based on facts or data compiled by other experts.[9]

You should also be familiar with the contents of Rule 704 of the Federal Rules of Evidence, which allow an expert to express an opinion on an ultimate issue (e.g., whether or not the defendant physician departed from the applicable standard of care), so long as the opinion will *assist* the jury.

DISCOVERY

The basis of any expert witness's opinions should be obtained before trial. Rule 26(b)(4)(A) of the Federal Rules of Civil Procedure provides for discovery of expert witnesses expected to testify at trial, their opinions, and the grounds for those opinions:

> (i) A party may through interrogatories require any other party to identify each person whom the other party expects

[8] 650 F.2d at 853.

[9] Barris v. Bob's Drag Chutes and Safety Equip., Inc., 685 F.2d 94, 101 n.10 (3d Cir. 1982).

> to call as an expert witness at trial, to state the subject matter on which the expert is expected to testify, and to state the substance of the facts and opinions to which the expert is expected to testify and a summary of the grounds for each opinion. (ii) Upon motion, the court may order further discovery by other means, subject to such restrictions as to scope and such provisions, pursuant to subdivision (b)(4)(C) of this rule, concerning fees and expenses as the court may deem appropriate.

Under the provisions of the rule, a party may require opposing counsel to state the substance of the expert's anticipated testimony, and the court may order further discovery. Ordinarily the order for further discovery addresses such issues as compensating the expert for the time given in responding to the interrogatories. Unless specifically prohibited in the jurisdiction, in most cases the court will allow depositions of the experts. There is no automatic right to depose an opponent's expert witness, and the basis for such depositions should be either by agreement or by motion.

Rule 26(b)(4)(B) prohibits discovery of experts retained as consultants, not trial witnesses:

> A party may discover facts known or opinions held by an expert who has been retained or specially employed by another party in anticipation of litigation or preparation for trial and who is not expected to be called as a witness at trial, only as provided in Rule 35(b) or upon a showing of exceptional circumstances under which it is impracticable for the party seeking discovery to obtain facts or opinions on the same subject by other means.

The protection against disclosure of consultants allows you to candidly discuss the case with persons who have specialized expertise in the subject matter. However, if the consultants later become trial witnesses, they become subject to normal discovery. A case that addressed this subject is *Williamson v. Superior Court*,[10] where the court stated the following:

> [T]he courts agree that the initial status of the expert as consultant changes once the expert becomes a designated

[10] 21 Cal.3d 829, 834-35; 148 Cal. Rptr. 39, 42-43; 582 P. 2d 126, 130 (1978).

> prospective witness. As the court stated in *Swartzman* . . . "[w]hen it becomes reasonably certain an expert will give his professional opinion as a witness on a material matter in dispute, then his opinion has become a factor in the cause. At that point the expert has ceased to be merely a consultant and has become a counter in the litigation, one to be evaluated along with others. Such evaluation properly includes appropriate pretrial discovery."

In other words, once a party elects to call an expert as a witness, all facts considered and opinions reached by that witness are discoverable regardless of the expert's status at the time the facts were considered or the opinions reached.

Note the exception written into Rule 26(b)(4)(A)—although usually exempt from disclosure, a consultant may be subject to disclosure upon a showing of "exceptional circumstances under which it is impracticable for the party seeking discovery to obtain facts or opinions on the same subject by other means."

When a consultant who doesn't testify is required to produce discovery because of "exceptional circumstances," the court *must* require the movant to pay for the consultant's time in responding to such discovery requests. Likewise, when a trial expert is ordered to respond to discovery beyond the original interrogatories, the fees and expenses incurred in complying with such "further discovery" *must* be paid by the movant. In both instances, Rule 26 uses the word "shall" to mandate payment.

DIRECT EXAMINATION

The following checklist is a useful guide to conducting the direct examination of an expert witness.

Identification and Occupation

Every effort should be made to humanize the expert by introducing his personal and family background to the jury.

Educational Background

Mention all institutions, colleges, and graduate schools attended in addition to any degrees that have been obtained, areas of study, and any specialized courses that might apply to the case involved.

Any positions held in the academic community should also be described for the jury.

Professional Training and Experience

Describe professional positions held by the witness including length of time and responsibilities. Specialized experience concerning issues involved in the case should be highlighted and explained to the jury.

Personal experience obtained in the field should also be highlighted, because "hands-on" experience is generally more impressive than an academic pedigree.

Under Federal Rule of Evidence 702, a witness may qualify as an expert on the basis of any one of five criteria: "knowledge, skill, experience, training, *or* education" (emphasis added). Of course, the more qualifications, the better. An expert witness need not be the most experienced on the subject, so long as the testimony aids the jury in its search for the truth.[11]

Practice Note

In presenting an expert's qualifications, choose carefully. An expert's long, arrogant, and pompous recitation of a string of qualifications may alienate the jurors and affect their ability to objectively consider the testimony.

Honors or Special Recognition

Awards and honors should be presented selectively to the jury. Only the most important should be mentioned by the expert; other qualifications will be in the resume, which should be introduced as an exhibit. In this way, any special recognition can be downplayed initially but highlighted to the jury later in the trial and during closing arguments.

Membership in Professional Organizations

This should also be stated in a selective manner with the previous considerations in mind.

11 Leichtamer v. American Motors Corp., 67 Ohio St. 2d 456, 424 N.E. 2d 568 (1981) (citing Alexander v. Mt. Carmel Medical Center, 56 Ohio St. 2d 155, 159, 383 N.E. 2d 564 (1978)).

Previous Testimony

Testimony by the expert in previous cases should be presented in a candid and direct manner. An expert who has previously testified on behalf of plaintiffs and defendants is more credible than one who always testifies for the same side. However, the expert should be cautioned against making any reference to previous employment by an insurance company—in most states, any reference to the subject of insurance is improper and frequently serves as a basis for a mistrial.

A fertile subject for cross-examination is the frequency of expert testimony; the inference is that the expert is a professional witness or a hired gun. The attorney presenting the expert can defuse such cross-examination by raising the issue during the direct examination.

Expert Witness Compensation

Expert witness compensation is another fertile area of cross-examination for implications of bias and/or economic interest and should be defused by proper handling during direct examination. Jurors fully expect expert witnesses to be fairly compensated for their time, so payment should be presented in a candid and tasteful manner.

Practice Note

> Once you have qualified the expert, then you should offer the testimony of the witness as an expert—it again underscores the fact that the witness is an expert.

Materials Received by Expert

Before expressing any opinion, the expert should list all materials received or reviewed in connection with the case.

Activities and Work Performed

Any preparatory activities taken by the expert should be specified for the jury. The expert should explain about visits made to the scene, tests or experiments conducted, statistical data studied, technical literature reviewed, photographs taken, and models or exhibits prepared. Although the expert may testify on data not admitted into evidence, her credibility will be enhanced if the data are admitted through the testimony of other witnesses.

Expert Opinions and Their Bases

The expert should specify each opinion he has formed and its basis to the jury. The only requirement under Rule 703 is that the opinion be based on a type of information that is reasonably relied on by experts in the same field and that this information is sufficiently trustworthy.

Many jurisdictions require that the opinion be stated in terms of a "reasonable degree of certainty or probability." In this case, the lawyer should clarify the expert's opinion by using the proper language required.

Practice Note

> Expert testimony is often complicated and tedious. Demonstrative evidence will help explain and animate the testimony. Studies have shown that jurors remember what they have seen much more easily than what they have heard. Therefore, a "show and tell" method is the best way to present expert testimony. Charts, maps, models, photographs, and simple drawings can be the key to effectively presenting an expert's direct testimony.

CROSS-EXAMINATION

The cross-examining attorney can attack expert testimony through a variety of techniques.[12] The approach varies with each expert and each case. Some of the most effective methods include the following:

Challenging the Facts Supporting the Opinion

An expert generally assumes the truth of certain facts; if any of these is untrue or not established, a fertile area for cross-examination exists. An effective cross-examination in this situation follows:

Q: Isn't it true that in expressing your opinion, you assumed that the vehicle was stopped at the time of the collision?

A: Yes.

12 For an excellent discussion, *see,* McElhaney, *Expert Witnesses—Nine Ways to Cross-Examine an Expert*, A.B.A. J., March 1989, at 98.

Q: If in fact the vehicle was moving, you would have to change your opinion, wouldn't you?

A: Yes.

If the expert refuses to change her opinion regardless of the change in facts, her credibility suffers substantial damage. An attack on the information relied on is particularly effective when the witness has conducted no factual investigation and instead has relied entirely on the reports of others.

Impeachment of the Expert

Under Federal Rule of Evidence 613 an expert witness may be impeached by a prior, inconsistent statement, and the statement can be introduced into evidence if the witness is given an opportunity to explain the prior statement. During discovery you should obtain articles written by the expert, as well as the expert's testimony and depositions from other cases. Since all of these materials contain statements or testimony previously made on the record, this is an extremely effective area for cross-examination.

Federal Rule of Evidence 803 (18) also allows an expert to be impeached through a learned treatise recognized as authoritative either by the witness, other witnesses, or judicial notice.

Demonstration of Bias

You are given great latitude in cross-examination to demonstrate any bias, interest, or ulterior motive held by the expert witness. Some experts are obviously court-wise and are susceptible to the inference that they are hired guns. An effective technique with this type of expert is to demonstrate that the expert has frequent contacts with or has taken compensation from the same law firm, party, or industry for whom he is now testifying or that he has taken identical positions in prior lawsuits. The jury may reasonably believe that an expert is biased if he has received or is receiving exorbitant fees from the industry or party on whose behalf he is testifying.

CONCLUSION

Authoritative, competent testimony frequently means the difference between winning and losing a complicated case. Therefore, the preparation and presentation of expert testimony should be carefully planned so that it achieves its purpose: assisting the jury in its search for the truth.

INSTRUCTIONS TO THE JURY

James J. Leonard, Jr. and Abraham Fuchsberg

In all jury trials, at some point before the case is turned over to the jury for deliberation, the judge must give instructions on the law so that the jury can properly fulfill its function. The most perfectly tried case may be marred, and ultimately reversed on appeal, if the jury is given incorrect, incomplete, or otherwise improper instructions on the law that it must follow.

Some trial lawyers suggest that you should draft a set of proposed instructions early in the processing of a case, particularly if novel issues of liability or damages will be a part of the case. You can then conduct every facet of the processing of the case, from preparation of pleadings to summation, knowing the language that will probably be used by the trial judge in advising the jurors of the law that will guide their decision. You will acquire substantial credibility if throughout the case you have been using language that the court then stamps with its imprimatur as the law.

Instructions are properly viewed as a very important element of the trial lawyer's attempt to communicate accurately, completely, and persuasively.

Jury instructions read by the trial judge carry substantial weight and authority with jurors. Most jurors do not realize that the instructions have been prepared by counsel for the respective parties. Rather, they view the instructions as coming from the court and as reflecting the clear and undisputed law of the jurisdiction. Although some jurors may not believe certain witnesses and may discount much of what is said by counsel, they typically look to the court as the source of impartial and controlling authority and will pay careful attention to the instructions the judge gives. In some cases, they place even more emphasis on the instructions than on the lawyers' arguments. Thus, a case can often be won in part by careful drafting and tendering of proper instructions to the court.

In some jurisdictions, jury instructions are given in writing to the jury, and the jurors are permitted to take the instructions into the jury room during their deliberations. Given a tool of this magnitude, prudent counsel should use no less care in ensuring carefully drafted instructions than he or she would use in preparing an important exhibit.

PRELIMINARY INSTRUCTIONS

In many jurisdictions, preliminary instructions are given before the trial to inform the jury in a general way what it will be asked to do at the end of the case. These instructions usually cover such procedural matters as identification of the parties; the order of the trial; and admonitions to the jurors not to discuss the case with anyone, including their family and fellow jurors; and not to read newspaper accounts of the trial or listen to television or radio broadcasts that touch on the case on which they are sitting. Such preliminary instructions also advise the jurors that they are not to form any opinions on the case until all the evidence has been presented and they retire to the jury room for deliberation.

These admonitions are frequently repeated throughout the trial, particularly before jurors are discharged for lunch or recess or at the end of the day. It is prudent practice for you to request that the admonitions be given at these times if you fear that the jurors might be exposed to media coverage or any other outside influence.

The substantive instructions dealing with the issues in the case are generally given at the completion of all the testimony. In some jurisdictions, the jury is "charged" after the parties have given final arguments; in other jurisdictions, the charge or portions of it may be given at the close of the evidence but before final arguments. Where a trial judge has discretion to give the jury the charge before argument, you may well ask the judge to do so.

Only after a jury has heard the law from the judge does it know what guidelines to apply. When you argue after the charge, you can refer to the judge's actual words and then use the facts, as you have proven them, to illustrate how the defendant violated a specific rule of law. The law has a majesty and the judge an authority that lawyers lack. When you argue after the charge has been given, you are able to wed that majesty and that authority to your version of the facts.

REQUESTED INSTRUCTIONS

Shaping the Final Outcome of the Case

The jury can be instructed on all legal issues incorporated in the pleadings and supported by the evidence. Almost universally, counsel submit requested instructions on the issues to the judge at some predetermined time before the close of evidence. In some jurisdictions, local rules dictate that proposed jury instructions be submitted at the time of the pretrial conference, at the time of jury selection, or before the close of the plaintiff's case. The prudent practitioner will learn well in advance of the pretrial conference the practice or procedure of the court and will present the initial jury instructions at the appropriate time. Typically, counsel for each party must submit sets of proposed instructions to the court and to each opposing counsel and retain one set. The attorney who does not prepare and submit a specifically adapted set of requested instructions that present the client's viewpoint on the legal issues in dispute is missing an important opportunity to shape the final outcome of the case.

Courts can generally be relied on to give proper instructions on the most obvious, noncontroversial issues in any case; thus, in a simple negligence action, it may not be necessary to prepare instructions on the definition of negligence, proximate cause, or burden of proof. Local practice will dictate whether you should submit such form instructions to the court or whether you should rely on the court to give these instructions unaided.

If the local jurisdiction has pattern or model jury instructions, and if you are satisfied with those instructions on specific issues, then use those instructions, with modifications if necessary. Obviously, if you disagree with an instruction, you should submit a proposed instruction to the court.

Complex Issues

You should always submit instructions you wish the court to read concerning the more subtle and complex issues. These issues may include status and duty in a premises liability action, violation of a statutory duty, determination of what constitutes permanent injury, the existence and effect of presumptions, and the right to recovery for the aggravation or lighting-up of a pre-existing condition. Preparing requested jury instructions in advance of trial—indeed, as suggested above, perhaps even before the complaint is filed—often will help you focus on the legal issues in the case and plan evidence presentation. Having prepared instructions in advance, you can look at the pleadings to see if they need to be amended and determine what evidence is needed to support the charges. Giving instructions that refer to theories or issues that have not been pled or upon which no evidence was presented will invariably result in error.

Early submission of instructions to the court will aid the judge in hearing the case and will likely influence the content of the final charge. If it is the custom or practice in your jurisdiction to submit trial briefs to the court before the commencement of trial, early preparation of requested jury instructions will assist you in briefing the disputed legal issues.

Pattern Jury Instructions

The highest courts of many states have adopted pattern or model jury instructions. These constitute an invaluable and necessary source for trial lawyers, and, in most instances, a strong argument will be required if you wish to persuade the trial judge to deviate from "stock" instructions bearing the imprimatur of a Bar Committee and perhaps the highest appellate court of the state. Pattern jury instructions generally contain detailed annotations and a text discussion of the points covered in the instruction.

In preparing requested instructions, you should first look to any model or pattern instructions that have been approved. If there are no model or pattern instructions for specific issues in the case, consult a general treatise on jury instructions. The opinions of the appellate courts are also a prime source for special instructions not covered by pattern charges. Frequently, appellate opinions contain approved instructions or statements of substantive rules of law that can readily be translated into the correct form for a jury charge. These opinions may persuade a judge to give an instruction outside the pattern instructions or on a novel, unique, or other particular issue.

Language

Jury instructions must not be framed in argumentative language. The novice trial lawyer may be tempted to use language that slants the statement of the law in the instruction in the client's favor. If the trial judge gives such an instruction (which she most likely won't), it may result in a reversal on appeal. Thus, be careful to use proper and balanced language in framing requested instructions and to avoid loading them with adjectives that belong in final argument. For example, don't submit a Request to Charge that speaks of "horrendous injury" or of the "relentless and unceasing conscious pain and suffering." An instruction should not merely contain an abstract proposition of law; it should integrate the applicable principle of law into the facts of the case.

The venire may contain jurors with limited education; therefore, instructions should contain words easily understood by the average layperson.

The following is a proper jury instruction based on the New York Pattern Jury Instructions:

> If you decide for the plaintiff on the question of liability, you may include in your verdict an award for the injury you find that he suffered and for conscious pain and suffering which you find to have been caused by the negligence of defendant. The plaintiff is entitled to recover a sum of money which will justly and fairly compensate him for his injury and for his conscious pain and suffering to date.[1]

In New York state, the highest appellate court has held that the award for conscious pain and suffering can include, in appropriate cases, "loss of life's enjoyment," called hedonic damages, not as a separate award but as part of the award for conscious pain and suffering. For example, if, as a result of the negligence of the defendant, the plaintiff is in a coma, then the charge should reflect the language of "loss of life's enjoyment." You should add such language

1 New York Pattern Jury Instructions 2:280.

to the instruction above and ask that it be charged. The instructions would then read as follows:

> . . . and for conscious pain and suffering which you find to have been caused by the defendant. The award for conscious pain and suffering includes loss of life's enjoyment, loss of the pursuits and pleasures of life, not as a separate award, but as a part of the award for conscious pain and suffering. . . .

The judge should be willing to charge your request or something like it.

Where the form charge uses the words "plaintiff" and "defendant," you should add the names of the plaintiff and defendant to personalize the charge.

Disputed Facts

In framing specific instructions, try to avoid assuming disputed facts. If any instruction assumes facts, the jurors can be misled into believing that those facts are no longer in dispute or that the judge has an opinion supporting one version of the evidence. Appellate opinions have repeatedly held that it is error for a jury instruction to assume the truth of disputed facts. This danger can often be avoided by using such phrases as "if any," "if you are reasonably satisfied from the evidence," or "if you so find."

Liability and Damages

Simple logic and common practice dictate that you first submit special charges on liability, and then on damages. When the issue of liability is being presented to the jury, you should draft damages instructions in such a way that the language of the charge does not presume the defendant's liability. The instructions should start with a phrase like, "If you find for the plaintiff on the question of liability, and if you find from the evidence that the plaintiff was injured as a direct and proximate result of the defendant's negligence, then . . ."

Format

The actual format of the instructions submitted will depend on local practice; know the state and local rules regarding jury instructions. It is generally considered good form to type each proposed instruction on a separately numbered sheet of paper. When this is done, the judge can select those she wishes to use and add them to the general charge. Numbering each requested charge separately facilitates discussion of the charges with the court and opposing counsel. It is also good practice to indicate the source of the particular charge requested at the bottom of each sheet. If the requested charge comes from a pattern or model instruction or a case, statute, or other authority, the cite should be included; if there has been a modification, this should be noted.

If the trial is in a jurisdiction where a set of the instructions are provided to the jury, it is wise—that is, the judge's clerical personnel greatly appreciate the courtesy—or it may be required to provide a "clean" copy of the instructions to the judge. A clean copy is one that gives no indication of which party offered the instruction nor any sources or citations.

The order in which instructions will be presented is worthy of careful consideration. Placing instructions in their proper order is an important element of persuasive communication; concepts such as primacy and recency warrant consideration.

Psychologists tell us first impressions are more lasting impressions; likewise last impressions are harder to forget. However, one party will usually have little effect on how the court orders its instructions, for example, liability instructions, damages instructions, and closing instructions.

Some attorneys believe that where jurors are given written instructions to take into the deliberations, you must see to it that the order in which the jurors are physically given the written instructions is not hurtful to the plaintiff. The written instructions should be arranged in the same order in which the jurors were given the oral instructions.

Affirmative Defenses

If the case involves affirmative defenses, you should submit proposed charges on these issues to the court. The same principles of balance and fairness that govern the framing of liability instructions and damages instructions should dictate the formulation of instructions on affirmative defenses. If the court declines to charge your version of affirmative defense instructions, there may be a basis for an appeal.

In many jurisdictions today, comparative, rather than contributory, negligence is the applicable rule of law. Impacting further on this substantive change is the abolition of joint and several liability in some jurisdictions and the adoption of new substantive law such as the Uniform Contribution Among Joint Tortfeasors Act. Preparing understandable, legally appropriate instructions in such jurisdictions is challenging indeed. It is advisable to sensitize the judge to problems of this magnitude as early as is feasible, for example, at the pretrial conference.

Undue Emphasis of a Point of Law

It is well settled that giving undue emphasis or influence to a point of law during a jury charge will constitute error. It is important that in framing written instructions, you avoid unnecessary capitalization or emphasis lest the judge, in adopting the suggested form, is led into error.

The greater danger is what the judge, sua sponte or at the suggestion of the defendant, may do to emphasize unfairly the defendant's position.

It is common error for a judge to give undue emphasis to a point of law during a jury charge. By undue emphasis we mean giving emphasis to one point of law to the exclusion of others or giving multiple instructions covering essentially the same issue. If, for example, during his oral charge the judge were to instruct on comparative negligence and repeat the charge or use the words more often than was warranted for the jurors to understand the charge, that would be undue influence. The jurors might get the impression that the judge thought the plaintiff was negligent. An appeal could be based on the added emphasis that point of law received.

Alternative Instructions

There is generally no prohibition against submitting more than one proposed instruction on a particular issue or point of law or against submitting conditional instructions. Where it is important that a particular point be covered in the court's charge, you should prepare alternative instructions. The most favorable version should be submitted first; if the court indicates that it will not give that instruction, you should except to the court's refusal of the first instruction and submit a modified or weaker statement of the same proposition. This will more than likely result in the coverage of the point in one form or another. Also, a trial judge's refusal to give the stronger instruction proffered may be used as an assignment of error in the event of an adverse verdict.

Some attorneys maintain a file of written instructions that have been approved in previous trials. The maintenance of such a file over the years can be of enormous benefit to the trial lawyer. Contact other trial lawyers if you need instructions that might have been given in cases tried on similar issues.

CHARGE CONFERENCE

Most jurisdictions provide for a "charge conference" to allow counsel to meet with the trial judge outside the presence of the jury to discuss the charge before final arguments. The entire conference should be recorded by a court reporter to preserve any rulings made by the court. Most judges recognize that a charge conference with counsel present will reduce the possibility of reversible error, and they therefore encourage counsel's participation in the determination of what instructions should be accepted. Remember that urging an instruction that does not reflect the law of the jurisdiction or the trend in which the jurisdiction is moving may result in reversible error.

The contents of final argument and the context of the court's charge are integrally related. It is only after you know what law will be submitted to the jury that you will be able to argue accurately certain aspects of the case. Although local rules usually refer to some point before or during trial where proposed instructions are to be exchanged, you should expressly request that this occur as early as is reasonably practical. By obtaining a set of instructions from opposing counsel, you can research the law, narrow the issues, and avoid potential error in the presentation of evidence. If the local rules do not expressly provide for a charge conference before argument, ask for one.

EXCEPTIONS

Because a large percentage of reversals are based on errors committed by the trial court in its charge to the jury, it is extremely important to take full and proper exception to the court's instructions. Although the results of an arduous trial may be completely eradicated by a single error or omission committed by the court in its charge to the jury, many lawyers find themselves less prepared to handle exceptions to the court's instructions than to any other part of the trial.

Previous portions of this chapter have addressed attempts by plaintiff's counsel to ensure that a fair verdict is obtained. The topic of "taking exceptions" is addressed to your efforts to ensure the reversal of an unjust verdict—or at least to ensure that you are in a position to challenge properly an unjust verdict resulting from errors in the court's charge.

Procedure

The two pivotal questions relating to the topic of taking exceptions are "when" and "how" to take them. The requisite procedures will vary from state to state, and state court practice is often different from federal court practice.

The suggestions that follow our discussion of when exceptions must be taken to the court's charge are based on the assumption that local rules do *not* provide for a charge conference or that a charge conference was not, in fact, conducted. If the trial judge does conduct a charge conference, you will at that time be able to make and record all necessary objections and exceptions to the instructions.

The when and how of preserving for review an error in the instructions may vary as to whether the charge is "given" or "refused;" the procedure for excepting to an oral charge may be different from the procedure for written instructions.

Local practice usually provides that you are accorded an exception to the court's refusal of your proposed written charge. If this is not the local practice, you must take steps to record your exceptions.

Local practice does not usually provide you with an exception to the court's giving of written instructions requested by the opposing party. Usually the procedure that governs is the same as that procedure for exceptions to the oral charge.

When it comes to excepting to a refusal by the court to give your written request, don't be shy. In this instance, more is better.

If there is a charge conference at which the judge tells you she will not charge one or more of your written instructions, take an exception at that time. Be sure the conference—or at least that part of it in which you take your exception—is on the record. There are no magic words, but these should work: "Your Honor, I respectfully except to Your Honor's refusal to charge ["give" in many jurisdictions] the following Request to Charge [Instruction] submitted by the plaintiff [read the Request into the record] on the following grounds [set forth each ground]: __________." After charging the jury, the judge may excuse the jury and ask counsel, on the record, if there are any exceptions or requests. At this point, you again except to the charge that the judge gave. The reason for this redundancy is to be certain that an appellate court does not get the impression that although you excepted at the charge conference, you later agreed with the charge as given and therefore waived exception.

The remaining discussion will be addressed to the typical procedure relating to when and how exceptions should be made to the court's *oral* instructions to the jury. The following suggestions are applicable whether the potential source of error is the giving of an erroneous charge or the erroneous refusal to give a proper charge.

When

Most local rules require that exceptions to the court's charge be taken outside of the jury's presence but before the jurors retire to begin their deliberations. Indeed, in some jurisdictions, appellate courts have ruled that objections to instructions are waived when counsel fails to raise the objections before the jury retires—even when the court and all counsel have stipulated to the procedure. Typically, the trial judge will call a short recess and excuse the jurors, rather than sending them back to the jury room, to provide counsel with the opportunity to state exceptions to the charge. If local practice requires that exceptions be taken before the jury retires to consider its verdict, and the trial court does not give you an opportunity to except to the charge, you may specifically have to request a recess for the court to "excuse" the jury, so both sides will have an opportunity to record their exceptions outside the jurors' presence.

How

Some jurisdictions still insist that the actual language of the charge to which you except be read to the trial judge by the court reporter. In any event, your reference to the portion of the charge to which you except must be specific enough that the trial court knows the precise portion of the charge to which your exception is addressed. Many lawyers first describe the topic, or the portion of the charge to which they wish to take exception, and then merely ask the trial judge to assent verbally for the record that he understands the specific portion of the charge to which counsel wishes to take exception. If local rules require the statement of grounds, you would then state the grounds of your exception.

This requirement of precise grounds is no longer uniform. Some states require that each ground of exception be stated with particularity and decline appellate review on those grounds not stated and recorded in the trial court; other states have eliminated the necessity of excepting to *any* portion of the court's charge, much less to the statement of grounds.

You should consider requesting an explanatory charge, if the court has not given one, at the conclusion of the court's instructions. The request for an explanatory charge may not only be a matter of good trial strategy, it may also be required to preserve a ground of error for appeal. The need for explanatory charges usually arises from the failure of the judge to instruct the jury on some topic that you anticipated would be covered in the court's oral charge. The appellate courts of many states still follow the practice of refusing to review the trial court's failure to charge on a certain point unless you preserved the error by requesting an explanatory charge.

VERDICT FORMS

General Verdict

After the court has completed reading its instructions, it will usually instruct on the form of verdict that the jury is to complete. In most jurisdictions, general-verdict or special-verdict forms are used. In a general-verdict form, the jury is simply instructed to state, "We, the jury, find for the plaintiff and award damages in the amount of __________ dollars," or, "We, the jury, find for the defendant." For preserving a favorable verdict on appeal, the simple general-verdict form is preferred. Special-verdict forms are more likely to result in error and reversal on appeal. However, as trial practice has become more complex, and with the passage of tort reform legislation bringing with it various forms of several liability, and of course with comparative negligence that has now been adopted in most jurisdictions in some way, the use of the special-verdict form is frequently not only justified, but necessary.

In jurisdictions with comparative fault and/or several liability, forms of verdict is a subject that requires the closest scrutiny and thorough preparation. The most carefully prepared and masterfully tried case can be compromised by lack of consideration in a relatively new or difficult-to-understand area of law.

Special Verdicts and Interrogatories

The rules of your local jurisdiction will generally dictate which form of verdict is preferred and which is allowed. Rule 49 of the Federal Rules of Civil Procedure and numerous state codes provide for special verdicts and for special interrogatories that may be used to "test" either special verdicts or general verdicts.

Generally, it is up to you to take the initiative in urging the use of special verdicts or interrogatories. In some states, judges do not ask the lawyers to submit verdict forms. Whether invited or not, you should submit your own version of the verdict sheet. A special verdict sheet is to be filled out by the jury, tracking from point to point, and in proper sequence, every question a jury must answer in arriving at the final verdict. A sample verdict sheet appears as an appendix to this chapter.

This sheet can be a source of reversible error. In some jurisdictions the only thing the jurors get to see, other than the evidence, is the verdict sheet. It directs their deliberations because they usually focus their attention on answering the questions in the order asked. The jurors hear the charge, then see and work with the verdict sheet.

A verdict sheet also can, if incorrect, form the basis for an appeal by an aggrieved party. It is in your client's interest, therefore, that the sheet be correct. A verdict sheet tends to become complex. You want it to be right. Why let a judge's clerk or secretary draw up this very important document for you?

You should ask the court before or during trial whether a general or special verdict will be employed. If the court indicates that special verdicts or interrogatories will be used, you should ask to submit proposed special verdicts or interrogatories framed in language that will avoid error on appeal. Your right to do so stems from the same principles that dictate that the charge on the law be determined before the presentation of closing argument. In jurisdictions where special interrogatories or verdicts are employed, consider carefully whether these should be discussed during argument. To the extent that your jurisdiction permits you to comment on the jury charge, you should also be permitted to comment on and explain the proposed special verdict or interrogatory.

Questions During Jury Deliberations

After the charge and the verdict form have been explained to the jury, the jurors retire for deliberation. Occasionally, jurors will have questions that they send out to the court during their deliberation. All such questions and inquiries should be preserved on the record. Local practice dictates how this is done.

In some jurisdictions, the jurors are required to submit their questions in writing to the court. In other jurisdictions, the jurors are recalled to the jury box, and the questions are presented orally to the court. Any responses made by the trial judge to inquiries of the jurors during their deliberations are to be considered additional instructions.

If you have any objections to the substance or form in which those replies are given, state the objections to preserve the record for appeal. You have the right and obligation to be present during the answering of any such questions, and you should make this known to the court if local practice permits you to leave the area of the courtroom during jury deliberations. You should never be absent when the court receives a question from the jurors or gives further instructions.

CONCLUSION

Jury instructions, properly framed and pertinent to the issues raised by the pleadings and evidence presented at trial, can be highly instrumental in producing a successful result. By exercising care in preparing requested charges and presenting them for the court's consideration, you can go far toward obviating any need for appeal by either side.

Instructions should not be viewed as a "necessary evil" to be thrown together on the evening before summation. Rather, you should view instructions as one other key element of the total package of your attempt to effectively persuade the jury.

APPENDIX

VERDICT SHEET—FULL TRIAL, COMPARATIVE FAULT, AND DAMAGES[2]

1. Was the defendant negligent?

   At least five jurors [five out of six are required for a verdict] must agree on the answer to this question.

   YES ______ NO ______

   [SIGNATURES]

   ______________________ ______________________

   ______________________ ______________________

   ______________________ ______________________

   If your answer is NO, proceed no further and report to the Court.

   If your answer is YES, proceed to Question 2.

2. Was the defendant's negligence a proximate cause of the collision [or other appropriate characterization of the occurrence]?

   At least five jurors must agree on the answer to this question.

   YES ______ NO ______

   [SIGNATURES]

   ______________________ ______________________

   ______________________ ______________________

   ______________________ ______________________

   If your answer to Question 2 is NO, proceed no further and report to the Court.

   If your answer to Question 2 is YES, proceed to Question 3.

2 New York Pattern Jury Instructions 2:36.

3. Was the plaintiff negligent?

At least five jurors must agree on the answer to this question.

YES ______ NO ______

[SIGNATURES]

______________________ ______________________

______________________ ______________________

______________________ ______________________

If your answer to Question 3 is NO, proceed to Question 6.

If your answer to Question 3 is YES, proceed to Question 4.

4. Was the plaintiff's negligence a proximate cause of the occurrence?

At least five jurors must agree on the answer to this question.

YES ______ NO ______

[SIGNATURES]

______________________ ______________________

______________________ ______________________

______________________ ______________________

If your answer to Question 4 is NO, proceed to Question 6.

If your answer to Question 4 is YES, proceed to Question 5.

5. What percentage of negligence is attributable to each of the parties?

DEFENDANT ______% PLAINTIFF ______%

Total of percentages must be 100%

At least five jurors must agree on the answer to this question.

YES ______ NO ______

[SIGNATURES]

____________________ ____________________

____________________ ____________________

____________________ ____________________

PROCEED TO QUESTION 6

6. What is the total amount of damages to which the plaintiff is entitled for medical expenses incurred to date?

   $ ____________________

   At least five jurors must agree on the answer to this question.

   YES ______ NO ______

   [SIGNATURES]

   ____________________ ____________________

   ____________________ ____________________

   ____________________ ____________________

PROCEED TO QUESTION 7

7. What is the total amount of damages to which the plaintiff is entitled for loss of earnings to date?

   $ ____________________

   At least five jurors must agree on the answer to this question.

   YES ______ NO ______

   [SIGNATURES]

   ____________________ ____________________

   ____________________ ____________________

   ____________________ ____________________

PROCEED TO QUESTION 8

8. What is the total amount of damages to which the plaintiff is entitled for future medical expenses?

$ ______________________

At least five jurors must agree on the answer to this question.

YES ______ NO ______

[SIGNATURES]

________________________ ________________________

________________________ ________________________

________________________ ________________________

PROCEED TO QUESTION 9

9. Over what period of time will future medical expenses be incurred?

____

At least five jurors must agree on the answer to this question.

YES ______ NO ______

[SIGNATURES]

________________________ ________________________

________________________ ________________________

________________________ ________________________

PROCEED TO QUESTION 10

10. What is the total amount of damages to which the plaintiff is entitled for future loss of earnings?

$ ______________________

At least five jurors must agree on the answer to this question.

YES ______ NO ______

[SIGNATURES]

____________________ ____________________

____________________ ____________________

____________________ ____________________

PROCEED TO QUESTION 11

11. Over what period of time will future loss of earnings be incurred?

____

At least five jurors must agree on the answer to this question.

YES ______ NO ______

[SIGNATURES]

____________________ ____________________

____________________ ____________________

____________________ ____________________

PROCEED TO QUESTION 12

12. What is the total amount of damages to which the plaintiff is entitled for pain and suffering to date?

$ ____________________

At least five jurors must agree on the answer to this question.

YES ______ NO ______

[SIGNATURES]

____________________ ____________________

____________________ ____________________

____________________ ____________________

PROCEED TO QUESTION 13

13. What is the total amount of damages to which the plaintiff is entitled for future pain and suffering?

$ ____________________

At least five jurors must agree on the answer to this question.

YES ______ NO ______

[SIGNATURES]

____________________ ____________________

____________________ ____________________

____________________ ____________________

PROCEED TO QUESTION 14

14. Over what period of time will future pain and suffering be incurred?

____

At least five jurors must agree on the answer to this question.

YES ______ NO ______

[SIGNATURES]

____________________ ____________________

____________________ ____________________

____________________ ____________________

REPORT YOUR VERDICT TO THE COURT

FINAL ARGUMENT

Philip H. Corboy and Susan J. Schwartz

Final argument is your last opportunity to persuade the jury that your client is on the right side of the lawsuit. You must assure those six or twelve people that they should award full, fair, and reasonable compensation for the injuries your client has suffered and will continue to suffer. During final argument, you must maintain credibility as you explain why your client is entitled to a verdict.

As the culmination of trial and your final contact with the jury, closing argument is the only time when you may coherently demonstrate how all evidence adduced at trial relates to the law. Use the law, which the judge has explained or will explain in instructions to the jury, to argue your case. Demonstrate how the law on liability and damages, applied to the evidence in the case, mandates a finding of liability as well as an award of substantial damages.

Long before trial, the vigilant lawyer develops the case's theme around which all evidence produced at trial will be structured. Your theme should be maintained in final argument. Use your theme to persuade the jurors that the law, applied to the facts, requires a single conclusion. Inherently, jurors want to do what is right.

If proximate cause is a critical issue, emphasize that instruction. Break down the definition of proximate cause into its component parts, adapt the facts of the case, and explain the concept to the jurors in language they will understand. When damages are significant, use an itemized jury verdict form to separately address each element of damages. The form can be made into a transparency and projected by overhead projector onto a screen, blown up onto a posterboard or featherboard, or drawn on a blackboard or butcher paper.

Jurors look for charisma, competence, and credibility in a trial lawyer, and they are still assessing you during final argument. Demonstrate your competence by logically applying the facts to the law. Admit any vulnerabilities in your case, but follow this admission by a demonstration of how the law, in its compassion, still allows your client to prevail.

GENERAL CONSIDERATIONS

Be Spontaneous

Never read your argument. An argument should not appear canned. Certainly a jury should not be lulled to boredom by counsel mumbling, reading trial notes, or shuffling through papers. You have lived and breathed this case during preparation and trial; you have planned your argument to parallel the theme of the case. This planned argument should be delivered as extemporaneously as possible. Notes are permissible. Even the most experienced counsel values an outline or checklist. Some still write a script, but never read it. Instead, highlight key words and phrases to remind you of crucial points to raise.

Watch Your Demeanor

Your demeanor in final argument, as throughout the trial, should be courteous. Deliver your argument with sincerity. Analyze the facts consistent with your theory of the case; don't just recite them.

A constant dulcet delivery will lull jurors to sleep. On the other hand, persistent shouting is equally ineffective and may smack of histrionics. Some vital points can be delivered by dropping your voice so jurors must strain to catch each word. Likewise, indignation is not out of place, and a raised voice is often appropriate. You must be the judge, for every case is different. Do what feels natural for you.

Feel free to emulate the style of other lawyers. Adapt borrowed bits and pieces of final arguments into a style that suits your personality. Charisma in the courtroom is attractive and persuasive to jurors. Some people are born with charisma, but many acquire it. When you are under the scrutiny of the jury, charisma will give you, and your client through you, a crucial persuasive edge.

Start and Finish Argument

Generally, each side is allowed equal time for argument. In many jurisdictions the plaintiff, who carries the burden of proof, is given the right to both start and finish the closing argument stage of trial. You may start with a closing argument and, after the defense argues, you have the opportunity to make a rebuttal argument. As counsel you may divide your allocated time, advising the court of how you expect to proceed.

Begin with a complete closing argument to seize the psychological edge of primacy. One of the most effective weapons in the plaintiff's arsenal is the right to be the first to give the jury the total picture. This weapon should be used to the fullest.

The inexperienced lawyer may favor a brief closing argument and plan a strong rebuttal. However, resist the temptation to save the best for last, because in the interim the defense has the opportunity to argue its entire case. The logical cohesiveness of the defense's statements may blunt the jurors' enthusiasm for any argument, even the strong finish you painstakingly prepared. Begin by taking the defendant to task; force the defendant to rebut *your* contentions. The jury will expect a counterattack from the defense that, if ineffective, may seal the decision for the plaintiff.

Many lawyers inform the jury that they do not intend to misstate the evidence. They explain that if they accidentally err, the jurors must recall and rely on their memory of the actual testimony. Do not, however, tell the jury that what you say is not evidence. Jurors could assume that everything you say is unimportant, as it is not evidence.

Use real language in final argument. Legalese is not persuasive. Would you use the term "motor vehicle" to persuade a friend at a cocktail party that your car is better than his? Jurors want to hear "after," not "subsequent to." Speak their language.

Do not tell the jurors what they must do; instead, lead them to the right conclusion. They want to do the right thing, but they do not want to be told what to do. They are the finders of fact—you are the persuader.

Use the Transcript

Key sections of testimony are often critical to the issues. Testimony can be transcribed daily during trial. If your jurisdiction allows you to use a transcript of testimony in argument, highlight the passages to be read to facilitate finding them later. In some courts, testimony may be enlarged or projected on a screen by overhead projector so the jury and court may view it as you read. This makes the jurors participants and assures them that the transcript is used accurately.

Transcribe defense counsel's opening to demonstrate any failure to deliver the proof promised.

If your jurisdiction does not allow verbatim transcript recital, summarize critical testimony, using witnesses' key words and phrases to refresh the jurors' recollections. The portrayal must be accurate, however—it must parallel the jurors' recollections, or you will lose credibility.

Incorporate Jury Instructions

In most jurisdictions, counsel has the right to learn which instructions will be given from the trial judge before final argument. To maintain the case's theme, structured around the relationship of the law and the facts as to both liability and damages, you should provide the court and other counsel with proposed jury instructions. Use these instructions to frame the proof, and then in final argument correspond the evidence to the law. This way, you can explain to the jury the significance of important instructions—use language from the instructions in the final argument as a basis for showing how the facts you have proven satisfy the law.

DELIVERY OF ARGUMENT

Address Jurors' Responsibilities

For most jurors, sitting on a jury is the only time other than voting in which they participate in their government—remind them of this. These people are called to serve in the judicial system that is our primary bulwark against tyranny. To serve is an honor and a duty that should not be taken lightly.

Express your appreciation of and respect for the jurors as "temporary officers of the court." Review the history of the jury system, beginning almost 800 years ago at Runnymede, England, when the feudal system ended and the Magna Carta was signed. Tell them that from that time until today, people in English-speaking countries have had the right to trial by jury, where six or twelve jurors combine their consciences, backgrounds, educations, common sense, and ethnicities to achieve justice in a dispute between citizens.

Emphasize the Oath

At the beginning of service, the jurors took an oath to follow the law. Remind them of that solemn oath and explain their duty to decide the case, according to the law and the evidence.

Tell the jurors that this trial will have been a charade if they fail to follow the law. Acknowledge that although lawyers have the right to tell them what the law is, if any lawyer supplies a version different from that given by the court, jurors should rely on the judge. The jurors must apply the law logically, reasonably, and properly to the facts in this lawsuit; even if the law as provided by the court seems unfair or unreasonable, they must follow it.

The jurors must be reminded that they are peers of the plaintiff. They represent the community. During juror deselection, ask the jurors to commit to following the law, despite disagreements with it. Then, in final argument, remind them of that oath to follow the law, again stressing the importance of their role. Also, if you emphasize adherence to the law, jurors might ask themselves, "Why is he stressing that I follow the law? Why is he reminding me that I said I would follow the law?" Subconsciously they may believe the law must favor the plaintiff.

Use the Facts

Jurors do not tolerate insincerity and dishonesty. Your approach should be one of complete candor. The lawyer who is perceived as insincere or dishonest is the lawyer whose client may be punished by the jury.

Facts may be laid out chronologically or by certain issues. The latter method can be particularly effective when liability is clear, but the defendant has denied negligence, and the court has directed a verdict for the plaintiff on the issue of liability at the conclusion of the defendant's case. An example of this type of presentation follows.

> This case started out when John's father retained me to represent his son. I filed a complaint, a charge of negligence.

> The defendant, as it had every right in the world to do in a country like ours, with a system like ours, denied that it was negligent. Anybody accused of running a stop sign and turning a healthy young man into what you know is John today has a right to a defense. The defendant filed an answer denying its liability. And it had a right to do that.
>
> Then the case developed. When the case began, counsel for defendant, as he had a right to do, told you in his opening statement that you would probably find his client responsible because at the accident scene, his client said that it was his fault. He said under oath that he was driving 45 to 50 miles an hour through a stop sign. He told the police officer he was reading a map, and that he thought the stop sign was tilted.
>
> So defense counsel was saddled with a tough situation, but he still had a right to defend his client. He said to you as a representative of his client, "Ladies and gentlemen, you will probably find against my client; but just keep your feet on the floor; remember, be fair, and think about it." He said to you, "Maybe the plaintiff in this case, John, contributed to this occurrence. Maybe you will find that the damages should be reduced somewhat because John contributed to the occurrence." Counsel had an absolute right to do that.
>
> Then this court, after hearing all the evidence, made a decision as a matter of law that my client had absolutely nothing to do with the collision that caused these tragedies. The only issue remaining for you to decide is the amount of damages to which my client is entitled as a result of the defendant's negligence.

Essentially, facts in argument are the lawyer's version of what the evidence has shown. Reminding the jury from whom the evidence came will credit your argument. Use facts to effectively explain concepts such as corporations or park districts:

> The best way to state my discussion of the facts in this case is to begin with, What is a park district?
>
> I say that because a park district is being sued here, and

some of you may have wondered, when we began this lawsuit, why the park district is being sued.

Let me just state what the uncontradicted evidence shows is the business of a park district. A park district is a municipal corporation that has many functions. Two of those functions are to supply recreation and to supply that recreation with safety to all of the people in the community. People have the right to use public property for recreation and to expect proper safety measures to be supplied when they use that property.

In planning a park, and again, this is uncontradicted, the activities to be conducted within a park, whether it be golf, tennis, shooting, sunbathing, boating, swimming, selling hot dogs, playing chess, diving, or just sitting in the sand, are all to be taken into consideration by a park district when it supplies recreation with safety.

Also, we know that laying out a park district and designing a park district has two considerations: (1) what recreations are to be supplied, and (2) how can it be done safely for the citizens of the community who are invited to use a park district in the park district's lands and lands adjacent to the park district.

We also know that one of the functions of the park district is to separate the activities of the park district. We don't have basketball and baseball going on in the same area. We don't have badminton and shooting going on in the same area. We don't have sunbathing and lawn bowling in the same area. We don't have horseback riding and shooting in the same area, and it is a maxim, uncontradicted and agreed by all of the witnesses and all of the parties to this lawsuit, that it is a rule—a standard—that you never, never ever have boating and swimming in the same area.

You just don't mix oil and vinegar. You don't mix matches and dynamite. You don't allow the mix of these two sports;

> and it is the duty of the park district, not some third party, not some third citizen, not some other municipality, but the duty of the park district to provide safe boating and safe swimming, separated one from the other. Ladies and gentlemen, this separateness, this maxim was stated by Mr. Smith, the general supervisor of beaches and pools for the park district, on the second day of the trial.
>
> When I specifically asked him, "Is it not a maxim that boating and swimming should always be separated?" he said, "Yes." And I asked him, "Was that maxim not violated?" and he said, "Yes."
>
> Another thing that a park district is supposed to do is to identify the hazards and to eliminate them. If boating is a hazard when it is close to a swimming area, you are supposed to eliminate one or the other. And another one of the responsibilities of a park district in the planning stage is to inform the public of what is going on in the park district. You don't let somebody go down to Lincoln Park and walk out onto a tennis court and be shot by some of the gun-shooters who are nearby.
>
> You don't let some 6-foot, 5-inch 15-year-old out bouncing a ball where bats are being thrown around. You don't allow people to swim in an area where boats are known to be, unless you are going to expect a tragedy.
>
> We know that boating is a national hazard. We know that 50 to 70 percent of the injuries that occur in the water result from a boat. The others are apparently slip, trip, and fall, but 50 to 70 percent of the people who get hurt in the water, get hurt because of a boat. It's a hazard, and a park district, as an expert in the recreation business and a public entity, has a responsibility to the people for their safety in those two sports.

Explain Burden of Proof

Television, books, and other media have misinformed jurors. If they "know" one thing, it's that the lawyer must prove the case beyond a reasonable doubt. Educate them. Telling the jury that a civil suit is not "that kind of case" is insufficient. You must explain that while the plaintiff has the burden of proof, the civil law in its wisdom requires only that the plaintiff prove each element of the case by a preponderance of the evidence.

Preponderance of the evidence is a simple concept. Something is proved by a preponderance of the evidence when, according to the evidence, it is probably more true than not true. Apply this simple test to the important issues of the case. Is it more probably true than not true that the defendant's conduct contributed in whole or in part to the plaintiff's injuries? Is it more probably true than not true that the plaintiff experienced pain and suffering before dying? Is it more probably true than not true that the defendant's agent was within the scope of her employment at the time she injured the plaintiff?

Argue Liability

A lawyer would be remiss in failing to explain the concept of duty. A juror might not understand why a defendant owes the plaintiff a duty or what that duty is.

The park district case is an example. A juror may not be comfortable with the concept that a park district owes a duty to a person who chooses to swim in an area not designated for that purpose. In that case, the plaintiff was struck by a motorboat while swimming in Lake Michigan. He had been swimming in the area for 20 years, even though he knew it was a designated no-swimming area. The park district's duty was explained in the following manner:

> You may have wondered when we started this case what the duty of the park district was. Let me show you what the court is going to tell you, specifically, is the duty of a park district. The court is going to tell you bluntly, and not casually, that it was the duty of the defendant, the park district, before and at the time of the occurrence, to use ordinary care for the safety of the plaintiff.
>
> That was the duty this district accepted when it created Lincoln Park, many years ago. All citizens of our city are the beneficiaries of that duty.

It was the duty of the park district to use ordinary care for the safety of the plaintiff. Now, what is ordinary care? The park district is going to tell you that ordinary care is nothing more or less than the responsibility of not being negligent toward the people in the park.

Specifically, that means that when supplying water, when supplying rocks, when supplying sand, and trees, they had the duty to supply them in an area that was safe.

Before going into the violation of that duty, I ask you to remember that the park district has 5,000 employees. They had 900 lifeguards. We're talking about a strip of land about one block long. The question to you will be whether or not the park district used ordinary care for the safety of plaintiff, an affirmative duty. We are not talking about the *plaintiff's* responsibility: we're talking about the park district's responsibility.

This may surprise some of you when we talk about that duty. You may say, "What did the park district have to do with somebody who was out using the water?" Whoever you thought it should be, the court is going to tell you that it was the duty of the park district. As far as you are concerned, they had the sole responsibility of supplying safe facilities to plaintiff.

When they supplied these "safe" facilities, they supplied boats, they supplied water, they supplied land, they supplied sunbathing beaches, and they supplied swimming areas.

Now, we know that there were at least five areas where serious swimmers swam. We know there is a difference between bathing and swimming. You can swim at the Planetarium. You can swim at the Oak Street Beach. You can swim at two other areas; and you can swim at Montrose Rocks. For many, many years it was tolerated, permitted, allowed, and even invited . . . for people to swim at Montrose Rocks.

Go back to what the uncontradicted evidence is: The function of the park district is to supply recreation and to supply it with safety. One of the things that the park district did was supply swimming facilities to people.

Every one of us has propensities. We all have desires. Every one of us has needs. Some kids in high school wouldn't think of doing anything in the summer except bouncing a ball. Other people wouldn't think of doing anything but batting a ball. Others wouldn't do anything but play chess down at the lake. Some people, because they are allowed to in a free society such as ours, want to swim.

The plaintiff was one of those people. As a matter of fact, he was taught how to swim in our own community at Von Steuben High School, and from 1935 until the day he was injured, he was an avid swimmer.

Now, when the park district creates a plan to put a park in a district of a city, they have a responsibility to anticipate the needs of the people who seek recreation. One of those people was the plaintiff. He sought swimming. He was a serious swimmer, and he was a good swimmer; not a speed swimmer, but good. He acquired a Red Cross Safe Guard badge in 1971, when he was in his late 40s.

The plaintiff is a kind, gentle, courteous, fragile man who didn't play chess. He didn't, at his age, play basketball or baseball; but he wanted to swim. The Chicago Park District supplied him with a place to swim. It was called Montrose Rocks, and they supplied it to him for 20 years, just as they supplied it to the little kids and the teenagers and everybody else who used those rocks to swim from for at least 20 years.

Now, you might say to yourself, "They stenciled the rocks." Public corporations do lots of things that we, the public, are either unaware of, or kept in the dark about. I don't have any idea whether the park district put stencils on an area where people were known to swim. I have no idea why they would put stencils on rocks and then let people swim right next to those stenciled rocks for at least 20 years, and do nothing about that.

We know that people sunbathed right next to the signs. Right next to the people who were sunbathing were other people who were coming in and out of the water; and they did that for 20 years.

Joe Pecorraro, the lifeguard who became the supervisor of the beaches, knew that people swam there. It had been designated a no-swimming area—an area where there were signs before he got the job—but he permitted it. Others permitted it. Five thousand employees, 900 guards, and not one of them, to our knowledge, ever stopped anyone from swimming.

Don't you think that if, in the last 20 years, there was a day when a lifeguard or one of the 5,000 employees of the park district had said, "Hey, kids, teenagers, 20-year-olds, 30-year-olds, 60-year-olds, get out of that water," don't you think somebody would have come in here and testified to it?

If one person had ever been ordered out of that water, wouldn't somebody have told us about it? Wouldn't they have brought somebody in here who would have said, "Sure, we kicked people out." You don't even have to be given a reason why they kicked somebody out. In any event, you heard several witnesses state they saw community residents swimming there often. Swimming right off the rocks.

So, the park district tolerated, permitted, allowed it, and even invited it.

Now, ladies and gentlemen, we know that in this lawsuit there was a lot of talk about the effect of stenciling. Let's accept the fact, for the moment, that the stenciling was beautifully written and it was in every language you needed to accommodate everyone in the community, and everybody who wanted to look down at the rocks could see the stenciled rocks: NO SWIMMING. NO DIVING.

> Even if that had been true, people still swam and were allowed to swim. Maybe there aren't many serious swimmers in this community. Hundreds and hundreds of people go to the bathing beaches, but at a place like this, the most we know of is about 50 people in the water.
>
> So, let them swim there. The serious swimmers want to be alone. They don't want to be where there are lifeguards and kids sitting around in the sand. They want to swim. So, let them swim there. And let them swim at over five other areas in the city; and sometimes we'll put lifeguards there for them, and sometimes we won't. In case we don't put lifeguards there, we are close enough to the beach, so we can get over there in less than a minute if somebody gets hurt. We can get over there in less than a minute when legs fall to the bottom of the water. And in this case, they did.
>
> We don't have to patrol it because it's a short distance away from us. We don't have to have lifeguards there because we have lifeguards over here. They can get there in a hurry. These are serious swimmers. They don't need our help. It's the little kids who don't know how to swim that we'll accommodate. They need discipline. It's those who won't want to swim beyond the buoys; we'll supply *them* with assistance and help, but we don't have to help these people any because they are serious swimmers.
>
> That was the judgment they made. They made that decision. But was it supplying ordinary care for the safety of those people?
>
> I respectfully suggest that the way that area was, the way those rocks went down into the water, it was an invitation to anybody who was an avid, anxious, desiring swimmer, who was entitled to use, did use, and was permitted to use that area to swim.

The best way to charge a defendant with negligence is to list for the jury each specific allegation of fault. Make it clear that the plaintiff need prove only one of the allegations of negligence, not all of them, to prevail. Weave this fact into the instructions with a statement that the court will tell the jurors that the defendant is responsible if any one of the allegations caused the occurrence.

Systematically, one by one, each allegation of fault should be discussed. You must help the jury relate the law of liability to the facts.

Uncontradicted or admitted allegations should be brought out first. Each and every allegation of fault should be detailed, followed by logical, reasonable support for the contention.

Maximize Damages

A personal injury lawsuit is a claim for money damages. A person who is hurt or disabled because of another's negligence is entitled to compensation. Why? Because that's the law. Don't hide this fact. Tell the jury that the plaintiff had a right to go about everyday life without any interference. Everyone has that right. And while the law recognizes that many persons are disabled, it also recognizes that if a person is disabled from the negligent conduct of another, that person is entitled to monetary damages.

Often during trial the defense will warn the jury that it should not act out of sympathy. You must then bluntly tell the jury that the plaintiff neither wants or needs its sympathy: "This is how our civil system works! We cannot snap our fingers and reattach the plaintiff's legs. The only thing you can do is award money damages, and in a cold, calculating way, you, the jury, must determine how to compensate this plaintiff for the elements of damage we are about to discuss." The jury must realize that sympathy won't pay the medical bills, won't return comfort to a painful world, and won't replace the paycheck the plaintiff can no longer collect.

The jurors must also know that it is their duty as officers of the court to compensate the plaintiff fully, fairly, and reasonably for all damages incurred; then they must be educated as to what is fair and reasonable. This can best be accomplished through suggestions of what those words do *not* mean. Fair and reasonable do not mean cheap. They do not mean mediocre or economical. They certainly do not mean bargain basement. Fair and reasonable mean full and complete, just and decent.

Use analogies to demonstrate these concepts. Had the defendant's negligence been responsible for the destruction of a tangible object, like a painting, and the art experts of the world agreed the painting was worth $1 million, the meaning of fair and reasonable would be apparent. If someone did not like the artist, or did not think the defendant deserved to be punished, and as a result awarded $500,000, that would be half justice. Half justice is worse than no justice.

Use an itemized verdict form when discussing damages, if permitted. Tell jurors that they should award "x" number of dollars for a particular element of damages, stick it on a shelf, forget about it, and move on to the next element of damages. This procedure should be followed for each individual element of damages to prevent jurors from lumping the awards together. Request individual verdicts for each element of damages.

Another successful technique is to show each element of damages on an instruction poster that mirrors the itemized verdict form. Cover each element of damages with a strip of cardboard attached to velcro. When disability is discussed, detach the strip covering this element. After explaining what disability means in terms of its interference with the dignity of human life, and after correlating the appropriate evidence, suggest a value and fill it in. When finished, replace the velcro strip over the figures. Then move to the next element of damages, pain and suffering; and so on. This method focuses the jury's attention on each single element of damages while diverting attention from the total amount being requested.

If counsel for the defense has not refuted damages, take full advantage. Hammer the jury with every instance of uncontradicted damages testimony. Discuss the testimony of witnesses who corroborated the noneconomic damages, and ask whether the defense provided any evidence to the contrary. Remind the jury that the doctor who testified, based on a reasonable degree of medical and surgical probability regarding the permanency of the plaintiff's injuries, pain, and suffering, was not even cross-examined.

Make the defense lawyer tell the jury why the figures suggested are too high for the plaintiff's noneconomic damages. Shift to the defense the burden of demonstrating why the amounts requested are unreasonable.

Address Comparative Fault

If comparative fault is an issue, you must address it and minimize its impact. For strategic reasons, discuss this issue only after having shown the defendant has violated an affirmative duty to the plaintiff and after arguing damages. Having asked the jurors to be fair, just, and reasonable, you must act accordingly. Remember, the jurors are constantly assessing your credibility. If your client's conduct could be considered to have been contributorily negligent, do not argue otherwise. Why? The jury exercising its collective wisdom may not adopt your analysis.

Do not concede fault, but deflect the jury's attention by demonstrating how the plaintiff was injured by the defendant's conduct. Make a distinction between the plaintiff's conduct and the defendant's negligence. The plaintiff's culpability, if any, is not as important as is the defendant's breach of duty. Your task is to minimize the percentage of fault attributed to the plaintiff's conduct.

In an automobile collision case, the defendant has the duty not to go over the centerline because such an action might hurt the plaintiff; the plaintiff has a duty not to go over the centerline simply not to be hurt. Make this distinction in a way the jurors will understand. Show that the defendant's negligence clearly stems from the failure to supply the plaintiff with safety, versus the plaintiff's failure to supply safety to self.

When you must address comparative fault—and you must whenever you believe it to be a legitimate issue in the case—consider placing this argument after your discussion of damages. Usually, in calculating the final award, the jurors must first determine a figure that represents the value of the lawsuit, without consideration of comparative fault. Then they determine the percentage of the plaintiff's fault and subtract proportionately to reach the final award (in some jurisdictions, the court does the math; the jury simply determines the percentage). It is extremely important that the jury does not subconsciously reduce that first figure before considering the percentage of the plaintiff's fault.

Discussing the plaintiff's comparative fault after damages allows you to attack the defendant again on the liability issues. This second chance to justify a very large award can be fruitful.

When arguing comparative negligence, be a zealous advocate for your client and never make unnecessary concessions. Give the jury logical, credible explanations for the plaintiff's conduct. "It is more probably true than not true that the plaintiff's conduct was not a cause of this accident." An example of a comparative negligence argument follows:

I would be remiss in my responsibility to you as a fellow officer of the court if I did not bring up a subject which, even though you do not yet know what the law is, some one of you, as an intelligent human being, may very well say to yourself, this fellow should not have been swimming.

Let's face that issue, point blank, staring it right in the face. This fellow shouldn't have been in there swimming. Well, I'm not conceding that he shouldn't have been there. To the contrary, I'm suggesting he had every right in the world to go there, as he was lulled into the security of safety of 20 years of swimming there.

But let's assume that you, in your wisdom, conclude—and I, respectfully, suggest you have that right—it would be inappropriate of me to suggest that you could not—determine that, perhaps, he, himself, contributed to this occurrence.

I'm sure that's entered your mind. Well, the court, ladies and gentlemen, is going to tell you what the law is. The court is going to tell you, first of all, that you are not required to set aside your own observations in experiencing the affairs of life; and you may consider all of the evidence in this case in light of your own affairs, and in light of your own experiences in life.

Therefore, you may say to yourselves, that when the authorities put these stencils on the rocks, that no matter how inadequate they were, he should have seen them. No matter how much of a lulling into a sense of security, as a grown man, he should have said, I won't go in here. I will go swim at the "Y" as I did this morning.

You may then say that the stencils should have kept him out. That's your prerogative. That's your job, not mine. But the law is compassionate. And the law, like a temporary officer of the court, is aware of the propensities of people.

The law is charitable; the law is aware; the law is gentle; the law is forgiving. The court is going to bluntly tell you that the plaintiff's contributory negligence, if any, is not a bar to his recovery. The court, in its wisdom, in following the law, is going to bluntly tell you that if it is your decision that this middle-aged man was negligent, you have the opportunity, quite simply, after determining what the full amount of fair and reasonable compensation is, to take that full amount, make the legal assumption that this occurrence was contributed to by two people, and making the legal assumption that 100 percent represents the total, combined negligence of the plaintiff and the defendant, you may find that a percentage of the negligence that was a proximate cause of the plaintiff's injuries attributed solely to the plaintiff, is a certain percent of that 100.

I respectfully suggest you do not have to put a figure in here any larger than zero. That is your job, not mine. If you find that somewhere between zero and some other figure, your responsibility would then be to reduce the total amount of damages by that figure and come up with the bottom-line amount.

Now, ladies and gentlemen, with reference to this man's activities, as I indicated, the law is perceptive and gentle and courageous and aware. You know, there are lots of country areas where there's an old, broken-down stop sign at a stop corner, and people just pass them and pay no attention to them at all because they are used to it.

If you walk right down here to Dearborn and Clark, outside the courthouse, you will see a sign that reads DO NOT WALK ON THE LIGHT. You will see people walking. Nobody's stopping them. As a matter of fact, the police will help you across if you need it.

You will see a red light. If there are no cars coming, you will cross against that red light. People do it, day after day after day. Plaintiff, day after day, week after week, month after month, year after year, decade after decade, like everybody else in that area, was allowed to, was permitted to, was enticed to, and was invited to swim.

> A tragedy occurred on this day, which I respectfully suggest that you will find was a result of one of those elements of negligence on behalf of the park district.

REBUTTAL

Usually the defendant's counsel will provide fodder during final argument to give you an opportunity to express indignation in rebuttal. Remember, however, you must maintain credibility. If anger is inappropriate, do not feign it.

If the evidence at trial and in your final argument did not contain the ingredients necessary to convince the jury to decide in favor of your client, rebuttal will not save the day. Facts and law will prevail. As always, thorough and detailed preparation is crucial to the ultimate disposition of any lawsuit.

Rebuttal can never be completely anticipated. Its purpose is to answer the contentions of the defense—to rebut. These are, however, your final words to the jury; do not waste them by being defensive. Rebuttal, like everything else, should be planned. Drive home your strengths. Raise the questions the defendant left unanswered. If you merely respond to the defendant's arguments, you may lend them credence. Stay on the offensive and lead the jury to follow your theory of the case.

BASIC MEDICAL ANATOMY

Mitchell A. Karton, M.D.

Illustrations by Jo Ann Clifford

At one time or another every personal injury lawyer struggles with the concepts of medical anatomy. You may find the subject particularly impenetrable—no law school treats the medical considerations of personal injury law in depth. Nevertheless, a personal injury lawyer spends a lot of time conferring with doctors, reading medical reports and records, taking medical depositions, and considering the implications of bodily injuries. You must be able to empathize with injured clients in order to represent them effectively; you must understand how an injury affects the workings of a tremendously complex structure—the human body.

With a little effort, you can learn enough about anatomy and the principal functions of tissues, organs, and systems to understand medical records, communicate with doctors, and appreciate a client's plight. Mastery of the first four systems considered in this chapter—skeletal, muscular, nervous, and cardiovascular—will enable you to effectively handle the medical aspects of most personal injury cases.

The basic units and the separate systems of the body comprise a single, integrated entity. In studying the building blocks of human anatomy, you must always remember that trauma is inflicted not on a single cell, tissue, organ, or system, but rather on a functioning whole person.

MEDICAL TERMS

Medical terminology can present a formidable psychological barrier to attorneys; nonetheless, a basic vocabulary is not difficult to acquire. By learning a few Greek and Latin roots, suffixes, and prefixes, the attorney can develop a basic understanding of medical terms. For example, the root for nerve is "neur," and the suffix "itis" means inflammation. Thus, "neuritis" means inflammation of a nerve.

It is important to understand the medical terminology detailing the positions, directions, and movements of the body. The following terms describe positions.

Anterior (or Ventral)—front
Posterior (or Dorsal)—back

Lateral—away from the midline
Medial—toward the midline

Proximal—toward the source
Distal—away from the source

Cranial—toward the head
Caudal—toward the tail

Superior—above
Inferior—below

The following describe movements.

Abduction—away from the center of the body
Adduction—toward the center of the body

Flexion—bending of a joint

Extension—straightening of a joint

Supination—turning upward
Pronation—turning downward

Eversion—turning outward
Inversion—turning inward

"Anatomical planes" identify "views" of the body. The more common anatomical planes include:

- *Median or Midline.* This is an imaginary plane that passes from the front to the back through the center of the body, dividing the body into right and left equal portions.
- *Frontal.* This plane divides the body into anterior and posterior portions. It passes at right angles to the median plane.
- *Transverse.* This horizontal plane passes at right angles to both the frontal and median planes, dividing the body into cranial and caudal parts.
- *Sagittal.* This plane sections the body parallel to the long axis of the body or parallel to the median plane, dividing the body into right and left unequal parts.

Some anatomical postures to which physicians frequently refer are as follows:

- *Erect.* The body is in a standing position.
- *Supine.* The body is lying flat on its back.
- *Prone.* The body is lying face and trunk down.
- *Laterally Recumbent.* The body is lying horizontally, either on the right or left side.

BASIC UNITS OF THE BODY

The human body is made up of four basic units: cells, tissues, organs, and systems. Cells are the microscopic building blocks of the body; they are the fundamental units and are not of immediate importance to the trial lawyer. Collections of cells similar in structure and function form tissues. The primary tissues are described below:

- *Epithelial and Endothelial*. These tissues cover external and internal surfaces of the body and viscera.
- *Connective*. These are tissues that hold organs in place and bind all parts of the body together.
- *Muscular*. These tissues carry out voluntary and involuntary functions, primarily motions.
- *Nervous*. These are the most highly specialized tissues. They coordinate and convey impulses to and from the central nervous system, both voluntarily and by reflex.

Organs (for example, the liver, heart, lungs, and pancreas) are different tissues that combine to perform a specific physiological task. Organs do not operate independently but within the framework of systems. Systems are groupings of organs that perform specific functions. The body may be divided into ten basic systems:

Skeletal	Respiratory
Muscular	Gastrointestinal
Nervous	Genitourinary
Cardiovascular	Endocrine
Lymphatic	Integumentary

The majority of injuries presented in a basic personal injury trial affect one, or all, of the first four systems.

SKELETAL SYSTEM

General Considerations

The skeletal system makes movement through its approximately 200 bones and connective fibers. The purpose of the skeletal system is to give support and shape to the body (see Figure 1) and provide attachment points for bones, muscles, and ligaments.

Anatomical Classification of the Skeletal System

The *axial skeleton* is composed of those bones lying near the midline of the body, such as the skull and spinal column.

The *appendicular skeleton* is composed of those bones that support the limbs.

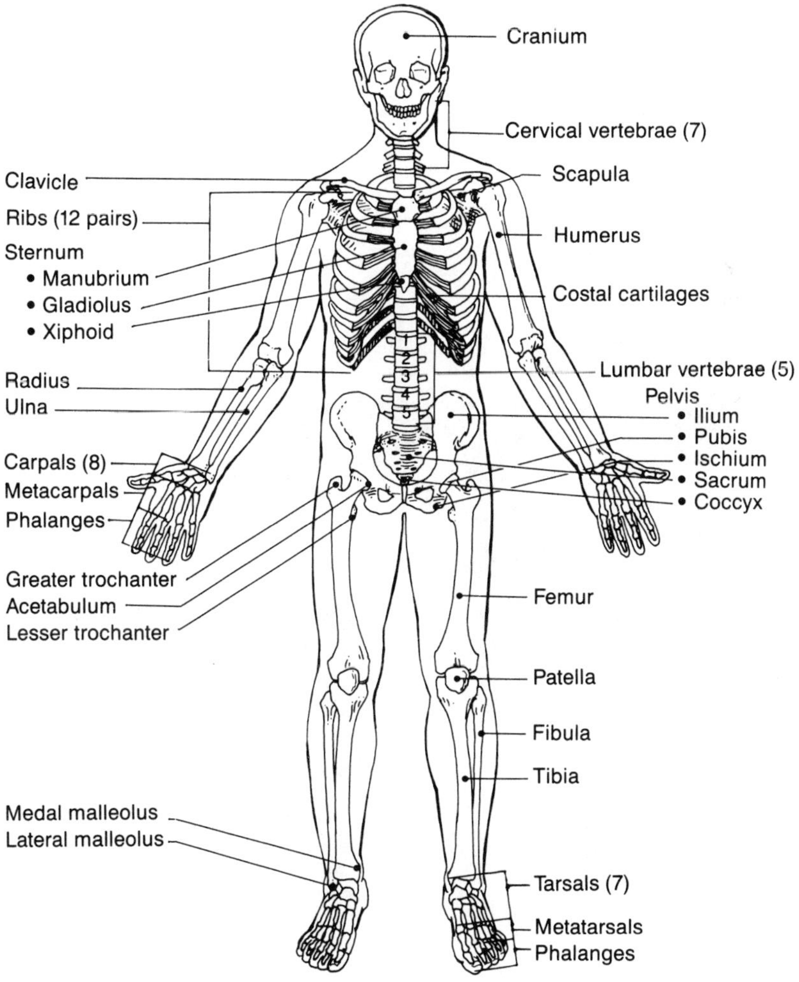

Figure 1
Skeleton

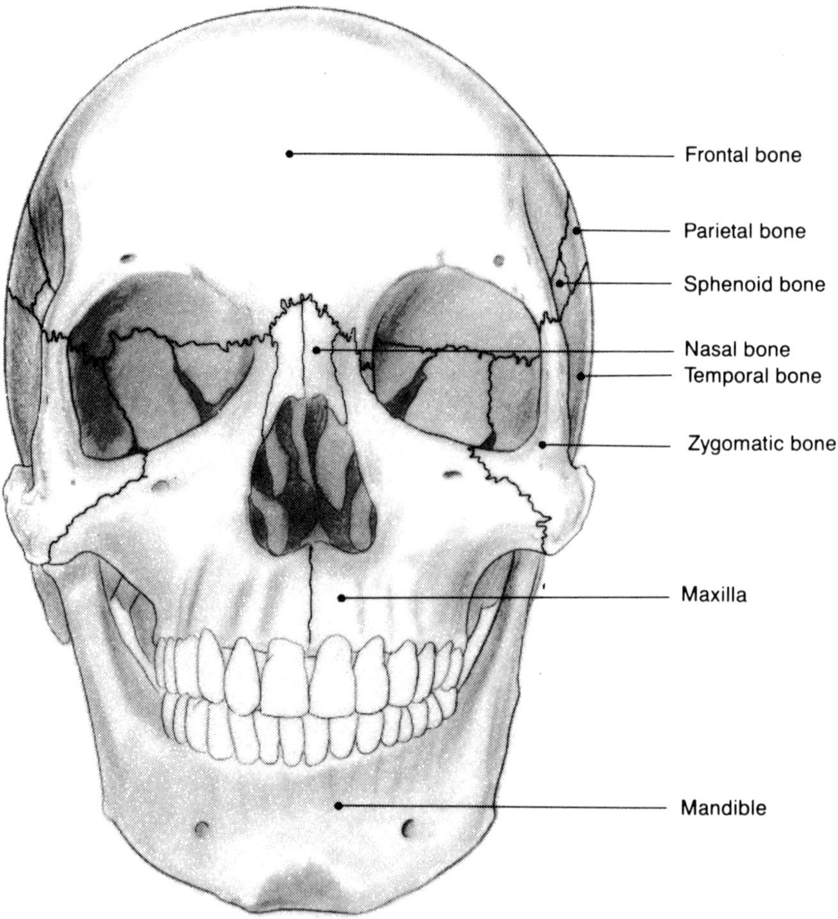

Figure 2A
Skull—Front View

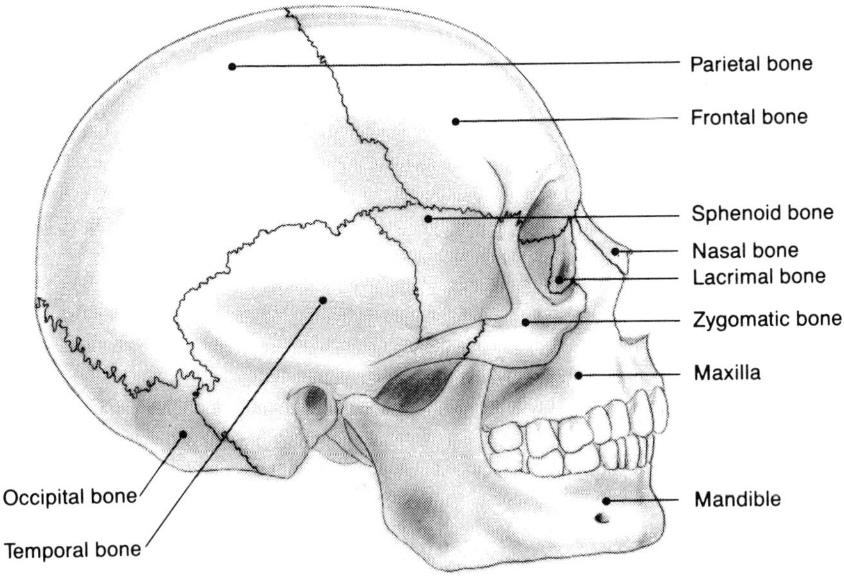

Figure 2B
Skull—Lateral View

Major Bones

You should be familiar with the following portions of the skeletal system.

The Skull (see Figures 2a and 2b)

Frontal bone	Mandible
Temporal bone	Zygomatic bone
Parietal bone	Sphenoid bone
Occipital bone	Nasal bones
Maxilla	Lacrimal bone

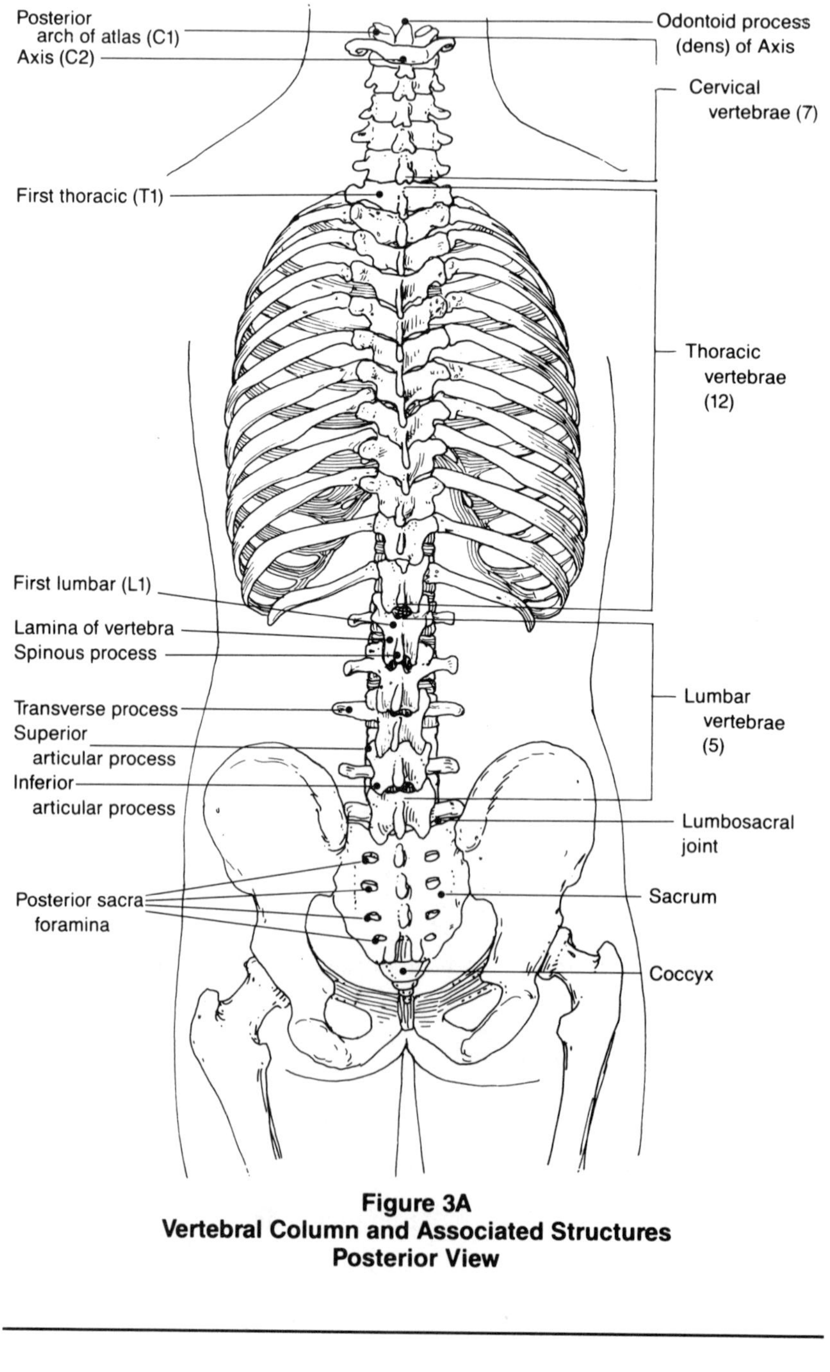

Figure 3A
Vertebral Column and Associated Structures
Posterior View

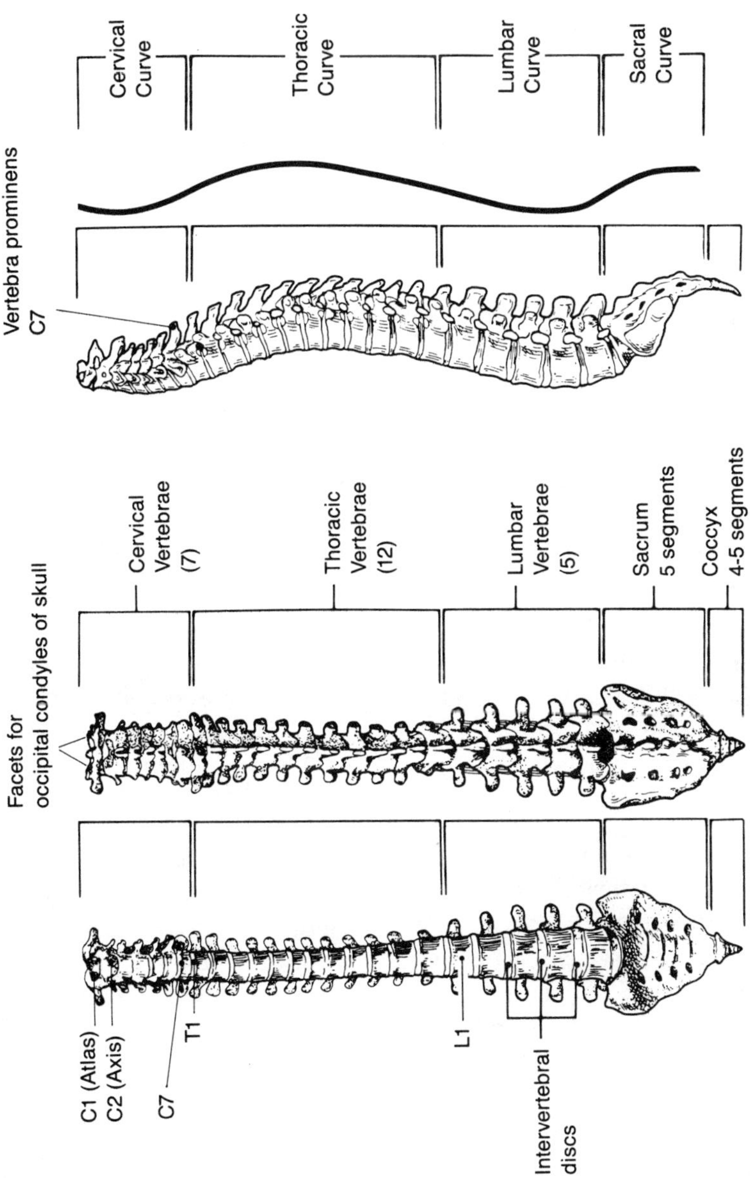

Figure 3B
Vertebral Column

Vertebral Column and Associated Structures
(see Figures 3a and 3b)

The importance of understanding the basic anatomy of the vertebral column (backbone) and its associated structures cannot be overemphasized. There are three major areas of the vertebral column: the cervical area, the thoracic or dorsal area, and the lumbar area. The bony structures that make up the vertebral column are known as vertebrae.

The cervical area, which supports the head, contains seven vertebrae (see Figure 4). The first of these is termed the "atlas." This structure supports the skull. The second cervical vertebra is called the "axis." The uppermost portion of the axis that articulates with the atlas is the odontoid process, also called the dens. This provides a point of rotation of the skull on the neck. The thoracic or dorsal area of the vertebral column is made up of twelve vertebrae. The lumbar area has five vertebrae. It is the lumbar area that is responsible for carrying most of the weight of the trunk. Immediately below the lumbar area is the sacrum. This structure consists of five fused vertebrae. Immediately below the sacrum is the coccyx, or "tail bone."

Between each pair of vertebrae is an intervertebral disc (see Figure 5). The outer portion of the disc, or the annulus fibrosus, is made up of a cartilaginous substance. Within the annulus fibrosus is a jelly-like substance known as the nucleus pulposus. Functionally, intervertebral discs serve a highly important, cushioning purpose.

Upper Trunk

The ribs are made up of twelve pairs of flat curved bones that are attached posteriorly to the thoracic portion of the vertebral column. Anteriorly the first seven pairs are attached to the sternum, the broad flat bone located in the midline of the chest (the "breast bone"). The eighth, ninth, and tenth ribs are joined to the cartilage of the seventh rib. The eleventh and twelfth are unattached anteriorly and are the so-called "floating ribs." The ribs, plus the sternum, compose the thoracic cage. This bony structure protects the vital organs of the chest and permits the expansion and contraction necessary in inhalation and exhalation.

Upper Extremities

This region contains the following bones:

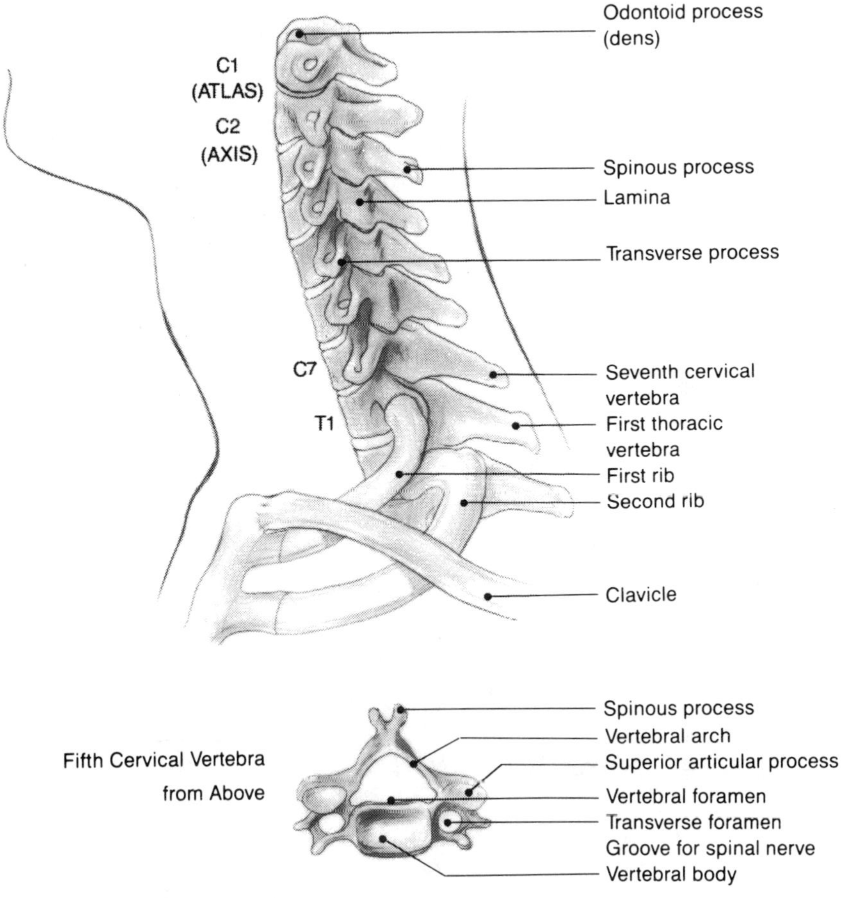

Figure 4
Cervical Vertebrae

- *Clavicle*. This is the collar bone.
- *Scapula*. This is the shoulder blade.
- *Humerus*. This is the upper arm bone.
- *Ulna and Radius*. These are the bones of the lower arm.
- *Carpals*. These are the eight bones of the wrist.
- *Metacarpals*. These are the five bones of the palm and posterior hand.
- *Phalanges*. These are the bones of the finger.

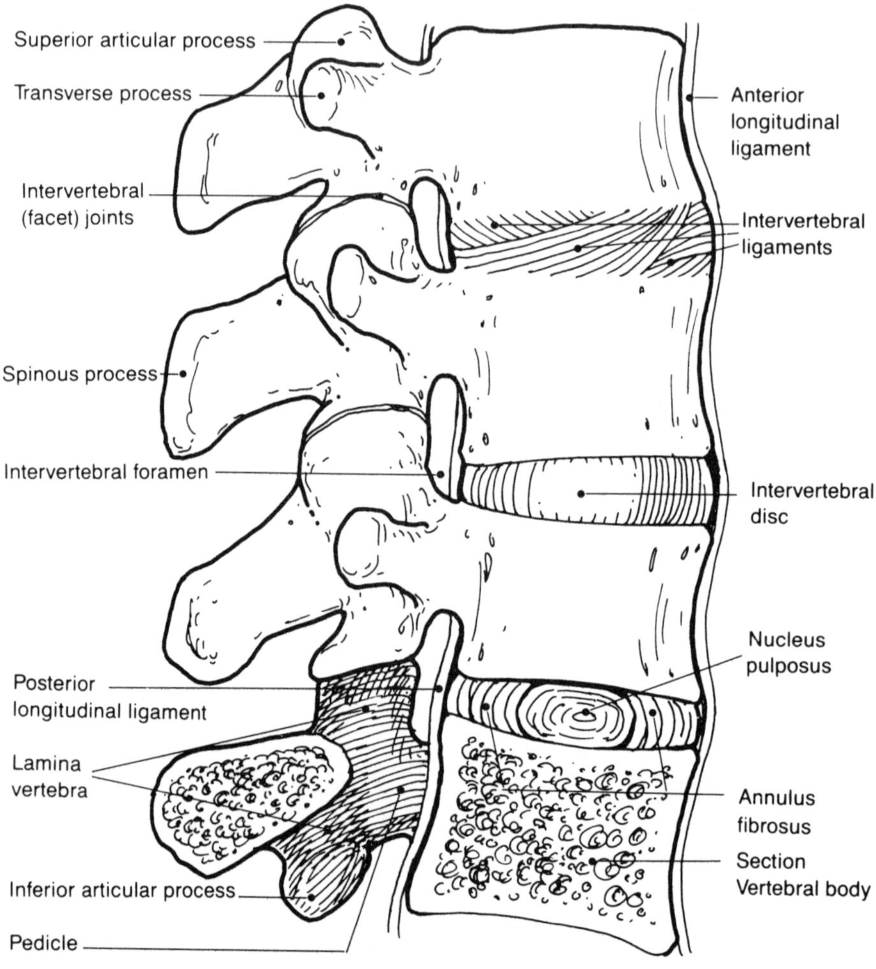

Figure 5
Intervertebral Discs

Lower Extremities

- *Pelvis.* The pelvis consists of two hip bones situated laterally and in front, with the sacrum and coccyx behind. The hip bones are divided into three parts: the ilium, the ischium, and the pubis; these three bones join to form the pelvic girdle.

- *Acetabulum.* This is not actually a bone, but rather a descriptive term for a large cup-shaped socket in the lateral aspect of the hip, into which the head of the femur fits.
- *Greater and Lesser Trochanters.* These are bony prominences located on the lateral and medial sides of the femur, for the attachment of muscles.
- *Femur.* This is the longest bone in the body; it is the bone of the upper leg.
- *Patella.* This is the kneecap.
- *Tibia and Fibula.* These are the bones of the lower leg. The tibia is the larger and is located medially.
- *Lateral and Medial Malleolus.* The lateral malleolus, at the lower end of the fibula and the medial malleolus, at the lower end of the tibia, are the ankle bones.
- *Tarsals.* These are the seven bones of the ankle.
- *Metatarsals.* These are the five bones in the sole and instep of the foot.
- *Phalanges.* These are the bones of the toes.

Joints

Joints are the places where bones are held together by connective tissue, such as ligaments, permitting certain movements while preventing others. Joints have certain common structural and functional features that allow them to be classified either according to the type of connective tissue that holds the bones together or according to the movement permitted.

The three major classifications of connective tissue are as follows:

Fibrous (Synarthrosis)

These are joints that are united by fibrous tissues. Little, if any, movement occurs with either of the existing two types.

- *Sutures.* These are joints, such as those in the skull, that are connected by several fibrous layers.
- *Syndesmoses.* These are fibrous joints in which the intervening connective tissue is thicker than a suture. An example is the tibiofibular syndesmosis, the joint between the lower ends of the tibia and fibula.

Cartilaginous (Synchondrosis)

These fibrous joints are united by fibrocartilage and serve as growth areas for the bones they join. Eventually, most of them are replaced by newly formed bone. The hyaline cartilage that joins the bones is a persistent part of the embryonic cartilaginous skeleton and, as such, serves as a growth zone for one or both of the bones that it joins. Most hyaline cartilage joints are obliterated, that is, replaced by bone, when growth ceases. The joint at the base of the skull beneath the pituitary gland is an example.

Synovial (Diarthrodial)

These tissues possess a fluid-filled space and are specialized to permit a wide range of movement. The articular surfaces are covered with cartilage, and the bones are united by the joint capsule and ligaments. All of the joints of the extremities are examples (elbows, wrists, knees, and ankles).

The three major classifications of joints with respect to movement are as follows:

Synarthroses

These are immovable joints, such as the sutures of the skull.

Amphiarthroses

These are joints with limited movement, as in the articulations between the vertebrae.

Diarthroses

These are freely movable joints, which include the following:

- *Plane Joint*. The articular surfaces of this joint are slightly curved, and permit gliding or slipping in any direction, like the carpal joints of the wrist and tarsal joints of the foot.
- *Hinge Joint*. This joint is uniaxial, and permits movement in only one place. An example is a joint between two of the bones (phalanges) of the finger or the toe.
- *Condylar Joint*. The articular area of this joint consists of two distinct articular surfaces. The knee joint is an example.
- *Ball and Socket Joint*. The shoulder joint is an example.

- *Ellipsoidal Joint.* The articulating surfaces of this joint are much longer in one direction than in another. An example is the radiocarpal joint.
- *Pivot Joint.* This joint is uniaxial; the axis is vertical. The axis-atlas joint of the neck that allows the head to turn is an example.
- *Saddle Joint.* This is a biaxial joint; an example is the carpometacarpal joint of the thumb.

MUSCULAR SYSTEM

General Considerations

All human activity is carried out by operation of the muscles. The human body contains 500 muscles that are large enough to be seen by the naked eye and thousands of muscle fibers that can be seen only through a microscope. Muscles, tissues of long slender cells, constitute about one-half of the body's weight; individual body shape is largely due to the muscle covering the skeletal framework. Tendons are also instrumental to the muscular system and are strong bands that attach muscles to bones or to other structures.

Movement of Muscles

Muscles are categorized by their primary movement:

- *Prime Movers.* These muscles actively produce movement.
- *Antagonists.* These muscles operate in opposition to prime movers.
- *Fixation Muscles.* These muscles steady a body part while others execute movement.
- *Synergists.* These muscles control movement of a proximal joint so that a prime mover may obtain movement of a distal joint.

Primary Muscles (see Figures 6a and 6b)

Neck

- *Sternocleidomastoid.* This large muscle bifurcates and inserts on both the sternum and the clavicle.

- *Paravertebral.* These slender muscles run the length of the spinal column.

Upper Trunk

- *Trapezius.* This triangular muscle is located between the back of the neck and the shoulder blades.
- *Pectoralis Major and Minor.* These muscles are located on the chest.
- *Latissimus Dorsi.* This is the broadest muscle on the back. It is located along the lateral aspect of the lower half of the back between the scapula above and the ilium below.
- *Deltoid.* This is a muscle capping the shoulder.
- *Triceps.* This muscle is located on the posterior aspect of the upper arm.
- *Biceps.* This is a muscle located on the anterior aspect of the upper arm.

Thoracic Wall and Abdomen

- *Intercostals.* These muscles are located between the ribs.
- *Subcostals.* These muscles connect a superior rib to the second and third inferior ribs.
- *Sternocostals.* These muscles connect the breastbone and ribs.
- *External and Internal Obliques.* These muscles support the abdominal contents and extend from the ribs to the crest of the ilium.
- *Rectus Abdominus.* These are long, vertical muscles in the front part of the abdomen, one to the right and one to the left of the midline, meeting along the vertical midline in the front of the abdomen. These are the muscles that bend the spine forward; they also support the abdominal wall.
- *Transversus Abdominus.* This girdle holds the abdominal organs in place.

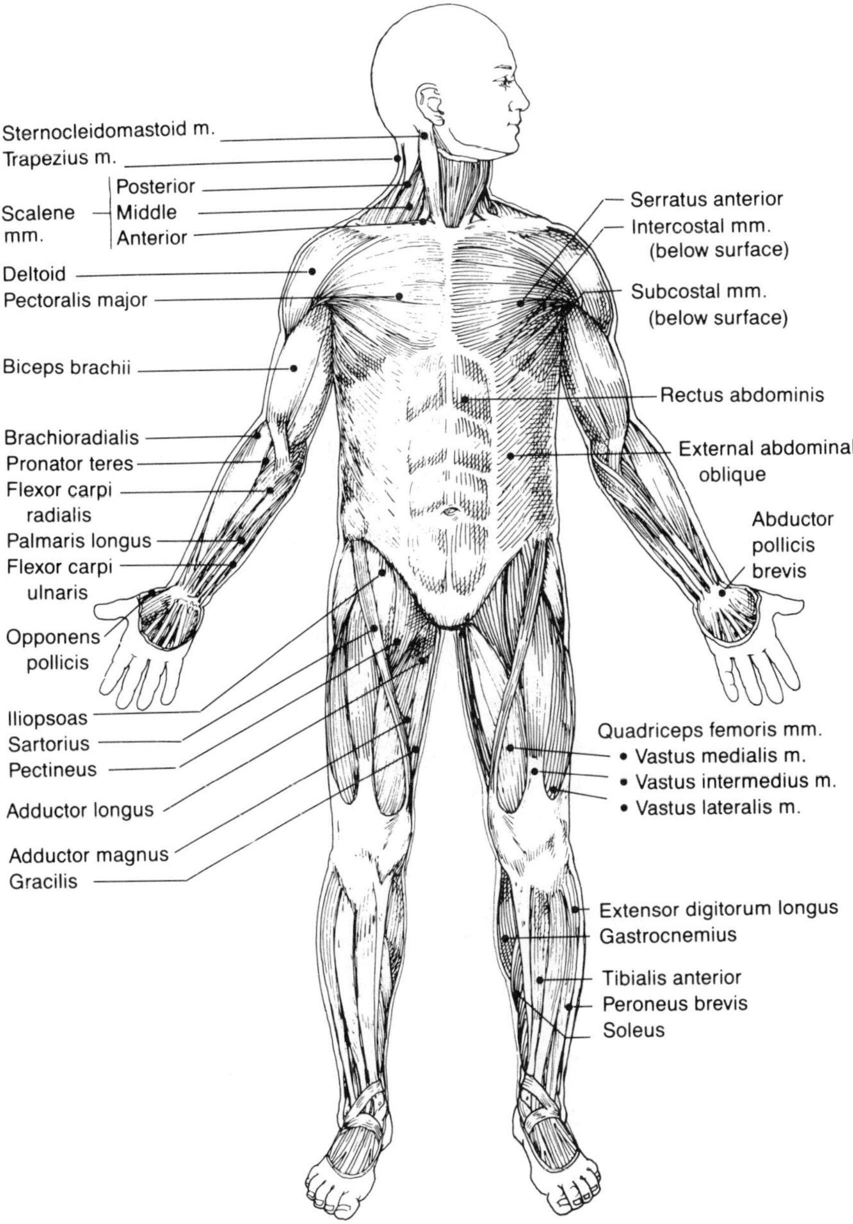

Figure 6A
Muscles—Anterior

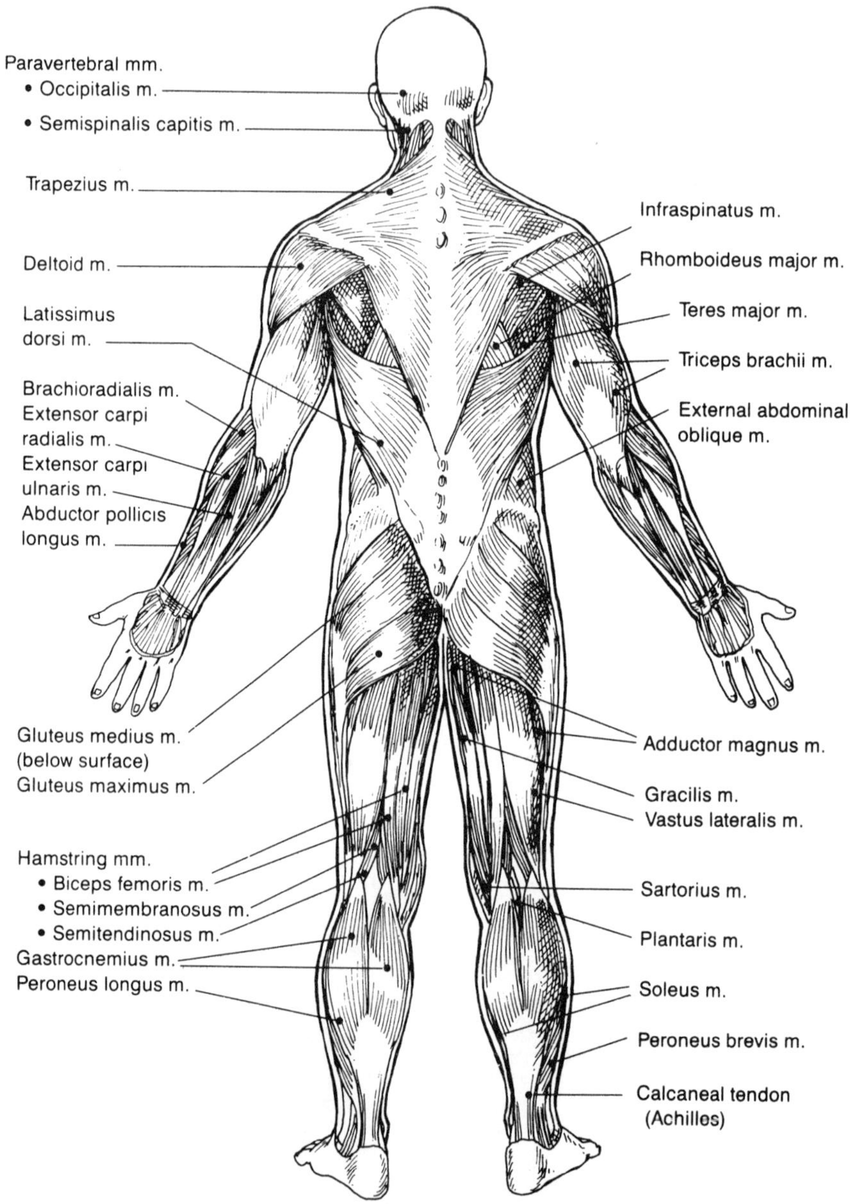

Figure 6B
Muscles—Posterior

Hip and Thigh

- *Gluteus Minimus, Medius, and Maximus.* These are the three muscles that form the buttocks.
- *Pectineus.* Located at the upper part of the inner thigh, this muscle bends the thigh at the hip joint to bring it toward the other thigh.
- *Adductor Longus, Brevis, and Magnus.* These three thigh muscles move the thigh to a position closer to the midline of the body.
- *Quadriceps Femoris.* This is a powerful thigh muscle, used in standing and walking, which straightens the leg at the knee joint.
- *Sartorius.* This muscle extends from the hip to the leg. Contracting it causes the thigh to bend at the hip joint and also to rotate outward; in addition, it helps to bend the leg at the knee.
- *Hamstrings.* These are three thigh muscles that bend the leg at the knee joint. The *semimembranosus* extends from the hip to the tibia. The *semitendinosus* extends from the back of the hip to the tibia. The *biceps femoris* is in the back of the thigh and extends between the femur and the lower part of the hip.

Lower Leg and Foot

- *Tibialis Anterior and Posterior.* These muscles are in the front and back, respectively, of the leg. They move the foot inward and outward and upward and downward.
- *Peroneus Longus and Brevis.* These are the leg muscles that turn the sole of the foot outward and lower the front part of the foot.
- *Soleus.* This is a muscle in the calf that extends the ankle joint, such as when the heel is raised to stand on the toes.
- *Gastrocnemius.* This is the outer calf muscle that bends the leg at the knee and bends the foot downwards.

NERVOUS SYSTEM

General Considerations

The human body has a "central authority" that issues orders to the rest of the body. The function of the nervous system, then, is to coordinate all of the activities of the body. The basic functional units of the nervous system are neurons, large cells that are specifically designed to carry impulses or messages rapidly over relatively long distances. There are two types of neurons: sensory neurons, which conduct impulses from sense organs to the spinal cord and brain, and motor neurons, which conduct impulses from the brain and spinal cord to the muscles and glands.

Anatomical Classification of the Nervous System

The nervous system may be divided into three main parts: the central nervous system, the peripheral nervous system, and the autonomic nervous system.

Central Nervous System

There is no more important part of the body than the central nervous system. When the body sustains serious trauma to this system, damage will in all probability be extensive. The basic components of the central nervous system are the brain, the spinal cord, and their coverings. Three membranes, known as the meninges, cover the central nervous system. The meninges serve supportive and protective roles. The meninges, from the outer to the innermost, are designated as the dura mater, the arachnoid, and the pia mater. (For further discussion of the meninges, see page 404.)

Brain (see Figures 7a, 7b, and 8)

The brain comprises 98 percent of the central nervous system and lies within the bony protection of the skull. The following may be designated as the major divisions of the brain and brain stem:

- *Medulla Oblongata*. This truncated cone of nervous tissue is continuous with the pons above and the spinal cord below. It lies anterior to the cerebellum. The medulla contains highly specialized nerve centers regulating heart action, breathing, circulation, and control of body temperature. It is in this area that many of the nerves cross over to the other side of

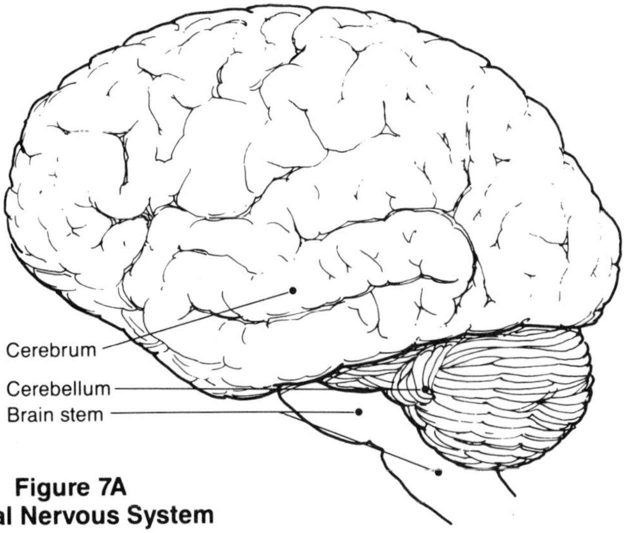

Figure 7A
Central Nervous System

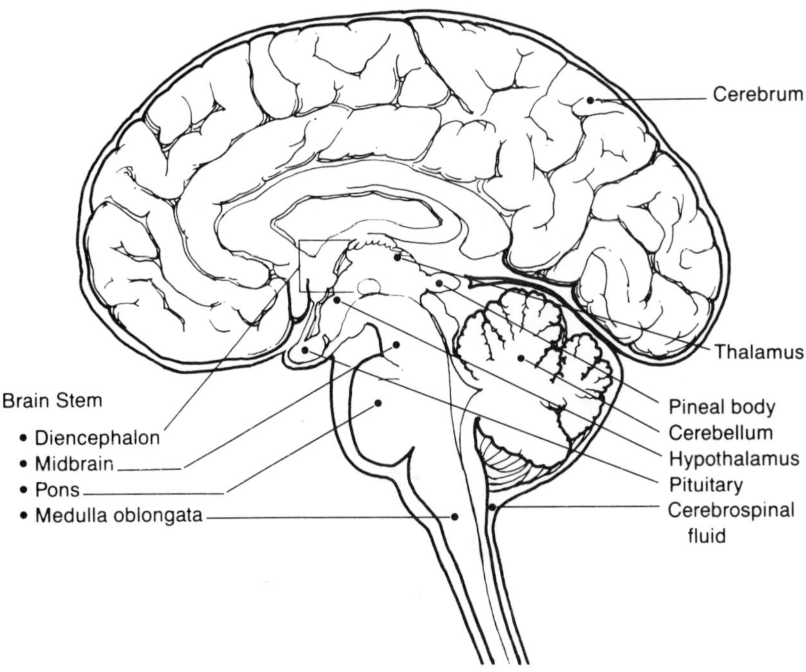

Figure 7B
Central Nervous System
(Cross Section)

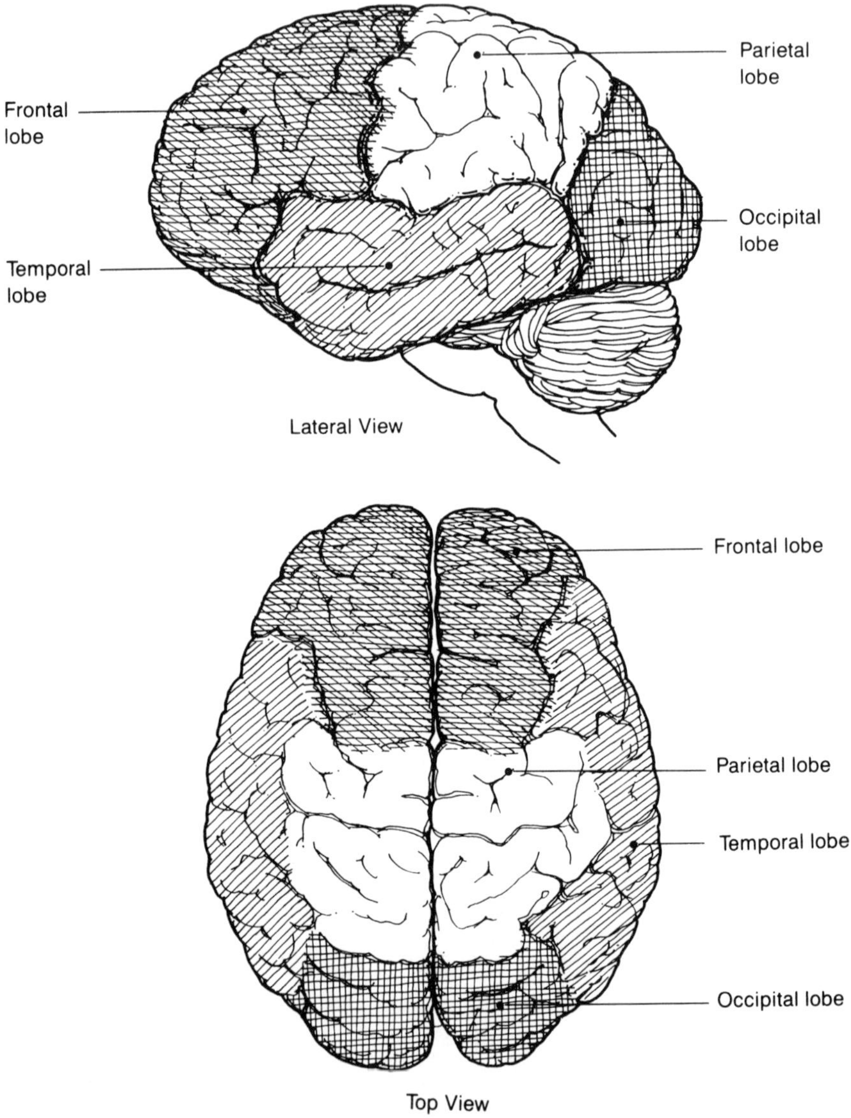

Figure 8
Cerebrum

the body. Thus, the right side of the brain controls the left side of the body, while the left side of the brain controls the right side of the body.

- *Pons*. This connects the medulla and the midbrain.
- *Midbrain*. This is where the cerebellum connects to the brain stem.
- *Cerebellum*. This is the second largest portion of the brain; it is located in the posterior aspect of the skull. The chief function of the cerebellum is to balance, harmonize, and coordinate motions of the body initiated by the cerebrum. The cerebellum integrates and correlates nerve impulses.
- *Diencephalon*. This is the portion of the brain between the midbrain and cerebrum. It contains the following:

  Thalamus. This is the integrating center of the brain, where tactile, olfactory, pain, and gustatory impulses are correlated with motor reactions.

  Epithalamus. This is the most dorsal division of the diencephalon.

  Subthalamus. This is the regulator of the muscles of emotional expression.

  Hypothalamus. This controls emotions that affect the heartbeat and blood pressure, as well as body temperature, carbohydrate metabolism, food metabolism, appetite, and sexual reflexes.
- *Cerebrum*. This occupies most of the cranial cavity and is the control center for higher cognitive functions. The cerebrum may be divided into cerebral hemispheres, and each hemisphere is, in turn, divided into four lobes: the *occipital* lobe, which is the control center for visual function; the *frontal* lobe, which is the center of voluntary movement and the seat of intellect and memory; the *temporal* lobe, which is the control center for auditory function; and the *parietal* lobe, which is the center of sensory and motor functions.

Cerebrospinal Fluid (CSF)

This is a clear, transparent fluid found in the spinal canal, specifically in the subarachnoid space (the area between the arachnoid and the pia mater). When a history of central nervous system pathology is suspected, physicians will draw out, or "tap," some of the fluid for the purpose of analysis. This fluid surrounds the brain and spinal cord and is, in large measure, protective in function.

Spinal Cord

The spinal cord can be compared with a highly complex telephone cable. It is enclosed in the vertebral column and has the three membranous coverings: the dura mater, the pia mater, and the arachnoid. Cerebrospinal fluid also surrounds the spinal cord.

The spinal column is split into an "ascending tract" (responsible for conducting impulses to the brain) and a "descending tract" (responsible for conducting impulses from the brain). It is through the spinal cord that the brain maintains its intimate functional relationship with the organs of the body. Thirty-one pairs of spinal nerves protrude from the lateral aspects of the spinal cord, through the vertebral foramina, or openings, and into the peripheral areas of the body; these nerves are, in effect, the cables that carry messages between the brain and the organs (see Figure 9). Spinal nerves are attached to the spinal cord by anterior and posterior roots. The nerves, after leaving the cord, are named after their corresponding vertebrae. Thus, the first eight spinal nerves are known as cervical (even though there are only seven cervical vertebrae); the next twelve, thoracic; the next five, lumbar; the next five, sacral; and the last pair, coccygeal.

Actual trauma to the cord itself may produce serious injury. If there is a severing of the cord, the body will function normally above the level of injury, while those portions of the body served by nerves emanating from the spinal cord below the site of injury will be paralyzed.

Peripheral Nervous System

This system is made up of nerves outside the brain and spinal column. The 31 pairs of spinal nerves and 12 pairs of cranial nerves that branch out into the body to send and receive messages to and from the brain are known as the peripheral nerves.

Twelve pairs of cranial nerves arise on each side of the brain:

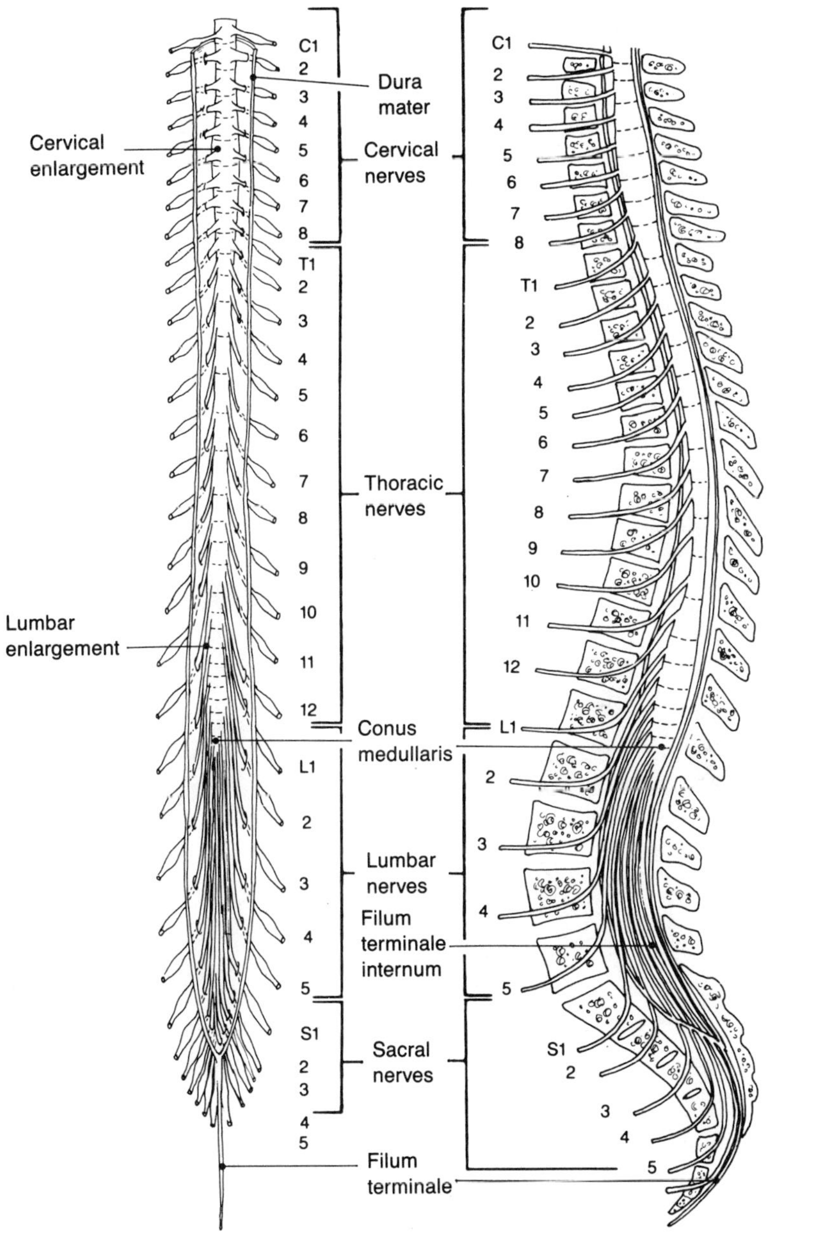

Figure 9
Spinal Cord
Posterior and Lateral Views

- *First Cranial Nerve.* This is the olfactory nerve; it is the nerve for the sense of smell.
- *Second Cranial Nerve.* This is the optic nerve.
- *Third Cranial Nerve.* This nerve controls eyeball movement and pupillary constriction and dilatation; it is also known as the oculomotor nerve.
- *Fourth Cranial Nerve.* This serves the eye muscle; it is also called the trochlear nerve.
- *Fifth Cranial Nerve.* Also known as the trigeminal nerve, this is the largest of the cranial nerves. It serves both a sensory and a motor function, and has three portions: the *ophthalmic*, serving the forehead; the *maxillary*, serving the upper cheek; and the *mandibular*, innervating the jaw and lower face.
- *Sixth Cranial Nerve.* This nerve also controls eyeball movement; it is also known as the abducent nerve.
- *Seventh Cranial Nerve.* This is both sensory and motor in function. It controls the muscles of the face, ears, and scalp and is known as the facial nerve.
- *Eighth Cranial Nerve.* This is the sensory nerve of hearing and equilibrium. The eighth cranial nerve is also known as the vestibulocochlear nerve.
- *Ninth Cranial Nerve.* This is known as the glossopharyngeal nerve; it serves both motor and sensory functions, carrying messages from the pharynx and back part of the tongue to the brain.
- *Tenth Cranial Nerve.* This is the vagus nerve, serving both motor and sensory functions for the thorax and abdomen.
- *Eleventh Cranial Nerve.* This is a motor nerve that supplies the muscles of the neck and shoulders. It is also known as the accessory nerve.
- *Twelfth Cranial Nerve.* This is the hypoglossal nerve. It is a motor nerve controlling the muscles of the tongue.

Once the spinal nerves have exited through the vertebral foramina, they divide and redistribute themselves into peripheral nerves with

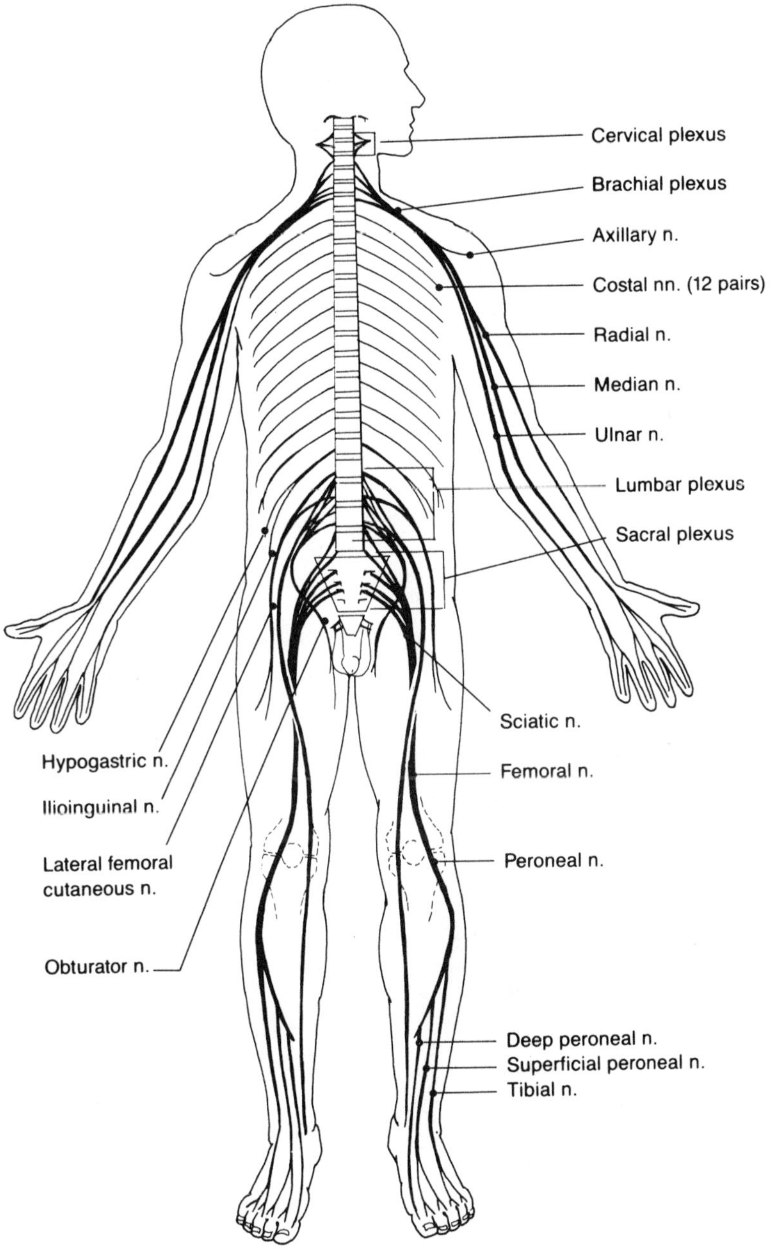

Figure 10A
Peripheral Nerves

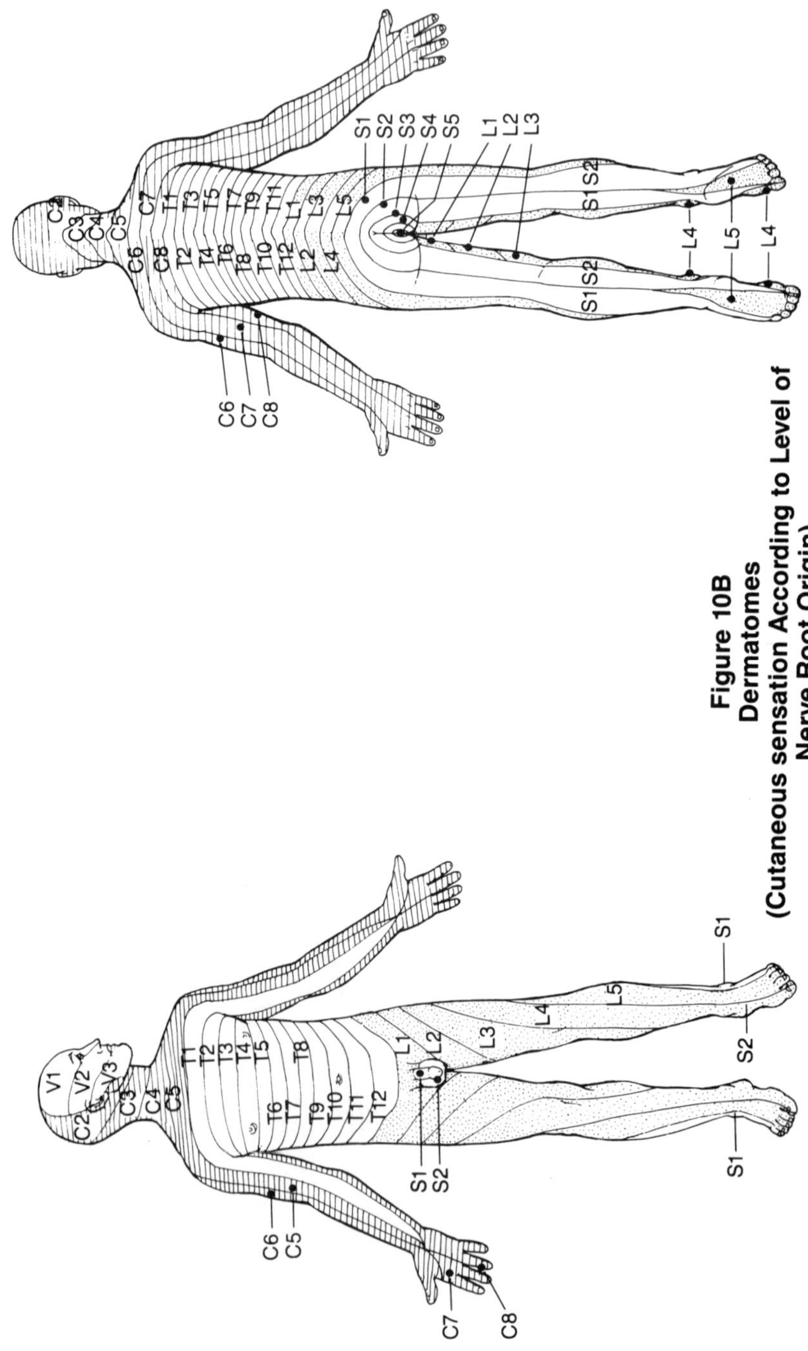

Figure 10B
Dermatomes
(Cutaneous sensation According to Level of Nerve Root Origin)

sensory, motor, or combined capabilities. A group of peripheral nerves that supplies a particular region of the body, but has not yet separated into terminal branches, is known as a nerve plexus (see Figures 10a and 10b).

Autonomic Nervous System

The autonomic nervous system functions automatically; it activates involuntary, smooth, and cardiac muscles, as well as glands. It serves the vital systems that function automatically, including the digestive, circulatory, respiratory, urinary, and endocrine systems.

The autonomic nervous system is broken down into two major divisions: the sympathetic nervous system and the parasympathetic nervous system. These two systems work in harmonious opposition and thereby balance and maintain the actions and reactions of various body mechanisms. For example, the sympathetic nervous system dilates the pupils, while the parasympathetic nervous system constricts them.

The trunk of the sympathetic nervous system lies in close proximity to the vertebral bodies and is composed of a series of masses of nerve tissue, known as ganglia, located on either side of the spinal column. The ganglia extend from the base of the skull to the coccyx.

The ganglia of the parasympathetic nervous system are located in the middle portion of the brain and the sacral region of the spinal cord.

CARDIOVASCULAR SYSTEM

There are five principal components of the cardiovascular system: heart, arteries, veins, capillaries, and blood.

General Considerations

The cardiovascular system consists of a muscular pump and a circulatory system whose functions are to provide oxygen and glucose as fuels to all tissues in the body.

Anatomical Classification of the Cardiovascular System

The five principal components of the cardiovascular system are described below:

Blood

Blood is a fluid tissue pumped by the heart through the body's arteries, veins, and capillaries. Its function is the transportation of oxygen, food, and water to all cells of the body and the return of carbon dioxide to the lungs for disposal (see Figure 11). All living tissue within the body must receive a continuous supply of oxygen-enriched blood. When tissue has a low supply of oxygen, the condition is described as "hypoxia." The total lack of oxygen is known as "anoxia."

Heart

The heart is a hollow, muscular pump. It is located behind the sternum in the front of the chest, slightly to the left of midline, between the lungs. The heart is enclosed in a membranous sac called the pericardium.

The heart is divided longitudinally into left and right sides by the septum, which passes through the apex to the base of the heart. Each side of the heart is subdivided into chambers: an atrium above and a ventricle below (see Figure 12).

Arteries

Blood is carried from the heart to all of the structures of the body by elastic tubes called arteries (see Figure 13). The arteries branch and rebranch as they course through the body, becoming smaller and smaller, until they are called arterioles. The arterioles feed blood directly into the capillaries. As the blood circulates through the capillary network, it releases oxygen and food to the adjacent tissues and picks up metabolic waste products, primarily carbon dioxide.

The aorta is the largest artery in the body. It originates from the left ventricle of the heart, arches upward, and passes down along the spinal column through the diaphragm. All along its route, the aorta branches off into other arteries that supply blood to the head, neck, arms, chest, and abdomen; it then divides into arteries that supply the legs and lower body. The following large arteries perform the indicated functions:

- *Innominate Artery.* This is also known as the brachiocephalic trunk. It is the first branch of the arch of the aorta and divides into the right subclavian and right common carotid arteries.

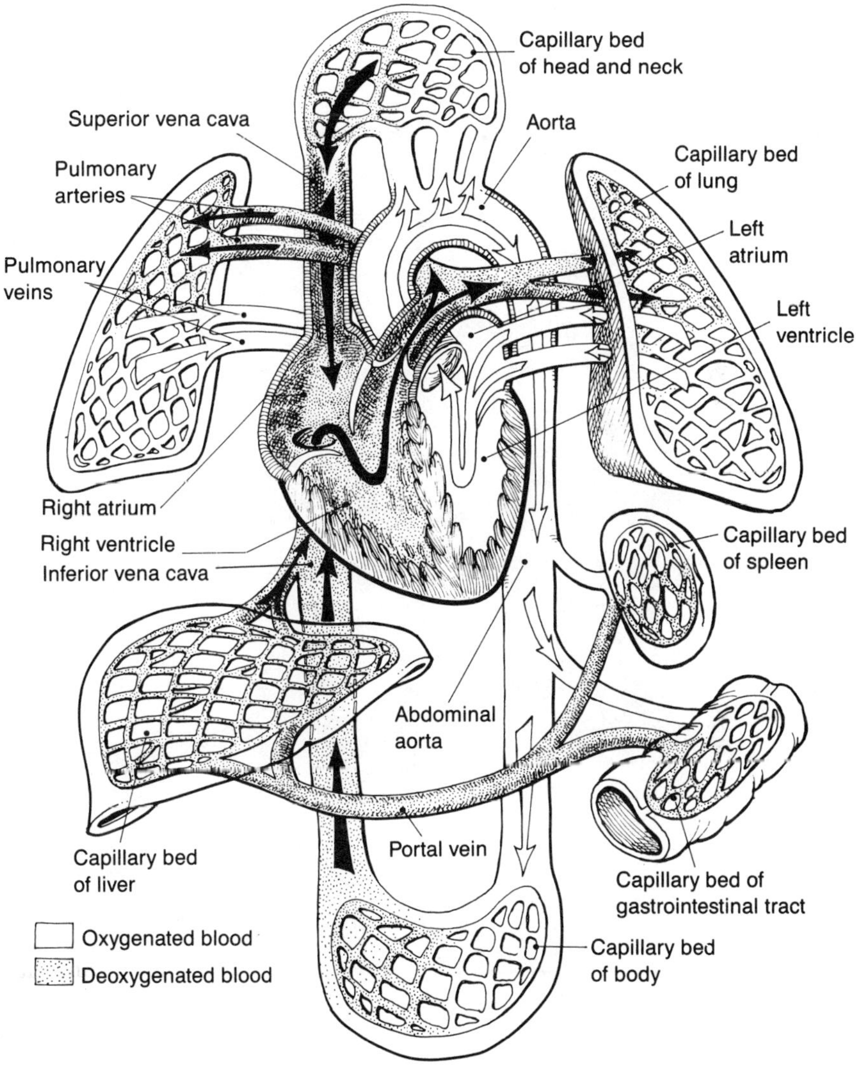

Figure 11
Circulatory System

- *Right and Left Subclavians.* The subclavian arteries, which are the main arteries carrying blood to the arms, are known by different names in different parts of their courses. The

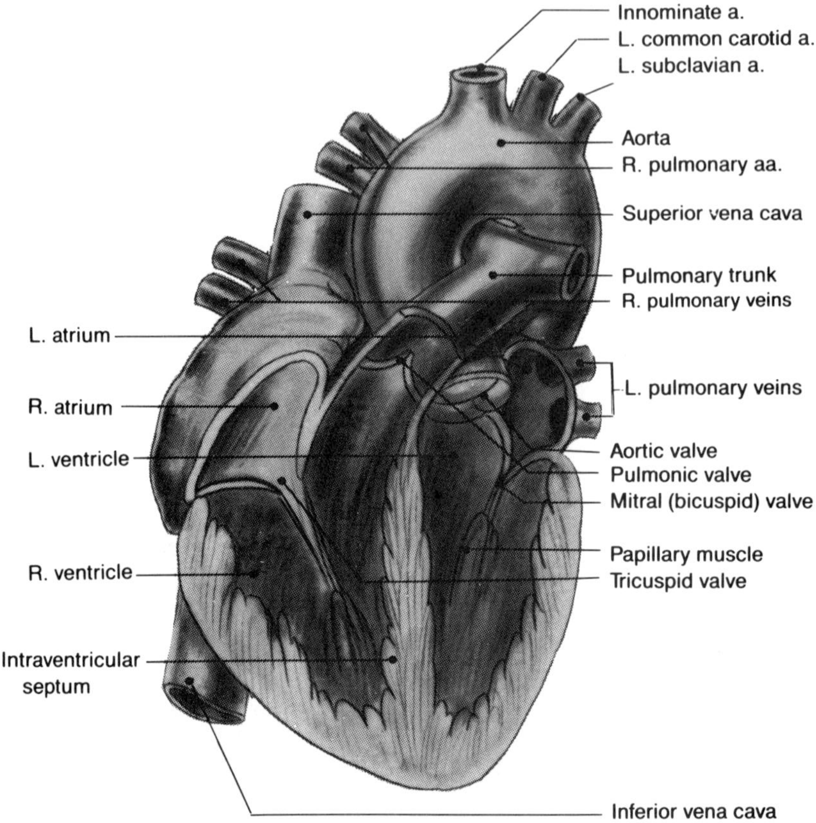

Figure 12
Heart Chambers and Valves

subclavian arteries themselves extend from behind the sternoclavicular joint to about the midpoint of the clavicle.

- *Right and Left Carotids.* These supply the right and left side of the head.
- *Internal Carotid.* This supplies the brain and eyes.
- *External Carotid.* This supplies the muscles and skin of the face.
- *Axillary.* This continuation of the subclavian artery supplies the upper arm.

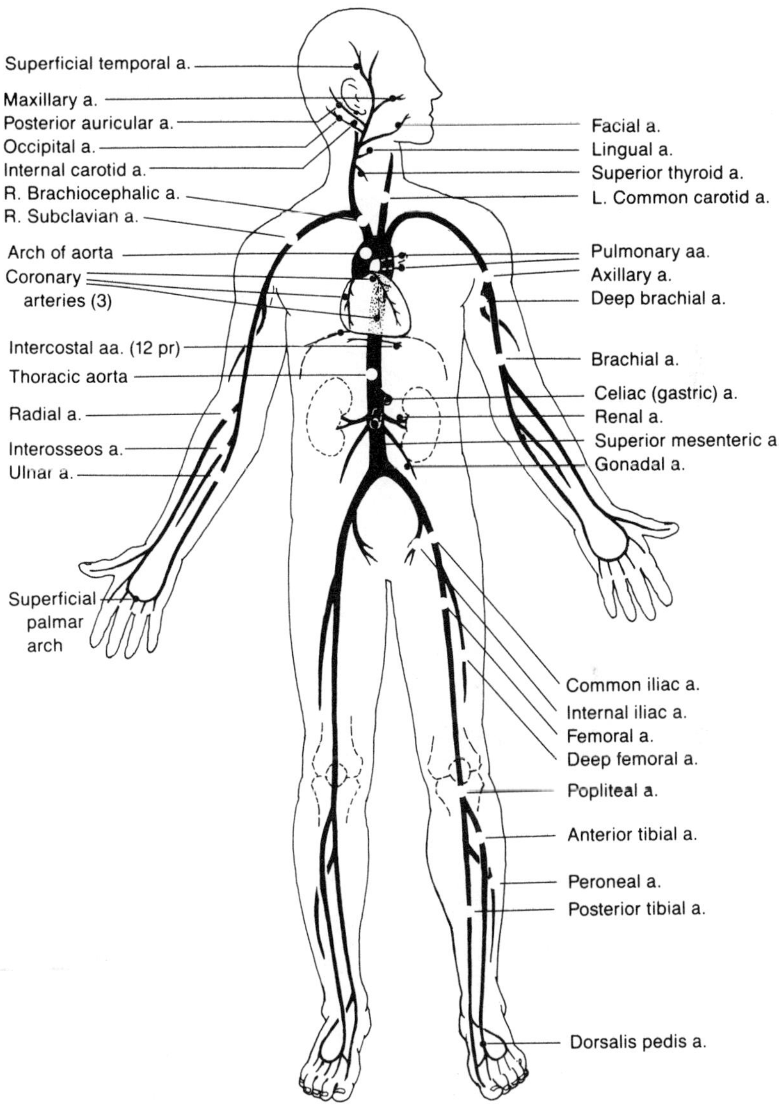

Figure 13
Arteries

- *Brachial.* This also supplies the upper arm. The brachial artery is a continuation of the axillary artery.

- *Radial and Ulnar.* These terminal branches of the brachial artery supply the lower arm.
- *Coronary.* The left anterior descending, left circumflex, and right main are the three major coronary arteries that supply the heart muscle.
- *Pulmonary.* This transports blood from the heart to the lungs to receive oxygen.
- *Gastric.* This supplies the stomach.
- *Splenic.* This supplies the spleen.
- *Hepatic.* This supplies the liver.
- *Superior Mesenteric.* This supplies the small intestine and proximal colon.
- *Inferior Mesenteric.* This supplies the distal half of the colon and rectum.
- *Renal.* This supplies the kidneys.
- *Abdominal Aorta.* This artery divides into the right and left common iliacs, which supply blood to the lower extremities.
- *Femoral.* This supplies the thigh.
- *Popliteal.* This supplies the knee.
- *Anterior and Posterior Tibial.* These supply the area of the tibia.
- *Peroneal.* This supplies blood to the lower leg.
- *Dorsalis Pedis.* This supplies blood to the foot.

Veins

The veins carry deoxygenated blood back to the heart (see Figure 14). They are hollow tubes, like arteries, though their walls are much thinner and without a muscular component. The small veins are known as venules; these venules collect blood from the capillaries, join larger veins, and finally return to the right side of the heart. There are two major systems of veins:

- *Systemic Venous System.* This system carries deoxygenated blood to the right atrium of the heart. The blood then flows into the right ventricle, which pumps it into the lungs.

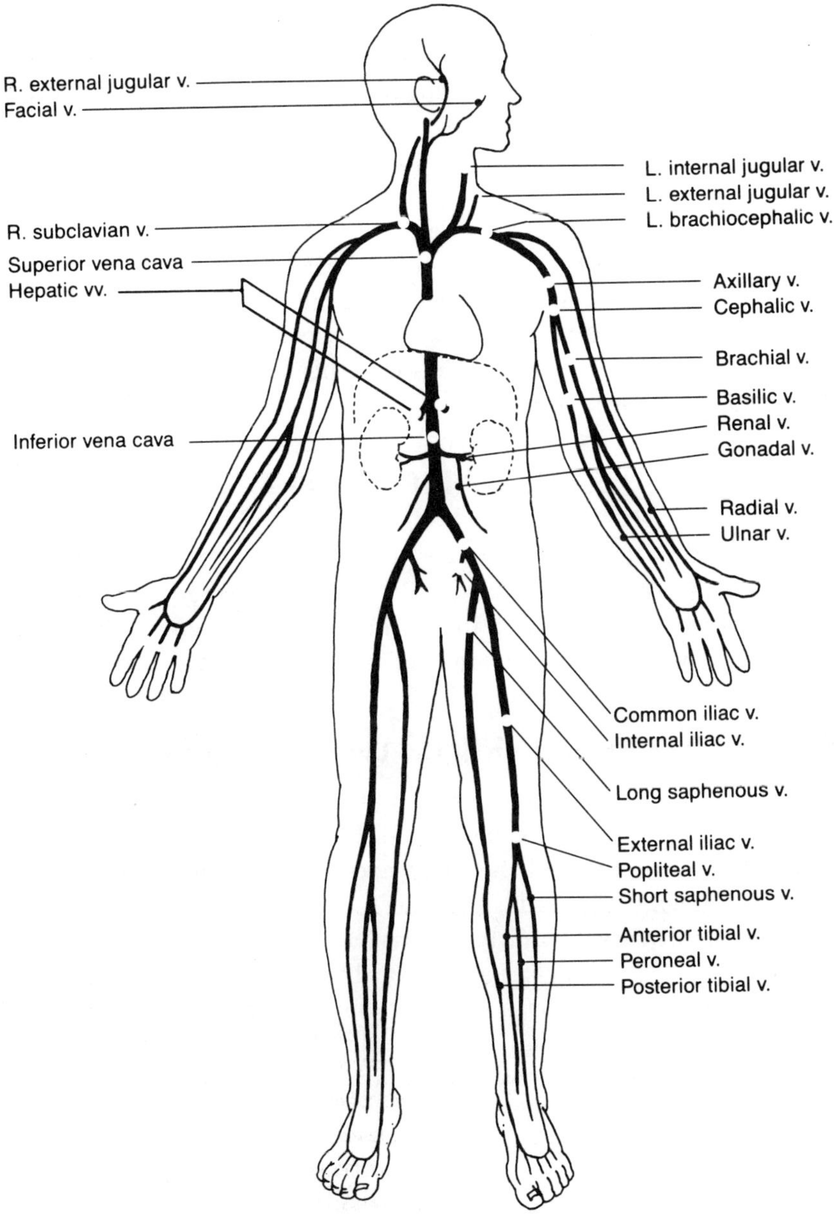

Figure 14
Veins

- *Pulmonary System*. This system comprises veins that carry freshly oxygenated blood back from the lungs to the left atrium of the heart. From the left atrium, the blood flows to the left ventricle from which it is pumped to the aorta for distribution to the entire body.

Capillaries

The capillaries compose a network of blood vessels into which arterioles (the smallest divisions of the arteries) empty. The capillary plexus provides an area in which oxygen and nutritive materials may pass from arterioles to active tissues. Deoxygenated blood may then pass from the capillaries into the venules, many of which join together to form veins.

LYMPHATIC SYSTEM

General Considerations

The lymphatic system is closely associated with the vascular system; the two systems run in parallel paths throughout the body. The lymphatic system provides surveillance and defense against infection.

Anatomical Classification of the Lymphatic System

Lymph is an almost colorless fluid rich in white blood cells. It is circulated throughout the body by the lymph vessels, which are located in every part of the body except the brain, spinal cord, eyeballs, internal ear, nails, and hair.

The lymph vessels and lymph tissue form a vast network that collects the lymph and carries it toward the heart, eventually opening into the thoracic duct and right lymphatic duct, which in turn empty into the left internal jugular and right subclavian veins. Like blood vessels, lymph vessels carry nourishment to and collect waste from the organs of the body.

The lymph tissue filters bacteria from the lymph system and also produces one kind of white blood cell (lymphocytes). The lymphoid tissue includes organs, such as the spleen, tonsils, and thymus; bone marrow; and lymph nodes (glands).

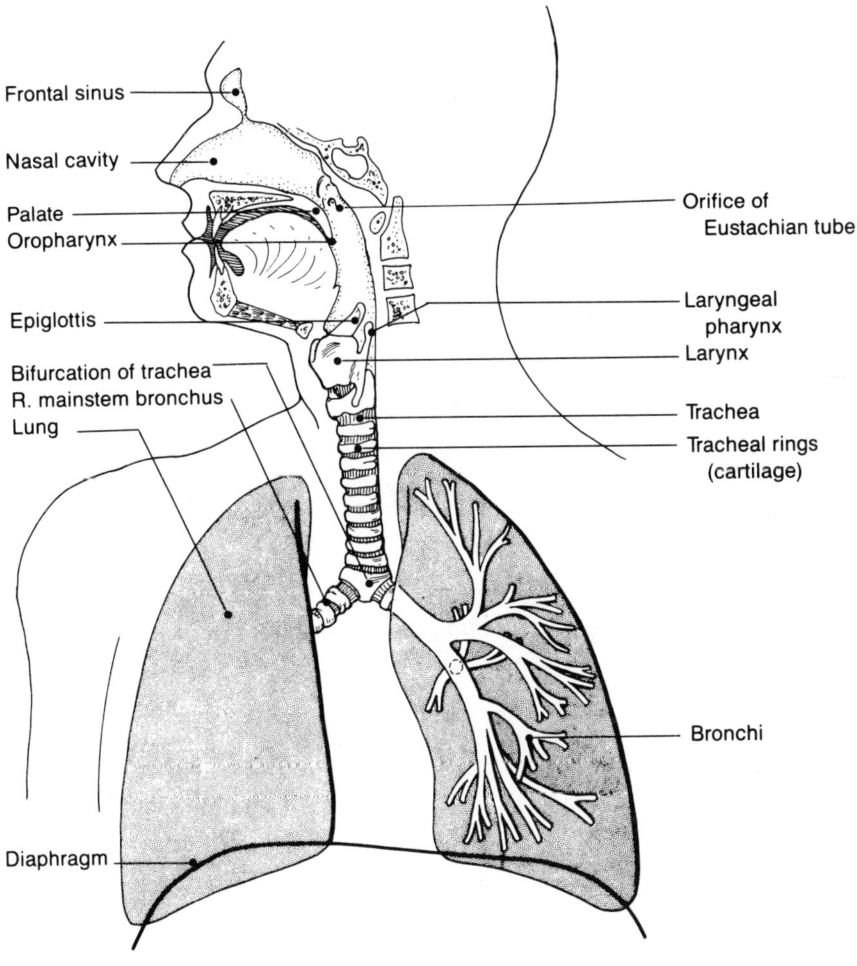

Figure 15
Respiratory System

RESPIRATORY SYSTEM

General Considerations

Respiration refers to the exchange of oxygen and carbon dioxide between humans and their external environment (see Figure 15).

Anatomical Classification of the Respiratory System

The principal structures of the respiratory system are as follows:

Nose

The primary organ of olfaction, the nose is also responsible for filtering and humidifying inhaled air.

Pharynx

Located at the back of the throat, the pharynx serves as an airway between the nasal chambers, mouth, and larynx. It aids in both respiration and digestion.

Larynx

This is the "voice box." It is located just below the pharynx and serves as a passageway for air, aids in swallowing, and allows vocalization.

Trachea

The "wind pipe" is a tube, approximately four inches long, formed of cartilaginous rings extending from the larynx to the bronchi.

Bronchi

The trachea divides into two main bronchi that carry air into the lungs. As the bronchi further branch within the lungs, they are known as bronchioles.

Lungs

The lungs are two large, closed membranous sacs located on either side of the chest. Both the lungs and the chest wall are lined by a viscous membrane called the pleura.

Mediastinum

This is a space that separates the chest into two cavities.

Diaphragm

This is a thin, musculotendinous partition separating the thoracic cavity from the abdominal cavity; it is the chief muscle of respiration and operates by lifting and lowering the lungs in the thoracic cavity, causing their contraction and expansion.

GASTROINTESTINAL SYSTEM

General Considerations

The gastrointestinal or digestive system includes the alimentary canal, which extends from mouth to anus, and its accessory organs (see Figure 16). The two major functions of the system are the digestion of food and the elimination of waste. The hepato-biliary system may be considered either separately or together with the gastrointestinal system.

Anatomical Classification of the Gastrointestinal System

The principal components of the gastrointestinal system are as follows:

Mouth

Food is broken down both mechanically and chemically in the oral cavity.

Pharynx

This is an oval, fibromuscular sac about five inches long. It is a passageway for both food and air.

Esophagus

This is a narrow muscular tube about ten inches long connecting the pharynx with the stomach.

Stomach

This is the widest part of the alimentary canal. It digests masticated food to a fluid consistency and passes it along to the duodenum. There are millions of gastric glands in the stomach and these secrete juices that aid in the chemical breakdown of food.

Small Intestine

This is a coiled, 20-foot tube that occupies the center and lower parts of the abdominal cavity. The greater part of digestion is completed in the three major divisions of the small intestine:

Duodenum. This is the widest, shortest, and most fixed part of the small intestine. It is associated with three organs that (among other functions) help break down foodstuffs and prepare nutrients for digestion.

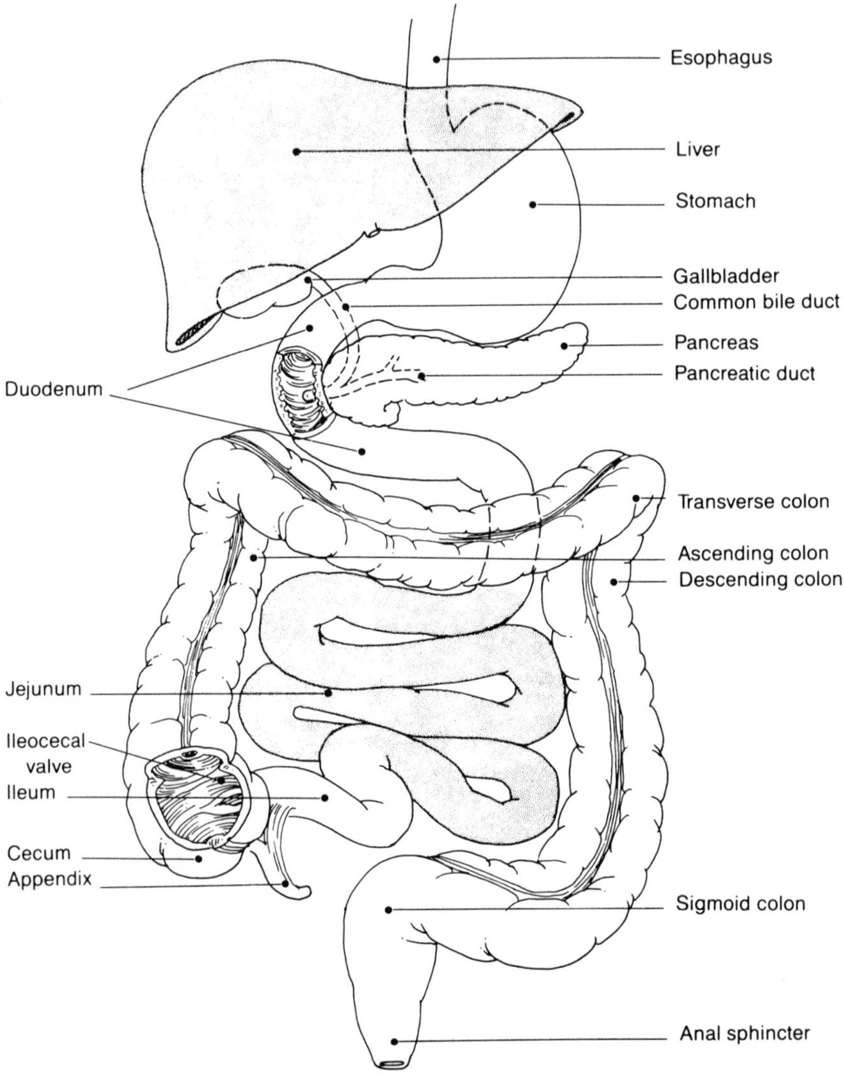

Figure 16
Gastrointestinal Tract

- *Pancreas.* This is a gland extending across the posterior aspect of the abdomen. It empties an alkaline digestive juice into the duodenum.

- *Liver.* This is the largest gland in the body. It lies in the upper abdomen, under the diaphragm, and above the duodenum. It secretes bile into the duodenum. The liver is also the most important organ of intermediary metabolism, for the storage and release of energy supplies.
- *Gallbladder.* This is a sac that adheres to the lower aspect of the liver. Its primary function is the storage and concentration of bile.

Jejunum. This is the portion of the small intestine that extends from the duodenum to the ileum.

Ileum. This is the longest part of the small intestine. Significant absorption of food takes place in the ileum.

Large Intestine

This organ, which is about five feet long, receives the products of digestion from the small intestine. Its chief function is the formation, transport, and evacuation of feces. This function requires motility, the absorption of water, and the secretion of mucous. The major divisions of the large intestine include the following:

- *Cecum.* This is a blind sac located on the lower right side of the abdomen.
- *Vermiform Appendix.* This is a narrow projection attached to the cecum.
- *Ascending Colon.* This long tubular structure is fixed in the right flank.
- *Transverse Colon.* This structure runs across the upper portion of the abdominal cavity.
- *Descending Colon.* This structure runs down the left flank to the brim of the true pelvis.
- *Sigmoid Colon.* This S-shaped part of the colon communicates with the rectum.
- *Rectum.* The terminal portion of the gastrointestinal system combines with the anal sphincter to control defecation.

GENITOURINARY SYSTEM

General Considerations

The genitourinary system comprises two major parts: urinary organs and reproductive organs (see Figures 17 and 18).

Anatomical Classification of the Genitourinary System

Urinary Organs

The urinary organs are common to both male and female and are essentially similar in both. The major components of the urinary system are as follows:

Kidneys

These are bean-shaped organs situated in the posterior part of the abdomen on either side of the vertebral column. They are the primary filters for bodily fluids.

Ureters

These are tubes 15 to 18 inches long, extending from the kidneys down the back of the abdominal cavity and emptying into the urinary bladder.

Urinary Bladder

This is a musculomembranous sac lying in the pelvis. It serves as a reservoir for urine.

Urethra

This structure serves a different function in the male and female:

- In the male, this is a membranous tube running from the urinary bladder to the penis and ending in a foramen. The urethra can convey either urine or seminal fluid.
- The female urethra is a short tube extending from the bladder to the anterior portion of the vulva. The sole function of the urethra in the female is voiding.

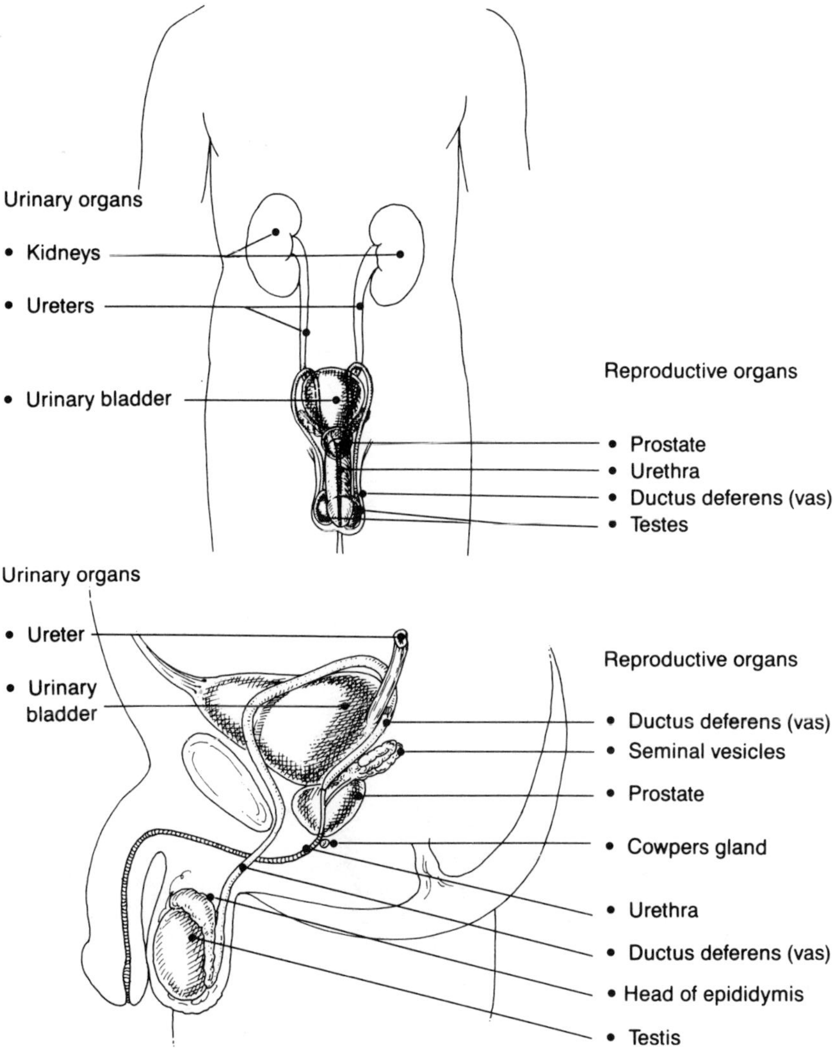

Figure 17
Genitourinary System (Male)

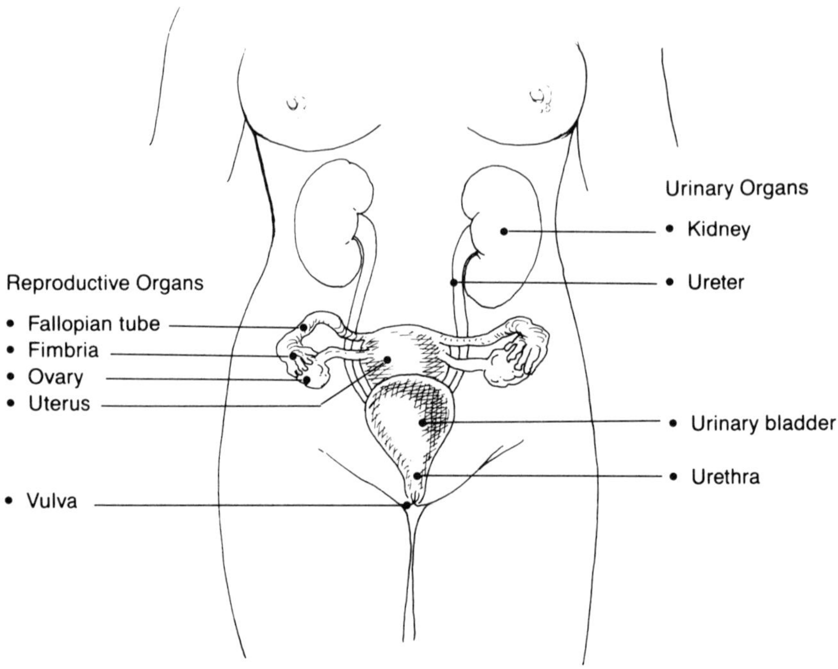

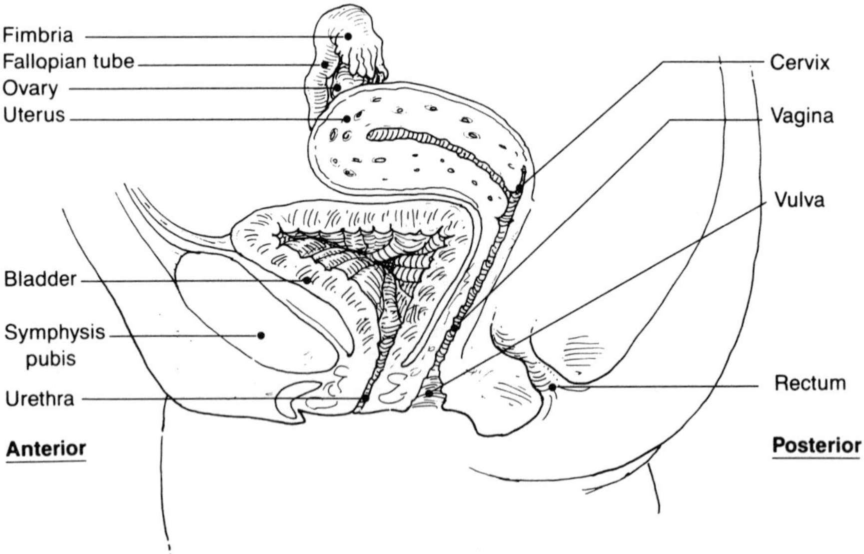

Figure 18
Genitourinary System—Female

REPRODUCTIVE SYSTEMS

Male Reproductive System

The essential organs of the male reproductive system are as follows:

- *Testes*. These are two organs suspended in a sac of skin (the scrotum). The epithelial cells of the testes produce sperm.
- *Epididymis*. This is a cordlike, elongated structure located outside of, but hugging the posterior portion of, the testis. It stores sperm.
- *Vas Deferens*. This tiny tube extends from the epididymis up through the inguinal canal toward the bladder. It carries sperm to the ejaculatory duct.
- *Spermatic Cords*. The spermatic cords comprise vas deferens, arteries, veins, lymphatic ducts, and nerves.
- *Ejaculatory Duct*. This is a short, narrow tube, less than one inch long, which is formed just above the prostate gland by the union of the seminal vesicles and the vas deferens.
- *Prostate Gland*. This gland secretes a thin alkaline substance that combines with the secretion of the seminal vesicles to form the bulk of the seminal fluid. The prostate gland is situated in the pelvis behind the pubic symphysis. It is structurally continuous with the urinary bladder that lies above it, but laterally and posteriorly a superficial groove marks a separation between the two organs.
- *Cowper's Glands*. These two structures are yellowish, rounded, lobulated, pea-sized bodies on each side of the membranous urethra opening into the urethra. They secrete a mucouslike substance, the function of which is obscure.
- *Penis*. This is made up of three muscular masses of tissue.

Female Reproductive System

The essential organs of the female reproductive system are as follows:

- *Ovaries*. These almond-shaped organs are approximately one and one-half inches in length and one inch thick. They lie on each side of the pelvis and are responsible for the production of the egg cells.

- *Uterus (Womb)*. This is a thick-walled, hollow, pear-shaped organ about three inches long and three inches wide at the upper, widest portion. It lies between the bladder and the rectum. It tapers to a lower part called the cervix and projects into the anterior wall of the vagina.
- *Fallopian Tubes*. These are two musculomembranous tubes about four inches long. They transmit the egg from the ovary to the uterus.
- *Vagina*. This is a fibromuscular tube that extends from the cervix or neck of the uterus to the vulva.
- *Vulva (Pudendum)*. This is the female external genital.

ENDOCRINE SYSTEM

General Considerations

The endocrine glands slowly discharge hormones into the bloodstream that biochemically regulate the body's activities. Complicated feedback loops allow for sensitive control of hormonal levels (see Figure 19).

Anatomical Classification of the Endocrine System

The endocrine system comprises ductless glands that secrete hormones directly into the bloodstream. The principal endocrine glands include the following:

Thyroid

The thyroid is composed of two lobes separated by a strip of tissue; it is located in front of the trachea. The main function of the thyroid gland is the secretion of thyroid hormones, which function as biochemical supervisors of growth and metabolism.

Parathyroids

These four glands, two on each side, lie posterior to the thyroid gland and are usually embedded in the thyroid. The parathyroids secrete hormones that regulate the calcium and phosphorus content of blood and bone.

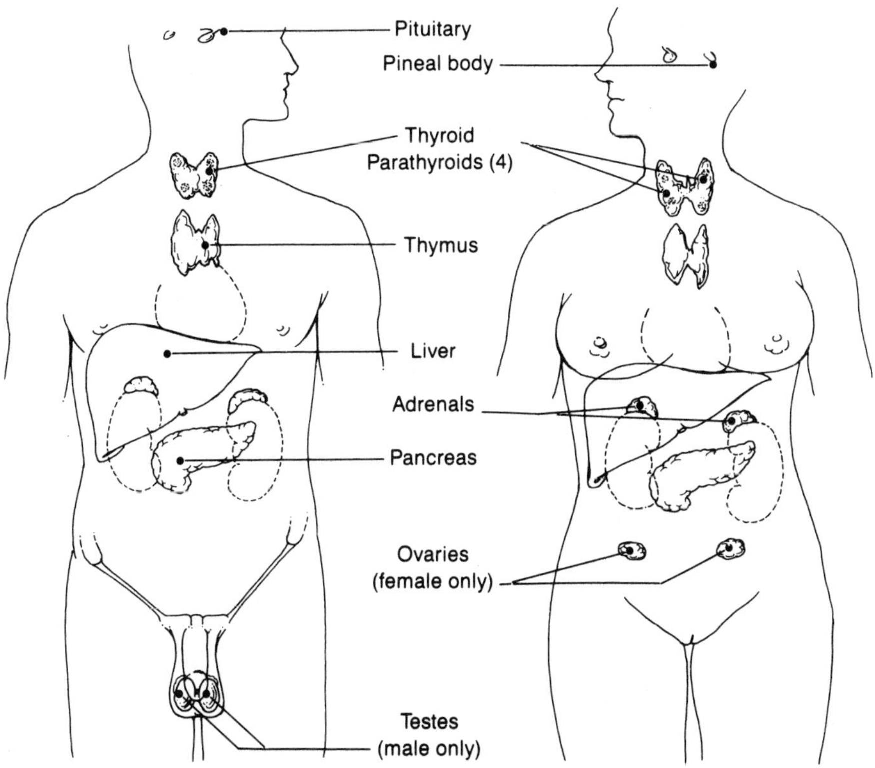

Figure 19
Endocrine System, Male-Female

Pituitary

The pituitary gland exercises control over many other endocrine glands. It is attached to the base of the brain and is divided into an anterior and posterior lobe.

Adrenals

The adrenal glands are located on top of each kidney and secrete hormones active in metabolism and sexual development. The adrenal glands also secrete epinephrine and norepinephrine, which stimulate in stressful situations and are major chemical components of the "fight-or-flight" response.

Gonads

The female ovaries and male testes produce hormones responsible for secondary sexual characteristics and vital for the functioning of the reproductive system.

Pineal

This gland is located near the base of the brain; its exact functions are not understood.

Thymus

This gland is situated in front of the trachea, partly in the neck and partly in the thorax. It is believed to be associated with immunological activities early in life.

Pancreas

This gland is the only gland that functions both with and without a duct. In a nonendocrine (exocrine) function, the pancreas secretes digestive juices that are delivered into the alimentary canal through a duct. It also contains sacs of specialized endocrine cells, called the Islets of Langerhans, which produce insulin and secrete it into the bloodstream.

INTEGUMENTARY SYSTEM

General Considerations

The integument protects the body from the elements and trauma and allows the dissipation of heat and water.

Anatomical Classification of the Integumentary System

The integument includes the skin, hair, nails, mammary glands, sweat glands, and sebaceous glands. The skin is the largest organ in the body.

MEDICAL EXAMINATION AND TESTING

Harvey F. Wachsman, M.D., J.D., F.C.L.M.
and Carole L. Gutterman, Ph.D., C.U.R.N.

Illustrations by William Meyer

This chapter will describe some common medical tests that physicians use in evaluating patients with head and neck injuries and injuries to the lumbar spine.

HEAD AND NECK

When a physician encounters a cervical (neck) injury, the initial examination and testing center on the neurologic disease process or injury as the physician checks for indications of nerve impairment. The pathology may manifest in the arm as muscle weakness, altered reflexes, or pain. Because these symptoms may be the result of interference with the peripheral nerves at the level of the cervical spine or may involve the brachial plexus or other nerves, the physician should perform an expanded neurologic examination to provide

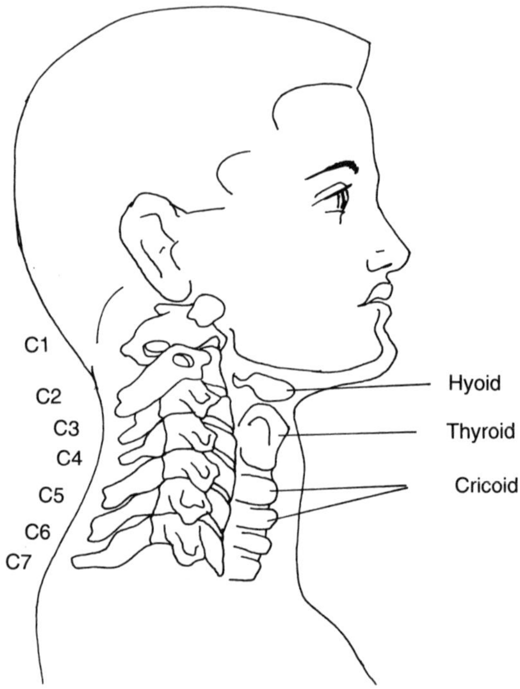

Figure 1
Anterior Aspect of Cervical Region

a better understanding of the integrity of the brachial plexus and of pathologic signs and symptoms in the arm as well.

The cervical spine serves to support and stabilize the head, to allow for the range of motion of the head, and to provide housing, protection, and transport for the spinal cord and vertebral artery.

The physician inspects the patient by noting the posture and attitude of the patient's head. Normally, the head is held erect, perpendicular to the floor, and moves in smooth coordination with body motion.

Palpation of Bony Structures

When the examination begins, the physician palpates (lays hands on) the patient's neck to examine the bony structures.

Hyoid Bone

The anterior (frontal) aspect of the cervical region (see Figure 1) comprises the hyoid bone, which is a horseshoe-shaped structure above the thyroid cartilage. The physician asks the patient to swallow; when the patient does so, the movement of the hyoid bone becomes palpable.

Thyroid Cartilage

This cartilage (see Figure 1) is commonly known as the Adam's Apple and marks the level of C4 vertebral body in the cervical portion of the spine, while the lower portion (below the Adam's Apple) designates the C5 level.

Cricoid

The first cricoid ring (see Figure 1) is just below the thyroid cartilage, opposite C6. It is immediately above the site for an emergency tracheostomy.

The C1 transverse spinous process of the bony vertebral column, which lies just behind the ear between the angle of the jaw and the skull's styloid process, has little clinical significance, but serves as an easily identifiable point of orientation.

Palpation of Soft Tissues

When examining the soft tissues of the neck, the physician begins with the area known as the anterior triangle. The anterior triangle is defined laterally by the sternocleidomastoid muscles, superiorly (upward toward the head) by the mandible, and inferiorly (downward toward the feet) by the suprasternal notch.

Sternocleidomastoid Muscle

This muscle is frequently stretched by hyperextension-hyperflexion (see Figure 2) injuries of the neck during automobile collisions. To test the muscle, the physician asks the patient to turn his or her head to the side opposite the muscle to be examined. This motion stretches the muscle so that it will stand out sharply near its tendinous beginning (origin). If the physician can feel a localized swelling of the muscle, the cause of the swelling may be a hematoma (bleeding). This swelling may cause the head to turn abnormally to one side (torticollis). Any tenderness the patient feels when the

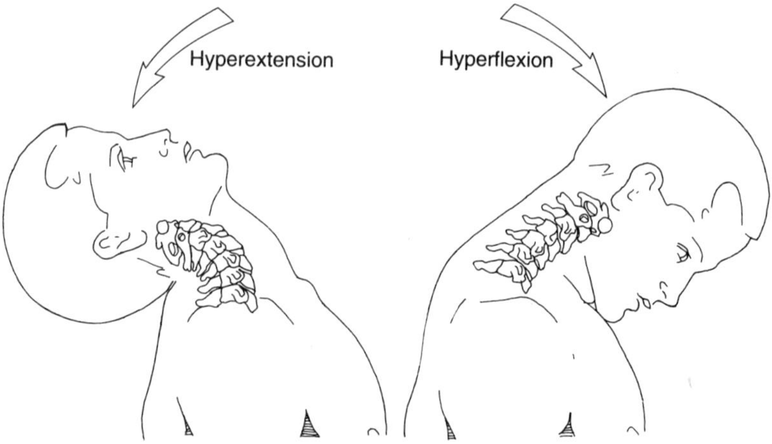

Figure 2
Hyperextension and Hyperflexion of the Sternocleidomastoid Muscle

physician palpates the sternocleidomastoid muscle may be associated with hyperextension-hyperflexion injury of the neck.

The physician should palpate the posterior (toward the rear or the back of the body) surface of the neck from behind, while the patient is in a seated position.

Trapezius Muscle

The broad origin of this muscle (see Figure 3) extends from the occipital notch (a bony landmark at the base of the skull) to T12 (the twelfth vertebra in the thoracic portion of the spinal column). The physician should palpate the trapezius muscle from origin to insertion. The superior portion of the trapezius is frequently stretched in flexion injuries (see Figure 2) of the cervical spine, such as may occur in automobile collisions. The physician may find that the patient experiences unusual tenderness and pain in the area of the trapezius; this symptom is due to the excessive stretching or tearing and consequent bleeding (hematoma) that results from a flexion-extension injury to the neck.

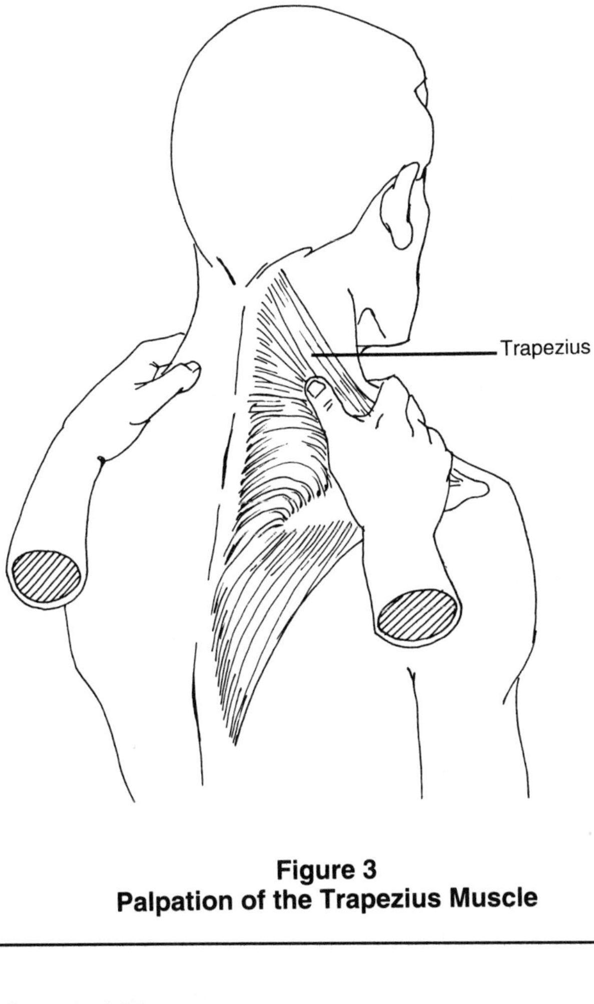

Figure 3
Palpation of the Trapezius Muscle

Greater Occipital Nerves

The muscles supplied by the greater occipital nerves (see Figure 4) are located at the base of the skull. If these muscles are inflamed as a result of the trauma sustained in "whiplash" injury, the greater occipital nerves are distinctly palpable. Inflammation of the greater occipital nerves commonly results in headache.

Superior Nuchal Ligament

This ligament (see Figure 4) rises from the occipital notch at the base of the skull and extends to the C7 spinous process. The liga-

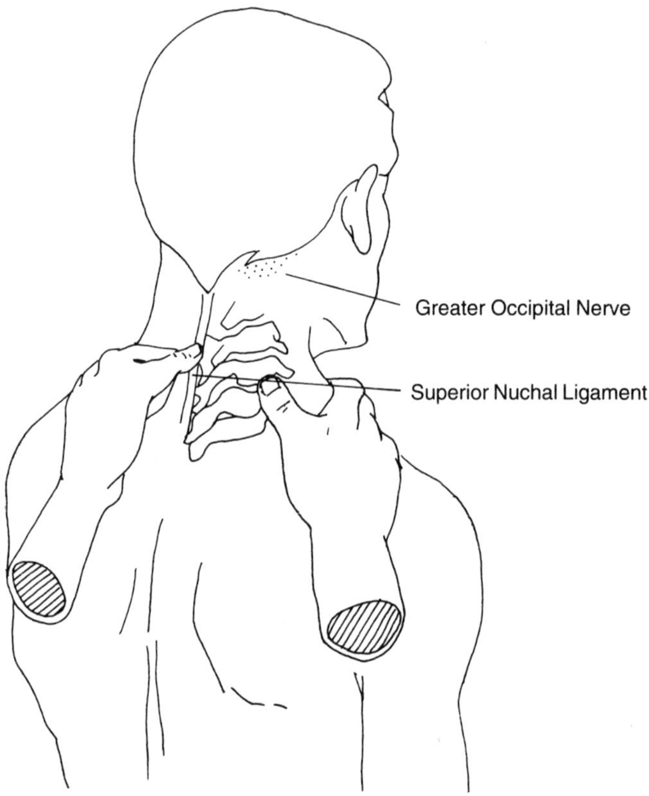

Figure 4
Palpation of the Base of the Skull

ment lies directly under the fingertips during palpation of the spinous process. Tenderness might indicate either a ligament that was stretched as a result of neck flexion injury or perhaps a defect or tearing within the ligament itself.

Range of Motion Testing

The range of motion in the neck includes the following movements: flexion (chin forward on chest), extension (head bent backward), lateral rotation (head turned to the side) to the left and right, and lateral bending (head tilted side to side) to the left and right. These specific motions are also used in combination, giving the head

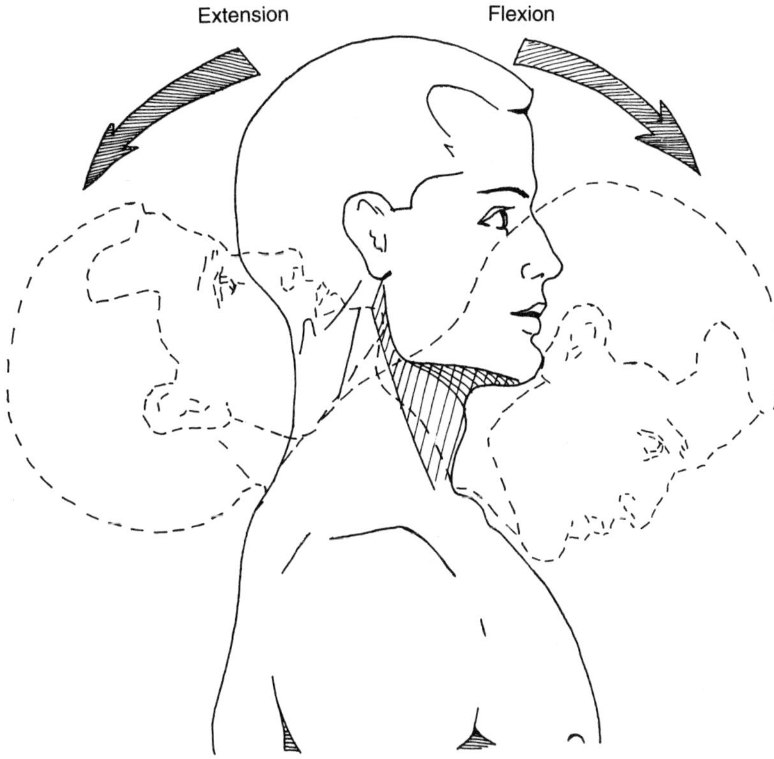

Figure 5
Passive Flexion and Extension of the Neck

and neck the capacity for widely diversified motion. Range of motion testing is a vital part of the physician's examination of an injury to the neck. For example, the condition known as torticollis, in which the neck muscles are distorted or contracted so that the neck bends and the head tilts, is typically accompanied by a limited range of motion in the neck. The patient's range of motion may be passively or actively tested.

Motion Testing—Passive

Flexion and Extension

To test the flexion and extension of the neck, the physician should instruct the patient to nod the head forward in a "yes"

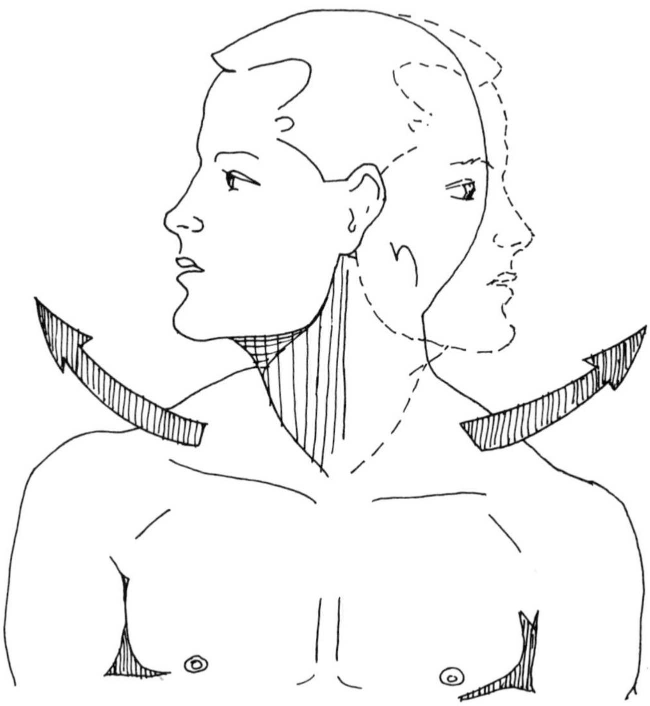

Figure 6
Passive Neck Rotation

movement (see Figure 5). The patient should be able to touch chin to chest (normal range of flexion) and to look directly at the ceiling (normal range of extension). Injury in the cervical area due to a soft-tissue trauma may result in a limitation in the range of motion and a disruption of the normal, smooth arch of motion.

Rotation

The patient should be able to move his or her head far enough to both sides (see Figure 6) so that the chin is almost in line with the shoulder. The motion should proceed with ease and in a smooth arch.

Lateral Bending

The patient in this test should try to touch ear to shoulder (see Figure 7), making certain not to compensate for limited motion by

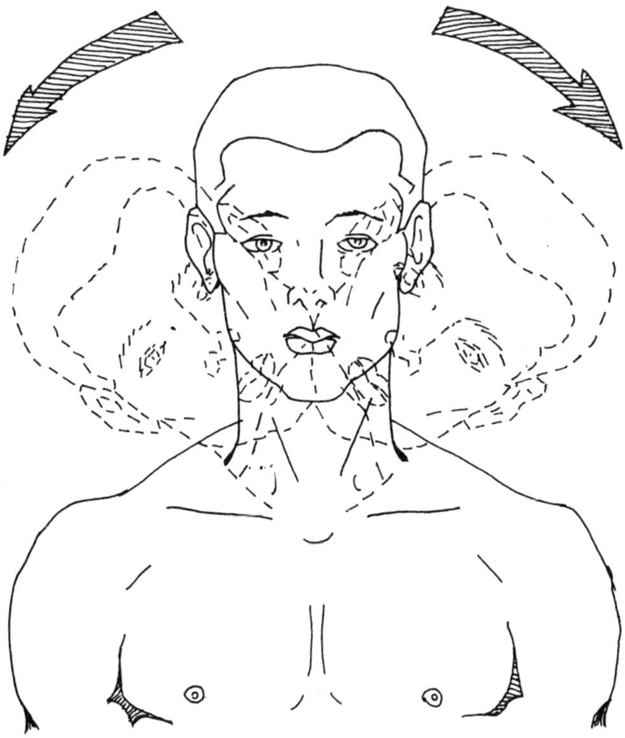

Figure 7
Passive Lateral Neck Bending

lifting the shoulder to the ear. Normally, the patient should be able to tilt the head approximately 45 degrees toward each shoulder. Enlarged cervical lymph nodes may limit motion, especially in lateral bending.

Motion Testing—Active

For the physician to test the innervation to the neck muscles, the patient should repeat the same motions of flexion-extension and lateral rotation-lateral bending just described. However, this time, the physician should place a hand or hands in position to prevent the rotation of the head, or flexion, or extension, to determine the ability of the patient's neck muscles to contract and maintain ade-

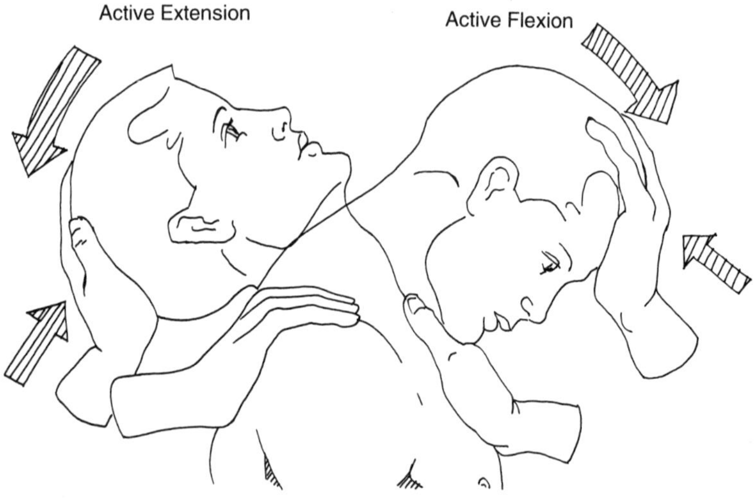

Figure 8
Active Flexion and Extension of the Neck

quate strength. If the muscle strength is limited or gives way, nerve pathology is indicated.

Flexion

The primary flexor muscles of the neck are the sternocleidomastoids, the scalenus muscles, and the paravertebral muscles, which are innervated by the spinal accessory nerve (cranial nerve XI). The physician tests these muscles and nerves by placing a hand on the patient's forehead and checking the maximum resistance that the patient can overcome (see Figure 8) .

Extension

The primary extensors of the neck are the paravertebral extensor muscles, for example, the splenius, semispinalis, capitis, and trapezius. Like the flexors, these muscles are innervated by the spinal accessory nerve.

The test for these muscles (see Figure 8) is similar to the test for the flexor muscles, except that the physician places a hand on the back of the patient's head. The physician again resists the motion of

Figure 9
Active Neck Rotation

the patient's head to determine the maximum resistance the patient can overcome.

Rotation

The primary rotator is the sternocleidomastoid, which is also innervated by the spinal accessory nerve. The physician tests for lateral rotation by placing a hand along the side of the patient's jaw and resisting movement to each side, observing the maximum resistance the patient can overcome (see Figure 9).

Lateral Bending

The primary muscles for lateral bending are the scalenus group. The physician tests these muscles by placing a hand on the patient's

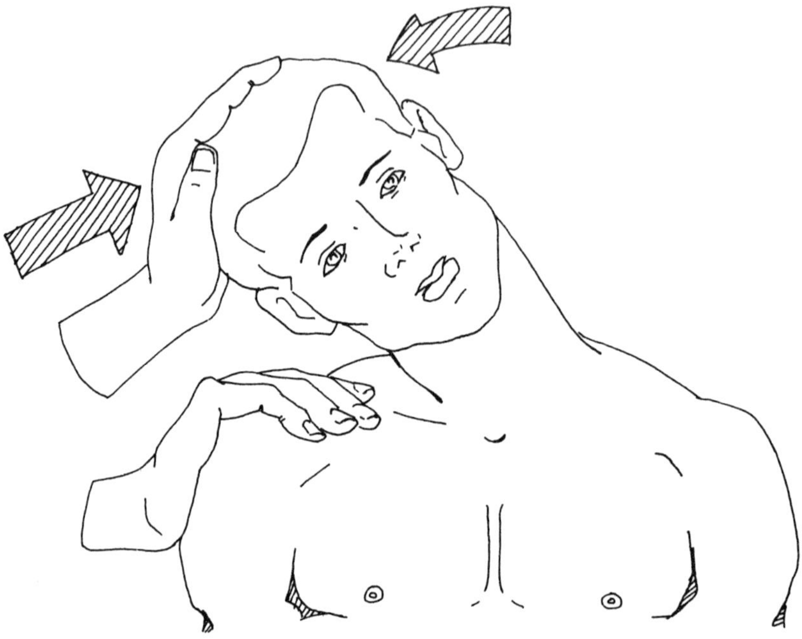

Figure 10
Active Lateral Neck Bending

shoulder to prevent shoulder elevation, and then placing the other hand on the side of the patient's head. Again the physician resists the patient's bending to determine the maximum resistance the patient can overcome (see Figure 10).

Central Nervous System Testing

Whenever cervical or head injury is suspected, the physician first examines the eyes to check for the normal response to light.

Pupillary Reflex

The pupillary reflex is the constriction of the pupil that normally occurs when light is flashed into the eye. The sensory receptors for this reflex are the rods and cones of the retina. The pupillary reflex is controlled by the optic nerve, cranial nerve II.

Consensual Light Reflex

The consensual light reflex is controlled principally by the oculomotor nerve, cranial nerve III, and is characterized by a constriction of the pupil that is similar to the pupillary reflex, but weaker. Therefore, when examining the patient, the physician flashes a light on the pupil to see if it will react normally by constricting. If the reflex is not elicited (if the pupils are fixed and dilated), brain pathology is strongly suspected, either (1) damage to the optic nerve or the oculomotor nerve or (2) unusually high pressure on the brain that increases pressure on the nerves that exit the brain, causing a serious and life-threatening situation.

Reflexes Associated with Focusing

When the eyes are directed to an object close at hand, three different reflex responses are brought into cooperative action:

- *Convergence*. When the eyes, as sense organs, pick up stimuli (lights, colors, shapes), the medial recti muscles contract to move the eyes into alignment so that the images are focused on the same part of the retina. Otherwise, the two images cannot be fused, and diplopia (double vision) will result.
- *Accommodation*. The pupil expands and contracts in response to light. Ciliary muscles control the pupil, changing the aperture in the eye. The lens, which is behind the pupil, is thickened when the ciliary muscles contract to maintain a sharp-focused image.
- *Pupillary Constriction*. This constriction does not depend on any change in light and is separate from the light reflex; the pupils narrow to regulate the depth of focus.

Protective Reflexes

If an object is thrust in front of the eyes without warning, the eyes will blink. This reflex response cannot be inhibited voluntarily. Nerve impulses are sent in neurologic pathways that run from nerve endings in the sense organ—in this case the eye—to the brain. The brain sends motor-response impulses back to the facial nerve (cranial nerve VII), which then activates the muscles around the eyelid to close the lid.

Visual Field

The destruction of one of the optic nerves blinds the eye. On the other hand, atrophy (withering) of the optic nerve affects some of its nerve fibers but spares others. Therefore, instead of total blindness, atrophy usually causes a loss of function in the peripheral parts of the field of vision of each eye.

The visual fields are a person's range of sight or boundaries of vision. They can be measured in detail with an instrument designed for that purpose called a perimeter, but there is a simple way of examining them for gross defects. While the patient's gaze is fixed straight ahead, the examiner introduces an object at some point beyond the normal periphery of vision and moves it slowly toward the line of vision. The examiner notes the point at which the patient first sees the object. After repeating the process from several directions, the examiner can estimate the scope of the patient's field of vision. With optic atrophy, there may be a reduction of both the right and the left visual fields, or a centrally located patch of visual loss (scotoma) may be found in each eye.

Some psychoneurotic patients who see everything as if they were looking through twin-barrelled guns (tunnel vision) will have restricted visual fields and tissue injury. These patients, however, do not stumble over objects, and if their visual fields are accurately measured on repeated occasions, gross inconsistencies in performance may be demonstrated. Tunnel vision may result from injury to the optic chiasma (point where the optic nerves join behind the eye) and may occur without loss of consciousness.

Vertigo

Vertigo is another common problem that may accompany cervical or head injuries. A person's ability to maintain balance and a sense of direction and motion is controlled by the vestibular branch of the acoustic nerve. The vestibular branch is connected to the semicircular canal and gives the sense of equilibrium. The semicircular canal is lined with cilia, or small hairs, that are attached to nerve fibers that run to the vestibular branch of the acoustic nerve. A fluid runs over these hairs and acts as a sort of level in the human ear. The impulses sent to the brain from the cilia through the vestibular branch allow the brain to give the motor commands that will achieve and maintain equilibrium.

Injury to the semicircular canals or the cilia cells causes disorientation or vertigo. Vertigo is a sensation of whirling. An individual suffering from vertigo may have a subjective feeling of rotation or may perceive that external objects are spinning around. A patient may describe feelings of giddiness, faintness, and light-headedness in terms similar to those mentioned above, but these feelings should not be mistaken for true vertigo.

Ménierè's Syndrome

Ménierè's syndrome is a disease of uncertain nature that is characterized by periodic attacks of severe vertigo, often accompanied by nausea and prostration. Tinnitus (whistling or ringing in the ears) and impairment of hearing are included in this syndrome. Ménierè's syndrome may be associated with repeated exposure to loud noises or with simple head trauma.

Petechial Hemorrhages

Acceleration-deceleration injuries involving the neck may cause microscopic or petechial hemorrhages in the brain. These small hemorrhagic areas will not elicit any gross brain pathology that can be diagnosed by neurologic testing, but they have been reported to cause headaches and discomfort.

Peripheral Nerve Testing in the Upper Extremity

Another problem that may arise from a hyperextension-hyperflexion injury to the cervical region is a herniated disc. A herniated disc is frequently diagnosed because of the patient's decreased motor function, decreased reflexes, and areas of altered sensation (pain) in the arm and shoulder. The upper extremity is innervated by cervical nerves C5 through T1. These nerves exit the spinal column through intervertebral foramina (holes) in the cervical spine to form a plexus (grouping of nerves) in the shoulder that is referred to as the brachial plexus. The diagnostic tests described here help to determine whether upper-extremity neurologic problems have a primary source in the neck.

To understand the tests that are performed for neurological injuries to the brachial plexus, one must first review and understand the components and functions of the brachial plexus. The brachial plexus originates chiefly from branches and divisions of the cervical nerves C5 through C8 plus the first thoracic nerve. These

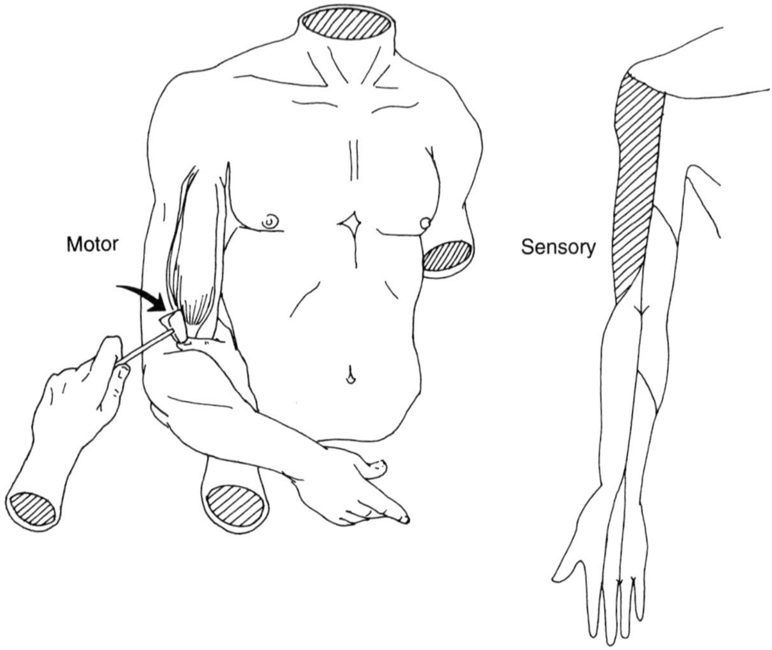

Figure 11
Biceps Reflex Test

branches divide and rejoin many times, ultimately forming the large nerves of the arm known as the median nerve, the ulnar nerve, the axillary nerve, the radial nerve, and the musculocutaneous nerve. The fifth cervical nerve supplies the lateral arm in the form of the axillary nerve. The C6 nerve supplies the lateral forearm, thumb, index fingers, and half of the middle finger. The C7 nerve supplies the middle finger, C8 supplies the ring finger and little fingers and the inside forearm, and T1 supplies the inside arm.

Each of the nerves that form the brachial plexus has a sensory function and a motor function. The innervation and action of the brachial plexus nerves are most easily understood by the use of reflex testing. Each reflex test is described individually below.

Reflex Testing of the Brachial Plexus

Biceps Reflex Testing (C5)

The deltoid and the biceps are two muscles that are innervated by

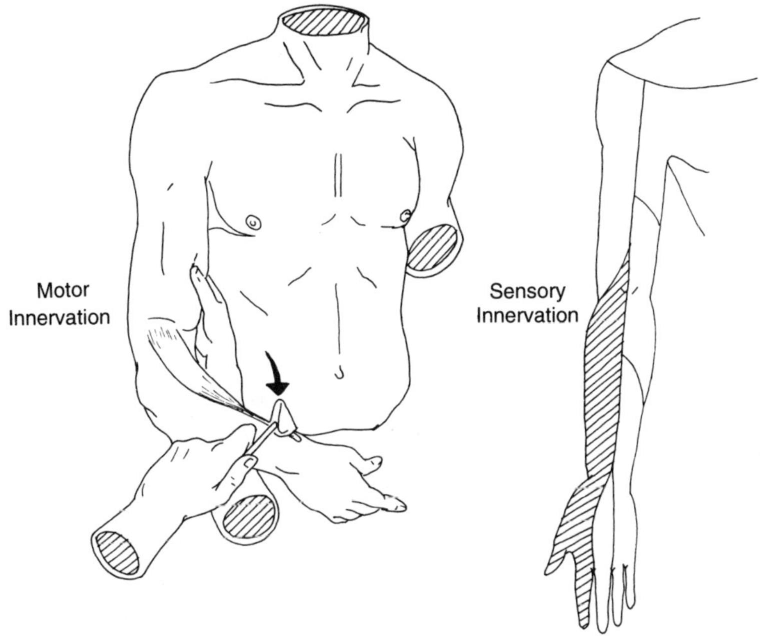

Figure 12
Brachioradialis Reflex Test

C5. The biceps reflex primarily indicates the neurologic integrity (intactness) of C5. However, this reflex also has a C6 component. For the biceps reflex test (see Figure 11), the patient's arm rests upon the physician's forearm. When the patient's arm is totally relaxed, the physician taps his or her own thumbnail with the narrow end of the reflex hammer. The patient's biceps should jerk slightly, and the physician should be able to see or feel the movement. If the muscle responds slightly to the tap of the reflex hammer, the C5 neurologic level (comprising the nerves that arise from the fifth cervical vertebra) is normal in its innervation of the biceps muscle.

If there is no perceptible response after several attempts to elicit a reflex, the C5 track is compromised somewhere: there may be a lesion at the C5 neurologic level anywhere from the root at C5 to the innervation of the biceps muscle. A decreased response may be caused by a lower motor-neuron lesion, such as a peripheral-nerve injury resulting from a herniated cervical disc.

The C5 neurologic level supplies sensation to the lateral arm in the skin covering the lateral portion of the deltoid muscle. (See Figure 11.)

Brachioradialis Reflex (C6)

The brachioradialis muscle is innervated by the radial nerve. During the reflex test (see Figure 12), the patient's arm is supported by the physician's forearm in the same manner used to elicit the biceps reflex. The flat edge of the reflex hammer is then used to tap the brachioradialis tendon at the far end of the radius to elicit the radial jerk.

The C6 nerve supplies sensation to the lateral forearm, the thumb, the index finger, and half of the middle finger. The C6 sensory distribution is often referred to as the "six shooter."

Triceps Reflex (C7)

The triceps muscle (see Figure 13) is innervated by the radial nerve. The triceps reflex is largely a function of the C7 neurologic level. To test this reflex, the physician keeps the patient's arm in the same position used for the two previous tests. The patient is asked to relax the arm completely. When certain that the patient's arm is relaxed (the lack of tension in the triceps muscle can be felt), the physician uses the narrow end of the reflex hammer to tap the triceps tendon where it crosses the back of the elbow. The physician should be able to see the reflex or to feel it as a slight jerk on the supporting forearm. The C7 nerve also supplies sensation to the middle finger. In some individuals, the middle finger's sensation is also supplied by C6 and C8.

Testing of C8

Because C8 has no motor reflex, muscle strength and sensation tests are used to determine its integrity. The muscles involved are the finger flexors, namely flexor digitorum superficialis and flexor digitorum profundus. The flexor digitorum superficialis receives innervation from the median nerve, while the flexor digitorum profundus receives half its innervation from the ulnar nerve and half from the median nerve.

To test finger flexion (see Figure 14), the physician curls or locks fingers with the patient's fingers and tries to pull the patient's fingers out of flexion.

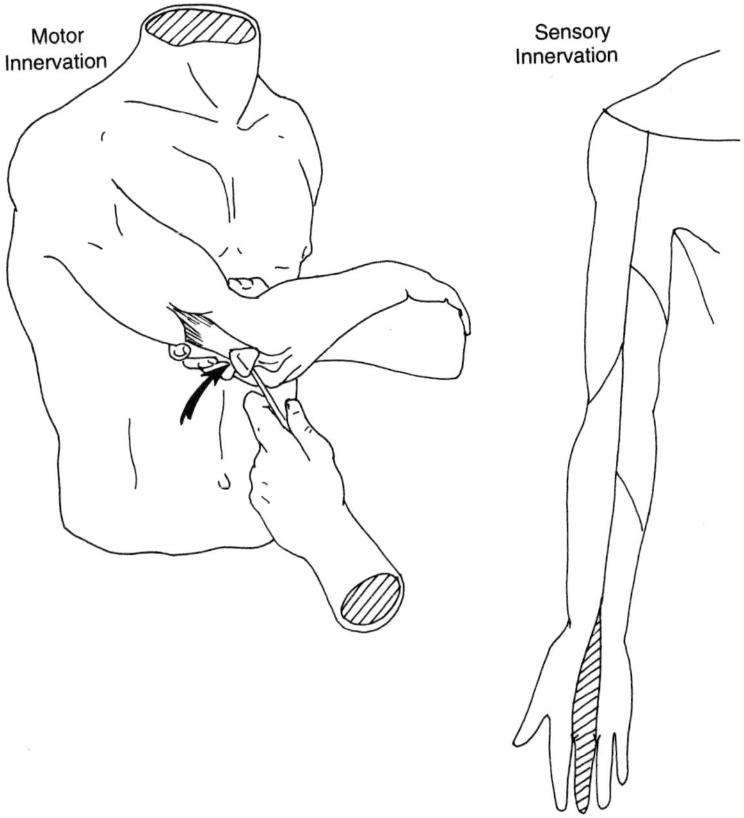

Figure 13
Triceps Reflex Test

The C8 nerve supplies sensation to the ring finger, the little finger of the hand, and the distal half of the forearm (ulna side). The ulna side of the little finger is the purest area (least likely to be innervated by other nerve fiber) for ulnar nerve sensation.

Testing of T1

Because T1, like C8, has no identifiable reflex, the physician evaluates its motor and sensory components by checking for finger abduction. The finger abductors—the dorsal interossei and the abductor digiti quinti—are innervated by the ulnar nerve and are

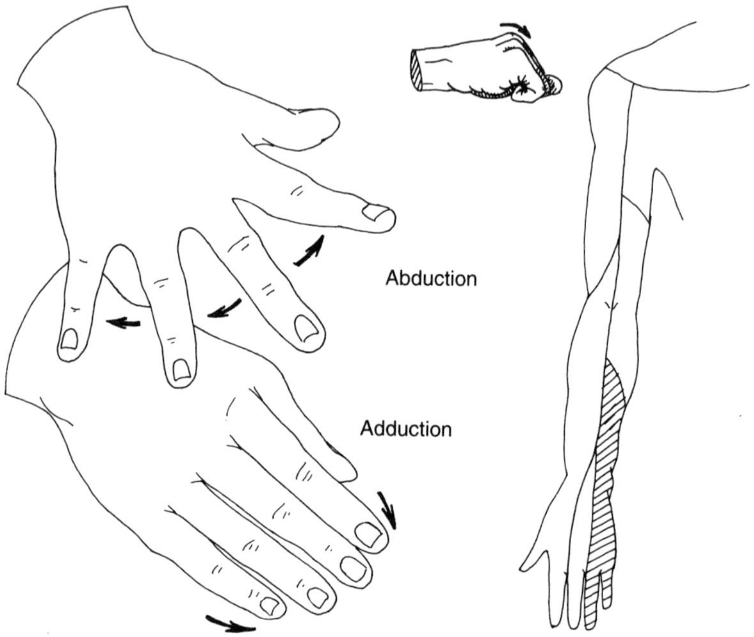

Figure 14
Finger Flexion Test

responsible for allowing the spread of the fingers from the midline (abduction). The physician evaluates abduction by squeezing the abducted fingers together and asking the patient to try to open them (see Figure 15).

Sensation is supplied to the medial (inner) arm by the medial brachiocutaneous nerve.

Other Tests for Upper Extremity

In addition to the tests that have been previously described, there are five other tests that are directly related to the cervical spine.

Distraction Test

This test demonstrates the effect that distraction may have in relieving pain. Distraction is the separation of two otherwise contiguous surfaces—in this case the separation of bone from nerve roots. By widening the foramen and therefore relieving nerve root com-

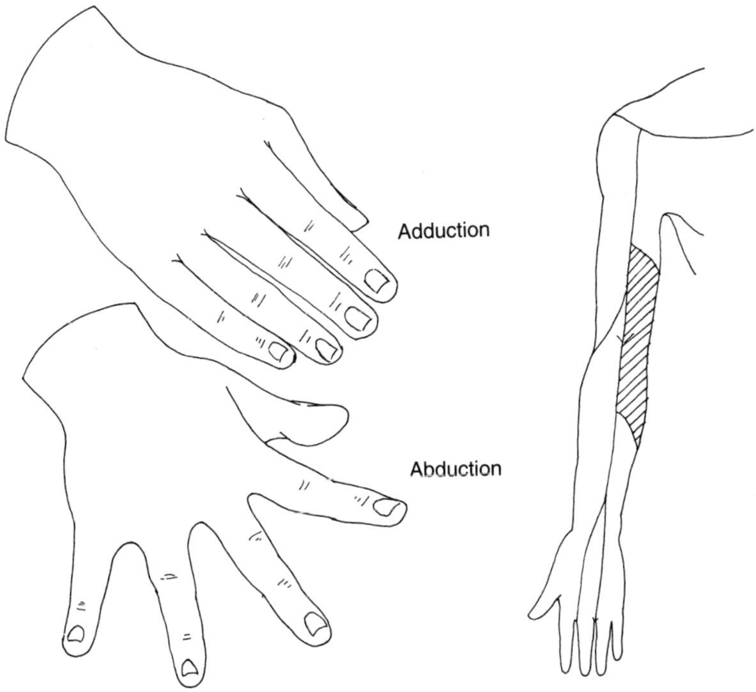

Figure 15
T1 Test

pression, distraction relieves pain caused by a narrowing of the nerve pathway through the vertebrae (neural foramen). Distraction also relieves pain of the cervical spine by decreasing pressure on the joint capsules. In addition, it may help alleviate muscle spasms by relaxing the contracted muscles.

The physician performs this test (see Figure 16) by placing the open palm of one hand under the patient's chin and the other hand on the patient's occiput. The physician then gradually lifts the patient's head to reduce the weight on the neck. If there is pain relief, then there is nerve root compression. If there is no change in the pain, nerve root compression is neither indicated nor ruled out.

Compression Test

A narrowing of the neural foramen, pressure on the vertebral joints, or muscle spasms can cause increased pain upon compres-

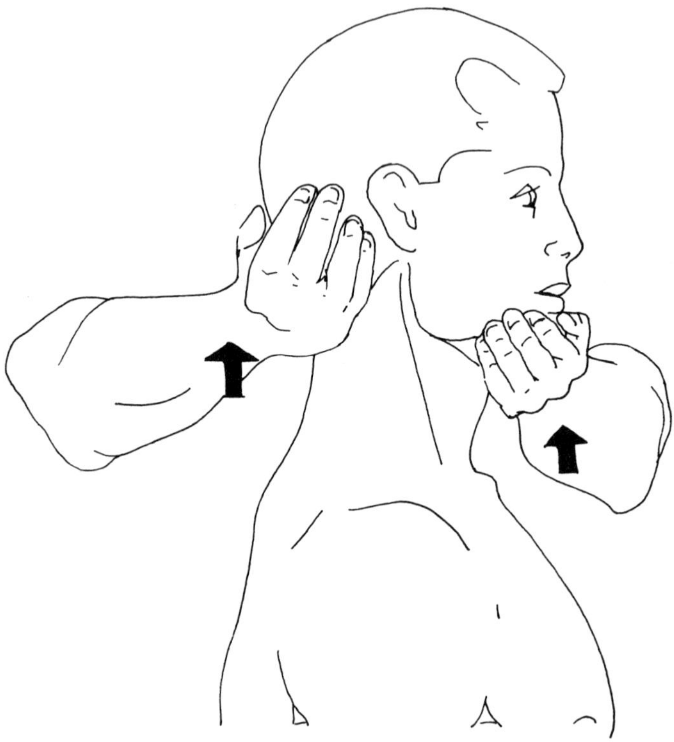

Figure 16
Distraction Test

sion. The compression test may reproduce pain referred to the upper extremity from the cervical spine and, in doing so, may help locate the neurologic level of any existing pathology. The physician performs this test (see Figure 17) by pressing down on the top of the patient's head while the patient is either sitting or lying down. If the patient feels more pain in either the cervical spine or the arm, the physician notes the exact distribution of pain. In a variation of this test, the physician rotates the patient's head to one side (usually rotating away from the injured side and thereby stretching the cervical nerves) before pressing down on top of it. The test is more sensitive when the head is rotated.

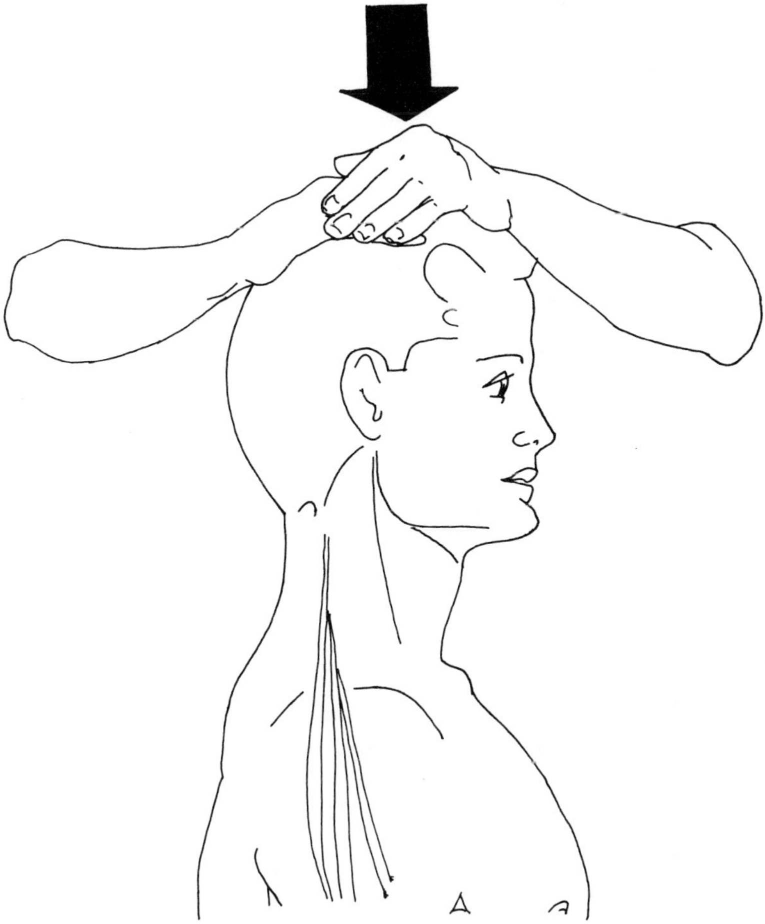

Figure 17
Compression Test

Valsalva Test

The physician performs the Valsalva Test by having the patient hold his or her breath and bear down as if moving the bowels. The physician then asks whether the patient feels any increase in pain, and if so, whether the patient can describe the location of the pain. If a space-occupying lesion, such as a herniated disc, is present in the cervical canal, the patient may develop pain in the cervical spine

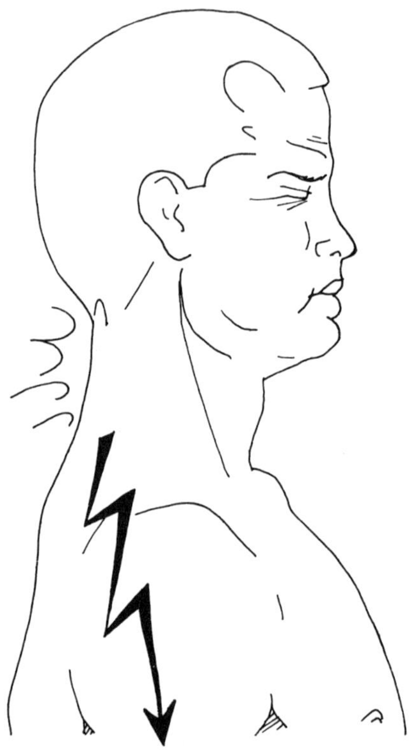

Figure 18
Valsalva Test

because of the increased intra-abdominal pressure. Pain may also radiate into the patient's arm. (See Figure 18.)

Adson Test

This test is used to determine the state of the subclavian artery, which may be compressed by an extracervical rib or by a tightened scalene muscle that can compress the artery where it passes to the upper extremity. The physician performs the Adson Test (see Figure 19) by taking the patient's radial pulse at the wrist. The physician continues to feel the pulse while pulling the patient's arm away from the body, extending the arm, and rotating it. The physician then instructs the patient to take a deep breath and to turn his or her head toward the arm being tested. If there is a compression of

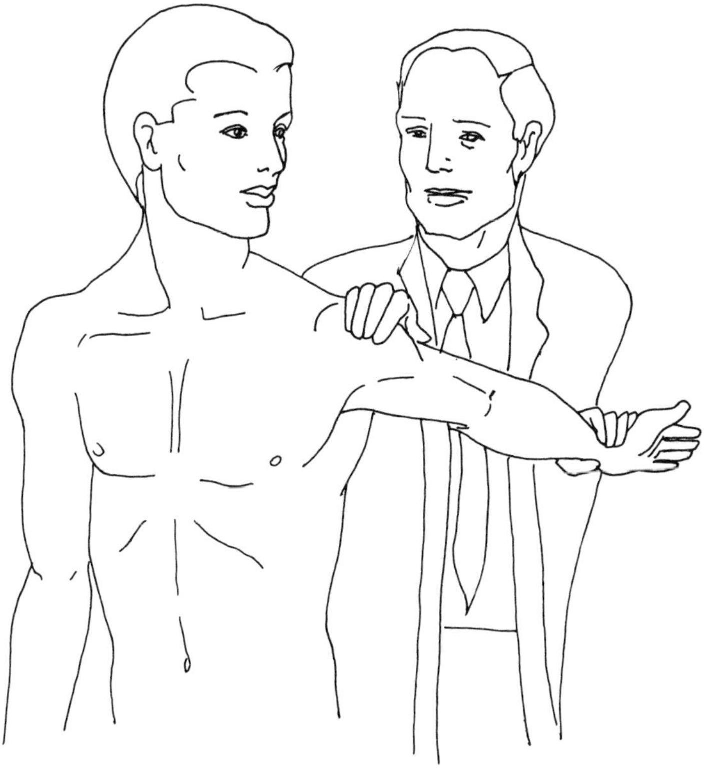

Figure 19
Adson Test

the subclavian artery, the physician will feel a reduction or absence of the radial pulse.

THE LUMBAR SPINE

The lumbar spine (see Figure 20) supports the upper portion of the body and transmits weight to the pelvis and lower extremity. It also transports the spinal cord, which at these levels is called the cauda equina (horse tail), and which supplies motor and sensory perception to the lower extremities. The absence of rib attachment gives the lumbar spine a wide range of motion.

When the patient enters the examining room, the doctor should

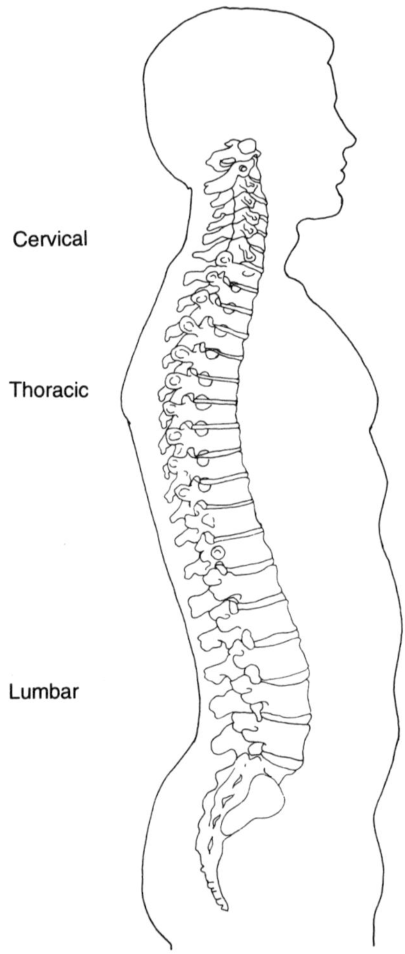

Figure 20
Spinal Column

inspect movements, posture, and spatial relationship (for example, twisting or tilting) in the horizontal and vertical axes of the pelvis. A patient with back trouble may hold the spine very rigidly to avoid bending, twisting, or other motions that could be painful. Any awkward or unnatural movement of the spine could also be a sign of some existing pathology.

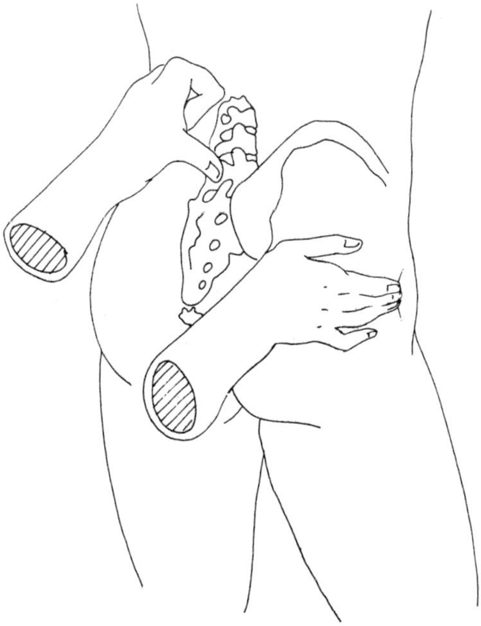

Figure 21
Pelvis and Components Palpation Test

Posture can graphically represent many spinal disorders and should be thoroughly analyzed. The shoulders and pelvis should appear level, and the bony structures, as well as the soft-tissue structures on both sides of the midline, should be symmetrical. When the patient is standing, an obvious inclination or listing to one side or the other may be a sign of congenital scoliosis or possible sciatic scoliosis caused by a herniated disc. From the side view, a smooth lumbar lordotic curve is normal. In certain individuals, however, it is not uncommon to find the normal lumbar lordosis (curvature) altered. In addition, abnormally exaggerated lumbar lordosis is a common characteristic of a weakened anterior abdominal wall. Kyphosis, another abnormality, manifests in increased convexity in the thoracic spine as viewed from the side (hunchback).

In addition to testing each vertebra and the movement and rotation of the vertebrae, the physician should palpate and check very carefully the patient's pelvis and all of its bony components (see Figure 21). This may be done with the patient either standing or lying down, whichever is more comfortable for the patient. Because the pelvis is a weight-bearing structure, however, some portion of this exam should be done while the patient is standing; in this position, pathology may become apparent under the stress of weight.

If the patient experiences pain when the physician palpates any of the vertebrae, this may indicate a defect in the spine such as a lumbar herniated disc. A visible or palpable step-off from one bony process to another may be an indication of spondylolisthesis (forward slippage of one vertebra over the body of another—most often L5 on S1, or L4 on L5). Spondylosis is a general term for degenerative changes due to osteoarthritis. Spondylolisthesis and spondylosis may cause back pain. In conjunction with these defects, there is the likelihood that a nerve root has been stretched or compressed or a disc herniated, causing pain down one or both legs.

Iliac Crest

The iliac crests are the bony protuberances at the waist. The physician palpates the iliac crests to see if they are level in relationship to each other. When they are not level, it is usually because of a pelvic or vertebral abnormality. (See Figure 22.)

Greater Trochanter

The physician can palpate the greater trochanter by sliding both hands down the iliac tubercles; the posterior edge of the greater trochanter will be felt as a bulge in the hip area. By palpating this area, the physician can detect if there has been a congenital dislocation of the hip or a hip fracture that has healed in a poor position. If either one of these two pathologies exist, the level of the trochanters may be unequal.

Range of Motion Testing

The bodies (central portions) of the lumbar vertebrae are separated by elastic, segmental, intervertebral discs, which are composed of an annulus fibrosis (tough outer part) and a nucleus pulposus (spongy inner part). Vertebral motion is greatest where the discs are thickest and where the joint surfaces are largest, as in the lower lumbar region between L4, L5, and S1. Where there is more motion, however, there is more chance of a breakdown, and herniated discs

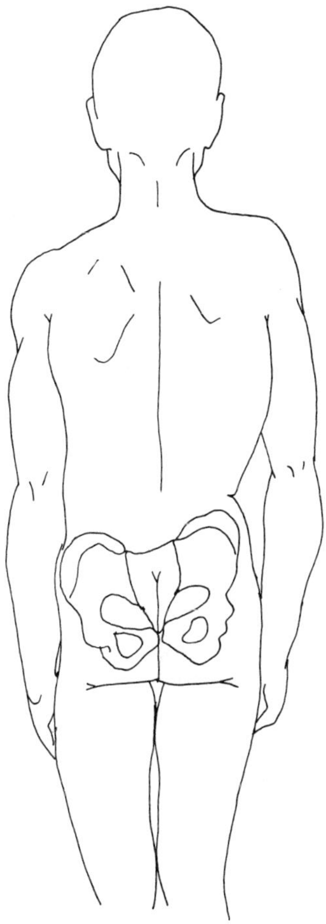

Figure 22
Abnormal Iliac Crest Level

and osteoarthritis are found in the lower spine much more often than in the upper lumbar spine. Because there are no restraining ribs in the lumbar spine, more flexion, extension, and rotation can take place in the lumbar spine than in the thoracic spine. Tests intended to demonstrate the range of motion in the lower back and hips are routinely performed where there is a likelihood that the patient has sustained an injury to the lumbar spine.

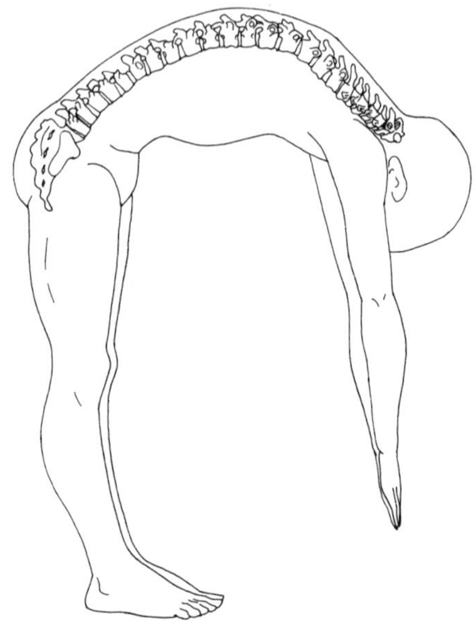

Figure 23
Spinal Flexion Test

Flexion

Major motion, such as flexion (see Figure 23), primarily involves motion in the hip; only an insignificant amount of movement actually takes place in the spine itself.

The physician tests flexion by having the patient bend as far forward as possible with knees straight, and try to touch his or her toes. If the patient cannot touch the toes, the physician may measure the distance from the patient's fingertips to the floor as a gross indication of flexion. However, a protuberant abdomen may preclude the patient from touching the floor with the fingertips.

Extension

The physician tests extension (see Figure 24) by placing one hand on the patient's lower back. Then the physician instructs the patient to bend backward as far as possible, using the physician's hand as a fulcrum for the motion.

The physician should estimate and record the range of extension

Figure 24
Spinal Extension Test

achieved. Spondylolisthesis causes increased back pain upon extension; patients with this condition may find some relief in flexion.

Lateral Bending

The physician tests lateral bending (see Figure 25) by first stabilizing the patient's iliac crest and then asking the patient to lean to the left and then to the right as far as possible. The physician notes how far the patient can bend to each side and compares left and right ranges of motion. Any discrepancy between the ranges of active (patient moving self) and passive (examiner moving patient) lateral bending of the lower back should be noted.

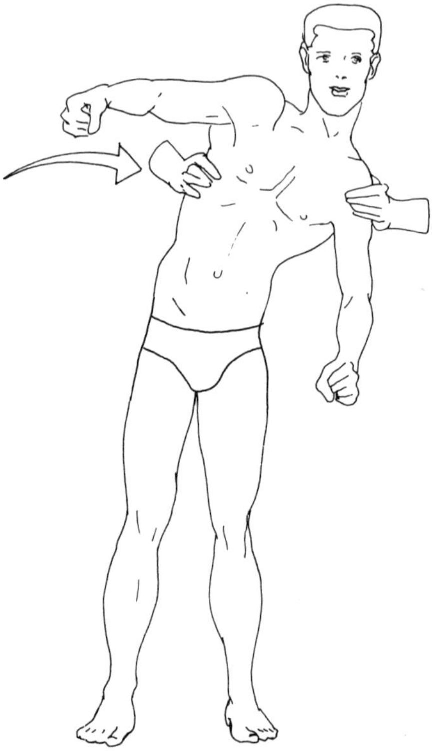

Figure 25
Lateral Bending Test

Rotation

To test rotation (see Figure 26) in the lumbar spine, the physician stands behind the patient and stabilizes the patient's pelvis by placing one hand on either the left or the right iliac crest and the other on the opposite shoulder. Then the physician turns the patient's trunk by rotating the pelvis and the shoulder posteriorly.

Neurologic Examination

The neurologic examination of the lumbar spine includes an examination of the entire lower extremity, since the spinal cord or cauda equina pathologies, such as herniated discs and nerve root

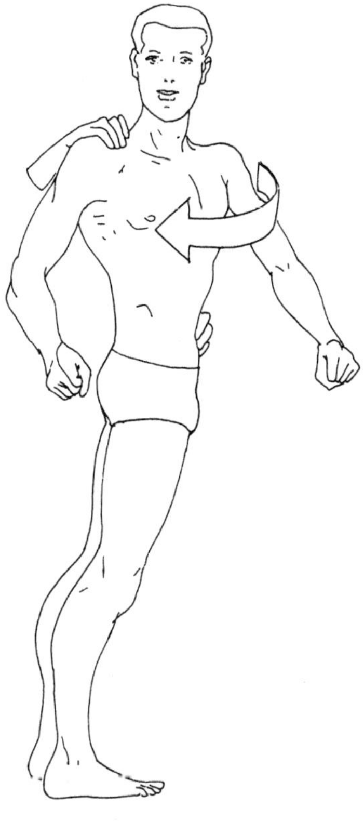

Figure 26
Spinal Rotation Test

damage, are frequently manifested in the extremity itself in the form of altered reflexes, sensation, and muscle strength. Therefore, this examination describes the clinical relationships among the various muscles, reflexes, and sensory areas in the lower extremity and their particular spinal cord levels, so that detection and location of spinal cord problems can be accomplished with relative accuracy and ease.

It is important for the physician to palpate and detect the level of the ischial tuberosity. The ischial tuberosity is in the middle of the buttocks at the approximate level of the gluteal fold (the crease formed by the back of the thigh and the lower buttock). The impor-

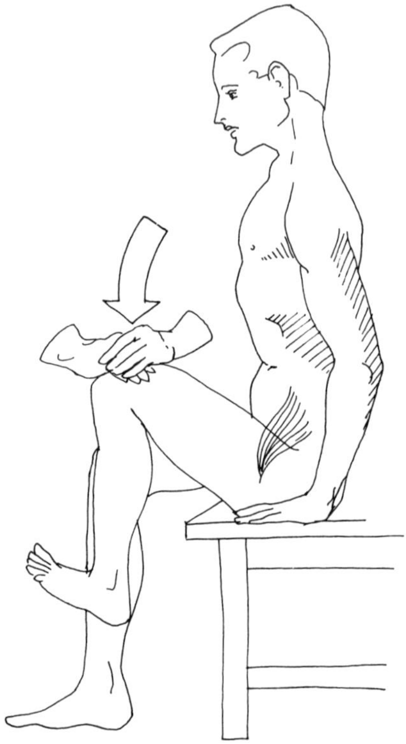

Figure 27
Lumbar Flexor Test

tance of testing or locating and palpating the ischial tuberosity and the greater trochanter is that the sciatic nerve is located midway between these two bony projections. If the physician presses firmly into the soft-tissue depression at the midpoint of the ischial tuberosity and the greater trochanter, the sciatic nerve may be felt underneath the fatty tissue. Tenderness of the sciatic nerve may be due to a herniated disc at the lumbar region, a muscle spasm, or direct trauma to the nerve itself.

There are no individual reflexes for the T12, L1, L2, or L3 levels, and they can only be evaluated from muscle and sensory tests.

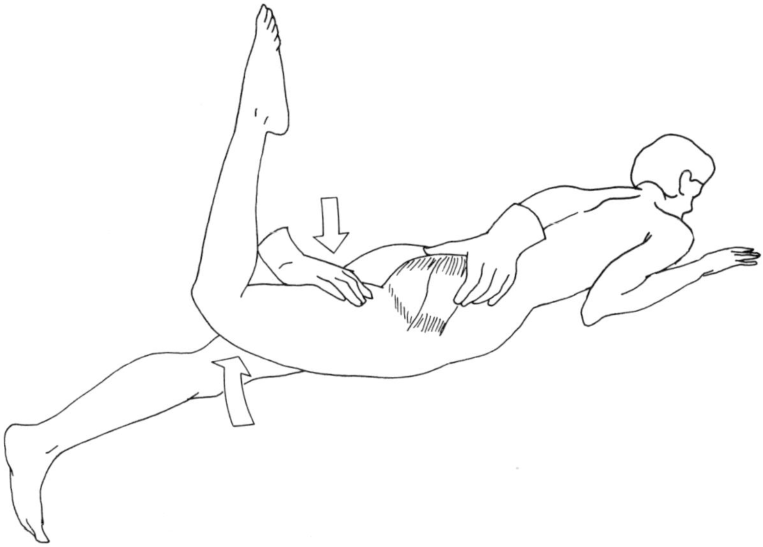

Figure 28
Lumbar Extensor Test

Muscle Testing—Lumbar Spine

The muscles should be tested in functional groups: flexors (muscles that bend or flex), extensors (muscles that stretch or extend), abductors (muscles that move away from the midline of the body), and adductors (muscles that move toward the body midline). Each functional group receives innervation from a different peripheral nerve and, in most instances, from a different neurologic level.

Flexors

The iliopsoas muscle is the main flexor of the hip. It is innervated by the femoral nerve, which is a combination of T12, L1, L2, and L3. The examiner tests the iliopsoas muscle (see Figure 27) by having the patient sit on the edge of the examining table with legs dangling. The physician stabilizes the patient's pelvis by placing both hands over the iliac crest and asks the patient to raise a thigh actively from the table. The physician then places a hand over the distal femoral portion of the patient's knee and asks the patient to raise the thigh further while the physician resists the motion. After

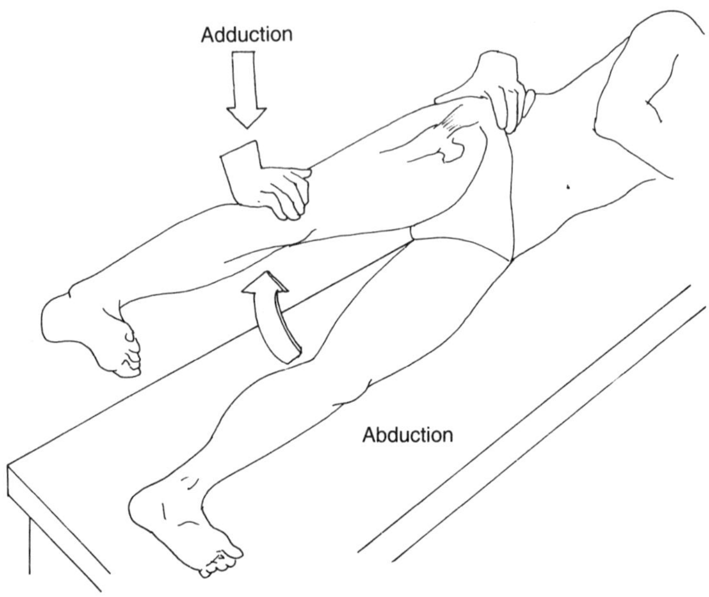

Figure 29
Lumbar Abductor and Adductor Tests

determining the maximum resistance the patient can overcome, the physician repeats the test for the opposite iliopsoas muscle.

Extensors

Gluteus maximus, the primary extensor muscle of the hip, is innervated by the inferior gluteal nerve, S1. The physician tests the extensor muscle group (see Figure 28) by asking the patient to lie prone and to flex one knee. This will relax the hamstring muscle so that it cannot assist in hip extension. The physician then places his or her forearm over the patient's iliac crest to stabilize the pelvis and asks the patient to raise a thigh from the table. Using the other hand, the physician offers resistance to this motion by pushing down on the posterior aspect of the patient's thigh just above the knee joint.

Abductors

Gluteus medius, the primary abductor of the hip, allows a person to move his or her leg away from the midline of the body. It is innervated by the superior gluteal nerve, L5. To test the abductor muscle group (see Figure 29), the physician has the patient turn on one side and stabilizes the patient's pelvis by supporting the iliac crest and tubercle. The physician then instructs the patient to abduct one leg (move the leg away from the midline of the body). When the patient does so, the physician tries to return the leg to adduction (toward the midline) by pushing against the lateral side of the thigh.

Adductors

Adductor longus, the primary adductor of the hip, is innervated by the obturator nerves: L2, L3, and L4. The physician tests for this group (see Figure 29) by having the patient lie on one side and abduct a leg. The physician then places a hand on the medial side of the patient's knee and asks the patient to try to pull that leg back toward the midline of the body against the physician's resistance.

Trendelenburg Test

This test is used to evaluate the strength of the gluteus medius muscle. The physician stands behind the patient and observes the dimples overlying the posterior-superior iliac spines at either side of the base of the spine. Normally, when a patient bears weight evenly on both legs, these dimples appear to be level.

The physician then asks the patient (see Figure 30) to stand on one leg. If the patient stands erect, the pelvis should be higher on the unsupported side. This elevation indicates that the gluteus medius muscle on the supported side is functioning properly (negative finding). However, if the pelvis on the unsupported side remains in position or actually descends, the gluteus medius muscle on the supported side is either weak or nonfunctional (positive test—indicates pathology).

Fractures of the greater trochanter or a slipped femoral epiphysis (the femoral epiphysis is a line of cartilage below the ball of the femur) can cause the gluteus medius muscle to become weak. Another possibility is a congenital dislocation of the hip, which not only brings the muscle's origin closer to its insertion, but also destroys the natural fulcrum around which the muscle functions. In addition, neurologic problems, including a nerve root lesion within the spinal canal, may cause paralysis of the gluteus medius muscle.

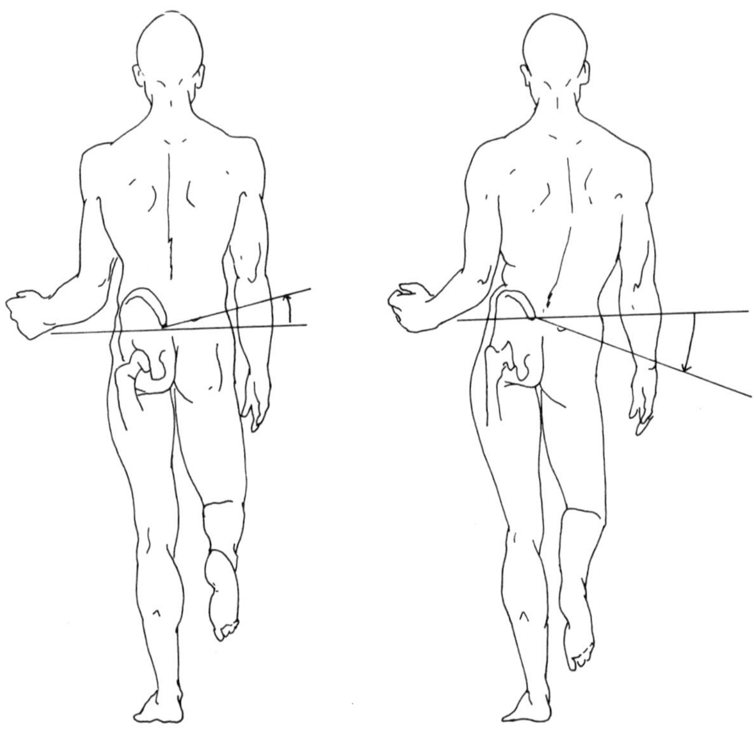

Figure 30
Trendelenburg Test

In addition to these tests, the physician should measure the patient's legs for any discrepancy in their lengths.

Range of Motion Testing—Hips

The hip has various degrees of motion through which it should be able to rotate. The following list describes the tests commonly used to determine whether there is any restriction in normal hip motion that may indicate an injury to the low back.

Abduction

The patient (see Figure 31) is asked to spread his or her legs

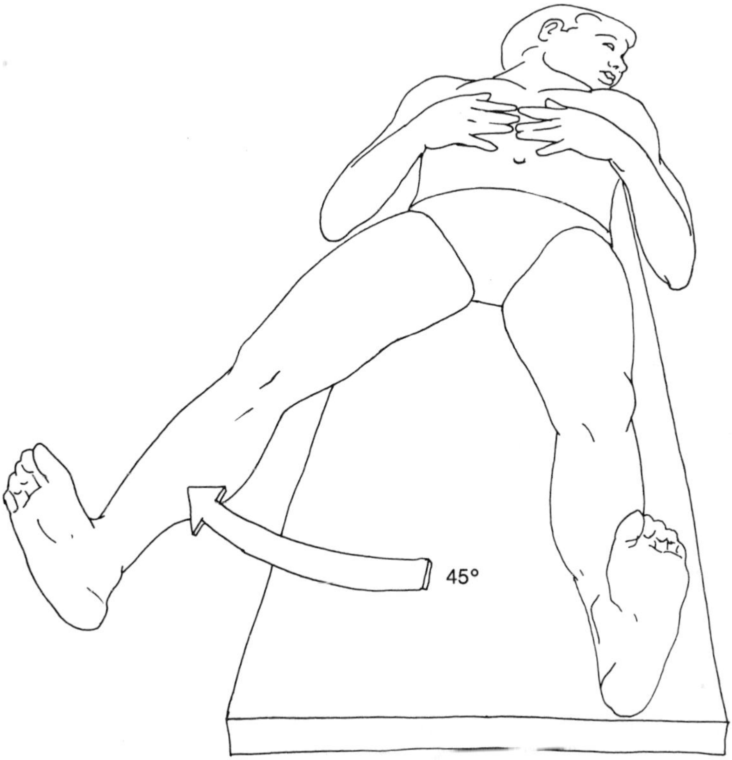

Figure 31
Hip Abduction Test

apart as far as possible. The patient should be able to abduct each thigh at least 45 degrees from the midline.

Adduction

The physician (see Figure 32) instructs the patient to bring the legs from the abduction position, and alternately cross them, first with the right leg in front and then with the left. The patient should be able to achieve at least 20 degrees of adduction.

Flexion

The physician instructs the patient to draw each knee toward the chest as far as possible without bending the back (see Figure

Figure 32
Hip Adduction Test

33). The patient should be able to bring the knees almost to the chest—approximately 135 degrees of flexion. The specific test for flexion is known as the Thomas Test.

Sensory Testing—Lumbar Spine

Nerves originating in the lower spines supply sensation to the hip, pelvic region, and thigh. The areas supplied by each neurologic level are broadly defined as bands, or dermatomes, which cover areas of skin. The dermatomes of the anterior abdominal wall run in transverse, slightly oblique bands. The strip approximately level with the umbilicus is supplied by T10, the strip immediately above the inguinal ligament is supplied by T12, and the area in between is supplied by T11. The sensory area of L1 lies immediately below the

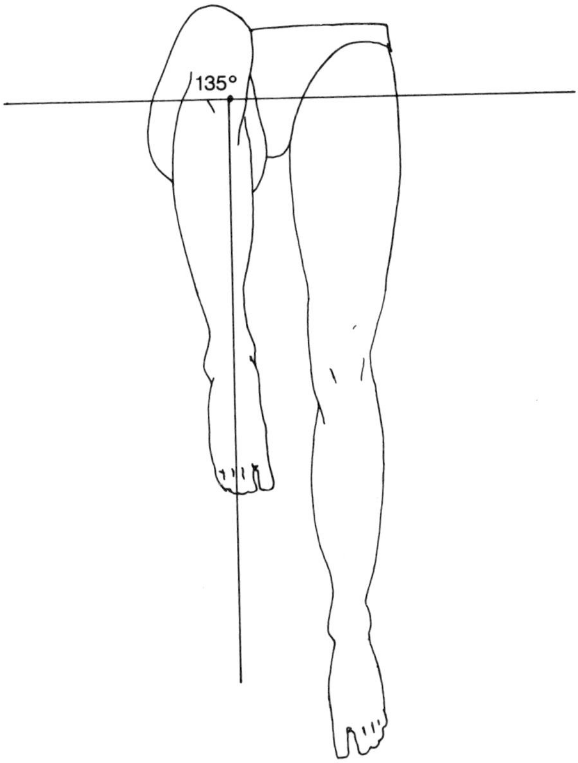

Figure 33
Hip Flexion, or Thomas, Test

inguinal ligament and parallel to it on the upper anterior portion of the thigh. An oblique band immediately above the kneecap represents L3, and the area between L1 and L3 on the midthigh is supplied by L2.

The cluneal nerves (divisions of L1-2-3) cross the posterior portion of the iliac crest and supply sensation over the iliac crest between the posterior-superior iliac spine and the iliac tubercle and over the buttocks. The posterior cutaneous nerve of the thigh (S2) supplies sensation to the longitudinal band on the posterior aspect of the thigh, extending from the gluteal crease to beyond the popliteal fossa. The lateral cutaneous nerve of the thigh (S3) supplies sensation to a broad, oval area on the lateral aspect of the thigh.

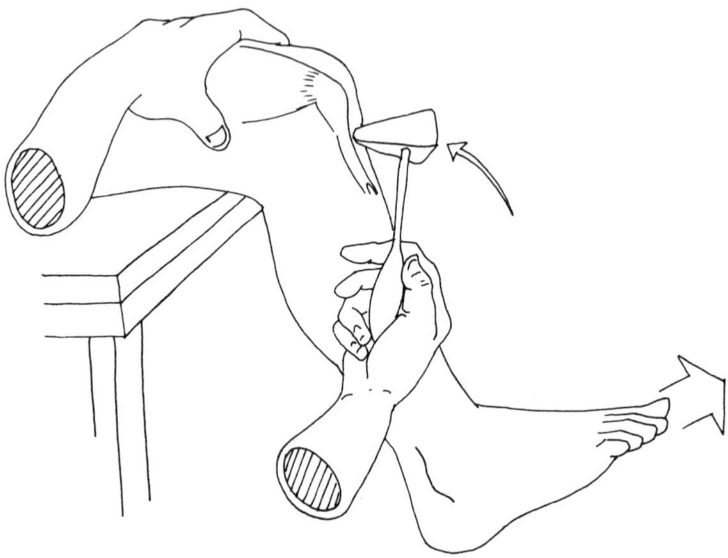

Figure 34
Patella Reflex Test

The dermatomes surrounding the anus are arranged in three concentric circles, receiving innervation from S2, S3, and S4.

Sensory testing determines which nerve-root supply in each dermatome has been damaged. This testing is done in several ways:

- The physician draws a wisp of cotton across the skin to see if the patient has any touch sensation.
- The physician uses a pin prick to see if the patient has any pain sensation.
- The physician determines the patient's ability to discriminate between two points of pain by using two pin-prick points next to each other.

Reflex Testing

The patella reflex (see Figure 34) is a deep tendon reflex, negotiated through nerves emanating from the L2, L3, and L4 nerve roots, but predominantly from L4. The patella reflex is considered an L4

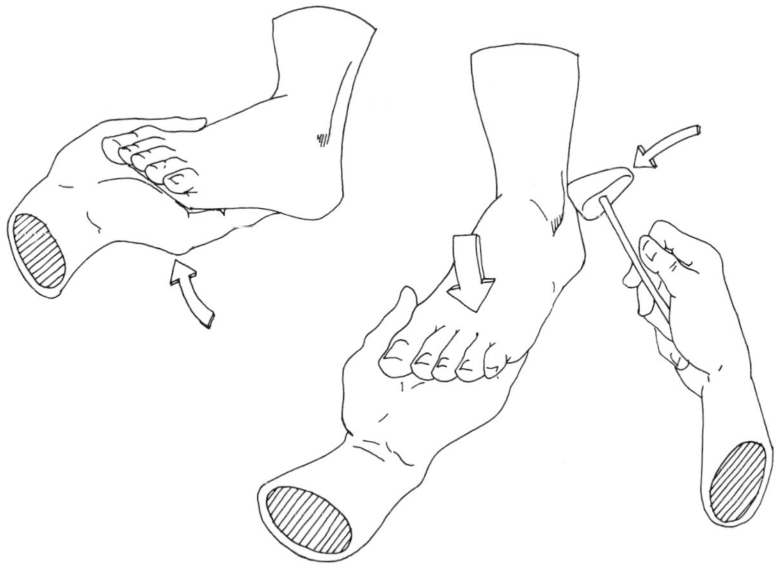

Figure 35
Achilles Tendon Reflex Test

reflex; however, even if the L4 nerve root is totally cut, the reflex is still present in significantly diminished form, because it receives innervation from sources other than L4. To test this reflex, the physician asks the patient to sit on the edge of the examining table with legs dangling free, or to sit on a chair with one leg crossed over the opposite knee. In these positions, the infrapatellar tendon is stretched and primed. The reflex is elicited when the physician taps the tendon with a reflex hammer at the level of the knee joint, using a short, smart wrist action.

Achilles Tendon Reflex

The Achilles tendon reflex (see Figure 35) is a deep tendon reflex, mediated through the gastrocnemius muscle. To test this reflex, the patient's foot is flexed to place the Achilles tendon into a slight stretch. The physician then strikes the tendon to induce the sudden, involuntary plantar (downward motion) flexion of the foot.

Superficial Reflexes

The abdominal, cremasteric, and anal reflexes are superficial, or upper, motor-neuron reflexes requiring skin stimulation. These reflexes are mediated through the central nervous system. The absence of any superficial reflex may indicate an upper motor-neuron lesion and has increased significance if associated with exaggerated deep tendon reflexes (spastic paralysis). Deep tendon reflexes are prevented from excessive reaction by the inhibitory abilities of the central nervous system; therefore, an exaggerated deep tendon reflex in combination with the loss of a superficial reflex is a double indication of cerebral or upper motor-neuron pathology.

Abdominal Reflex

The physician tests the superficial reflex by having the patient lie supine on the examining table. The physician then uses the sharp end of a reflex hammer to stroke each quadrant of the abdomen, noting whether the umbilicus moves toward the point being stroked. The lack of an abdominal reflex indicates an upper motor-neuron lesion. The abdominal muscles are innervated segmentally: the upper muscles from T7 and T10, and the lower muscles from T10 to L1.

Cremasteric Reflex

The superficial cremasteric reflex may be elicited by the examiner's stroking the inner side of the male patient's upper thigh with the sharp end of the reflex hammer. If the reflex is intact, the scrotal sac on that side is pulled upward as the cremasteric muscles (T12) contract. An absence or reduction of both cremasteric reflexes indicates an upper motor-neuron lesion, while a unilateral absence suggests a probable lower motor-neuron lesion between L1 and L2.

Anal Reflex

The physician tests the anal reflex simply by touching the perianal skin. The external and anal sphincter muscles should contract in response (S2, S3, S4).

Babinski Test

The physician performs the Babinski Test (see Figure 36) by stroking the bottom of the outer border of the patient's foot with a blunt object (usually the handle of the reflex hammer). By noting

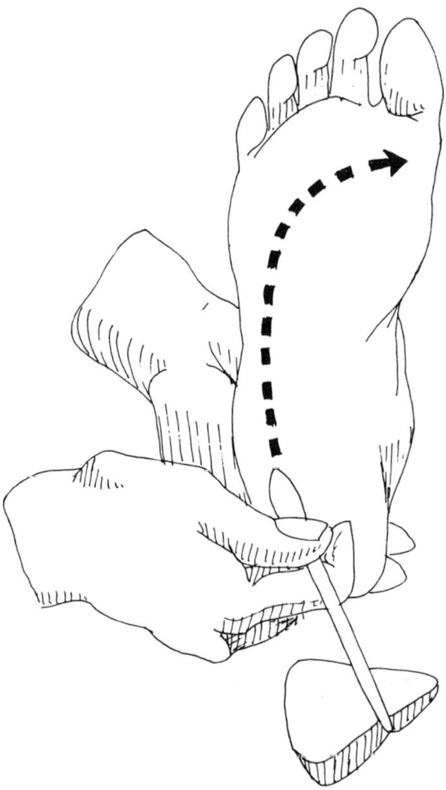

Figure 36
Babinski Test

the reaction of the toes of the patient, the physician can determine if there is injury to the descending motor pathways (nerve fibers descending from the brain into the spinal cord). The normal response in adults is the plantar flexion of the toes, but if Babinski's Sign is present, there is a slow dorsiflexion (upward and back) of the great toe accompanied by a fanning of the lateral toes (see Figure 37). The purpose of this test is to determine whether there is an injury to the motor pathway of the brain or spinal cord (upper motor-neuron lesion). The Babinski Sign is present in clinical cir-

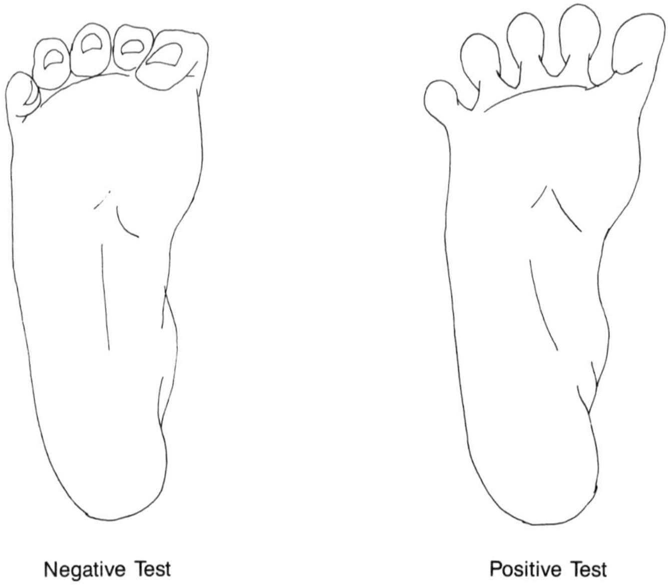

Figure 37
Negative and Positive Babinski Test

cumstances of a spastic paralysis. If there is an injury to the peripheral motor nerve as it leaves the spinal cord, there will be a flaccid (limp) paralysis (lower motor-neuron) of that leg, and there should be no Babinski Sign.

Straight Leg Raising Test

This test is designed to reproduce back and leg pain so that the physician can determine the location of its cause. The physician instructs the patient to lie supine on the examining table. The physician then lifts the patient's leg upward by supporting the patient's foot around the ankle (see Figure 38). The knee should remain straight; to ensure that it does, the physician places a hand on the anterior aspect of the patient's knee to prevent the knee from bending. The extent to which the leg can be raised without discomfort or pain varies, but normally the angle between the leg and the table measures approximately 80 degrees. If the straight leg raising

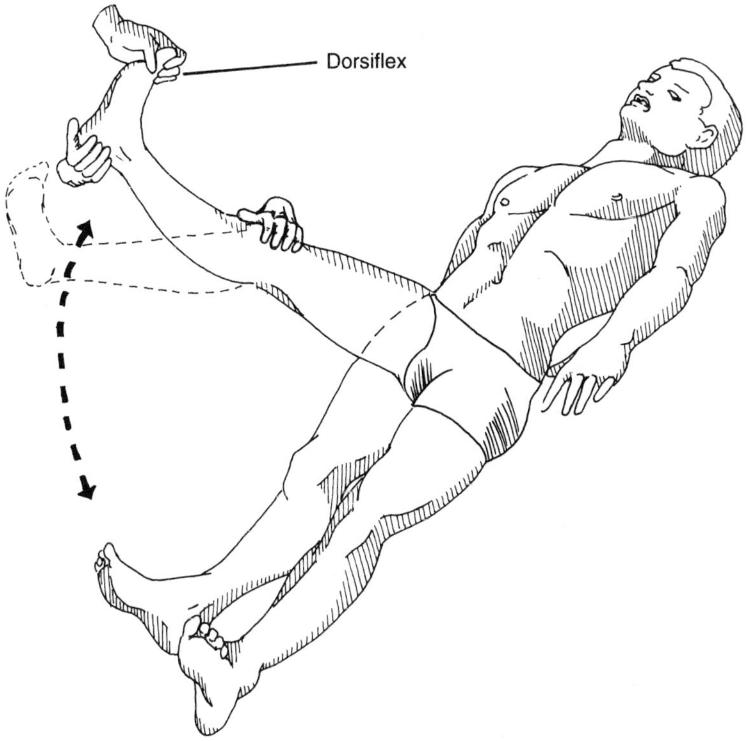

Figure 38
Straight Leg Test

is painful, the physician must determine whether the pathology is due to problems in the sciatic nerve or to hamstring tightness. Hamstring pain involves only the posterior thigh, whereas sciatic pain can extend all the way down the leg. The patient may also complain of low back pain and, on occasion, pain in the opposite leg. At the point where the patient experiences pain, the physician lowers the leg slightly and then dorsiflexes the foot to stretch the sciatic nerve and reproduce sciatic pain (see Figure 38). If the patient does not experience pain when the physician dorsiflexes the foot, the pain induced by the straight leg raising is probably due to hamstring tightness. If there is a positive reaction to the straight leg raising test and the dorsiflex maneuver (also called the Lessuge

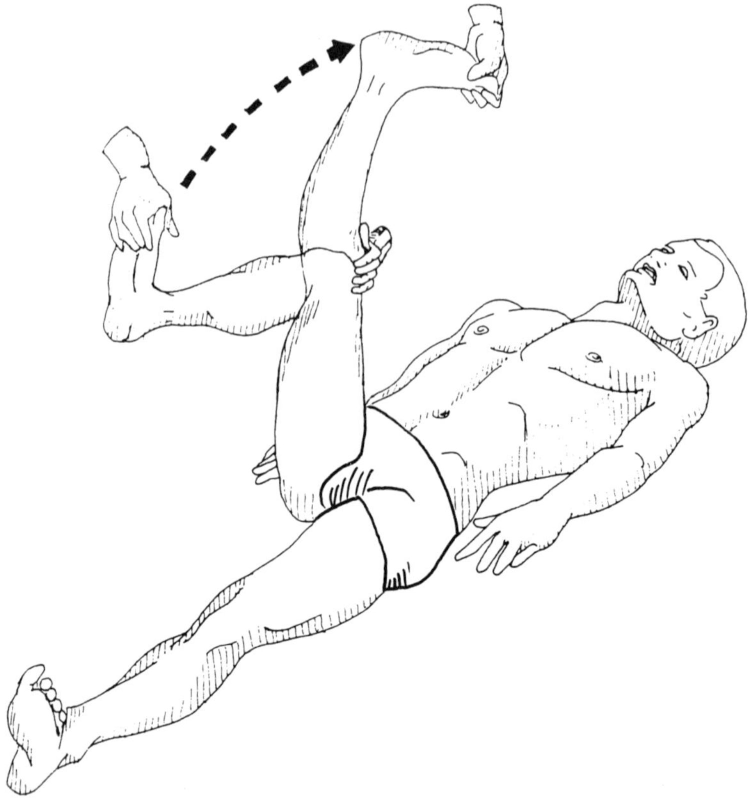

Figure 39
Alternate Straight Leg Test

Test), the physician asks the patient to locate, as nearly as possible, the source of the pain.

Next, with the patient lying supine, the physician raises the uninvolved leg. If the patient complains of back and sciatic pain in the opposite (involved) side, there is a good possibility that there is a space-occupying lesion such as a herniated disc in the lumbar area. This test is referred to as the positive cross leg–straight leg raising test.

In a variation of the straight leg raising test (see Figure 39), the physician raises the patient's leg with the knee bent. When the knee is extended, the extension will stretch the sciatic nerve and cause

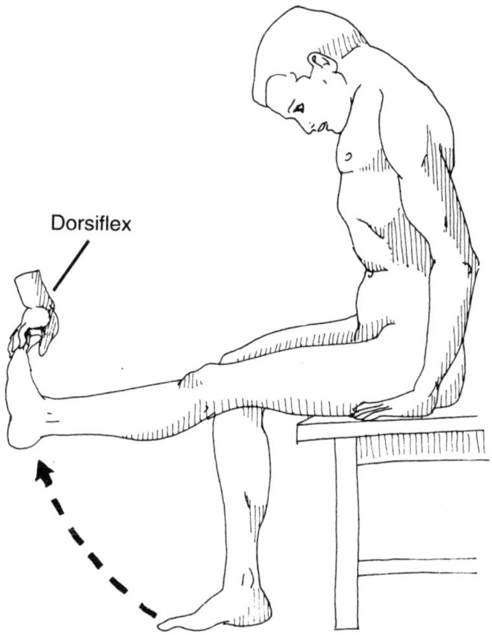

Figure 40
Seated Straight Leg Test

pain; dorsiflexion of the toes will also cause pain. There is another variation of the test (see Figure 40) with the patient seated on the edge of a chair. Again the knee is bent. When the knee is extended, the sciatic nerve is stretched and the patient experiences pain. However, when the straight leg raising test is performed with the patient in a sitting position, the patient has a natural tendency to lean back and not to complain of pain. Therefore, the straight leg raising test is considered more accurate when the patient is lying down, because then the patient's back is immobilized.

Patrick, or Faber, Test

This test (see Figure 41) is used to detect pathology in the hip, as well as in the sacro-iliac joint. The patient should lie supine on the table and then place the foot of the involved side on the opposite

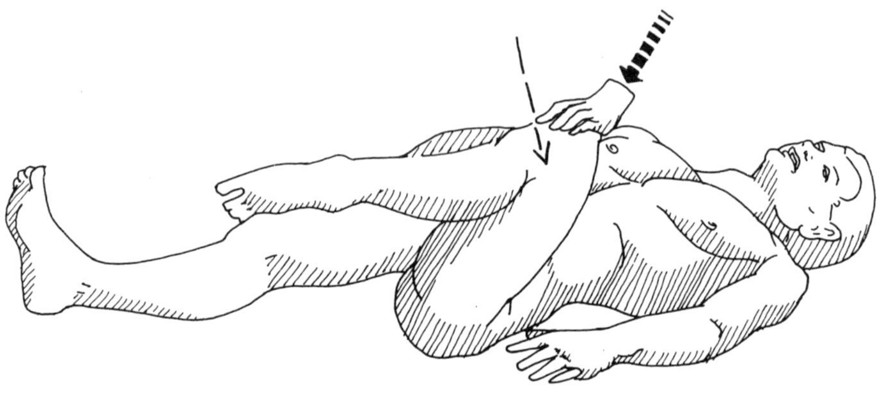

Figure 41
Patrick, or Faber, Test

knee. The hip joint is now flexed, abducted, and externally rotated. In this position, inguinal pain indicates pathology in the hip joint or its surrounding muscles. When the end point of the hip joint's flexion, abduction, and external rotation has been reached, the femur is fixed in relation to the pelvis. To stretch the sacro-iliac joint, the physician extends the range of motion by placing one hand on the flexed knee joint, placing the other hand on the anterior-superior iliac spine of the opposite side, and then pressing down on each of these points. If the patient complains of increased pain, there may be pathology in the sacro-iliac joint.

Sacro-Iliac Joint Test

For this test, the physician asks the patient to lie prone (see Figure 42) on the examining table. The physician then places both hands on the patient's iliac crests, with thumbs on the anterior-superior iliac spine and with palms on the patient's iliac tubercles. The physician then forcibly presses the patient's pelvis toward the midline of the body. If the patient complains of pain around the sacro-iliac joint, there may be pathology in the joint itself, such as infection or problems caused by trauma.

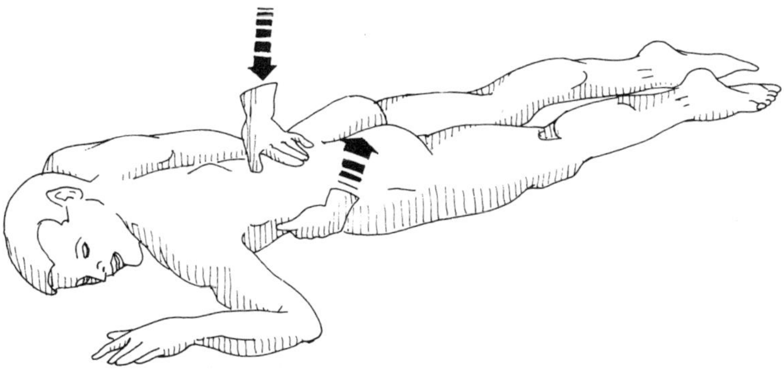

Figure 42
Sacro-Iliac Test

NEURODIAGNOSTICS

Neurologic examination today can include a variety of diagnostic tests, both invasive and noninvasive.

Conventional Radiography

The most common diagnostic tool is conventional radiography, which entails using ordinary X-ray beams to obtain a two-dimensional view of the bony skeleton. To produce a conventional film, X rays are focused into beams that are aimed at the approximate target. These beams pass through the body to a metal or plastic cassette or film holder that contains the X-ray film. Within the cassette and on either side of the film are enhancing screens that turn some of the X rays into light, so that both X rays and light rays hit the film. The exposed X ray is then developed, resulting in negatives similar to those in conventional photography.

The spinal column is three-dimensional. Thus, a minimum of two films are required for adequate evaluation of the spinal column. Furthermore, the angularity of the parts of the spinal column requires various angled views. The treatment of patients with cervical spine injuries where a spinal cord injury is suspected requires that the patient be immobilized and that a single lateral view of the cervical region be obtained by the technician. Most serious pathology of the cervical spine can be detected on the initial lateral view.

Therefore, the lateral film is the single most important film in this clinical setting.

In conventional radiography, the area most likely to be abnormal or injured is positioned closest to the X-ray film, because the area near the film is the area most likely to be seen clearly. Such positioning prevents loss of anatomical detail. The specific views are named for the direction of the X-ray beam as it passes through the patient to reach the film. For example, the P-A film is a posterior-to-anterior film (back to front). Because the body part closest to the X-ray film is seen with greatest clarity, the organs within the various body cavities will be most distinct. In an A-P (anterior-to-posterior) film, the spinal column will be closest to the X-ray film and thus the clearest in definition. Apart from positioning, definition is changed through the use of different exposure times as well as different voltages. Changes in exposure time and voltage can alter the depth of X-ray penetration, thus affecting the intensity of the body structure on film.

In cervical spine injuries, a lateral view allows the radiologist to analyze not only the cervical vertebra but also the anterior and posterior arches of C1, the odontoid process of C2, the remaining cervical spines, the discs, the processes, the overlapping facet joints, and the soft tissues adjacent to the spine. The radiologist not only assesses alignment but looks for subluxation (overriding), facet-joint widening, and motion of the spinous processes on flexion and extension.

Xeroradiography

Xeroradiography, a technique used since the 1950s, employs a conventional, single X-ray beam to produce a dry-paper picture. The detail produced by xeroradiography is unsurpassed and obviates the need for a cumbersome view box. Xeroradiography is excellent in defining soft-tissue lesions and is most useful in evaluating cervical soft-tissue masses, foreign-body tendonitis, synovitis, and very subtle fractures that may be missed by a conventional X ray. The utility of xeroradiography lies in its ability to indicate sharp changes in density. Thus, contiguous areas of differing density such as bone and surrounding soft tissue are seen more clearly. Xeroradiographs can highlight nonopaque foreign objects as well as calcific lesions far better than plain X rays.

Xeroradiographs are produced when X rays strike film in a

cassette containing a positively charged, selenium-coated aluminum plate rather than film. The X-ray beam passes through the body and strikes the plate, which discharges portions of itself in proportion to the amount of X rays that strike it. Various tissues permit different amounts of X rays to pass through to the plate. Thus the different densities of tissues are imaged. Xeroradiography is not without its difficulties. It is costly, and its images can be obscured by contaminating images, known as artifacts, that are caused by the weight of body parts.

Conventional Tomography

Conventional tomography was introduced in the 1930s and is advantageous because it blurs out overlapping, extraneous structures. It employs a single X-ray tube and an X-ray cassette attached to each other by a rod that moves them about a fixed fulcrum at a constant speed, in two parallel planes, in opposing directions. Motion blurs the structures above and below the target plane, while the target plane remains focused and clear. Conventional tomographic films are a valuable tool for detecting subtle fractures. Recent modifications in conventional tomography permit complex motions of the tube and film, producing greater blurring and consequent increased obscuring of extraneous structures.

Computerized Tomography

Computerized tomography (CT) is among the more popular diagnostic tools that have gained increased acceptance recently and are now more widely available. CT scanners are X-ray machines that employ a series of highly columnated, narrow X-ray beams to produce sectional X-ray images that have better contrast resolution than conventional X rays. A computerized scanner is composed of an X-ray source, a computer that analyzes data from the X-ray detector, and a display console. The computer divides the scanned area (for example, arm, leg, back) into a matrix of small squares called pixels. The computer assigns an X-ray attenuation (clarity) coefficient to the scanned area (every substance that exists has an attenuation coefficient) and then assigns each pixel a number related to its attenuation coefficient, with water density at the baseline number of zero. The numbers assigned by the computer are represented on the final X-ray image as various shades of gray on a "gray scale," with the highest number (air) as black and lowest number (bone) as white.

A CT scan can be performed with the patient in one position, making the CT scan a superior diagnostic tool for a severely injured patient. The CT scan's high-contrast resolution makes it most useful in assessing spinal injuries, anatomy, and pathology. The CT scan is ideal for assessing structures (for example, disc material) within the spinal canal that might not be visible on conventional X rays and tomograms. The CT scan will not demonstrate all fractures and is not intended as a routine screening tool, but has greatest application in examining specific areas of *known* injury.

Since its introduction in 1972, CT scanning has been greatly refined. The first-generation scanner required 30 minutes to adequately evaluate the entire cranial contents. With the introduction of the second- and third-generation scanners, a single slice through the cranial contents can be performed in about two seconds. A unique diagnostic tool, the scanner now affords the physician the ability to detect subtle differences in soft-tissue density. Thus, computerized tomography has proved to be invaluable in detecting various traumatic intracranial lesions such as intra- and extracerebral hematomas, infarcts, contusions, and edema.

In cases of head injury, 10 to 15 conventional slices, each covering a surface area of at least 10 square centimeters of intracranial contents, are scanned. The patient is moved one centimeter between slices. This movement results in multiple contiguous images, each image corresponding to a one-centimeter-thick reconstructed section of the brain.

The first-generation scanners tended to produce a poor image. They were slow, and patients' unnecessary movement produced technically inferior images clouded by artifact. With the advent of the third-generation rapid scanners, motion artifact has been virtually eliminated.

Often, in addition to conventional computerized tomography, scanning after injection of contrast material (dye or radioactive isotopes), though clearly invasive, provides enhancement of lesions not well visualized on nonenhanced scans. Contrast scans are particularly helpful in defining A-V (arterio-venous) fistulas (holes between an artery and a vein where blood spills) and A-V malformations (congenital anomalies), among other vascular conditions. Taking scans both with and without contrast (double scanning) is beneficial in demonstrating traumatic lesions.

Computerized tomography is not without pitfalls. Often patients with focal neurologic deficits (minute bleeds or lesions) have normal CT scans. However, conducting a series of scans over time to see the lesions evolving will frequently reveal the focal neurologic deficit. Other drawbacks are that a CT scan exposes patients to large X-ray doses and the equipment is sophisticated and expensive.

Magnetic Resonance Imaging

Magnetic resonance imaging (MRI) is a new technique that uses a combination of magnetism and radio-frequency pulses to measure the differences in proton density between tissues (for example, bone compared with connective tissue). This technique uses computers to produce multiplanar anatomical pictures on X-ray film. The essential characteristic of MRI images is that bone, cartilage, and ligament are poorly imaged. Thus the surrounding tissue is clearly seen, without interference from bone and other structures. In MRI, soft tissues have the highest degree of contrast. Therefore MRI has its greatest application in soft-tissue injury and in pathology of the brain and spinal cord. The radio frequency used with MRI precludes its use for patients who have pacemakers or implanted hardware or who use life-support equipment. MRI equipment is costly and because it is so new, its long-term effects on patients are unknown.

Additional diagnostic tests particularly useful in neurologic conditions include a group of invasive studies still employed in specific clinical circumstances.

Myelography

Myelography, which permits study of the spinal cord and nerve roots, involves an injection of a contrast medium into the spinal fluid. Myelography uses conventional X rays but may be done in conjunction with CT after injection of contrast material. Myelography is rarely used for acute spinal-cord trauma because its use in this clinical setting has been all but supplanted by CT and MRI scanning. Myelography is most useful in confirming the presence of bony spinal pathology or spinal-cord pathology that impedes the flow of cerebral spinal fluid. Myelography requires a lumbar puncture, which is generally done below the L2 level, where the spinal cord tapers to the conus medullaris. By puncturing the patient at this location, the physician avoids the danger of directly injuring the spinal cord with the needle used to inject the contrast material.

Although myelography is useful in determining spinal cord and nerve root pathology, it requires a long test time and long X-ray exposure and is not as accurate as newer scanning techniques.

Angiography

The final diagnostic to be considered is angiography, which involves the study of blood vessels using contrast material. Newer forms of angiography include digital and subtraction angiography, which use computers to remove or subtract bony structures from the image. This permits greater definition of vascular structures, because the blood vessels are not obstructed by overlying bone. Angiography is performed in conjunction with varying forms of photography (including motion picture film and videotape) to preserve the results for future and more thorough analysis. Angiography is a valuable tool in assessing vascular injury. However, it is cumbersome, requires the use of multiple catheters, and incurs the risk of iatrogenic mechanical vascular injury (puncture, laceration, or aneurysm) and renal damage because of the large volumes of contrast material required for the study.

With the adjunct diagnostics now available, a neurologic examination can hardly be complete without using at least one of the new, sophisticated tests because of their ability to define a lesion quickly and accurately. Injuries to the cranium should be verified by either CT or MRI or both. Injuries to the cervical spine should be examined first by conventional radiography, followed by tests aimed at either soft-tissue or bony-structure definition. Spinal-cord compression lesions may require myelography for visualization. Subtle fractures may best be identified with plain tomography. Foreign objects may be readily visualized on xeroradiograph.

Diagnostic tools are intended to be adjuncts and cannot replace the thorough history and physical examination conducted by the practitioner. Such examination and history serve to guide the physician's judgment in ordering various invasive and noninvasive studies to confirm the diagnosis and localize the injury. Interpretation of these tests should be left to the experienced radiologist or neuroradiologist, who should review the tests with the practitioner to ensure correct diagnosis and an appropriate plan of treatment.

COMPUTERS IN PERSONAL INJURY LITIGATION

Douglas B. Abrams

The advent of computers represents an advance of overwhelming importance and potential for plaintiffs' lawyers. Plaintiffs' attorneys can benefit from using computer technology even more than defense attorneys. Generally, the defendants have sufficient resources to hire whatever person-power they require. With computers, plaintiffs' attorneys can balance the superior resources of the defendants to organize and prepare cases with increased efficiency.

Unfortunately, to many attorneys, using a computer seems unrealistic. Perhaps an attorney's reluctance to use a computer stems from the fear of failure. "I've practiced successfully without computers for 25 years and I'm not about to change now," is a typical reaction from longtime trial lawyers. Yet a computer is no more difficult to use than a video cassette recorder. Another concern may be the perceived high cost of computers; the proliferation of computer equipment and software, however, has lowered the price of a basic computer hardware system to less than that of an expensive stereo system.

The time is rapidly approaching when the use of computers may be necessary to maintain an efficient law office. More important than office efficiency, however, is the responsibility the lawyer owes to the victims of negligence. Not only are these victims entitled to be represented by lawyers with advanced trial and negotiation skills, they deserve attorneys who will develop their cases using all available and feasible technology. The use of computers will eventually be so widespread and necessary that the following principles may come to apply:

- it is economically feasible to use computers;
- using computers will assist the plaintiff's lawyer in advancing the plaintiff's cause; and
- it is unacceptable to fail to use economically feasible and technologically available means to increase the chance of the plaintiff's case succeeding.

This chapter presents an outline of the methods for computerizing, as well as a discussion of computer uses in a personal injury law practice.

COMPUTER USE

Concepts and Definitions

A general understanding of basic computer language is helpful for lawyers who are converting to computer use. The following is an elementary glossary.

Hardware

Hardware is the physical machinery used with computers, including the components. A basic computer hardware system usually consists of the computer itself, a monitor, a keyboard, and a printer.

Software

Software is the term used for computer programs that perform various tasks. Word processing, accounting, database, and communication programs are examples of different types of software.

Modems

Modems enable a computer to send and receive information via telephone lines. These devices can be either external (fitting outside the computer) or internal (fitting inside the computer). Modems vary in speed—defined in bauds (the number of characters per second)—the higher the speed of transfer, the greater the cost. Speeds range between 1,200 bauds and 9,600 bauds.

Operating Systems

DOS (disk operating system) is a software that controls the basic operation of the computer. The company that developed DOS, Microsoft, continues to refine the system, and therefore different versions of it are available. Unix is another operating system. Novell's NetWare is a personal computer–based network operating system. Unix and NetWare were designed as multitask and multi-user systems.

RAM

RAM (random access memory) chips enable the computer to do functions such as word processing and mathematical calculations. Functions performed in RAM occur very rapidly—because they are performed by electrical pulses rather than by a mechanical device—but generally are lost when the computer is turned off.

Hard-Disk Drives

Hard-disk drives store information the same way cassette tapes or videotapes do; data is magnetically stored on a medium—for a hard disk, the data is stored on a metal platter. Hard-disk drives vary greatly in their speed and in the amount of information they can store. The amount of information that can be stored is measured in megabytes. A megabyte is approximately one million bytes or characters of information. For example, hard-disk drives having 80 megabytes of storage capability can store almost 84 million characters of information, which is roughly equivalent to 40,000 pages of double-spaced text.

Floppy Disks

Floppy disks are removable disks, usually 5-1/4" or 3-1/2", that are inserted into the computer's disk drive.

Networking

Networking is the process by which several computers are linked together. A network usually has a central computer called the "file server." This computer stores software and data files that other computers in the network may use and share. Networking requires not only the actual physical linkage of computers, it also requires networking programs or software.

Multitasking

Multitasking is the process by which a computer may be programmed to do different functions at essentially the same time. The computer cannot actually perform the functions simultaneously, but its speed is so rapid that the functions appear to be simultaneous.

Word Processing

Word-processing software packages allow the user to compose text by typing on the computer keyboard. Major word-processing packages enable the user to use footnotes or to move and copy words or paragraphs within a document or from one document to another.

Data Processing

Data-processing software enables the computer to analyze and compare information that is typed into the computer. Data-processing software lets the user create an "electronic file-cabinet" and combine, sort, and store information with amazing speed.

Computer-assisted Research

The computer user can do research by using the computer and a modem to enter large commercial databases. The organizations supplying these research database services generally charge fees based on usage time. (Legal databases include Lexis and Westlaw.) After connecting with a database, the user can instruct the computer to search for specific information.

Laptop Computers

Laptop computers are small computers, usually capable of running on batteries, that can be easily carried from place to place.

ASCII

ASCII is one of the standard formats for representing the characters used in programming. Use of ASCII symbols enables information to be shared between programs. ASCII stands for American Standard Code for Information Interchange.

PURCHASING CONSIDERATIONS

In general, the world of computers is divided between IBM-compatible computers and Apple/Macintosh computers. The Macintosh computer is made by Apple Corporation and is used primarily in business. Apple Corporation still makes other models under the Apple name, but those are home computers rarely used in business.

IBM-compatible machines are the computers most widely used in the business world and specifically by attorneys. More business software programs have been written for IBM-compatible computers than for Apple/Macintosh computers. However, many users advocate Apple/Macintosh computers because they are user-friendly and have easy and effective graphics capability.

Apple/Macintosh computers are more expensive than IBM-compatible computers. Furthermore, the hardware and software necessary to allow Apple/Macintosh computers to communicate with IBM-compatible computers is currently expensive.

The widespread use of IBM-compatible computers gives an important advantage to the office maintaining an IBM-compatible system. Many times the user of an IBM-compatible computer can simply take or send a floppy disk to another law office and transfer information from the disk directly into the other law office's computer.

Office Analysis

If you are deciding whether to purchase computer hardware and software, a systematic review will help you avoid frustration and economic woes. First, diagram your present office arrangement. The flow of work is an important consideration. Second, talk with other attorneys with similar law practices to discuss methods of handling computerization. Third, read computer magazines to become familiar with computer jargon. Fourth, interview independent computer consultants, being careful to avoid hiring anyone who is more interested in selling a particular brand of hardware or software than in developing a workable system for you.

In analyzing an existing computer system to determine whether or not to upgrade, you should also do a systematic review. First, diagram your present office arrangement, listing all existing equipment. Second, diagram the flow of work. Third, hold a staff meeting to discuss whether the staff has difficulties with the present system. Fourth, seek an independent consultant to review the present system.

Hardware and Software Options

Networking

Networking, when effective, may offer advantages such as increased uniformity in the information available to the lawyers and staff. For example, networking simplifies the use of forms by allowing all lawyers and staff members immediate access to the same files. Efficiency is touted as another advantage of networking; a network user can send information directly from one computer to another without walking. Generally, the larger the office, the more advantages arise from networking. However, networking has its own problems. For example, many security issues arise, particularly with information requiring different levels of confidentiality. In addition, equipment failure can be more disruptive when all computers are connected. Nevertheless, in the future, as the software for networking improves, networking will be the rule for almost all professional offices.

At present, in deciding whether to network, the considerations would be whether to use a DOS-based or a Unix-based system. A detailed analysis of the differences between DOS-based and Unix-based systems is beyond the scope of this chapter. Generally, when a Unix-based system is first installed, it tends to need more sophisticated programming than a DOS-based system would need, and therefore may require more start-up time. However, proponents of Unix-based networks claim that Unix-based systems are inherently more powerful and more efficient that DOS-based systems. Furthermore, proponents of Unix assert that recent developments have made Unix easier to use.

A network generally costs more than stand-alone computers. Networks require additional programming and hardware. Networking also requires more interaction between computer users and computer system designers and programmers.

Novell is a company that provides software for networking called NetWare. Novell-based networks are among the most common types of personal computer (PC) networks.

DOS, Unix, and NetWare are operating systems that run on a PC. DOS was designed as only a non-networking, non-multiuser system, whereas Unix and NetWare were designed with networking and multitasking in mind. DOS and NetWare can use standard PC software, whereas generally Unix needs special versions of software. However, within the next few years this incompatibility is likely to be overcome by software programs.

Again, a common failure of networking occurs when the file server (the central computer for the network) has inadequate processing speed and inadequate storage. In the present state of hardware, an 80386-based machine would be the minimum computer to serve as a file server. Similarly, in a law firm setting, the lawyers should consider providing hard-disk drives on the network terminals (usually referred to as work stations) to minimize the likelihood that the file server will become burdened with vast amounts of correspondence. If the network terminals do not have hard disks for storage, relatively unimportant items such as letters could slow and clutter the file server.

Word Processing

The use of computers for word processing is remarkably important to the trial lawyer. The most effective use of word processing is for the lawyer to draft documents directly on the computer. To use a word processor, an attorney simply needs to learn how to type.

PC Magazine summarized major word-processing programs.[1] You may get the article at a library or from *PC Magazine*.

According to the editors of *PC Magazine*, WordPerfect Version 5.1 and Microsoft Word Version 5.0 ranked high in suitability for law office use. Many lawyers use WordPerfect 5.0 or 5.1 as their word-processing software. Microsoft Word Version 5.0 is another well-regarded word-processing system. MultiMate is an effective, but less-used, brand of word-processing software. Virtually every well-recognized type of word-processing system is acceptable.

1 PC MAGAZINE 9 (Dec. 11, 1990): 107-192.

Lawyers who draft their own documents have a significant advantage over lawyers who are not able to use computers. This is especially true for those with access to laptop computers. For example, during a trial it sometimes becomes necessary to make a motion on a particular point. To supply the necessary document, some law offices will create a crisis atmosphere and require staff to return to work after hours. A less stressful and more effective solution is for the lawyer to take a portable computer to the office or home and draft the document. A laptop computer is extremely useful when the lawyer is handling a case in a county or state away from the home office.

Word processing also permits more efficient use of forms. A memorandum of law or discovery drafted for one case can readily be redrafted for use in another lawsuit. Using computers to prepare documents, a lawyer may also share memoranda and briefs with another law firm by sending or taking to the other firm a floppy disk containing the information. Furthermore, depositions may be placed on computer disks and sections made readily available for use in motions and memoranda. Today, many court reporters will supply not only the traditional paper copy of a deposition but also a copy of the deposition on floppy disk, formatted in ASCII. In this format, the text of the deposition can be accepted by virtually every word-processing program.

In some situations, a lawyer can bring either a laptop portable computer or a transportable computer to a deposition. When seeking information concerning a particular document from a recalcitrant witness, the lawyer can draft a request for production during a recess and, back on the record, ask the witness whether the witness understands the character and nature of the document requested.

Exhibits can also be prepared during the deposition for use in the deposition and later at trial. This procedure can be extremely effective during videotaped depositions because it provides visualization of evidence or illustrative embellishment of the witness's testimony.

In-house brief banks should use word processing or data management. With texts of briefs stored on the word processor, material from long-closed cases can be used and customized for a new case. An example of a brief bank on a database system is attached as Appendix A. In addition, surveys can be rapidly developed for submission to potential witnesses (see Appendix B).

Databases

Over the past few years, extremely powerful and inexpensive database software packages have become available. The uses of data processing are limited only by the creative intellect of the user. These software packages permit the lawyer to store and retrieve vast amounts of information quickly. A database is the computer equivalent of a file cabinet replete with files. The lawyer is able to create different indexes to organize the material. One example of how a database can be useful is the creation of a list of all cases in which a particular expert testified in a products liability case with regard to the inadequacy of warnings and the cases in which warnings were held adequate. Rather than fumbling through endless files during a deposition, the lawyer can pause, check the computer (or the printed copy of the database file), and then question the witness.

In cases involving numerous documents, data management and a database are very helpful. The lawyer can gather from many sources answers to interrogatories from other cases where the defendant admitted knowledge of the defect and can enter this information in a database. Because each database management and processing system is different, this chapter will not address the methods of creating such systems.

The use of data management works well when the lawyer carries the system with a portable computer; the data management system may then be used during depositions or in other lawyers' offices.

A lawyer beginning to use a database should consult an independent consultant. Programming a system can be done either by the firm's staff or by the independent consultant.

Research

The widespread use of the computer has led to the availability of computerized legal and medical research. The cost for joining a research system is comparatively small and can be well justified. Westlaw and Lexis are the major vendors of computerized legal and medical research services. Each has its own proponents, but either would be satisfactory for most law firms. The services, moreover, extend well beyond legal research. For example, services such as Medline are available for conducting medical literature searches.

By using a portable computer and a modem, a lawyer can access the entire body of case law and medical journals from an office.

Computerized research services are developing rapidly and will soon, if not already, be a necessity.

Law Office Management

Law office management systems have been available for the last several years. These software packages perform a wide variety of tasks, including maintaining witness lists, tracking case status, and, most importantly, docket control. As integrated comprehensive systems are developed, lawyers stand to benefit even more. These systems, working with word processing, will take variables for a particular case and create pleadings and discovery documents—in minutes rather than hours. These systems will also address and print standard letters from a computer checklist. Attending an ATLA Convention and touring the vendors' booths is an excellent way to learn about state-of-the-art systems.

These systems have some degree of sophistication and expense. Systems that can be programmed to fit a particular law firm's practice are more desirable than systems that cannot be customized. For maximum efficiency, a law office management system should not be undertaken until the entire staff, including lawyers, is familiar with a word-processing system, such as WordPerfect, Wordstar, or MultiMate. In some law firms, only a few of the lawyers understand the use of the firm's entire computerized system, and the usefulness of the system is undermined. All the staff must be trained on the system. One way to increase efficiency of training is to hire an independent consultant to train the staff and have the session videotaped. Often the information the consultant gives seems clear at the time of the presentation, but later confusion develops. In this situation the training videotape can be a helpful reference. Also, a person having difficulty can view the videotaped session privately to reinforce what's been taught.

A system known as the PINS computer system is one of the best-known law office management systems.

Communications

Communication software packages can be of great benefit to the trial lawyer. These software packages, now quite inexpensive, work with modems to transmit information over telephone lines. Lawyers using communication packages can rapidly transmit briefs from one law firm to the next much as documents are sent by fax. However, with communication packages, documents can be put into the computer without retyping.

Additionally, using a modem, the lawyer can have access to his or her own office computer file from home, from another lawyer's office, or from a hotel. This increased access to the lawyer's main office computer would be quite valuable.

In the same vein, some lawyers within ATLA are proposing a system of communication between different law firms using electronic bulletin boards. An electronic bulletin board is a message- and file-transfer system in which messages and files may be transferred by modem to any computer that calls the bulletin board. New developments in cases would be posted on the boards. The use of electronic bulletin boards will probably increase rapidly over the next five years, and they may become an important tool in the trial lawyer's practice.

Carbon Copy Plus is a software program that permits a computer user to transmit information from one computer to another. This type of package is sometimes referred to as a "remote computer access" program. For example, a lawyer located in another city could call the home office to engage Carbon Copy Plus. Thereafter, by calling the home office number, the lawyer could have the same access to the computer as if she or he were at the office.

Accounting and Billing

The usefulness of computerized accounting and billing may be self-evident. Many accounting software packages are available. Independent consultants should be retained to analyze the law firm's accounting systems and perhaps to customize the firm's bookkeeping software package. Available software packages include Moneycounts, Quicken, and Timeslips III.

Computerized Depositions and Searches

Hardware that can store many depositions on computer disks is available. Software packages are also available that can rapidly search through the computerized depositions for specific parts of the deposition. Where numerous depositions are taken in a case, this tool can be invaluable for assessing areas in which defendants have contradicted themselves. The use of computerized depositions will increase rapidly over the next several years.

Word Processing and Database Integration

For attorneys using word-processing and database packages, transfer of data between these two types of programs is a continuing issue. Many word-processing programs, such as WordPerfect 5.1 and MultiMate Advantage, permit the word processor to accept or "import" data from database programs. Promotional material for a recent software package entitled "Outside In" claims that the software can import and export files from data-processing programs to and from word-processing programs. Similarly, software packages are available to convert entire documents from one word-processing format to another.

Form Documents

An important use of the computer is to develop forms for use in litigation. The user enters data, and the computer substitutes these data—names or descriptions—for the variables in a form document. For example, in products liability cases, interrogatories can be drafted so that the computer will substitute the identity of a specific product in appropriate places throughout the document. A sample of this type of interrogatory form is attached as Appendix C to this chapter.

SUMMARY

The potential for the use of computers in personal injury cases is overwhelming, and lawyers who make full use of available technology will have substantial advantages in their representation of clients. The process of computerization is neither difficult nor unduly expensive; the time when computers will be used by lawyers as frequently as dictating machines is not far off.

APPENDIX A

BRIEF BANK

Title of Document	Contents	Letter	Number
Accident Reconstruction	Admissibility of Speed— Article in The Litigator	A	663
Accident Reconstruction	Frederick Ryder	A	465
Accident Reconstruction	N.C. Case Law re: Accident Reconstruction Opinion—List of cases compiled by Jay Trehy	A	483
Accident Reconstruction	Testing	A	526
Accident Reconstruction	Questions for Experts	A	646
Accident Reconstruction Evidence	Peggy Abrams's Paper: Evidentiary Problems in the Use of Reconstruction Testimony	A	495
Account Stated	Requested Instructions	A	38
Accountant's Liability		A	206
Accountant's Malpractice Liability		A	265
Administrative Law	Effectiveness of Oral Notice of Resignation— Haley v. North Carolina State University (1978)	A	241

APPENDIX B

QUESTIONNAIRE

3-WHEELED ALL-TERRAIN VEHICLES

To: Mr. John Thomas Jones
100 Maple Street
Raleigh, NC 27607
919/833-4509

Please Circle Your Responses to the Questions Below

1. Did you know that the United States Government has *banned* further sales of 3-wheeled A.T.V.'s by manufacturers in this country?

   Yes No

2. What *type* of A.T.V. did you purchase from Honda of Raleigh?

   3-wheeler 4-wheeler other

3. What *year* did you purchase your A.T.V.? ________________

4. What was the *engine size* of your A.T.V.? (in cubic centimeters)

   250cc 200cc 175cc 125cc 110cc 70cc other ____ cc

5. Who was the A.T.V. purchased *for*?

Child Only	Adult and Child	Adult Only

6. Did you tell the Honda salesman who would be riding the Honda A.T.V. you purchased?

   Yes No

7. If you were purchasing the A.T.V. for regular or even occasional use by children, what *size* A.T.V. did the Honda salesman *recommend* to you?

   250cc 200cc 175cc 125cc 110cc 70cc other ____ cc

8. If applicable, was the *child present* at Honda of Raleigh when the A.T.V. was purchased?

Yes No

9. If applicable, state *age* of child(ren) present.

5-8 years 9-11 years 12-14 years 15-16 years over 16 years

10. Did the Honda of Raleigh salesman *demonstrate* the Honda A.T.V. by riding it around the premises or parking lot?

Yes No

11. If you were given a riding demonstration of the A.T.V., did the Honda salesman *wear* the following:

a. A crash helmet? Yes No

b. Safety goggles? Yes No

c. Protective gloves? Yes No

d. Safety boots? Yes No

Thank you, Mr. Jones, for taking the time to answer these questions. A postage paid envelope is enclosed for your convenience in returning this questionnaire.

[Name of attorney/firm]

[Address]

APPENDIX C

IN THE UNITED STATES DISTRICT COURT
FOR THE EASTERN DISTRICT OF NORTH CAROLINA
RALEIGH DIVISION
CIVIL ACTION NO.: ________

________ Plaintiff	)	
	)	
v.	)	INTERROGATORIES
	)	(Products Liability Cases)
	)	
________ Defendant	)	

PLAINTIFF'S FIRST INTERROGATORIES TO DEFENDANT
____

Pursuant to Rule 33 of the Federal Rules of Civil Procedure, the Plaintiff hereby requests that the Defendant, ___________, through its officers or agent, serve upon the Plaintiff within forty-five (45) days after service of the Summons and Complaint sworn answers to the Interrogatories set forth below:

DEFINITIONS

The following definitions apply to terms used in this set of Interrogatories.

1. The words "you," "your," and "your company" mean the corporate defendant separately answering these interrogatories; its parent(s); its merged, consolidated, or acquired predecessors, divisions, subsidiaries, and/or affiliates, including present and former officers, directors, agents, employees, lawyers, legal assistants, and all other persons acting or purporting to act on behalf of the corporate defendant or its predecessors, subsidiaries, and/or affiliates. "Predecessor(s)" means any business firm, whether or not incorporated, that had all or some of its assets purchased by you or came to be acquired by you, whether by merger, consolidation, or otherwise. "Successors" means any business firm, whether or not incorporated, that purchased all or some of your assets or that

acquired you or any of your predecessors, whether by merger, consolidation, or otherwise.

2. As used herein, the words "document" and "documents" include any written, printed, recorded, or graphic matter; photographic matter or sound reproductions; or computer input or output, however produced or reproduced, that (1) are now or were formerly in the possession, custody, or control of the defendant company (including documents at any time in the possession, custody, or control of their domestically domiciled subsidiaries or merged or acquired predecessors); or (2) are known or are believed to be responsive to these interrogatories, regardless of who now has or formerly had custody, possession, or control.

3. As used herein, the words "person" and "persons" include natural persons, firms, partnerships, associations, joint ventures, corporations, and any other form of business organization or arrangement.

INSTRUCTIONS

1. If the interrogatory asks for information that could have at some time been answered by consulting documents that are no longer in existence, then do the following in answer to such interrogatory:
   a. identify what information was maintained;
   b. identify all the type(s) of documents that contained such information;
   c. state the time period during which such documents were maintained;
   d. state the circumstances under which such documents ceased to exist;
   e. state the date when such documents ceased to exist;
   f. identify all persons having knowledge of the circumstances under which such documents ceased to exist; and
   g. identify all persons who have knowledge or had knowledge of the documents and the contents thereof.
2. The Defendant is reminded of its duty to supplement its responses, pursuant to FED. R. CIV. P. 26(e)(1) and (2).

PROCEDURE

If the Defendant exercises its option under Rule 33(c) of the Federal Rules of Civil Procedure to produce business recordings in lieu of responding to any interrogatory, the following procedure is to be followed:

1. In response to each such interrogatory, the Defendant shall state
    a. the identity of the records containing the answer;
    b. whether other copies of each record presently exist and if so, identify (1) the location of other copies by stating the name(s) of the file(s) in which they are kept and (2) the person(s) who received copies thereof;
    c. whether other copies of each record ever existed and if so, for each record identify (1) each file in which a copy was maintained, (2) the dates during which such record was in existence, (3) the circumstances under which such record ceased to exist, (4) all persons having knowledge of the circumstances under which such record ceased to exist, and (5) all persons receiving copies of such records; and
    d. the identity of all persons reviewing such documents.
2. In producing such records, the defendant will produce such records separately and will designate the interrogatory or interrogatories to which such record responds, as well as the identification of the file(s) from which the documents were segregated.

INTERROGATORIES

1. Identify and describe the responsibilities of the officer or officers of the Defendant who are supplying the answers to these interrogatories.
2. Identify the officer or officers or employees of the Defendant who were responsible for negotiating and executing the sale of the subject [describe the product or equipment] (hereinafter referred to as equipment) to whomever you sold it.
3. Identify the buyer and describe the marketing process that placed the subject equipment into commerce, identifying every distributor or "middleman" who handled the unit.
4. Do you have a predecessor or successor that was or is involved in the manufacture or marketing of the equipment? If so, identify the predecessor or successor and the predecessor's or successor's relationship to the present Defendant.
5. As applies to the equipment, state the following:
    a. the date the equipment was first commercially sold;
    b. the date and place where the equipment was designed or developed;
    c. the identity and present whereabouts of the person or per-

sons responsible for the design of the development of the equipment;

d. the identity and present location of all records describing and dealing with the design and development of the equipment; and

e. the identity and present location of all records dealing with the testing of the equipment.

6. Specify with particularity every safety precaution that the Plaintiff could have taken in placing the equipment [or its component] in operation.

7. Do you have a manual or instruction pamphlet or other literature that is normally supplied to the purchaser of the subject equipment? If so, describe it with particularity, or in lieu thereof attach copies of all such literature to your answers to these interrogatories.

8. At the time of the development of the equipment did you attempt to determine whether the product complied with the then applicable safety standards, safety orders, regulations, laws, rules, and design requirements of any city, county, state, or the federal government of the United States? Describe all such investigations.

9. With respect to the [component] of the equipment, state whether there has been any change, alteration, or modification (hereinafter collectively called "change") from when it was first developed to the present. If so, state

a. the nature of each such change,

b. the reason for each such change,

c. the details of how the changed equipment differed from the original product, and

d. the date each change was accepted by you and made commercially available.

10. Describe every known occurrence of a failure on the part of the [component].

11. Do you know the cause of or have a reasonable hypothesis to explain the failure of the equipment as alleged in the complaint? If so, please describe your hypothesis.

12. How could you have prevented the failure of the equipment?

13. Have you ever considered having a safety device or design or mechanism built on the equipment as to prevent the failure of the equipment?

14. If you have ever considered such a safety device or design or mechanism, identify all documents or any policy discussed or adopt-

ed with respect to such device.

15. Describe any meeting at which such safety policy or device was discussed.

16. Are any warnings about use and dangers inscribed on or otherwise physically attached to the equipment? If so, please identify the location and content of the warnings.

17. Are any warnings, cautions, or other notices of danger supplied in any manner whatsoever to users or maintenance personnel of the equipment? If so, please describe the manner and content of these warnings.

18. Have any persons other than the Plaintiff ever been injured in an accident involving similar equipment? If so, identify each such person.

19. If claims have been asserted or filed by any of the persons named in the answer to the preceding interrogatory, identify for each such person his or her attorney, the court in which any actions were filed, and the outcome of any such action.

20. Identify the sales contract and invoice for the sale of the subject equipment, or in lieu thereof, attach a copy of the contract and invoice.

21. Describe any warranties, written or oral, and any disclaimer of warranties, written or oral, made by you to the purchaser of the equipment that injured the Plaintiff.

22. Describe any orientation or training procedures followed by you, your agents, or your distributors when your equipment is purchased.

23. Describe any change in the warning applicable to the equipment that caused the injury to the Plaintiff, subsequent to the equipment's being manufactured.

24. Identify any known complaints or injuries involving possible dangers or risks in the subject equipment that have been filed with the Occupational Safety and Health Administration, the Consumer Product Safety Commission, or any other federal, state, or local government agency.

25. Identify any expert you intend to call at the trial of this matter, the subject matter on which the expert is expected to testify, the substance of the expert's facts and opinions, and a summary of the grounds for each opinion.

26. Identify the engineer or other person on your staff who is most familiar with the design and manufacture of your [equipment] in-

cluding the [component].
27. Identify all documents, including but not limited to reports, internal memoranda, transcripts, statements, statistical charts, patents, or blueprints that relate in any way to the [component] and your [equipment].
28. Identify the name and address of your insurance company or companies.
29. Identify your insurance policy number or numbers and state the limitation of coverage for each policy. If you have excess coverage, please give the identical information for your excess coverage policy.

The ______________ day of __________________ , 19 __ .

[NAME OF ATTORNEY/FIRM]

____

[Name of attorney/firm]
[Address]
[Telephone number]

ALTERNATIVES TO LITIGATION: MEDIATION AND ARBITRATION

Michael S. Gillie

The courts of this country should not be the places where the resolution of disputes begins. They should be the places where disputes end—after alternative methods of resolving disputes have been considered and tried.
— Justice Sandra Day O'Connor

ALTERNATIVE DISPUTE RESOLUTION

Introduction

It is often difficult for tort victims to handle the delay, expense, and stress of litigation. While litigation is essential in many cases, there are now relatively new forums (at least in a tort litigation context) that may assist in resolving litigation before trial. This chapter discusses these alternatives to resolving litigation and explains why all parties to a dispute have an incentive to use them.

The two major forms of alternative dispute resolution (ADR) are *mediation* and *private arbitration*. In mediation, the parties attempt to settle their differences by meeting with an impartial expert who has no authority to force an agreement or render a decision. As will be discussed in this chapter, mediation is often more effective than direct negotiation, and thus it enhances the parties' ability to reach an early settlement. In a variety of legal areas, mediation has a success rate of 80 percent or better, making it a sensible step for many parties.

In private arbitration, parties present their case to a neutral third party for a legally binding decision. The arbitration proceedings are outside the court system, but arbitration statutes allow the arbitrator's decision to be enforced like a court judgment. Mediation and arbitration are often used together—mediation to define the dispute and settle as many issues as possible, arbitration then being available for any unsettled issues. Using this approach, the parties are able to settle their dispute fully without venturing into the court system.

The increased use of ADR enjoys broad-based support. Many local bar associations support ADR in a variety of ways—from establishing committees to funding programs. Courts are actively using ADR, and many judges are working to increase such use. In addition, the business community, led by the insurance industry, is rapidly moving to increase its use of such alternatives. Most major insurance companies now have formal in-house programs to encourage their claims representatives to use mediation, and hundreds of corporations—the heart of corporate America—have pledged to use more ADR techniques for their disputes. As a result, the use of mediation and arbitration is growing at a geometric rate, and numerous ADR programs, both public and private, have been established to meet this demand.

This chapter begins with an analysis of the way ADR affects attorneys and the practice of law. This is followed by an explanation of how the insurance industry, and business in general, is using these alternatives. The heart of the chapter is a detailed description and analysis of mediation and private arbitration. Finally, more specialized types of ADR, such as mini-trials, summary jury trials, and class action administration, are discussed.

Philosophy of Dispute Resolution

The goal of dispute resolution is to settle the case swiftly and fairly and with the least possible intervention by an outside third party. Thus, assuming quality representation on all sides, an agreed-upon settlement is always better than a rendered decision. Mediation—a process with a proven ability to achieve settlements—should be considered in every case. Arbitration, which compares favorably with the court system in terms of speed and expense, still involves a binding decision by an outside party—a decision that one side or the other could be dissatisfied with. Thus mediation is the favored alternative.

It is important to note that ADR is not a replacement for the jury system—ADR requires a strong court system to be effective. This is particularly true with regard to mediation, where the parties analyze what will happen to the case if it isn't settled. As in direct settlement negotiations, the threat of litigation and a jury trial is what causes defendants to make reasonable offers.

ADR and the Practice of Law

The expanding use of mediation and arbitration is having an effect on the day-to-day practice of law. Traditionally, the options available to an attorney handling a claim were to settle the case through direct negotiations or go to trial. On this very basic level, there wasn't any difference between handling one claim and the next—the approach was always the same. Mediation and arbitration have changed that situation by offering sensible alternatives that should be considered for every case. If the client needs a relatively quick, final decision, arbitration may be appropriate. If the disputing parties would benefit from an in-depth analysis of the strengths and weaknesses of the claim, you should consider proposing mediation. ADR isn't right for every case, but it can be effective in many cases. Thus the lawyer's role is to select the right approach for each particular case, rather than to proceed automatically to trial.

Stated another way, the law is evolving not only substantively—through statutes and case law—but procedurally as well. Few areas of law are changing as quickly as dispute resolution procedures—each year brings numerous new applications and innovations. And every year the number of attorneys and businesspeople who become believers in ADR increases dramatically. These changes have made ADR a part of the day-to-day practice of law.

Finally, the increased use of ADR techniques alters the role of the attorney in the dispute resolution process. As noted above, advising a client already involves considering a number of options, and those options will increase. But attorneys also have a prominent role in the processes. As the use of ADR increases, so does the need for mediators and arbitrators. Attorneys are already the most prominent professionals in ADR, and many attorneys have developed a significant practice acting as mediators, arbitrators, ADR administrators, and designers of customized ADR programs. From a professional point of view, every practicing attorney should be familiar with ADR techniques.

How Insurance Companies and Other Businesses Approach ADR

Insurance companies have a greater incentive to use ADR than any other type of business. This is because an insurance company's litigation expense is a disproportionately large part of its operating budget, and if the company can lower its litigation costs, it can increase its profits substantially. It is not surprising that the insurance industry has taken the lead in using ADR techniques.

In the early 1980s a number of insurance companies—notably The Travelers, The Hartford, and Maryland Casualty—established pilot projects to test the effectiveness of mediation and arbitration. The companies were generally pleased with the results, and their programs were expanded. Since the mid-1980s, most other major insurance companies, and many smaller and regional companies, have established ADR programs.

The insurance companies are using ADR to cut down on their litigation and administrative expenses. ADR, by providing early resolutions, helps the companies save attorney fees, expert costs, discovery expenses, and administrative time. Industry estimates of savings range from $1,000 to $3,000 for soft-tissue automobile accident cases to much higher savings for bigger cases. Settlements also help remove uncertainty from the planning process and free up reserves so additional business can be written. For these reasons, the insurance industry is very enthusiastic about ADR.

Although ADR approaches differ from company to company, the basic approach taken is usually as follows: the company announces a corporate policy in favor of using ADR and sets ever-increasing goals for the number of cases to be submitted to this process. It establishes a home office ADR director whose job it is to promote the use of alternatives within the company. That person develops educational materials and an approved list of mediation/arbitration agencies that the field claims offices may use.

Many companies also establish an ADR expert in each claims office. To increase the number of cases sent to ADR, some companies use a quota system—"you will send ________ cases to mediation each month"—while others use incentives such as days off or trips to Hawaii as awards for case submissions. Motivating field people can be difficult, and many companies do not have as many submissions as they would like. They are thus often receptive to proposals by the plaintiff's bar to mediate or arbitrate (this is usually done through an ADR agency, with the agency having the ability to go directly to the claims manager or the company's ADR director if necessary).

Following the lead of the insurance industry, other businesses and industries are also making ADR a part of their day-to-day claims processing. Many of the Fortune 500 companies are self-insured, which requires them to maintain in-house claims departments. Therefore, these companies have the same incentives as the insurance companies to participate in ADR.

Finally, it is worth noting that in this insurance/business area, mediation has generally been found to be a more satisfactory process than arbitration. This is because mediation takes much less time and expense to complete, and the parties keep control of the outcome. These reasons, coupled with the fact that mediation is successful in the vast majority of cases, make mediation the most popular and fastest-growing ADR method for tort and commercial cases.

MEDIATION FOR CIVIL CASES

Introduction

Mediation is a method of settlement negotiation where the parties to a dispute sit down with an impartial third party, the mediator, and attempt to resolve their differences. Unlike arbitration, the mediator has no power to render a decision or force the parties to accept a settlement. Instead, the mediator uses a variety of procedures and techniques to help the parties arrive at a resolution.

Mediation is frequently successful, and, as mentioned above, it is not uncommon for mediation programs to have settlement rates of 80 percent or better.

Mediation has been effectively applied in a number of legal areas. Consider the following descriptions of cases that have been successfully mediated around the country:

- A young boy was killed when the cover of a dumpster slammed shut on his neck (Portland, OR).
- A tourist's easily treated problem was misdiagnosed, causing permanent blindness (Honolulu, HI).
- Defective warning as to torque capability of tongs that hold the drill pipe in place on an offshore oil rig resulted in serious injury (New Orleans, LA).
- Farm machinery lacked sufficient guard and injured a worker's leg (Milwaukee, WI).
- A child was killed as the result of defective highway design (Rochester, NY).
- A sponge was left in a patient after surgery (Phoenix, AZ).
- A dental device caused the patient to suffer a serious infection (Indianapolis, IN).
- Defective grain treatment caused a farmer to suffer crop loss (Seattle, WA).
- A commercial hand drill shorted out, throwing its user against a wall and causing him to suffer serious back injury (Philadelphia, PA).
- A home swimming pool filter exploded, injuring the owner (St. Louis, MO).
- A front-end loader had a defective shifting mechanism that caused it to run over the driver (Chicago, IL).
- A child was electrocuted by a short in an electric fan (Atlanta, GA).
- A pharmacy gave a wrong medication that nearly killed a patient (Boston, MA).
- A person attending a rock concert was pushed and suffered serious injury (Los Angeles, CA).
- A pit bull with a "propensity for roaming and attacking"

attacked a motorcyclist. The motorcyclist was seriously injured; the dog was killed (Denver, CO).

- A lawyer failed to file two personal injury lawsuits before the statute of limitations ran out (Phoenix, AZ).
- A leaking gasoline storage tank contaminated surrounding groundwater (Casper, WY).
- A claimant stopped to help a disabled vehicle and was hit by third vehicle (Salt Lake City, UT).
- A highway was designed defectively (Missoula, MT).
- A doctor and hospital were sued for a practical joke involving the doctor taping peanuts onto a "certain part of the male anatomy" following disc surgery, causing embarrassment and concern to the patient and his spouse (location withheld by request).

Agreement To Mediate

By agreeing to mediate, parties are simply agreeing to take part in a settlement negotiation with the help of a neutral expert. They are not agreeing to settle, and the mediator has no authority to force them to do so. Either party may terminate the mediation process at any time without cause.

Convincing all sides to mediate is often the most difficult aspect of the mediation process. This is largely due to a lack of knowledge about the process, coupled with a fear that anything being offered by the other side must be detrimental. These barriers will come down as attorneys become more familiar with the process, and they realize that there is little to lose—and everything to gain—by participating in a mediation session. In short, all sides usually benefit from an early settlement, and mediation increases the chances of achieving that goal.

Parties typically sign a written mediation agreement that deals with such matters as identification of the mediator, fees, and guarantees of confidentiality.

Mediation Session

All sides to a dispute will be present at the mediation session. For example, participants in an automobile collision case will usually include the plaintiff and her attorney, an insurance company representative, a defense attorney, and the mediator. Usually the mediator will be an attorney with expertise in the particular area of law who has received training in mediation techniques.

The typical first step is a joint session where all sides will sit down together in a conference room. After introductory remarks by the mediator, each side will be given the opportunity to explain its position and describe the evidence it will offer if the matter goes to trial. Such presentations, preferably in the form of a relatively short and informal opening statement, help everyone understand the case so that they can effectively analyze the risks.

After the joint session, the mediator will meet with each side individually. These separate meetings, called caucuses, are confidential, and it is very common for the mediator to have a number of caucuses with each party. In each caucus the mediator will discuss the risks of the case—best and worst outcomes, quality of evidence, and costs of litigation. This helps everyone—particularly the clients—understand the case.

The mediator will also confidentially explore possible settlements with each side and attempt to determine where the case might be settled. This helps remove the posturing from the negotiations by allowing a party to propose its true settlement position without disclosing it to the other side and thereby appearing to be weak or caving in.

A case history follows:

> A head-on collision between a truck and a car resulted in the deaths of the automobile driver and his three passengers. Wrongful death claims in excess of $2.5 million were brought against the owner of the truck. There was evidence of drinking on the part of the automobile driver, and cross-claims were filed among the plaintiffs.
>
> Discovery showed that eyewitness testimony and experts' accident reconstructions were conflicting and contradictory. The case also involved a significant jurisdictional issue. After the case had been languishing in court for a number of years, the defendant's insurance company and the four plaintiffs' attorneys agreed to mediate and a mediation session was scheduled. The parties selected an experienced personal injury attorney as the mediator.
>
> The mediation session was attended by the plaintiffs' attorneys and representatives of each estate, insurance represen-

tatives and defense attorneys, and the mediator. It is worth noting that this was the first time that all the parties described above had been in the same room together. The parties first participated in a "joint session", where each side was given the opportunity to explain its position. The mediator then met with each party privately, beginning with the plaintiffs. Strong points, weak points, and conflicting evidence were analyzed in detail and it became clear that, as is often the case, a jury trial would be a substantial risk for all involved. In a separate meeting with the plaintiffs' attorneys and their clients, the mediator was able to achieve a tentative agreement as to how the cross-claims would be handled if the plaintiffs could reach a settlement with the insurance company. Also in separate meetings, the mediator obtained a settlement figure from both sides. These settlement positions were to remain confidential unless each side gave the mediator figures that would settle the case. Each side moved into a realistic settlement range, and after a 4-hour mediation session, the parties reached a substantial settlement.

The insurance company involved has since sent literally hundreds of cases to mediation. The plaintiffs' attorneys have also mediated numerous cases and have addressed bar association meetings about the merits of using ADR.

A good mediator typically does *not* give his or her opinion on the settlement value of the case—giving an opinion can lock a party into a position and impair settlement efforts. The key to this approach is to remember that most cases eventually settle anyway, indicating that the parties are able to reach a meeting of the minds. The mediator's role is to help them accomplish this as early as possible, with minimal mediator intrusion. In addition, if the parties know that the mediator will be rendering an opinion, it will probably affect how candid they will be concerning their real settlement positions, and this will adversely affect the mediator's ability to help them agree to settle. Thus, opinions by the mediator can distort the process.

If a settlement agreement is reached, the parties will usually execute formal settlement documents. This may take place at the end of the mediation session, or the parties may do it by mail thereafter. If a settlement agreement is not reached at the mediation session, the parties and the mediator may continue the discussions by phone if further progress is possible, and in some cases a second mediation session will be scheduled. If a full settlement is not reached, the parties are free to pursue other options such as arbitration or litigation.

Why Mediation Works

A very legitimate question is "What does mediation add to the negotiation process?" The mediator doesn't render a decision and can't force a party to accept a settlement, and anyone can terminate the mediation at any time. What does mediation accomplish that the parties can't themselves? Consider the following points:

Mediation Brings the Parties to the Bargaining Table as Early as Possible

Every attorney knows that most cases settle at some point: before trial, during trial, or even after trial. Cases often take on a life of their own, and incur considerable expense, before the parties engage in serious settlement negotiations. If any one party won't participate in settlement discussions—which can happen for many reasons other than simply to delay the proceedings—then the other parties have no choice but to wait. Proposing mediation is a new option to help break that impasse and get negotiations moving.

Another way to analyze this aspect of mediation is to recognize that most cases settle because of a deadline—whether an upcoming trial date or a scheduled round of discovery. People, including many busy trial attorneys, tend to put things off until there is no avoiding the situation. Mediation imposes an early deadline. It requires the parties to sit down at an established time and place to seriously discuss settlement. Once everyone's attention is focused, the chances of settlement improve.

Mediation Educates the Participants and Provides a "Day in Court"

Communication between disputing parties is often very poor, and for a variety of other reasons people can have misperceptions about what is involved in a dispute and how it could be settled. Mediation helps solve these problems.

Remember the flow of a mediation session: a joint session attended by all parties where everyone explains his or her position, followed by private meetings with the mediator where the case is discussed in detail and settlement possibilities are explored. These discussions are designed to help everyone understand the case. Many attorneys have indicated that their client would not have accepted a reasonable settlement if the client hadn't attended the mediation session—and it is clearly in the client's interest to have a full understanding of the case as early as possible. In addition, the attorneys and insurance representatives gain a better understanding of the case and the personalities involved. Even if the case doesn't settle, the participants usually feel that mediation was worthwhile.

There is also a psychological aspect to resolving disputes. Many people need to be listened to—to have their "day in court"—before they accept a reasonable settlement. Most experienced practitioners will be familiar with this element of dispute settlement. Consider the typical automobile collision plaintiff: she suffered a significant injury that has greatly affected her life. She is totally unfamiliar with what is involved in litigation or how to place a value on her injury. The insurance company denies her claim and months or years go by with relatively little communication taking place. She talks to her friends and family, reads about jury verdicts in the paper, watches while the insurance company sponsors golf tournaments, and, most important, lives with her condition on a day-to-day basis. It is not surprising that she will benefit by having everyone involved in her case sit down as early as possible to discuss it. For example,

> An automobile mechanic was injured when his hand was caught in a hydraulic tire changer. He sued the manufacturer, claiming that the tire changer had been defectively designed because it did not have a locking device to prevent a lever from springing backwards. The plaintiff made a settlement demand, and the manufacturer denied any liability, claiming that the plaintiff had operated the machine improperly and in disregard of stated warnings. The case also involved a workers' compensation lien.
>
> A mediation session was attended by the plaintiff and his attorney, insurance company representatives and defense attorneys, a workers' compensation representative, and an attorney/mediator. During the mediation session, the detailed discussion of the case helped the plaintiff realize that

> litigation would be very expensive and that he could possibly have his award reduced by comparative negligence. It also prompted the workers' compensation representative to become more flexible with its lien amount. The defense became convinced that it had substantial exposure and that the plaintiff and plaintiff's attorney would be effective at trial. As a result, the case settled.

The Mediator Can Work Behind the Scenes To Develop a Settlement

A great deal of posturing takes place during negotiations—neither party wants to appear to give in. Plaintiffs start high; defendants start low. Neither discloses its real position too early. Yet most cases settle before trial, which means that the parties agree on the bottom line analysis of the dispute.

Mediation is designed to avoid this posturing. In the private meetings each party can give the mediator a settlement position that is to remain confidential unless it will actually produce a settlement. By going back and forth between the parties, the mediator is often successful at finding common ground. For example,

> In an automobile collision case the plaintiff demanded \$100,000, and the defense offered \$30,000. Neither side wanted to alter its position for fear that it would be interpreted as a sign of weakness, although each was willing to settle at a different figure.
>
> During a mediation session, both sides privately gave the mediator their true settlement positions. These were given on the understanding that they would not be revealed unless a settlement could be obtained. As it turned out, the evaluations of the parties were similar, and the case settled.

Certain types of cases involve so many parties that any one participant may have trouble even exploring settlement possibilities. A mediator can often be effective at working out a settlement in such cases by simply organizing the discussions. Also, since the mediator has no stake in the outcome, the parties are more likely to be candid with him or her when discussing possible settlements. The mediator can talk confidentially with each party to determine what its real interests are, and then work to develop a settlement formula that will be acceptable to everyone. For example,

> Every spring a housing development experienced severe drainage problems that flooded basements and made septic systems inoperable. As a result, the 25 homeowners sued everyone connected with the project, including builders, architects, financing agencies, and governmental agencies. Counting the insurance companies, the case involved more than 70 parties. Trial was expected to last 15 weeks and cost hundreds of thousands of dollars. The parties were unable to effectively organize settlement discussions, and a month before trial all settlement efforts had broken down. As a last resort, one party asked a mediation agency to become involved.
>
> The agency quickly contacted all significant parties and obtained their agreement to participate in a mediation session. A mediator then met with all the parties and discussed settlement possibilities. Based on some positive indications at the session the mediator was able to convince the parties to agree to postpone the trial for two months. As a result of further confidential discussions, the mediator was able to develop a settlement formula that was accepted by all parties. The formula included adjustments of mortgages, buyouts, repairs, and monetary damages. All sides agreed that the case would have gone to trial without the efforts of the mediator.

For a discussion of additional approaches to multiple-party situations, see the Class Action Administration and Mass Tort ADR Programs in the section of this chapter headed "Other Alternative Dispute Resolution Methods."

Note

> None of the above points—bringing the parties together as early as possible, educating them, and working behind the scenes to put together a settlement—rely on the mediator giving an opinion or pressuring a party to alter its settlement position. That's not part of mediation. Mediators don't settle cases; they simply use the mediation process to enhance the chances of the parties arriving at an early settlement.

Administrative Agencies

Usually an administrative agency whose purpose is to facilitate mediations and other dispute resolutions is used to help coordinate the mediation.

Typically, one party will ask the agency to contact the other parties involved and propose mediation, or both parties, having agreed to mediate, will contact the agency. Most agencies will send informational materials to the parties and then follow up by phone to explain the mediation process and obtain everyone's agreement to mediate. An agency often can be more effective than a party at convincing other parties to participate—an agency is not associated with any side of the case, and thus it is less likely that there will be a knee-jerk reaction against the proposal. In addition, mediation needs to be properly explained for an unfamiliar party to see its value, and agencies are generally more adept at this.

Agencies also provide panels of trained mediators and a general administrative structure, and it is not uncommon for an agency to help the parties coordinate premediation materials. An agency's mediation procedures will include provisions as to mediator selection and payment, the hearing process, and confidentiality.

The agencies usually charge an administrative setup fee and an hourly fee for the mediator's time. Many agencies do not charge any fee if they are unable to set up the case.

To select an appropriate agency, analyze the following points:

- the experience of the agency with the type of case you want to submit;
- the possible mediators and the type of mediator training they have received;
- the agency's success rate at obtaining agreements to mediate. Does it charge a fee only if the other side agrees to participate?
- the agency's settlement rate;
- fees; and
- references.

Mediator

There are no restrictions on whom the parties may use as a mediator. In tort cases, the mediator is usually an attorney with experience in tort litigation. The attorney should have considerable mediator training and should have a nonjudgmental personality (meaning that he will be able to keep his opinions to himself). If you have any questions about the abilities of a proposed mediator, ask for references.

How To Prepare for a Mediation Session/Discovery

A mediation session involves a discussion of the case, as opposed to the presentation of evidence such as would take place at a trial or an arbitration hearing. Therefore, preparing for a mediation session is much easier. There is no need to organize witnesses or other evidence. And there are usually no formal premediation pleadings, although it is generally desirable to provide a mediator with a mediation brief, or letter, together with supporting exhibits, as you would provide to an arbitrator or panel of arbitrators.

A critical element of a successful mediation is that each side must be represented by a person with adequate authority to settle the case. This typically means that clients should attend the mediation session, a business or governmental entity should be represented by a high-level manager, and insurance carriers should be represented by an adjuster or claims person with settlement authority.

As described earlier, at the mediation session each side is given the opportunity to describe the liability and damage issues in its case to the other parties. Settlement positions are usually not discussed at this stage, to avoid the possibility of a party locking itself into a position. In addition to preparing an opening presentation, the attorney should determine whether her client should actively participate in this presentation, and brief the client accordingly. For instance, plaintiffs are sometimes given the opportunity to explain how the injury has affected their day-to-day life (particularly if the client will make a good impression).

After the joint meeting, the parties meet privately with the mediator to discuss the strengths and weaknesses of the case and to explore settlement possibilities. Obviously, an advocate needs to be familiar with the factual and legal issues involved in the case and be prepared to discuss them. Negotiation strategy is beyond the scope of this chapter, but basically the advocate should determine in advance where she wants the negotiations to lead, how to get there, and what facts or circumstances brought out at the mediation session might change that strategy. In a real sense, mediation is simply a matter of condensing the negotiations—parties make the same moves they would have anyway, but over the course of a few hours instead of months or years.

Finally, a party should determine if there are any facts it doesn't want to disclose to the other side. If so, the party should either keep the information to itself or tell it to the mediator in confidence. However, remember that one purpose of mediation is to convince the other side that your position is the correct one. If there are favorable facts of which the other side will become aware through formal discovery, there is probably little to lose by disclosing them at the mediation. It may make a difference as to whether the case settles now or later.

How To Select Cases To Send to Mediation

Mediation has proven effective in a variety of legal areas, including personal injury, products liability, business contracts, medical negligence, real estate, construction, and wrongful discharge. This is true whether liability is admitted or hotly contested, whether the case is in litigation or not, and whether the case involves a few thousand dollars or millions of dollars. Mediation is basically an analysis of risks, and risks are present in virtually any type of case.

Obviously, mediation is not intended to take the place of direct negotiations—most cases will still be settled by direct communications between the parties. But mediation is a new tool that can help move a case toward settlement, and law firms are now analyzing their caseloads to determine if mediation should be proposed in certain cases.

A previous section discussed why mediation works: (1) it brings the parties to the bargaining table as early as possible; (2) it educates them; and (3) it lets the mediator work behind the scenes to facilitate a settlement. In the following situations these aspects of mediation can be applied to specific cases.

- ▸ It has been three months since the parties discussed settlement; or the case is more than two years old.

  Comment: Mediation is a way to get the settlement discussions moving again. The administrative agency will contact the other side and will usually be able to persuade it to participate. There is nothing to lose by trying.

- Your phone calls or letters to the other side go unanswered.

  Comment: Before mediation, your only option was to put the case aside and wait. Now, when you send a case to a mediation administrative agency, the agency will contact the other side and propose mediation. This communication from a neutral party is usually more successful at getting the other side's attention.

- You—or the other side—are having client control problems.

  Comment: The careful analysis that takes place at the mediation session is often very helpful in giving clients a realistic view of the case, and it is in their interest to understand such issues as early as possible. Many attorneys have said that this was critical to their client's accepting a reasonable settlement. Obviously, you should also consider proposing mediation if you believe that the other side is having client control problems. An example of this would be a business manager of a self-insured company who does not really understand his vulnerable situation.

- A lawsuit will soon be filed.

  Comment: One purpose of mediation is to save litigation expenses. Proposing mediation may avoid the filing of the lawsuit.

- The other side is not furnishing you with the information you need to discuss settlement.

  Comment: As the administrative agency discusses the case with the other side, it is common to ask for the updated information you need. Usually it is just a matter of working out a schedule for such information to be furnished before the mediation session.

- The case is in litigation and a substantial round of discovery is coming up.

  Comment: The discovery necessary to knowledgeably discuss settlement is usually much less than that necessary to go to trial. Proposing mediation may avoid additional expense.

- The case is in litigation, and it is time to begin preparing for trial.

Comment: Most cases settle—many at the "courthouse steps"—after the time and expense of trial preparation. Using mediation may help the parties avoid trial preparation.

- The case involves a large number of parties, and you are having trouble putting together a comprehensive settlement.

  Comment: The mediator can play a major role in simply organizing the settlement discussions. The mediator can work closely—and confidentially—with each side to explore settlement possibilities and to put together a settlement package.

- The case involves co-defendants or co-plaintiffs who are unable to agree among themselves on settlement possibilities.

  Comment: For the same reasons that mediation works for disputes between plaintiffs and defendants, mediation can work for disagreements among parties on the same side. The mediation would proceed just like any other, with all participants first meeting jointly and then each privately with the mediator.

- One party to a case—or the party's attorney—is driving up everyone's litigation costs by engaging in unnecessary discovery or procedural maneuvers.

  Comment: The mediation session is usually attended by clients as well as attorneys. This can help rein in an overzealous attorney. The mediation session will also help focus a less experienced attorney on the important issues of the case.

- You are handling numerous similar cases.

  Comment: Consider using mediation to pull all the parties together so that all the claims can be handled at the same time. Another approach would be to use mediation to bring about early settlement negotiations in a sample group of cases so that you can develop guidelines and strategies for resolving the remaining ones. In this regard, see also the discussion of Class Action ADR Programs and the Mass Tort ADR Programs under the section headed "Other Alternative Dispute Resolution Methods."

- Your experience tells you that this case will settle.

  Comment: In a confidential meeting a party can give the mediator a settlement figure that will not be disclosed unless it will settle the case. This avoids the posturing that takes place in the usual negotiation process and enhances the possibilities of a settlement.

Legalities of the Mediation Process

There is little case law or legislation on the use of mediation. An analysis of the legalities of mediation must therefore be by analogy to other areas of law. Such an analysis must rest on legal principles that may well differ from jurisdiction to jurisdiction. The following analysis is very basic and should be used by practitioners only as a starting point.

- Is a mediated settlement agreement legally binding?

  A mediated settlement agreement is usually just like any other voluntary settlement of a claim. It is a contract, and its construction is governed by legal principles applicable to all contracts. The law generally favors compromises and is inclined to hold that they are final and binding. If the mediated agreement is not intended to be a binding contract, or if there are contingencies, the agreement should obviously cover such matters.

- Is the mediation process confidential?

  Remember that during the mediation session the parties make presentations to each other and also have confidential caucuses with the mediator. The issues here are whether a party's disclosures at the mediation may be used at a later trial and whether the other party—or even an outside party—may discover what was told to the mediator in confidence. There are a number of ways to approach these issues.

  Offer of Compromise—Settlement Negotiations

  The mediation session is a settlement negotiation. Under the Federal Rules of Evidence and similar rules in most states, offers of compromise and statements made during settlement negotiations are inadmissible as evidence at a later trial. Note that the details of this principle, such as what types of statements will be excluded and who may assert it, will differ from jurisdiction to jurisdiction. It's also probably safe to assume that, under any theory, evidence that is otherwise discoverable will not be rendered inadmissible simply because it was mentioned at the mediation session.

Mediation Confidentiality Statutes / Special Programs

By far the most effective protection for the confidentiality of mediation is found in statutes specially designed for that purpose. A rapidly growing number of states have such statutes. Sometimes these statutes apply to mediation generally, sometimes only to special programs such as dispute resolution centers or court-annexed programs.

This is an area where the law is developing very quickly, and any listing would soon be outdated. Check your state law.

Breach of Contract / Privilege / Public Policy

In the absence of a statute providing confidentiality, principles of contract law, privilege, or public policy may protect the confidential nature of mediation.

Usually the parties sign a mediation contract that states that the mediation proceedings are to remain confidential. Any party who later tries to discover the content of private conversations with the mediator would be breaching that agreement.

As to the privilege, mediation does not fall under any formal statutory privilege, but some courts have allowed a nonstatutory privilege in certain circumstances. *Wigmore on Evidence* sets forth the elements of such a privilege as follows:

(1) The communications must originate in a *confidence* that they will not be disclosed.

(2) This element of *confidentiality must be essential* to the full and satisfactory maintenance of the relations between the parties.

(3) The *relation* must be one which in the opinion of the community ought to be sedulously *fostered*.

(4) The *injury* that would inure to the relation by the disclosure of the communications must be *greater than the benefit* thereby gained for the correct disposal of litigation.[1]

It would appear that the mediation process would fit all four requirements—particularly when the parties sign a mediation contract providing for confidentiality.

Related to the idea of privilege is a general public policy argument that confidentiality is very important to the mediation process, and the judicial system should view with favor—and even encourage—the parties' attempts to settle their differences.

► Is a contract clause requiring mediation enforceable?

Because mediation is consensual, it is difficult to force parties to mediate. There is some moral suasion to a contract clause, however, and participating in a mediation could be a condition precedent to some other dispute resolution step. Conceivably, a failure to mediate could be used as evidence of bad faith.

PRIVATE ARBITRATION

Introduction

Private arbitration enables the parties involved in a dispute to present the case to an impartial third party for a legally binding decision, removed from the formal court system. Arbitration can be less expensive, quicker, and less stressful than a formal trial, yet the arbitrator's award has the same force and effect as a civil court judgment.

Note

Please note that this section analyzes private arbitration under various state and federal statutes and not specialized arbitration programs such as court-annexed Mandatory Arbitration programs, or the Mass Tort ADR Programs. For a further discussion of these specialized programs, see the

1 8 J. Wigmore, *Evidence* §2285, at 527 (McNaughton rev. 1961).

section headed "Other Alternative Dispute Resolution Methods." Please also note that labor law arbitration, which is governed by different statutes and legal requirements, is also beyond the scope of this section, although many of the same principles apply.

Arbitration Statutes

Forty-eight states have enacted statutes giving legal effect to a private arbitration process. The federal arbitration statute, typically used for interstate matters, is 9 U.S.C. §§1-15 (1988). These statutes set forth various arbitration requirements and procedures and provide for court enforcement of the arbitrator's award. Most state statutes and the federal statute are basically model act statutes, so there are many similarities from jurisdiction to jurisdiction. However, there are also differences, and reviewing the arbitration statute and related case law is typically the first step in analyzing arbitration law.

Some states still recognize "common law" arbitration, in addition to statutory arbitration. Common law arbitration, which developed through case law, predates the modern arbitration statutes. It is typically a matter of contract, with enforcement of the arbitrator's award requiring an action for breach of contract. In many states the enactment of a modern arbitration statute has been held to supersede common law arbitration, meaning that the parties must comply with the arbitration statute to have a valid arbitration proceeding. Even in the states where common law arbitration still exists, it is little used because it is cumbersome, time consuming, and ill-defined when compared with statutory arbitration.

Contract To Arbitrate

Arbitration statutes require that the parties enter into a contract to arbitrate. By agreeing to arbitrate, the parties are giving up their constitutional right to go to court and have a judge or jury hear the case. The terms of the contract to arbitrate dictate the scope of what is to be arbitrated, and thus it is critical that the contract be drafted correctly. Although courts liberally interpret a grant of authority to the arbitrator, the arbitrator, unlike a court of equity, cannot allow a party to unilaterally add additional issues.

An arbitration contract typically defines the dispute and the relief that may be awarded. While many such contracts are very general in such terms, the parties can closely define or limit the arbitrator's authority. Following are two approaches that are popular for tort cases:

- *High-Low*: "The arbitrator may award no less than $25,000 and no more than $75,000." The plaintiff is assured of a recovery, while the defense avoids an extremely high award.
- *Baseball*: "Fifteen days before the hearing each side will submit a final offer to the arbitrator and the arbitrator must select one or the other final offer as his award amount." Patterned after major league baseball's arbitration procedures for player-owner salary disputes, this arrangement is designed to move parties into a settlement range before arbitration.

An agreement to arbitrate can take either of two forms:

- *Submission Agreement*: This is a contract between the parties to a dispute, agreeing to submit the dispute to arbitration. Such an agreement is entered into after a dispute has arisen, an example being the arbitration of a third-party automobile collision claim.
- *Arbitration Clause*: This is a contract clause that provides for the arbitration of future disputes. In many jurisdictions, uninsured/underinsured motorist policy provisions include an arbitration clause for contested cases.

In drafting either an arbitration contract or arbitration clause, you may wish to consider adding provisions for the awarding of attorney fees if a party fails to comply with the arbitration provisions.

Court Enforcement of the Arbitration Process

The arbitration statutes allow the parties to operate outside the court system but provide methods to bring the power of the court to bear if a party refuses to cooperate. Typical statutory provisions include (1) the ability to obtain an order to compel arbitration, (2) the staying of court action pending arbitration if a party sues another when there is an arbitration clause in the underlying contract, and (3) in some instances provisions for preaward attachment of property. The statutes also set forth procedures to give the arbitrator's award civil judgment status, thus allowing such things as attachment and garnishment.

What Disputes Can Be Arbitrated?

Almost any civil case can be arbitrated, including medical negligence, products liability, and other types of personal injury cases (many uninsured/underinsured motorist provisions include arbitration clauses).

There are a number of areas where arbitration is not allowed because public policy dictates that the courts should hear the controversy. Child custody, criminal cases, probate, and adoption are generally governed by statutory and constitutional mandates requiring court action. Consumer protection, antitrust, and claims for punitive damages are often not arbitrable, although jurisdictions differ in their approaches to these subjects. Here again, the practitioner should review applicable statutes and case law before proceeding with arbitration.

Arbitration Process

Initiating the Arbitration Process

As described above, there are two methods of contracting to arbitrate: a *submission agreement* for existing disputes and an *arbitration clause* for future disputes.

In a submission situation, the agreement is sufficient to begin the process. When an arbitration clause is involved, however, statutes set forth certain procedural requirements designed to give the noninitiating party notice of the claim. Typical provisions require that the noninitiating party be served, personally or by registered mail (check your statute carefully), with a Notice of Intent to Arbitrate.

Role of the Administrative Agency

Many arbitration agreements designate an agency to administer the arbitration proceedings. Each agency has a panel of impartial arbitrators with expertise in various areas. Each also has a detailed set of arbitration rules, designed to allow for the orderly, impartial administration of cases. Such rules dictate the selection of arbitrators, the collection of the necessary fees, and how to deal with many procedural issues. The parties work with the agency rather than the arbitrator to handle such matters. Thus, use of an agency helps the parties select an impartial arbitrator, helps to avoid unnecessary communication between the arbitrator and a party, and provides structure and order to the process.

Appointment of an Arbitrator

As noted above, the arbitration agreement usually designates an administrative agency's arbitration rules to govern the proceedings. Such rules set forth the procedures to be used to select an arbitrator. Arbitration being a matter of contract, the parties can also agree on their own formula for arbitrator selection. In the event the manner of selection fails or is unclear, arbitration statutes usually allow the court, on application of a party, to appoint an arbitrator or determine a method of arbitrator selection.

There can be one or a number of arbitrators, depending on the agreement of the parties. Usually the agreement provides for either one or three arbitrators. Some agency arbitration rules set forth the number of arbitrators to be used, subject to change by the parties. In a situation in which more than one arbitrator hears a case, usually a majority determines any question and renders a final award.

There are no restrictions on who the arbitrator can be as long as the parties agree to use her. For tort cases, usually the arbitrator is an attorney experienced in tort matters or a former judge. Sometimes the parties desire a particular expertise in the arbitrator, for example, asbestos litigation. In any event, if the parties have any restrictions or expectations regarding the arbitrator, they should include a provision to that effect in their contract to arbitrate.

The arbitrator, of course, must be impartial and has a duty to disclose any circumstances or relationships from which it would be reasonable to infer the presence of bias, absence of impartiality, or interest in the welfare of one of the parties. The basic rule for the arbitrator should be to disclose any possible problems in this regard and let the parties decide whether to proceed.

Arbitrator's Powers

Arbitration statutes typically enumerate a number of arbitrator powers including the rights to set the time and place for the hearing, administer oaths, and compel the attendance of witnesses and subpoena records and documents—backed up by the court's contempt powers.

Although the arbitrator's duties and powers are subject to the agreement of the parties, administrative rules, and basic due process considerations, the arbitrator has broad discretion in the conduct of the arbitration proceedings and in determining what evidence, and in which form, is necessary to the decisional process.

Discovery

Discovery has traditionally been an area of uncertainty in arbitration, and attorneys who are expecting the wide-open discovery provisions of most court rules may be shocked. Again, the practitioner should look to the agreement of the parties, the agency arbitration rules, the arbitration statute, and any related case law. Many arbitration statutes specifically provide for depositions, although in some cases they require arbitrator approval. The arbitrator usually has the authority to compel the attendance of witnesses and the production of documents at the hearing. The availability of discovery such as interrogatories and production of documents is less clear and will depend on the contract to arbitrate, the administrative agency's procedures, and the arbitrator's perception of his authority to order such discovery. The practitioner should either be comfortable with the statute's and agency rules discovery provisions, or take steps to clearly set forth discovery provisions in the contract to arbitrate.

Arbitration Hearing / Evidentiary Standards

The format of an arbitration hearing is usually the same as that of a trial: opening statements; presentation of evidence by each party, subject to cross-examination; and closing arguments. However, arbitration is flexible and may be customized to fit the needs of a particular case. For instance, in a construction case involving numerous claimed defects, the arbitrator may find it beneficial to receive evidence on site, "defect by defect," rather than follow the usual trial format of having each party testify about all defects and then having the other party do the same.

Because private arbitration is separate and apart from the court system, formal court procedures and rules of evidence may not apply. This is another area in which the agreement of the parties and/or the administrative rules may limit or define the arbitrator's authority. As a result of the absence of formal evidentiary rules, more evidence is probably considered by the trier of fact than would be at a court trial. It is also worth noting that there is no formal record of arbitration proceedings unless requested by a party and no requirement for the preservation of exhibits. Thus, objections to the evidentiary rulings for-the-record have little value.

Basic due process considerations—notice and opportunity to be heard—do apply to arbitration proceedings. With regard to the latter, if basic evidence is excluded by the arbitrator there may be grounds to vacate the award (see the section headed "Vacation, Modification, or Correction of an Award" below). This is another reason why evidence is often "let in for what it's worth." With regard to the notice of the proceedings, statutes often require written notice by certified mail or personal service, although some only require "reasonable notice." Most statutes provide that if a party fails to appear after receiving such notice, the arbitrator may nevertheless proceed to hear and determine the controversy upon the evidence presented.

Arbitration Award

Award

After a hearing, the arbitrator decides the case and renders an award. The arbitration statute and/or the arbitration agreement may set forth any time limits as to when the award should be rendered. The award should be in writing and signed by the arbitrator. In the event the arbitrator fails to comply with the applicable time limit, some statutes provide that the court may order the arbitrator to perform. Most awards are in the form of money damages. However, in the proper case, the arbitrator may have the power to grant injunctive or other equitable relief.

Enforcing the Award

In most cases, parties voluntarily comply with the award. If not, however, arbitration statutes provide for court enforcement of the award. Usually this requires an application to the court to confirm the award. Confirmation of an award is not a trial; it is simply a motion to enforce an order already made by having a judgment entered on the award, and statutes typically provide for a quick confirmation process. The judgment has the same effect, and may be enforced, as if it had been rendered by the court after a trial.

Note that some arbitration statutes allow a party to make application for a preaward court order to preserve property or otherwise secure satisfaction of the award.

Vacation, Modification, or Correction of an Award

Most arbitration statutes allow an award to be modified or corrected when there is an evident miscalculation or mistake in identification of a person, thing, or property in the award. Some statutes allow the arbitrator to make such changes; some call for the court to make them.

A more substantive issue is what recourse, if any, a party has if it disagrees with the arbitrator's decision. A basic policy of arbitration is to provide the parties with finality, as opposed to appellate rights in the court system, and thus the arbitrator's award is subject to a very limited court review. Unlike a judge, the arbitrator is deemed to be the judge of both the facts *and the law*, and unless the award "on its face" shows the adoption of an erroneous rule or mistake in applying the law, an award will not normally be vacated or modified. Most awards are very short (e.g., a two-sentence decision), which leaves very little for a court to review.

Arbitration statutes typically set forth grounds for vacating an arbitrator's decision. The federal statute 9 U.S.C. §10 (1988) is a good example. This statute provides that an award may be vacated in the following circumstances:

- where the award was procured by corruption, fraud, or undue means;
- where there was evident partiality or corruption in the arbitrators, or either of them;
- where the arbitrators were guilty of misconduct in refusing to postpone the hearing, upon sufficient cause shown, or in refusing to hear evidence pertinent and material to the controversy, or of any other misbehavior by which the rights of any party have been prejudiced; or
- where the arbitrators exceeded their powers, or so imperfectly executed them that a mutual, final, and definite award upon the subject matter submitted was not made.

Where an award is vacated and the time within which the agreement required the award to be made has not expired the court may, in its discretion, direct a rehearing by the arbitrator.

Note that the statute states that the award may be vacated by the court, not overturned with a different result entered. Thus, at best the complaining party will obtain a new arbitration hearing. The grounds for vacation are seldom present and they are difficult to prove; therefore the arbitrator's award is usually final.

Finally, the parties in their contract to arbitrate may set forth an appeal process, or the agency arbitration rules may do the same. However, any such provisions may go against the basic arbitration policy of finality.

When To Select Arbitration

Arbitration has a number of attributes that may make it a sensible approach in a particular case.

Resolution Is Quick

Speed is perhaps arbitration's greatest advantage when compared with the court system. An arbitration hearing can be set up on short notice and, in any event, arbitration is usually much quicker than waiting for a trial date. The trade-off necessary to obtain a quick, final decision is to give up rights to appeal. With arbitration you generally get one, nonreviewable decision.

Savings in Time and Money

Arbitration can usually save the parties time and money. Discovery in an arbitration is usually less burdensome than in litigation. Arbitration hearings are set up at convenient times and places and begin on time, thus avoiding lengthy courthouse waits. Relaxed procedures and rules of evidence typically allow an arbitration hearing to proceed faster than a court trial.

An "Expert" Decides the Case

The expertise of the arbitrator is another reason some cases are arbitrated. In technically complicated matters such as specialized tort litigation, the parties may find it attractive to use a trier-of-fact who is also an expert in the field. This can cut down significantly on the time and expense necessary to educate the decision maker, and, at least in theory, helps assure that the decision will be a well-reasoned one.

Lower Stress Levels

All of the above-described advantages make the arbitration process less stressful than trial on the parties. Lowering the stress level that your clients experience can be appropriate advocacy.

There may be some instances when arbitration would not be in your client's interests. The most common reason is that the plaintiff does not wish to give up his or her right to have the case decided by a jury. Another reason is that a party wishes to use the case to set a legal precedent or at least preserve full appellate review of any decisions made in the case. Finally, arbitration is not available if the other side won't agree to arbitrate—they may feel that there is an advantage in delaying the proceedings, or they may wish to preserve their rights to a jury trial and appellate review.

OTHER ALTERNATIVE DISPUTE RESOLUTION METHODS

In addition to arbitration and mediation, there are a number of more specialized ADR options. Some are court-annexed; some are in the private domain. Most are a derivative of basic mediation or arbitration or a mixture of the two and, as noted earlier, this is a very rapidly evolving area. What follows are brief descriptions of the most popular ADR formats.

Referee—"Rent-A-Judge"

Many state statutes allow the parties to a lawsuit already filed with the court to select (and pay for) a referee to hear their case. The referee, who is usually an attorney or retired judge, conducts a trial that includes the formalities of any court trial such as compliance with the Rules of Evidence and a court reporter. After the trial the referee renders a court judgment that has the same force and effect and is subject to the same appellate review as a decision rendered by a sitting judge.

Basically, the referee statutes allow litigants to obtain a trial earlier than they otherwise would while at the same time preserving their right to a formal appeal.

Mini-Trials

A mini-trial is a form of mediation that has proven very effective at resolving complex cases such as multimillion dollar commercial disputes. Because of the need to condense the large amounts of information involved, mini-trials are more structured than the mediation process described earlier in this chapter.

Parties enter into a "mini-trial agreement" that sets forth such things as discovery provisions and how the hearing will be conducted. A mini-trial neutral—usually an attorney or retired judge—

presides. Each side is given a set period of time—four hours for example—to make an abbreviated presentation about its case. After the presentations, the parties' representatives meet to discuss possible settlements. The mini-trial neutral may act as a mediator or render an advisory decision, depending on the wishes of the parties.

Mock Jury Trial

An abbreviated case may be presented to a mock jury for a decision. In some cases, one side will use a mock jury to help it analyze possible outcomes before a real jury. In other instances, both sides will make shortened presentations before a mock jury for an advisory decision, or even a binding one.

As with a mini-trial (above), an administrative agency will usually work with the parties to develop a "Mock Jury Agreement" that will set forth how the mock jury session will be conducted.

Class Action Administration

Certain types of cases such as products liability or consumer protection actions can involve large numbers of claimants. As a result these cases can be very expensive to litigate and cumbersome to settle. This is particularly true where claims are not uniform but instead include people who have been injured—and should be compensated—in varying degrees.

Using ADR can be an effective approach to such cases. An administrative agency can either be selected by the parties or appointed by the court. The agency typically will design a set of claims procedures and related forms and then will be responsible for sending out information, taking in and screening claims, and sending accepted claims through a mediation/arbitration process. The agency also keeps statistics and often oversees restitution payments. By using ADR in this way both sides save substantial litigation expenses and bring the matter to a close as quickly as possible.

Mass Tort ADR Programs

In the 1980s, ADR programs were established under products-liability-related bankruptcy plans, the two best known examples being the Manville Personal Injury Settlement Trust for asbestos health claims and the A. H. Robbins bankruptcy relating to the Dalkon Shield. These bankruptcy plans involve trusts that are established to pay legitimate claims. To keep transaction costs as low as possible to preserve the trust funds for claimants, mediation and/or arbitration procedures were negotiated as part of the bankruptcy plan. In the Manville Trust situation the ADR procedures have worked well, although the Trust itself has had financial difficulties. At the time of this writing, the Dalkon Shield arbitration program was only just beginning. In any event, it is clear ADR will play a significant role in resolving mass tort situations. Here again, practitioners should familiarize themselves completely with the specific ADR procedures that will be used.

Court Programs

Around the country court systems are using various forms of ADR, including the following:

- *Settlement Conferences*. Settlement conferences have long been a part of many court systems. Typically the parties submit a written description of the dispute to the settlement judge and then appear in person for a short discussion of the case. Usually the judge will render an advisory opinion.
- *Mandatory Arbitration*. This is an increasingly popular form of court ADR. Typically, certain types of cases—usually tort or contract claims involving, in most jurisdictions, smaller damage cases—are required by court rule to go through an arbitration process before they can proceed to trial. If a party appeals the arbitration award and proceeds to trial, which it has a constitutional right to do, there are usually sanctions such as having to pay the other side's attorney's fees if the appealing party doesn't improve its position.
- *Mediation*. Mediation has not been used widely by the court system, except in the area of family law where numerous mediation programs have been established. Some federal and state courts have established mediation programs of commercial and tort cases, and the number of these programs is expected to increase.
- *Summary Jury Trials*. Like the private mock jury trial, a summary jury trial is an abbreviated presentation of the case before an impartial jury. The jury then renders an advisory decision.

CONCLUSION

It is important to remember that alternative dispute resolution is not a replacement for the jury system. Instead, ADR complements the court system and adds to the "arrows in the quiver" of the practitioner, by providing sensible options to jury trials in appropriate cases. With the proper approach, using ADR can be very effective representation.

INDEX

C

N

O

P

Q

U

V

W